GREAT DEAF AMERICANS:

THE SECOND EDITION

"At a time like this I have some very
irresistible temptations to make some very
profound statement. And the first of these is
that **deaf people can do anything that
hearing people can do . . . except hear.**
The second one of these is that ears are cheap.
It's what's between the ears that counts."

—Fred Schreiber,
"Potentials for Employment
of the Deaf at Levels in Keeping with
Their Intellectual Capabilities," 1972

GREAT DEAF AMERICANS:
THE SECOND EDITION

By
Matthew S. Moore
and
Robert F. Panara

With a foreword by Yerker Andersson
Chair of Deaf Studies, Gallaudet University

Deaf Life Press
a division of

MSM
PRODUCTIONS LTD
A MULTI-MEDIA COMPANY

Rochester, New York
1996

Great Deaf Americans: The Second Edition
Copyright © 1996, by MSM Productions, Ltd.

Cover Design: Matthew S. Moore
Vignette credits: **Laurent Clerc**: From a portrait by Charles Willson Peale, *circa* 1820/American School for the Deaf. **Juliette Gordon Low**: National Historic Preservation Center, Girl Scouts of the U.S.A. **Thomas Scott Marr**: Tennessee School for the Deaf. **Shelley Beattie**: Ms. Beattie. **Curtis Pride**: Joe Rizzo/Better Hearing Institute. **John Yeh**: Michael Sparks; courtesy of Mr. Yeh. **Gertrude S. Galloway**: Dr. Galloway. **Erastus "Deaf" Smith**: From a portrait by Thomas Jefferson Wright/San Jacinto Museum of History. **Dr. Robert Davila**: Dr. Davila. **Regina Olson Hughes**: Gallaudet University Archives. **Heather Whitestone**: Kim Jobe, **The Daily Corinthian**, Corinth, Mississippi.

Library of Congress Cataloging-in-Publication Data
Moore, Matthew Scott, 1958-

Great Deaf Americans: the second edition / Matthew Scott Moore
and Robert F. Panara; with a foreword by Yerker Andersson.
        p. cm.
    Includes bibliographical references
    ISBN 0-9634016-6-1 (alk. paper)
    1. Deaf—United States—Biography. I. Panara, Robert.
II. Title
HV2534.A3M66 1996
920'.00872
[B]—DC20   96-24582
                                                                    CIP
Printed in the United States of America

The paper use in this publication complies with the Permanent Paper Standard issued by the National Information Standards Organization (Z39.48-1984) (∞)

10 9 8 7 6 5 4 3 2
Second Edition
First Printing, July 1996
Second Printing, September 1998

Acknowledgements

Anyone who has ever attempted a work of "collective biography"—to use the technical term—soon learns what a dauntingly complicated task it can be. We are indebted to many, including the living "profiles" themselves, and the families, friends, and colleagues of the deceased ones, as well as authors, scholars, editors, secretaries, newspaper-library staffers, teachers, administrators, photographers, researchers, public and institutional librarians, and archivists for providing assistance, information, updates, input, corrections, and photographs. Frank G. Bowe, Jack R. Gannon, Henry Kisor, Jack Levesque, Peggie Parsons, Judith Viera Tingley, and Frank Turk not only sent us information about themselves, but helped with other profiles, or suggested other sources.

Charles F. Bancroft helped with the technical aspects of the book's design—the preparation of the photos and illustrations.

With deepest gratitude, we thank Michele Listisard of **Science** Magazine. She did considerable "sleuthing" in the Potomac area, Washington, D.C., and Gallaudet campus, as well as serving as our E-mail wizard.

And a very special thanks to Linda Levitan for her many long months of ongoing research, assistance, labor, and support.

We apologize for any inadvertent omissions or errors.

To all of those who helped make this book a reality, our thanks!

Sherry Adams, Librarian, **Houston Chronicle**; • Eric Albronda and Mildred Albronda; • Elaine B. Alexander, Director of Instruction; and Martha J. Emrey, Librarian, Tennessee School for the Deaf; • Lisa Allphin, Executive Communication Liaison, DCARA; • Judith A. Anderson, Librarian, Alexander Graham Bell Association for the Deaf; • Yerker Andersson; • Joan Ankrum; • Marianne K. Avery, Assistant Director, Information Services; and James Stuart Osbourn, Senior Reference Librarian, New Jersey Information Center, Newark Public Library; • Robert K. Baker, Office of the Director, NTID; • Paula Bartone-Bonillas, Editor, **Hearing Health**; • Caroline Becher; • Bennett, **South Dakota Magazine**; • Karen Bentley, Coordinator, Deaf/Hearing Impaired Program, Lewis & Clark Community College, Godfrey, Illinois; • J. Stephen Bolhafner, Librarian, **St. Louis Post-Dispatch**; • Patricia L. Bowen; and Joseph J. Rizzo, Executive Director, Better Hearing Institute; • Beatrice M. Burke; • Lawrence S. Burr; • Brian Butcher, San Jacinto Museum of History; • Brad Cafarelli, Bragman, Cafarelli & Nyman; •Patricia L. Campbell, Western History Association, University of New Mexico; • Dr. Clifton F. Carbin, author, **Deaf Heritage in Canada**; • Virginia Carter, Resource Center Coordinator, SWCID; • Ruth Cella, Director, Development and Public Relations, The Pennsylvania School for the Deaf; • Susan Chockley, Library Assistant, Public Services; and

Sandy Trybalski, Assistant Archivist, Tennessee State Library and Archives; • Shirley Clark, Staff Assistant, University of Oklahoma Libraries; • Sandy Cohen, Director, Library Service for the Hearing Impaired, Nashville Public Library; • Tracey Collins, Administrative Assistant, **Entrepreneur** Magazine Group; • Nancy Creighton, Editor, **NAD Broadcaster**; • John R. Cronin, Chief Librarian, **Boston Herald**; • Mary Degenhardt, Archivist; and Mary Levey, Director, National Historic Preservation Center, Girl Scouts of the U.S.A.; • Robin Dettre, Art Inventories, National Museum of American Art; • Loraine DiPietro, Marguerite Glass-Engelhart, and the staff of the National Information Center on Deafness at Gallaudet University; • M. Stephen Doherty, Editor-in-Chief; and Lynne Moss, Administrative Assistant, **American Artist**; • Edward Duarte and Mary Jane Kinney, **Sports Illustrated for Kids**; • George F. Epps; • Steve Farhood, **The Ring**; • Randy Fisher, James K. Goodwin, and Steven R. Sandy, AAAD Committee for "Dummy" Hoy; • Lawrence Fleischer, President; Shirley Platt, Executive Director; and Lisa Ivey, Managing Editor, **Deaf Sports Review**; AAAD; • Charles A. Frankenberry, Executive Assistant to the President; and Denise Hanlon, Office Services Supervisor, Gallaudet University; • Julie Franklin, General Manager, Weitbrecht Communications, Inc.; • Victor Galloway; • Lilah C. Gillis, **Yankton Press & Dakotan**; • Artie Terrell Grassman, Community Relations, Kentucky School for the Deaf; • Jonathan Green, Globe Photos; • David Halberg, Curator, Clerc-Gallaudet Historical Room; and Chris Thorkelson, Public Relations, American School for the Deaf; • Jerry Hassell; • Ken Hirsch; • Al and Peggy Hlibok; • Marjoriebell Holcomb; • Samuel Kay Holcomb; • Thomas Kay Holcomb; • Suzie Jacobs, California School for the Deaf Historical Museum, Fremont; • Kim Jobe, **The Daily Corinthian**, Corinth, Mississippi; • Michael P. Kaika, Department of Public Relations, Gallaudet University; • Maxine M. Kelley, Legal Assistant, Kutak Rock; • Ann Keplinger, Librarian/ Archivist; and Tod Ruhstaller, Director, Haggin Museum; • Sherri Kimmel; • Kim Klein, Photo Researcher, **The Washington Post**; • Marge Klugman, Editor-in-Chief, **GLAD News**; • Dick Koles, New Jersey Newsphotos; • George Kosovich, Rehabilitation Services Administration; • Dan Kubick, History and Social Science Department, Omaha Public Library; • Patti Kunkle, Office of the President; Gallaudet University; • Colleen Lane, Media Specialist, Ultratec; • Dr. Harlan Lane; • Dr. Harry G. Lang, Department of Educational Research and Development, NTID; • Gary Layda, Photographer, Metro Government of Nashville; • John R. Lovett, Western History Collections, University of Oklahoma Libraries; • Jack Lyness, Editor, and Stephanie Secrest, Photographer, **The Argus**, Fremont, California; • Marilynn Madison • Helene Maram, Hearing Loss Link; • Tony Landon McGregor; • Pamala Micheaux, Managing Editor, **American Annals of the Deaf**; • **Muscle & Fitness**; • Joe Nathan, Archives Assistant, **The Sporting News**; • National Air and Space Museum; • Lisa Nelson, AP/Wide World Photos; • Marjorie Norwood; • Michael J. Olson and Ulf Hedberg, Gallaudet University Archives; • Nancy Oppel, Sunsource, **Baltimore Sun**; • Edna Paananen-Adler; • John Panara; • Pauline ("Polly") Peikoff; • Anna B. Peebler, Photo Archivist, Rosenberg Library; • George Potanovic, Jr.; • John Pride; • Dr. Robert W. Read, Botanist Emeritus, Smithsonian Institution; • Kim Readmond, Publications Coordinator, Central Institute for the Deaf; • Marthada Reed and Richard D. Reed, Missouri School for the Deaf; • David

Reynolds, Indiana School for the Deaf; • Arlene Rice, Executive Assistant, New York School for the Deaf; • William M. Roberts, Acting Curator, Pictorial Collections, Bancroft Library; • Dr. Ross J. Roeser, Director and Professor, Callier Center for Communication Disorders, University of Texas at Dallas; • LaVera Rose, Cultural Heritage Center, South Dakota State Historical Society; • Nancy and Clifford Rowley; • Andrea Saks and Mrs. Jean Saks; • Philip Saltonstall; • Dr. Jerome D. Schein; • Patrick Seamans; • Deb Sisum, Deputy Keeper, Catalog of American Portraits, National Portrait Gallery; • Rev. Dr. Clayton F. Smith; • William Bruce Sparks; • Frank B. Sullivan, NCI; • Alice Tangerini, Staff Illustrator, Department of Botany, National Museum of Natural History, Smithsonian Institution; • Angela K. Thames, President, T.J. Publishers, Inc.; • Gretchen Viehmann, Assistant Photo Editor; and Laura A. Harris, Head Librarian, **New York Post**; • Ann Walding-Phillips, Omaha **World-Herald** LibraryLink; • Martina Walker; • Vickie Walter, Editor, **Gallaudet Today**; • Ed Waterstreet, Artistic Director, Deaf West Theatre; • Melinda Weinrib; • Carol Wetherson, Office of Public Information, Western Maryland College; • Kathy Winter, Librarian, South Dakota School for the Deaf.

Also: the staff at the Rundel Memorial (Central) Library, Rochester, New York—Central Reference, Circulation, and the Art, Literature/Biography, Business, History, and Periodicals Departments; and Carol and Maria at the Highland Branch.

Grateful acknowledgement is made to the following for permission to quote excerpts from the following articles:

Gigi Anders, "Beauty and the Battle," **USA Weekend**, March 3-5, 1995.
Phil Bowie, "The Fastest Woman on Earth," **The Saturday Evening Post**, March, 1977.
Diane Casella Hines, "Morris Broderson: Speaking Through His Art," **American Artist**, October 1980. Copyright © 1980, BPI Publications. Reprinted with permission.
Mary Johnstone, "Making an Impact," **Gallaudet Today**, Winter 1990-91.
Michael Kelly, "A silent roar for Kenny Walker," **Omaha World-Herald**, November 3, 1990. Reprinted with permission.
Erika Kotite, "Personal Best: When Abilities Outshine Disabilities," **Entrepreneur Magazine**, April 1991. Reprinted with permission.
Cynthia Merrifield, "Interview" with Kitty O'Neil, **Hearing Health,** August/September 1994. Reprinted with permission.
John Dishon McDermott, "A Dedication to the Memory of George E. Hyde," **Arizona and the West: A Quarterly Journal of History**, University of Arizona Press, 17(2), 1975.
Harold Scarlett, "Russ Colombo trains on beer, defies undertow," **Houston Post**, May 8, 1966. Copyright © 1966, **Houston Post**. Reprinted with permission. All rights reserved.
Nancy Wahonick, "'Discovering' Hillis Arnold," **December Rose**, July/August 1988.
Mel Williams, "David Peikoff . . . Man of Action," **The Silent Worker**, July 1951.
The excerpts from Laura Redden's "A Few Words About the Deaf and Dumb," **American Annals of the Deaf**, Volume 10 (1858), and Harold J. Domich's "John Carlin: A Biographical Sketch," **American Annals of the Deaf**, Vol. 90, No. 4, September, 1945, are reprinted with permission.
The excerpt from Fred Schreiber's 1972 speech, "Potentials for Employment of the Deaf at Levels in Keeping with Their Intellectual Capabilities," is taken from **A Rose for Tomorrow** by Dr. Jerome D. Schein. Copyright © 1982 by Dr. Schein and the National Association of the Deaf. Reprinted with permission.

A Brief History of
GREAT DEAF AMERICANS

The first edition of **Great Deaf Americans** (T.J. Publishers, 1983) was co-authored by Robert F. Panara and his son John Panara. It achieved a modest degree of success.

As time went by, its shortcomings became increasingly obvious. Of the 33 profiles in the book, for example, a mere 7 were women. There were two Black men, but nobody from Hispanic or other racial/ethnic backgrounds. At least one critic found fault with the overemphasis on sports and the performing arts.

In 1993, by which time the first edition had finally sold out, I approached Bob Panara, my old friend, with a proposal. I told him that, knowing the importance of making this book readily available to the widest possible readership—now that Deaf Studies courses were growing in popularity—that Deaf Life Press would like to pick it up. I explained that I wanted to produce a completely revamped version—revised and expanded, with photographs, and containing a larger number of profiles to better reflect the diversity of the Deaf community.

He enthusiastically agreed. He functioned as consultant-advisor and specialist in Deaf Studies. He provided biographical information, and his sizable collection of articles and clippings about the "old" profiles and a few new ones. He also suggested several names. I undertook the actual work of contacting the sources, getting updated information, photographs, quotes, and permissions. I redesigned the book from scratch. I also rewrote the text almost completely, with the help of Linda Levitan, who provided the meticulous research. This edition contains more than twice as many profiles as the original one.

I want to thank Bob Panara for giving me the freedom to shape the revision as I saw fit.

Matthew S. Moore

Table of Contents

Dedication

To the memory of the deaf achievers of our past (especially those whose achievements have been forgotten or lost); to the success of our current deaf achievers, famous and obscure; and to those who proudly extend our achievements into the territory of the future.

And to my good teachers at Indiana School for the Deaf, supporters, and friends, and those who have worked diligently with me.

Matthew S. Moore

To John Panara, who helped make this work possible by collaborating on the first edition.

Robert F. Panara

Foreword

Great Deaf Americans: The Second Edition, by Matthew S. Moore and Robert F. Panara, has again confirmed my opinion that Deaf Studies is a gold mine for those who want to know not only about deaf people and their history but also how their culture has enriched the United States' heritage.

More and more universities are establishing academic departments or centers specializing in the study of selected variations in human groups, such as African Studies, Asian Studies, or in religion—e.g., Catholic Studies or Islamic Studies. Following this trend, a few universities have even created Deaf Studies as a specialized field. Researchers, scholars, and interested readers now have the great responsibility to make sure that the compilation of our heritage will not exclude any human group from its contents any longer. We have repeatedly acknowledged that cultural or linguistic contributions made by any human group in a given country have been either overlooked or belittled in the compilation of its national heritage. Human groups in any country can survive and can enhance their culture only if they can appreciate their differences and similarities both between and within themselves. Isolation and the refusal to appreciate the contributions by outside groups will likely weaken the solidarity within a human group. For example, Native Americans can no longer be dismissed as an unimportant cultural variant. There is much evidence that American Indians made many significant contributions to the emergence of the United States as a country. This acknowledgment has apparently helped the Native Americans to appreciate their own culture. We also know that African-Americans played an important role in the many wars fought by and within the States, beginning with the American Revolution. In 1945, the prestigious Arlington National Cemetery finally agreed to offer burial sites to African-American war veterans. Their participation in U.S. military history had been officially recognized.

In our case, we find that the invention of the TTY coupler by Robert Weitbrecht, Andrew Saks, and James C. Marsters, has made revolutionary changes in telecommunications. These changes have helped to integrate hearing individuals, government agencies, legislative assemblies, and the private sector, with deaf people. Another example: researchers' discoveries that sign languages in fact existed among deaf people before schools for the deaf were established have forced us to abandon the old myth that the founders of schools for the deaf were credited for creating sign languages. In my opinion, such development of a sign language was possible just because the dominating society at that time was fascinated by, not hostile to, the attempt of deaf people to become a part of its culture.

Jack Gannon's **Deaf Heritage** has given a powerful impetus to the proliferation of books on sign languages and deaf people as a cultural variation, histories of local, state or regional, national and international organizations of the deaf, biographies of outstanding deaf Americans, and artistic expressions such as paintings, drawings, and ASL poetry. I venture to predict that this stimulating growth will definitely recognize deaf people as an integral part of the United States' heritage instead of as a pathological group.

Hero worship is valued in every country, so it is not surprising that children, whether deaf or hearing, always seek, consider, and adopt adults as their possible role models. In 1984, UNESCO urged schools for the deaf to employ deaf adults so the latter could function as role models for students. Although this trend has not yet become international, its importance has now been recognized in many industrialized and developing countries. Meeting this important challenge, Matthew S. Moore wisely decided to update the popular book **Great Deaf Americans** by publishing a second edition.

This decision is commendable, as schools and universities offering Deaf Studies are in desperate need of biographies of successful deaf individuals. Such information is needed as it will certainly encourage children to adopt great deaf Americans as possible role models and to make greater contributions to deaf culture as well as to the national heritage. Furthermore, this book will certainly make adults aware of what contributions great deaf Americans have made to their country. The publication of **Great Deaf American: The Second Edition**, therefore, is in line with the current attempt to include the consideration of all human groups in any national heritage.

Questions may be raised on the selection of deaf persons for this book. Readers may ask themselves whether the selected Americans are typical of culturally deaf people or what scientists call "Deaf;" whether other great deaf Americans have been overlooked; whether it is too early to include some young deaf Americans in this book, and so on. The selections of deaf scientists, artists, performers, award winners, administrators, and leaders in other books or magazine articles has already been questioned. Let interested readers continue to discuss such questions! It may stimulate scholars to publish more research findings or reexamine the national heritage. This kind of intellectual growth will help us to rank Deaf Studies as an equal partner with African Studies, Asian Studies, Women's Studies, Religious Studies, and so on. In that sense, **Great Deaf Americans: The Second Edition** must be welcomed as a significant factor in the evolution of Deaf Studies as an academic field.

Yerker Andersson, Ph.D.
Chair and Professor of Sociology
Gallaudet University
June 1996

Yerker Andersson

A native of Sweden, Yerker Andersson is from a family of teachers, and came to the United States in 1955 to further his education. (He and his younger brother Svante were born deaf.) He received his Bachelor's degree in Sociology from Gallaudet College (1960) and his Master's in Counseling from Columbia University, and his Ph.D. in Sociology from the University of Maryland. He first worked as a guidance counselor for two years at New York School for the Deaf (Fanwood) before joining the Gallaudet faculty in 1964. He is currently Professor of Sociology and Chair of the Department of Deaf Studies at Gallaudet University. His special interest is cross-cultural comparative studies of deafness and other disabilities. President Clinton appointed him to the National Council on Disability.

Originally involved in Swedish local and national Deaf organizations, Dr. Andersson expanded his involvement to an international level. He served as President of the World Federation of the Deaf for 12 years (he was the first deaf leader to address the United Nations General Assembly), and is now an honorary member. He's also been active in numerous organizations and committees at Gallaudet University and in the National Association of the Deaf. He has written dozens of papers and articles, given many lectures at international meetings, and conducted leadership-training workshops; he's fluent in Gestuno (International), Swedish, and American sign languages.

Dr. Andersson is married to Nancy Timko of New Jersey (Gallaudet '58); they live in Frederick, Maryland. He is a skilled woodworker and model-ship builder.

Introduction to the Second Edition

This book contains 77 brief biographies of deaf persons who have had impact of varying degrees on their generations, ours, and the future. Our purpose is to highlight the achievements of a sampling of deaf citizens, and to suggest the variety of the Deaf experience—which ranges from oral-deaf (Robert Weitbrecht, Bonnie Poitras Tucker, Heather Whitestone) to culturally-Deaf (Fred Schreiber, Phyllis Frelich, Bernard Bragg) to eclectic (Marlee Matlin) to late-deafened (Juliette Low, Michael Chatoff, I. King Jordan) to deaf/blind (Helen Keller, who isn't included here, her story being sufficiently well-known).*

When Bob Panara chose his original 33 "Great Deaf Americans," he used the criteria of "contributing to the cultural development of America," of making a national or international impact. A number of these people were already well-known in the community-at-large—the legendary Juliette Low and TV stars Linda Bove and Lou Ferrigno. Others weren't. Others had already achieved fame in the Deaf community—local heroes and heroines. Still others were downright obscure.

In preparing this revision, we have done a certain amount of necessary reshuffling—keeping the "must-haves," eliminating some names from the roster of prospects to make room for others from the past who, we feel, have a stronger claim to warrant inclusion, and adding some "new" names from the present. (All but one of Dr. Panara's 33 notables have been retained.)

What is "greatness," anyway? Who is "great"? What is the difference between those who are "great" and those who are merely "good"? Who decides? And by whose standards, anyway?

Only time tells.

Some achievers are included here because of the cumulative work of a lifetime; others for a series of accomplishments, others for one or two notable things—reaching the top of their professions. It simply isn't possible to compare the achievements made by a TV or film performer or athlete with those made by a research scientist. The TV star's renown may outshine that of the scientist, but the scientist may have a greater claim on posterity. Or vice versa. And an entertainer—say, one from an ethnic-minority background—may wreak a change in public attitudes, with potentially significant social repercussions. A case in point: the growing popularity of American Sign Language classes in public high schools, directly or indirectly attributable to the popularity of an actress like Marlee Matlin. The best we can do is gather together a colorful variety of those who have made notable achievements, and let their own lives "do the talking."

Great people don't work completely alone. Nobody achieves anything in a vacuum. There's an old saying, "Behind every great man stands a woman," and a more recent bitter-funny variation, "Behind every great woman stands a man who tried to stop her." I propose yet another variation: "Behind every great achiever stands a dedicated team." The aviator, racer, or astronaut who breaks world records is lionized as a hero or heroine and becomes (willingly or not) an instant celebrity in the full glare of publicity. It's too easy to forget that each of them depends on the hard work of a dedicated crew who rarely get their share of credit/media attention/publicity (and who may well prefer to do without it in the first place). For each public hero, there is a support system—a squadron of assistants, apprentices, coaches, recruits, volunteers, friends, families, spouses, children, employees, teachers, mentors, angels, all more or less in the background. The spotlight usually prefers to focus romantically and dramatically on the individual while leaving the crew in shadow. Many deaf people devote their careers to the furtherance of someone else's achievement, at the cost of their own. And, conversely, many deaf achievers are aided by hearing supporters.

Unfortunately, there is a scarcity of deaf heroines. This is not because deaf women have accomplished less than deaf men in what they set out to do, but that they have long been discouraged (or simply prohibited) from pursuing their own ambitions and encouraged, wholesale, to be wives, mothers, and housekeepers. Usually, though not invariably, the more "untraditional" their ambitions, the more overt the discouragement. Society's expectations for girls were, and still are, different from its expectations for boys. (Case in point: Women were not admitted to the newly-established institution now known as Gallaudet University for 24 years. It was feared that their presence would prove disruptive and "promote immorality.") Even so, one could argue that deaf boys as well as deaf girls have been denied their right to dream and to achieve their full potential. Deaf women have endured a double burden of oppression: as deaf persons and as females.

Likewise, we have a scarcity of African-American/Black, Hispanic, (Native) American Indian, and Asian-Pacific Americans here. Most of the profiles are of white males. Once again, it's the old story of exclusion. Deaf Blacks were sent to segregated schools (if they received schooling at all), and Gallaudet College was long off-limits to them. There is still a disproportionately large number of Black and Hispanic students at Kendall Demonstration Elementary School and Model Secondary School for the Deaf (both on Gallaudet's Kendall Green campus in Washington, D.C.), but disproportionately few Black students at Gallaudet University—and virtually no representation on the faculty. In 1994, however, Dr. Glenn B. Anderson became the second Deaf chairman of the Gallaudet Board of Trustees. He was already its first African-American member. Progress is made in fits and snatches, in bursts and trickles.

Politics, the arts, technology, law—closed doors of opportunity are gradually being coaxed, or forced, open to us. Deaf people are fighting for the right to serve on juries (and some undaunted ones have already served), enter nontraditional and lucrative professions (e.g., human and veterinary medicine), and to do everything that hearing society has allowed and encouraged "normal" folks to do. As we approach the 21st century, we see that the barriers are still formidable, although less apparent. This partly explains the high proportion of deaf people represented here in the arts (performing and fine)—it affords us creative and communicative freedom.

We are still barred from military service, although Erastus Smith's remarkable career shows that deaf people, in those rougher, pre-Emancipation times, had a bit more freedom in some respects than we do. They also had considerably less bureaucratic red tape to contend with. William and Eliza Willard came to Indianapolis from Ohio, got permission from the state legislature to found a school for deaf children, advertised, rented a building, rounded up some pupils, and went straight to work. Within a matter of months, they had founded a school—now Indiana School for the Deaf, one of the finest of its kind. We wonder what sort of procedures the Willards would have to go through now—and they held no teachers' certification. All they could do was—teach. And they did.

In assessing their achievements, it's wise to avoid lumping all deaf people together into one category. We may all be more or less audiologically-deaf, but our differences define as well as divide us.

For one thing, we need to take into account the age of onset of deafness. The challenges facing a child born deaf to hearing parents differ from those facing a child born deaf into a deaf family. A born-deaf or early-deafened child in a hearing family has a much more difficult time coping with the inevitable communication/language barriers than a deaf child of deaf parents or a child who became deaf at age 8 or 12, or even 5. In terms of the acquisition of English (hearing, speaking, reading, and writing it), children who lose their hearing after age 5 have an easier time of it—they've lived several years as hearing persons and have acquired spoken and written language skills. The challenges are formidable for born-deaf children of hearing parents, who may not know how to communicate with their child at all (and may possibly *never* learn).

Thus, deaf children of deaf parents often start life with a significant advantage: their parents know how to communicate with them from the day they're born. They're exposed to language from the start, and tend to have a particularly secure identity and self-image. They also tend to become the leaders, the transmitters of ASL and Deaf culture to other deaf children at school. (E.g., Bernard Bragg, Phyllis Frelich, Gertrude Galloway.)

The parents of "oral successes" (and the grown-up "successes" themselves) often brag about their achievements in speech and speechreading. Some of Alexander Graham Bell's top pupils (notably Mabel Hubbard, whom he ultimately married) had lost their hearing *after* they'd learned to speak. Yet the public was led to believe that they had been born without the faculty of hearing. In effect, Bell was perpetrating a sham. The odds are overwhelmingly against a born-deaf child's developing clear, articulate speech. We have to be realistic.

Therefore, the ability of a late-deafened person to function in the "hearing world" should not be measured against that of a born-deaf person to the detriment of the latter. Each deaf person is an individual.

One must also take into account the cultural affiliation of deaf people themselves. Do they consider themselves "Deaf," "deaf," or insist on identifying themselves as "hard-of-hearing" or "hearing-impaired"? Howard E. "Rocky" Stone, founder and first executive director of Self Help for Hard of Hearing People, Inc. (SHHH), has long been legally deaf, but prefers to identify himself as "hard-of-hearing." He isn't included here. Kitty O'Neil, stuntwoman and racer, became profoundly deaf as an infant, but has apparently never felt any connection whatsoever with the Deaf community. Unlike Rocky Stone (who gave a signed speech when he received an honorary doctorate from Gallaudet University), she has disdained signing. Mabel Hubbard Bell, one of the most notable "oral successes" (and who learned to speak *well before* she became deaf at age 5), despised other deaf people and took pains to avoid them. (We have omitted her from the second edition.) Juliette Low struggled to cope with her severe deafness, but remained and worked in the hearing community. (It was only a few years before her death that disabled and deaf girls were admitted into Girl Scout troops, or formed their own.) Steve McQueen, the late actor/producer, never publicly acknowledged that he was partially deaf. (It didn't jibe with his macho public image.) Thomas Alva Edison, the most famous American inventor, progressively deafened, functioned as hard-of-hearing. Where do you draw the line? It can be exceptionally difficult.

When choosing those for inclusion in this book, we tried to use several criteria: a variety of backgrounds, age of onset, cultural affiliation. We wanted to emphasize deaf people who identified with the Deaf community, cared about other deaf people, and (although not invariably) advocated for Deaf rights. Even if they were not "Deaf advocates," we considered their impact on both Deaf and Hearing communities. Again, this is a difficult task. While Steve McQueen arguably had no impact on the Deaf community, can it be said that Kitty O'Neil has? Of course, McQueen concealed his deafness, while O'Neil has always been honest about hers.

However, there are a good number of medically-deaf persons who, for all practical purposes, have functioned as culturally-Hearing, such as Lou Ferrigno and Heather Whitestone. Even Marlee Matlin, who won an Oscar for a signing/nonspeaking role, falls into this category. We have the freedom to take signing or speaking roles, if we feel comfortable with them; to use our voices if we please; to depend on our speechreading skills if that's what we prefer. It's a matter of comfort and choice. But it also has political ramifications.

Is deafness a catastrophe? Or, as the tabloids are fond of saying, a "tragedy"? We think not. Is it a "handicap"? Some of feel that it is; others call it a "minor inconvenience," a "challenge" (to use that increasingly abused word), or even a "way of life."

All of us, to some extent, have battled long-standing societal prejudices and the still-prevalent attitude: that you cannot succeed in an upscale career or public life unless you can speak. (Even Helen Keller aided and abetted the oralists by her friendship with Alexander Graham Bell, endorsement of his cause, and public pronouncements like "Speech is the birthright of every child.")

In some ways, it was easier in 19th-century America: the early schools for the deaf produced a few generations of educated and accomplished deaf people who never used their voices, nor were pressured to—let alone forced. (E.g., John Carlin.) That was before the advent of oralism in the States. The term "oral failure" had not yet been coined. "Oral failures" didn't yet exist. Until Bell.

You will note that most deaf achievers of the past came from hearing families and were early-deafened. (Spinal meningitis and scarlet fever were among the most common causes of childhood deafness.) A higher proportion of recent achievers are from Deaf families. You will also note a preponderance of deaf achievers from the latter half of the 19th century and the first half of the 20th who attended oral schools. By the time they were born, there was no longer any choice. Even the state/residential schools for the deaf abandoned the use of sign language in the classroom and adopted a rigid pure-oral approach. Sign language as it was originally used in the residential schools—as Laurent Clerc and his many students used it—has yet to make a complete comeback.

While the oral/auditory approach was rigorously enforced in the classroom and corridors, sign language (what we now call ASL) was used in the dormitories, or, as a better surety against discovery and punishment, in the toilets. Thus deaf children were introduced to the public and private faces of the Deaf reality. This tension underscored the achievements of Fred Schreiber, Bernard Bragg, and Phyllis Frelich. They weren't content to "act Hearing;" they wanted freedom to be first-class Deaf citizens. They wanted pride. The DPN student leaders took that a step further: they wanted full representation as Deaf people.

Do the stories of past generations of deaf people have anything to say to us? They do indeed.

They underscore the importance of attitude, of refusing to take "can't" as an answer. (Far too many deaf children have been—and are still being—taught that they "can't," not that they *can*.)

It is our modest hope that these biographical sketches inspire and provoke our readers—to do further research into the lives, times, and achievements of these people, to seek out other "forgotten" deaf achievers, and, perhaps, to reach for some "inaccessible" star themselves. We now have a galaxy of deaf people busy accomplishing things. We owe much to the achievers of the past (and present), those who made it possible for us to have the freedoms and the choices we take for granted. Our current achievements are still to be assessed and sifted out by time; our future achievements are yet to be chronicled.

Matthew Scott Moore
Rochester, New York
April 1996

*The term "deaf" (small "d") is used in its broadest sense to describe medical/audiological deafness, irrespective of cultural affiliation (oral or signing). "Deaf" (with a capital "D") is used to indicate cultural affiliation or identity—being a member of the Deaf community that uses American Sign Language (ASL) as an everyday means of communication. "Deaf" is an attitude as much as a quasi-ethnic affiliation. Some hearing people are very much part of the Deaf community; a number of deaf persons are not. "Hard-of-hearing" can mean an audiological condition *or* an attitude.

GREAT DEAF AMERICANS:
THE SECOND EDITION

The aged Laurent Clerc, an original oil portrait by John Carlin, circa 1860-66.
(Kentucky School for the Deaf)

CHAPTER 1

Laurent Clerc

1785-1869

The French legacy

When Louis Laurent Marie Clerc was born on December 26, 1785, his prospects were comfortable. His father, Joseph François, was *notaire* (royal civil attorney), justice of the peace, and mayor of La Balme-les-Grottes, a tiny village 26 miles east of Lyons, France. His mother, Elisabeth Candy, was a notary's daughter.

When he was a year old, Laurent toppled from his high chair into the kitchen fireplace. One side of his face was severely burned, and a resulting fever left him deaf and deprived him of the sense of smell. (He later thought that he had been born deaf, however.) He was also left with a prominent scar on his right cheek. This scar became the basis of his sign-name (the index and middle finger brushing the right cheek, near the mouth, downward twice)—still used today in the States and France.

His parents sought medical advice and tried a variety of treatments in a desperate attempt to cure his deafness. All efforts failed. Laurent, it seemed, was destined to spend his life without an education and a means of communication. He enjoyed some degree of freedom, though, playing in the La Balme's cavernous grottoes and fighting imaginary monsters there.

Fortunately, he had a devoted uncle-godfather, also named Laurent Clerc, who heard about a school for the deaf in Paris. When he was 12 years old, his uncle brought him to Paris and enrolled him in the Institut National des Jeune Sourds-Muets, directed by the Abbé Roch-Ambroise Sicard. Clerc's first teacher and chief mentor was Jean Massieu, once an illiterate shepherd boy, now one of the first truly educated deaf people. Massieu had devoted himself to the education of other deaf people. He was a colorful, eccentric, literate, witty personality. A hero.

Sicard's and Massieu's methods of instruction, utilizing sign language and the manual alphabet, awakened Laurent's dormant intellect. He made rapid progress, completing the course of study in 8 years. By 1816, he was in charge of the highest class. He was a brilliant teacher, loved by his students.

That year, something happened that changed the course of his life. While participating with Massieu in one of Sicard's public demonstrations in London, he met an idealistic young Yankee Congregationalist minister, Thomas Hopkins Gallaudet.

Sicard gave him a free ticket to the next demonstration—Gallaudet was impressed—and a generous invitation to visit the Institute. He finally did.

Mason Fitch Cogswell was a physician and leading citizen of Hartford, Connecticut. His daughter Alice (born 1805) had been deafened by "spotted fever" (spinal meningitis). And there were no schools for the deaf in the States. Gallaudet was Cogswell's neighbor. He took an interest in Alice (a beautiful child, bright and alert, but virtually languageless) and discussed her plight with Cogswell. Both agreed that she could—and should—be educated. Cogswell already had Sicard's treatise on deaf education, **Théorie des Signes** (and loaned it to Gallaudet). He "networked"—enlisted the support of other wealthy parents of deaf children, helped sponsor a census of the deaf population of Connecticut, and after determining that there were a sufficient number to warrant the venture, collected funds and organized a meeting of city fathers to sponsor the establishment of a school for deaf children. They unanimously chose Gallaudet, financed his trip, and sent him abroad to learn the best methods of educating the deaf.

Although Gallaudet could only spend 3 months at the Institute (he was running out of funds), he had numerous opportunities to observe Clerc, whom he called "a master teacher." Gallaudet quickly sized up the situation and his needs. He realized that Clerc had the expertise to help him fulfill his mission of founding the first school for the deaf in America. Accordingly, he made a bold offer (one not anticipated by Dr. Cogswell or the others)—he asked Clerc to come to the States with him and help establish the school. And Clerc boldly volunteered to go.

Even though it meant that Clerc would be leaving his homeland, family, friends, students, Sicard, Massieu, his native language, the delights of Paris—everything he cherished—for a raw, new (and anti-Catholic) country, the challenge appealed to his adventurous streak and his empathy for Alice and the other deaf children of the States, languageless, untaught. He was also ambitious.

Permission was granted to him by Sicard, who also gave him his blessing, although he was sorry to lose his star pupil. He and Gallaudet drew up a detailed contract; Clerc was to spend 3 years in the States "on loan." Four days later, on June 18, 1816, they sailed from Le Havre on board the *Mary Augusta*.

The crossing lasted an overlong 52 days, but Clerc and Gallaudet made good use of their time. They tutored each other, Gallaudet polishing Clerc's English (although he already had a working knowledge of it) and Clerc teaching Gallaudet sign language. The two were to remain friends and colleagues. Clerc's writings in English show a remarkable clarity and elegance of expression.

They arrived in New York on August 9, and then journeyed by stagecoach to Hartford, where Gallaudet planned to establish the school. Gallaudet introduced Clerc to the Cogswell family, and Dr. Cogswell was delighted and reassured—here was an educated deaf man, a gallant gentleman. Alice, of course, was ecstatic.

First, however, it was necessary to enlist public and legislative support and raise the needed funds. With Gallaudet as his interpreter, Clerc gave many speeches and educational demonstrations, much as he had done in London. From October 1816 to April 1817, they traveled throughout the East, from Boston to Philadelphia, also interviewing parents of deaf children and rounding up prospective students. From the public, they raised $5,000, which was matched by the Connecticut General Assembly—the first such appropriation in American history.

Their mission accomplished, they returned to Hartford. The new school (originally called the "Connecticut Asylum, For the Education and Instruction of Deaf and Dumb Persons") rented a building and opened its doors to seven pupils on April 15, 1817, with Gallaudet as the principal and Clerc as head teacher. Alice Cogswell was the first to enroll.

In 1818, Clerc became the first deaf person to address Congress, and got a standing ovation—and funding for the growing school.

Clerc used French signs ("natural" and "methodical") in class, but complained that his students were "changing" them. (This suggests that they already had some form of native sign language.) They took Clerc's signs, borrowed many, and modified others to their own usage. From this blend evolved today's American Sign Language. Some two-thirds of ASL signs—still used today—are derived from the French—Clerc's "graceful signs." He thus played a vital role in the development and enrichment of ASL.

Students ranged from ages 6 to 40. Classes were intensive, and used the simplest equipment—primers, slateboards and chalk, quill pens, ink, and paper. All instruction was in sign. Speech wasn't taught, as it was considered a waste of time. Yet many of those students became educated, highly literate, productive adults. Many became teachers of the deaf themselves. Several—like William Willard—even founded schools for the deaf, carrying Clerc's influence and example across the States.

For two generations, Clerc was the single most influential character in Deaf education. His teaching career at "Old Hartford" spanned 41 years. He also trained hearing teachers of the deaf. As new schools opened up in the States, their administrators came to Hartford from New York, Pennsylvania, Quebec, Virginia, Kentucky, and Indiana to receive training in communication and methods of instruction. (The Kentucky School for the Deaf was the first "Hartford satellite.") From August 1821 to March 1822, Clerc was acting principal of the Pennsylvania Institution in Philadelphia (now Pennsylvania School for the Deaf).

On May 3, 1818, Clerc married the vivacious and intelligent Eliza Crocker Boardman, one of his former pupils. It was the first recorded Deaf marriage in the States, and a happy one. Four of their children survived infancy. Clerc remained in Hartford, revisiting France three times (1820, 1835, and 1846). He retired in 1858, age 73. In 1864, he spoke at the inauguration of the National Deaf-Mute College (now Gallaudet University) in Washington, D.C. He received an honorary M.A. degree from Trinity College and citations from Dartmouth College and the University of Lyons.

On July 18, 1869, he died, full of honors, at the ripe age of 84.

In 1874, an impressive black-granite memorial shaft with a bronze bust was unveiled at "Old Hartford," with the inscription: *The Apostle to the Deaf-Mutes of the New World . . . who left his native land to uplift them with his teachings and encourage them by his example.*

In 1921, "Old Hartford" moved to a new campus in West Hartford and was renamed The American School for the Deaf. On April 15, 1992, ASD kicked off its 175th Anniversary celebration.

Clerc continues to inspire Deaf people. There have been plays written and performed in the States and France to honor his pioneering achievements. *Laurent Clerc: A Profile* (1976), by ASD alumnus Gilbert Eastman, was performed by the Gallaudet College Players when ASD's Clerc Residence Hall was formally dedicated in 1976. *La Vie de Laurent Clerc,* by Christian Cloux and Michèle Bonnot, was performed in 1994 in La Balme to celebrate the Laurent Clerc Association's 10th anniversary. There have been video-documentaries and plans to produce a feature film—and to establish a memorial in Hartford's Spring Grove Cemetery, where Laurent and Eliza Clerc are buried.

In Harlan Lane's **When the Mind Hears**, a monumental history of the Deaf experience in 18th- and 19th-century Europe and the States, Clerc is a central *persona*; the first half of the book is written from his own viewpoint, recounting the history of deaf education and the follies of some of its practitioners, the political and social turmoils of his age, his contemporaries, and his own life and adventures.

Thus, the spirit of Laurent Clerc lives on—in stone and bronze, books, drama, and video, the expressive language of signs that he brought over from France—and, above all, in the Deaf community he helped create—an immortal legacy.

Thomas Jefferson Wright's original oil portrait of "Erastus "Deaf" Smith,
commissioned by Sam Houston in 1836. (San Jacinto Museum of History)

CHAPTER 2

Erastus "Deaf" Smith

1787-1837

"The eyes of the Texas army"

Erastus Smith was born on April 19, 1787, near Poughkeepsie, New York, to Chileab and Mary Smith, devout Baptists. Little is known about his early life. Illness in infancy left him with a chronic lung ailment and may have deafened him, but it's possible that he was progressively deafened. He grew into a frail, quiet youth. Although not totally deaf, he was unable to follow group conversations, but could manage nicely on a one-to-one basis. Solitude was what he preferred.

The Smith family moved to the Mississippi Territory when Erastus was 11, and set up a farm. He became strong and vigorous, active in outdoor life, helping his family work their farm (which he disliked) and spending his free time hunting and fishing (which he enjoyed).

Ultimately, he caught "Texas fever"—a craving for the vast spaces of the frontier, and for their fabled riches. He first visited in 1817, then settled in San Antonio de Béxar, a center of Tejano (Hispanic-Texan) culture, raising and selling cattle. Around this time, 1821, Mexico won its independence from Spain, putting the Texas territory under the rule of the Mexican government. With the rapid settlement of Texas, Smith gained a reputation as a scout and was often employed as a land surveyor or hunting guide. He also fought "hostile" Indians.

He married Guadalupe Ruiz Duran, an aristocratic 25-year-old Castilian widow, in 1822. His marriage automatically made him a Mexican citizen. He happily absorbed the language and customs of the Tejanos, who called him "el Sordo" (the deaf one). Texians (Anglos) called him "Deaf" (pronounced "Deef") to distinguish him from other Smiths. He and 'Lupe had four children: Susan, Gertrudes, Travis, and Simona.

Tensions between the growing population of Texians and the Mexican authorities escalated, and finally, on October 2, 1835, broke into open war. Smith, although innocent of any involvement (and trying to remain neutral), immediately fell under suspicion by the Mexican army.

On October 19, he returned from a buffalo hunt and found Béxar surrounded by Mexican soldiers. He was denied entry to visit his wife and children, but told to come back the next day. He did, and when he saw cavalrymen coming after him, realized that it was a trap. He fired his rifle, then both pistols, at his pursuers, and didn't stop riding until he reached the camp of the Texas revolutionists, commanded by Stephen Austin, the former colonizer-diplomat-turned-radical. When General Cos, President-General Santa Anna's brother-in-law, posted a $1,000 reward for the capture of *el Sordo*, Smith made his decision. He enlisted as a volunteer in Austin's army, and placed a mere $500 bounty on Cos' head, saying that was all *he* was worth.

On his first mission, Smith guided a Texian company behind enemy lines. He fired the first shot at the Battle of Concepción on October 27. The surprise attack against Cos' forces, in a thick fog, ended in a stunning victory for the Texians. Thereafter, *el Sordo* became a key figure in the Texas Revolution. He participated in the "Grass Fight" (November 27). Wounded in the shoulder during the Battle of Béxar (December 5-8), he was granted 3 months' leave to join his family in Columbia and recuperate. (Cos surrendered and withdrew all forces from Texas.)

When Smith learned that Cos had returned to Texas with Santa Anna and 6,000 troops, he was furious. Santa Anna was on his way to Béxar—on a mission of vengeance. Smith rejoined the army on March 7, 1836, the day after the Alamo fell.

His keen eyes, intimate knowledge of the territory, exceptional ability to "smell out" a trail, and bravery impressed Sam Houston, commander-in-chief of the Texas Regular Army, who appointed him "personal scout and spy with the rank of private," and put him in command of his own company. Smith gave Houston unwavering loyalty. Asked if his deafness was a hindrance, he replied, "No, I sometimes think it is an advantage—I have learned to keep a sharp outlook and I am never disturbed by the whistling of a ball [bullet]—I don't hear the bark till I feel the bite." Some called him "the eyes of the army."

When Houston learned about the "massacres" at the Alamo and Goliad, he had the messengers arrested as liars, then sent Smith towards Béxar to get more information, accompanied by his equally brave and resourceful companion scout, Captain Henry Wax Karnes. They soon met the only Anglo survivors: Susannah Dickerson, whose husband Almeron, an artillery captain, had just been slain in the siege, her 14-month-old daughter Angelina, and Joe, Travis' black slave. At least twice during the ensuing eastward retreat, Smith helped capture dispatch pouches from General Sesma's couriers to Santa Anna—useful intelligence for Houston. Twelve miles from the Texian camp at Harrisburg, Smith and Karnes captured three Mexicans, including Captain Bachiller, a special courier from Mexico City carrying dispatches for Santa Anna. It was a decisive stroke of luck—a coup.

The turning point occurred on April 21, 1836. Santa Anna, pursuing the fleeing Texas government, had amassed a large army that, with Cos' newly-arrived reinforcements, outnumbered the Texian force (1,250 to some 870), near Buffalo Bayou, which emptied into the San Jacinto River (just east of the modern city limits of Houston). Surrounded by "treacherous marshes," the grassy plain was reached directly through Lynch's Ferry on the east or Vince's Bridge—a sturdy little construction of cedar timbers—8 miles to the west. Heavy rains had flooded the surrounding embankments.

With his dark, leathery, sunburned face and a sombrero pulled over his reddish hair, Smith could easily pass as a Tejano. He disguised himself as a ragged, barefoot field hand and scouted the Mexican camp. When questioned, he played dumb or answered in

Spanish. He then reported to Houston. By some accounts, Smith proposed a daring stratagem: if the Texians staged a surprise offensive, he could destroy the bridge. The enemy would then be trapped, without a means of retreat. Nor could they receive reinforcements. It was a bold—and risky—plan, but Houston agreed to it. Six volunteers led by Smith chopped down Vince's Bridge with their axes.

But whose idea *was* it? Houston's? One of the men in Smith's detail? Or Smith himself? The various accounts disagree. Even if Smith was just carrying out orders, that doesn't lessen his valor.

Houston waited until mid-afternoon. The Mexicans weren't expecting the Texians until next morning. They relaxed. Even Santa Anna was enjoying an afternoon siesta. Amazingly, they didn't even have sentries posted.

So sudden and so devastating was the Texian assault that the Battle of San Jacinto lasted less than a half-hour—18 minutes, by several accounts. Smith returned in the nick of time, waved his axe high overhead—to show that he had accomplished his mission— and shouted in his high-pitched, squeaky voice, "I have cut down Vince's Bridge! Now fight for your lives and remember the Alamo!"

The next day, Santa Anna, disguised as a common soldier, was captured. (Smith's vigilance helped prevent his escape and as-sured his capture. He wasn't in the party that captured Santa Anna, but he did—unknowingly—help capture Cos, his archenemy.) The Texians all wanted Santa Anna lynched without further ado, but Houston wisely recognized *El Presidente's* importance as their only bargaining chip. Santa Anna agreed to an armistice—a cease-fire and immediate withdrawal of Mexican troops from Texas. At this historic event, which marked the birth of the Texas Republic, Smith was given an honored place, right next to Houston.

This scene was later depicted in an enormous painting (1886) by William Henry Huddle in the Texas State Capital. Under a great live-oak tree, Houston reclines on a colorfully-striped Mexican blanket, his shattered right leg bandaged in rags, as he gestures to Santa Anna to take a seat on an upturned artillery crate. Promi-nently placed in the foreground, wearing a fringed buckskin shirt and cradling a rifle against his knee, is Deaf Smith, who cups his ear to hear, if he can, the terms of surrender.

Smith was delegated to deliver a dispatch to General Filisola, Santa Anna's second-in-command, and brought back his scribbled reply. He was then assigned to spy on the retreating army and see that the terms of surrender were carried out.

Shortly afterwards, Houston commissioned Thomas Jefferson Wright to paint Smith's striking portrait from life—one of the few honors he lived to enjoy. He soon retired from military duty and went to Richmond, where he embarked on a new business venture—land transactions—with John Borden, youngest of the Borden brothers (of dairy-dynasty fame). He'd hardly begun when, with the onset of cold, wet Gulf weather, his health took a turn for the worse. Famous, but never fortunate, he died on November 30, 1837, age 50. The cause: "consumption."

Writing to his friend Anna Raguet, Sam Houston grieved: "Deaf Smith, my stay in my darkest hour, is no more!" 'Lupe and the children were visiting relatives in Mexico when it happened, so they weren't at the funeral.

As time went by, Smith's gravesite was lost, and never relocated. A monument was set up by the state at the approximate site and later moved to Richmond courthouse. The inscription reads: "So valiant and trustworthy was he, that all titles sink into insignificance before the simple name of 'Deaf' Smith." In 1840, Smith's portrait appeared on Republic of Texas $5 bills. The granite marker on the site of Vince's Bridge commemorates the role played by Smith's detail in the Battle of San Jacinto.

In 1876, a vast area of land in the Texas Panhandle, adjacent to New Mexico, was named Deaf Smith County; it's famed for its mineral-rich farmlands. **The Deaf Smith Country Cookbook** was published in 1973. That year, a "spaghetti Western," **Deaf Smith and Johnny Ears**, was released. Cleburne Huston engaged in a more successful endeavor: his meticulously-researched but lively biography, **Deaf Smith: Incredible Texas Spy**, was published in 1975. (It's now a collector's item.) Smith remains a folk hero in Texas.

William Willard, after an old daguerreotype.
(Courtesy of Indiana School for the Deaf)

CHAPTER 3

William Willard

1809-1888

Founder of Indiana School for the Deaf

On November 1, 1809, Sarah Goodrich Willard, of the small community of Rockingham, Vermont, gave birth to her seventh child. Her husband Isaac had died two months earlier. The baby was named William after Isaac's father. Sarah provided for her family, and William contributed to its livelihood. He was taught to do an honest day's work, and to value education. (Several members of the family had been early students at Harvard College.)

At age 6, William was deafened by spotted fever (spinal meningitis). Sarah sought help in getting an education for him, and refused to give up. She discovered that only two years after William had been deafened, the "Hartford Asylum" opened. She took William to Hartford and enrolled him there on May 22, 1824, as its 132nd student. He was 14 years old and eager to learn.

He became Laurent Clerc's student and thrived under his tutelage; he spent what must have been an exciting and fruitful 5 years at Hartford with Clerc and making lifelong friendships with his classmates. Clerc instilled in young Willard his dream of providing an education for all deaf people in the States.

In 1829, Willard left Hartford. Although he lacked a degree, he was a man of superior intelligence. His first endeavor was to establish a private school for deaf children in New York City. He worked diligently as a tradesman as well. But the New York Institution for the Deaf and Dumb (later New York School for the Deaf, still popularly known as "Fanwood"), which had gotten off to a shaky start in 1818, had taken most of his potential students.

His efforts failed. But that initial failure was brief. Soon afterwards, he was offered, and accepted, a position as one of the first teachers at the newly-established Columbus Asylum for Mutes (later the Ohio Institution for the Education of the Deaf, now Ohio School for the Deaf). He remained in this position for the next 10 years, a diligent teacher and energetic Presbyterian.

Around this time, he met Elizabeth (Eliza) Young, a student at the Columbus Asylum. She was born on December 16, 1817, in Summerville, Ohio. Very little else is known about her. They were married on September 17, 1839, in Oxford, Ohio. They had six children (all hearing) and were to enjoy a long, happy marriage that was also a successful educational partnership.

They already had two young daughters when they decided to move to Indiana. Once again, William planned to start a private school. It was to be a joint venture, with Eliza as teacher/caretaker to the female students.

In May 1843, Willard rode to Indianapolis and presented himself with credentials to the General Assembly, proposing the establishment of a school for deaf children. He later wrote: "I first started for this state traveling on horseback from Ohio. At this time the country was sparsely settled and covered with grand, tall trees. After days of difficult traveling, I reached the capitol, fresh and full of spirits." Those high spirits were well rewarded. On May 30, the General Assembly enacted a resolution endorsing Willard's interest in opening a school and proposing that he visit various parts of the state to stir up interest in the education of deaf people.

He posted announcements of his plan in newspapers around the state: "For their tuition I will make no charge. Boarding can be had for $1.50 a week." He spent the greater part of the summer of 1843 riding across the state on horseback, at his own expense, scouting for potential students. Eliciting public support, he demonstrated his methods and explained the benefits of instruction to anyone who was interested, and recruited students for his school. Fundraising was not his objective. Finding deaf people was. Supt. Thomas MacIntire later wrote of him: "Being a gentleman of no ordinary intelligence, of pleasing manner and affable address, he was eminently successful in the object of his tour."

On October 1, 1843, William and Eliza Willard opened their semi-private school in what is now downtown Indianapolis, with 12 students in attendance. The school prospered. During its first year, the total enrollment climbed to 23.

When the General Assembly convened the following December, they felt duty-bound to take up support of the Willard School. An Act of January 15, 1844, established the "Indiana Asylum for the Education of the Deaf and Dumb." It was the sixth state school for the deaf—but the first one to provide free education. Willard was appointed principal, at a salary of $800 a year. But Eliza Willard's direct connection with the school ended.

The state rented for it a newly-built, roomy 2-story frame house with spacious grounds. To accommodate the ever-increasing number of students, it soon relocated to an even larger building.

According to the official guidelines for the school, admission age ranged from 10 to 30 years. Pupils were required to take a 5-year course to earn a certificate. The school was open to out-of-state students whose families paid $100 per annum. Sessions ran from the first Monday in October to the last day in July.

In 1845, Willard filled a small composition book with samples of his students' handwriting (for the edification of visitors). The text, which he must have written for his students to copy, presented an analysis of "the sign language" used at the school. Thus, he was probably the first to analyze and record basic grammatical rules of what we now call ASL. His "extract" discusses "descriptive" and "indicative" signs, and concepts that are now called iconicity, concrete, abstract, and universal signs, classifiers, and sign-mime. In doing so, he predated Dr. William Stokoe—the first hearing scholar to subject ASL to linguistic analysis—by nearly 150 years.

The school continued to grow, and soon needed to relocate again. This time there was some disagreement as to where. Several cities vied for the honor; Indianapolis finally "beat" the top contender, Bloomington.

In 1846, Willard purchased around 80 acres of land just outside of the eastern city limits of Indianapolis. A spacious parcel of land adjacent to Willard's property was purchased for the campus; he undoubtedly used his influence with the city. It was just off the old National Road—once the main Midwestern highway. As soon as the impressive Greek Revival main building was finished in 1850, the school moved there. The splendid campus featured an orchard, shade and forest trees, various flowers, a conservatory, "winding walks and drives," a vegetable garden, a pasture for crops and the teaching of agricultural methods, and a baseball diamond for the "Silent Hoosiers." With Willard's property to the north of the National Road and the school's 124 acres to the south, the area just to the east of the city limits was an enclave for Deaf people and the beginning of a Deaf cultural center in Indiana. The school remained at this location 61 years, until October 1911.

Willard's surviving letters indicate some tension between himself and the school's Board of Trustees (all hearing). When his salary was reduced by $100 during the 1861-82 school year—the only teacher to have his pay docked—he responded in a forceful and dignified letter.

He taught for 20 years, until 1864, when he (according to the school's annual report) "was, on account of ill health, relieved from duty . . . and has retired to private life." Since Willard lived for another 24 years, active almost to the end, his health was apparently *not* in decline. Was he forced into retirement by the Board? Possibly.

After his retirement, Willard visited each classroom regularly, greeting his "old students." They also visited him at his home, as did other prominent citizens. Rev. Thomas Gallaudet (Thomas Hopkins Gallaudet's eldest son) visited the Willards on November 14, 1868. He had, of course, known William in Hartford.

Buying and selling real estate, purchasing bonds, renting his farmlands, selling cattle and produce, Willard remained an active businessman. He acquired wealth and helped support his children and their families in hard times.

On April 19, 1886, William's beloved Eliza died. Around that time, he developed a malignant tumor in his cheek. He died at home on February 15, 1888.

In 1904, the state approved the construction of a handsome new 80-acre campus, nearly 5 miles directly north of the old one. After the old campus was demolished in 1911, the grounds became a public park, officially named "Willard Park." ISD's Student Council placed a commemorative plaque there in 1966. (It was ultimately stolen.)

On October 1, 1993—Founder's Day—ISD officially kicked off its sesquicentennial celebration. A new historical marker was unveiled by Willard's descendants, and a memorial wreath was placed at the Willards' gravesites in Crown Hill Cemetery.

By the time Willard died in 1888, the "Dark Ages" of the American Deaf Community had begun. The perception that hearing people automatically knew what was best for deaf people went unchallenged for more than a century. ISD became an oral school.

The "Deaf President Now!" uprising at Gallaudet University in March 1988 sent shock waves through the Deaf community and beyond. Across the nation, schools for the deaf began actively seeking and hiring qualified deaf candidates as superintendents, administrators, faculty, and staff. Things began to change at ISD as well—or, more accurately, the pace of change was speeded up. Between ISD's first and second Deaf superintendents was a distance of 149 years. In 1992, Eddy Laird became ISD's second deaf superintendent.

ISD had emerged from the oralist twilight to become a pioneering school again. It quietly reinstated and recognized signing, gradually working towards full acceptance of ASL as a language of instruction. In 1967, Roy Holcomb popularized "Total Communication" while teaching there. Today ISD is one of the top deaf schools—a fully accredited national resource center recognized for its leadership in education, its advocacy of ASL, and being the first state deaf school to adopt a Bilingual/Bicultural approach— using ASL to teach English (1991).

Willard and his students were proud Deaf people who expressed themselves fluently in ASL and written English. They saw themselves as full-fledged citizens. Today we call this the "Bi-Bi" goal. In a sense, the wheel has come full circle.

Edmund Booth: "Like King Saul of old, 'higher than any of the people from his shoulders and upward.'" (Gallaudet University Archives)

CHAPTER 4

Edmund Booth

1810-1905

Forty-Niner, journalist, leader

Edmund Booth lived a long and adventurous life—farmer, teacher, pioneer settler, Forty-Niner, newspaper publisher, Deaf leader. He was born on August 24, 1810, on a farm in Chicopee, Massachusetts, near Springfield. When he was 4 or so, an outbreak of "spotted fever" (cerebrospinal meningitis) killed his father and left him partially deaf and totally blind in one eye. As he later recalled in his autobiography, **Forty-Niner**: "It so continued until the age of seven or eight when, with another boy, I spent nearly a day sporting in an old pond. The next morning I was totally deaf and have so continued since." But he "never lost the power of speech." Before he became totally deaf, his mother taught him how to read. (He became a lifelong reader.) He had a bit of schooling. When he was 12, he went to live at the farm of his kindly Uncle David, who died when Edmund was 16. That year, he had an encounter that changed his life:

> . . . in the spring of 1827, a man called and wished to see me. His name was Flavel Goldthwaite, son of an old neighbor who, with his family, lived a mile or so down street. I was called into the parlor where he was and he began to use the hand alphabet, with which I was familiar, and now and then a sign, the language of the deaf. He told me of the Hartford school and that I could go there for education. I was then sixteen years old, and no one had ever hinted the possibility of my going.

He negotiated with his family, and, since "the quota of Massachusetts was full," waited for the next vacancy. He was admitted to the Hartford Asylum in 1828, and studied under Laurent Clerc,

Thomas Hopkins Gallaudet, and Lewis Weld, Gallaudet's successor as principal. He completed his studies in 1830. But instead of
returning to Springfield, he stayed on as a teacher, first substitut-
ing for Frederick A. P. Barnard, who was ill. (Barnard, himself
deafened as a young man, later became tenth president of Columbia College [later University] in New York.) Weld was so pleased
with Booth's teaching that he offered him a permanent post and
regularly increased his salary. In 1834, Booth, two other students,
and Weld "sailed from New York to South Carolina and Georgia.
Had exhibitions before the legislatures of those two states, and
both passed laws sending pupils to Hartford."

In May 1839, Booth resigned, "glad to be free and my own
master." He decided to move West—to Iowa. He had suffered an
attack of pneumonia, and desired a more active life than teaching
afforded, and possibly a better salary (even though he was earning
the decent sum of $600 a year). Not coincidentally, Iowa was where
Mary Ann Walworth's family now lived. Mary Ann had been one
of Barnard's students, and he wanted to see her again.

Booth journeyed by railroad, stagecoach, canal, and lake steamer
to eastern Iowa. There was one extraordinary incident: "After
leaving Chicago, then a village of possibly twenty houses, and
while stopping at Galena, a small town near the Mississippi,"
Booth was "detained and his baggage examined"—he was mis-
taken for "a fugitive murderer from Ohio . . . a tall man with one
eye and black hair." Luckily, Booth had *light* hair.

His destination was Anamosa, a wilderness with a few widely-
scattered log cabins. As an 1898 biography put it: "Indians, deer,
wolves, rattlesnakes, and the like belongings to a frontier life, or a
sparsely populated district, were abundant, and might almost be
said to have been his daily companions." He "accepted the first
thing that offered in the way of employment;" he built mills, dams,
houses, and made a "fair living" at farming. His family soon joined
him, and he and his brother-in-law built the first "comfortable
house," frame-style, in Jones County. In July 1840, he married
Mary Ann Walworth in that house. He held a number of minor
offices, including three terms as Recorder of Deeds (1841 to 1846),

and Enrollment Clerk to the Iowa House of Representatives (1844). Although nominated as county treasurer, he declined, not wanting to relocate.

When Iowa became a state in 1848, Booth convinced the state legislature to send its deaf children to Illinois School for the Deaf (founded 1846) to be educated, at Iowa's expense. He helped found Iowa School for the Deaf in Council Bluffs; it opened in 1855.

In 1849, after the Gold Rush began, Edmund left Mary Ann and their three children to join the migration to California. It took 6 months to reach "the land of gold." The hardships were plentiful; he survived cholera and smallpox. He mined for gold near Sonora, and—as **The Silent World** of Toronto put it—"was successful in a fair degree," sending home enough money for Mary Ann to purchase a 5-acre tract of land. At night, he read, kept a journal, and wrote letters home: "I am staying here chiefly for the children. They must have as good an education as possible." (Later, in addition to overseeing his children's education, he helped his neighbors' children with theirs, using the library he had brought from Hartford.) When he returned to Iowa in 1854, via the Isthmus of Panama, he brought "a considerable sum of money."

In 1855, John Jacobus Flournoy, a wealthy and exceedingly strange deaf character from Georgia (and a co-founder of Georgia School for the Deaf), publicly proposed the establishment of a Deaf commonwealth—a self-governing state—in the West. He was convinced that unless deaf people separated from hearing society, they would experience nothing but oppression. In his view, deaf people would always be "contemned, scorned, degraded and abhorred" by the hearing majority.

Back and forth, the debate continued for a couple of years in the **American Annals of the Deaf**. Flournoy had several notable critics, deaf and hearing. One of the most forceful was Booth. He argued that Flournoy's scheme was economically and socially impracticable. "While tracing out his castles in the air, [Flournoy] gives but superficial attention to the nature of the materials with which it is to be built, or the foundation on which it is to be laid." Booth had never felt oppressed or discriminated against, and moved comfortably in both deaf and hearing society. (John Carlin likewise criticized Flournoy's proposal, but was much less tactful.)

In 1856, Booth began his career as an editor and publisher. One of the few people in Jones County with any degree of literary skill, he was asked to contribute an article for the first issue of the weekly **Anamosa Eureka**. His writings became lead editorials.

In 1858, he paid Matthew Parrott $1,000 for a half-share in the **Eureka**. Under Booth's editorship, it was successful and influential. In 1862 he bought out the other half-share, using money from the sale of his farm. He managed the enterprise by himself until 1868, then took his older son Thomas into partnership; the new firm was called "E. Booth & Son." The **Eureka** was the "leading official paper of Jones County." It was printed on northern Iowa's first Hoe Power Press, which Booth bought in 1866. (He also built a brick printing office for it.) He continued to contribute articles to the **Annals** and published several poems in Deaf periodicals.

Booth held strongly Abolitionist views, and expressed them in print. He even got involved in face-to-face but one-way arguments with pro-South Northeners on the street. He denounced the U.S. Census for its malicious bias against blacks.

In 1880, Booth received an honorary Master of Arts degree from National Deaf-Mute College (renamed Gallaudet College in 1894).

In August 1880, the first National Deaf-Mute Convention was held in Cincinnati, during which the NAD was established. Booth, 70, was elected chairman *pro tem*. Although nominated for the presidency, he "modestly declined to serve," fearing that his age might be a problem, and helped elect Robert P. McGregor, 31, to the post. (NAD's other co-founder, Edwin A. Hodgson, became its second president.)

As noted in the **Deaf-Mutes' Journal**, edited by Hodgson:

> To him is accorded the unique distinction of being the first man to preside at a gathering of the representative deaf from all parts of the United States. In a large hall on one of the hill-tops overlooking the City of Cincinnati, in the year 1880, he called to order the meeting that was to organize the present National Association of the Deaf. That was twenty-five years ago, but even then he was called "the venerable Edmund Booth." Tall and muscular, with hair and beard as white as

drifted snow, he fulfilled the functions of temporary chairman of the first and greatest assemblage of deaf-mutes that up to that time the world had ever known.

Booth agreed to chair the NAD's National Executive Committee, and for the rest of his life, played an active role in advocating for the rights of deaf people in the States.

Although bothered by an occasional recurrence of his old lung trouble, Booth enjoyed a vigorous old age. As Thomas wrote:

Father went to the world's fair in Chicago in 1893. There was a world's congress of the deaf, including teachers and others, held in the Art Institute Building, and he came into their midst with his two sons. Several of these teachers recognized him and hurried toward him with hands and fingers flying. Instantly there was a rush, and greetings and demonstrations of affection followed that were to the writer pathetic beyond the language of pen or tongue to describe. There stood father in the midst, six feet, two and a half inches tall, and of massive frame, and, like King Saul of old, 'higher than any of the people from his shoulders and upward'—a veritable patriarch among the representatives of his class from the four quarters of the globe. He was then the oldest living ex-teacher of the deaf in the United States, and probably at the time of his death there was not another in the world who exceeded him in age.

When he was 90, he was quoted by **The Silent World** (Toronto): "Life with me has been agreeable, as a rule, the exceptions being hardly worth notice, and those exceptions being almost entirely out of memory."

He died on March 29, 1905, at the then-remarkable age of 94 years, 7 months, and 5 days. Edward Allen Fay, first vice-president of Gallaudet College and longtime editor of the **Annals**, described Booth as "a man of strong convictions, hating shams, pretensions and injustice, and sometimes expressing what he felt with too little regard for the feelings of others. He was kindhearted, liberal-minded, and generous, however."

Ironically, Frank Walworth Booth, Edmund's younger son, headed the American Association to Promote the Teaching of Speech to the Deaf (later renamed the Alexander Graham Bell Association for the Deaf), the chief political adversary of the NAD—which his father had co-founded. He was an ardent oralist. For all that, he wrote an affectionate tribute to his remarkable father for the AAPTSD's **Association Review**.

John Carlin, from an engraving in **Harper's New Monthly Magazine**, 1884.
(Courtesy of Pennsylvania School for the Deaf)

CHAPTER 5

John Carlin

1813-1891

Artist, Writer, and Advocate

John Carlin was a gifted artist, poet, and writer; an eloquent signer who promoted the cause of higher education of the deaf (although highly critical of sign language); he contributed greatly to the welfare and cultural life of the Deaf community. What makes his achievements all the more remarkable is that he began life in poverty and had only 5 or so years of formal schooling.

Born in Philadelphia on June 15, 1813, Carlin was deafened in infancy, as was his brother Andrew, 3 years younger. Their father, a poor on-again, off-again cobbler, could scarcely provide for them, much less give them an education.

As for his first artistic endeavor, Carlin's biographer, Harold Domich, quotes an older biography: "[H]e was accustomed to trace with chalk fantastic figures upon the floor, and which his mother would quickly deprive of their immortality by the application of the mop." Unschooled, languageless, and pretty much on his own, he roamed around the streets of Philadelphia. He was fascinated by what he saw of the charming old city with its domes, steeples and towers, beautiful parks, and landscapes.

In 1820, Carlin was spotted on the street by a kindly old merchant, David G. Seixas, who took him aside and tried to communicate with him. As Carlin himself later wrote: "I was picked up in Kensington, and for that deed of practical philanthropy, learned to love and respect Mr. Seixas' memory." Seixas took in deaf streetchildren, gave them food and clothing, and conducted a makeshift school in his house, where he taught them "the primary elements of a common school education," using self-invented sign language. Some 15 children of various ages were enrolled when Carlin began. He was bright, and began to learn.

That same year, the state took over Seixas' school. It also hired a few "competent" teachers of the deaf. One of these was Laurent Clerc, on loan from the Hartford Asylum as a visiting teacher-administrator, helping the new Philadelphia school get started. Although Clerc stayed for only one year, his influence was profound—and it touched John Carlin. The "Mt. Airy School" (now Pennsylvania School for the Deaf), was successfully launched, and Carlin thrived. As Domich noted: "He had an unquenchable thirst for more knowledge and a great desire to paint." But since each teacher used a different self-invented sign-language system, Carlin had difficulty understanding them, and his early frustration probably caused his later distaste for sign language—even though he became an effective "public signer" himself.

He graduated in 1825, at the age of 12. Domich: "Graduation put Carlin on his own again . . . His father was unable to provide sufficient funds for him to attend school any longer, and so he had to fall back on his own resources." For 7 years, he supported himself as a sign- and house-painter. At night and whenever he could, he studied. By the time he was 19, he not only had a solid background in art history but had also mastered English and five foreign languages.

In 1833 and 1834, using his earnings to pay for his art education, he studied drawing under John Rubens Smith, and portrait and genre painting at the Artist's Fund Society in Philadelphia. He also studied portraiture under John Neagle in New York. He knew he had talent and "became firmly resolved to succeed at his painting." Even though he ran out of money and had to give up his studies, he went back to work, saved his money, and in 1838, went "to visit Europe to observe the old masters and study under the famous teachers of the day."

First he went to London to study the British Museum's celebrated antiquities. He then went to France, where he studied portraiture under the famous teacher, Paul Delaroche. "It was here that his previous study of French, one of the languages he had mastered through his own efforts, stood him in good stead." He progressed rapidly in his studies. He also used pad and pencil to help Delaroche communicate with another American student—a hearing man who knew very little French. He did illustrations for **Paradise Lost** and **Pilgrim's Progress**, and practiced his own verse, struggling to attain "correctness."

In 1841, having run out of funds, Carlin returned to the States, set up a studio in New York, and began working as a miniaturist. His specialty was painting miniature portraits on ivory. (In pre-photography days, miniatures were mounted and worn as jewelry, given as tokens of love and affection, and treasured with family keepsakes.) Among his patrons were members of the Knickerbocker Families of "old New York." These were the first contacts that Carlin would make with prominent figures in society.

In 1843, he married Mary Wayland, who had attended Fanwood. She was the niece of William H. Seward, Governor of New York, later U.S. Senator and Secretary of State under President Lincoln. The Carlins raised five children, all hearing.

As Carlin's work became greatly in demand, many famous Washington personalities and diplomats sat for him. He knew Jefferson Davis, who was Secretary of War under President Franklin Pierce, and who commissioned Carlin to paint his son's portrait. He became friends with First Lady Jane Pierce, Senator Seward, Hamilton Fish, Thurlow Weed, and Horace Greeley.

When photography became popular, decreasing the demand for small-scale portraiture (miniatures soon became a virtually extinct genre), Carlin switched to more profitable landscape, genre subjects, and large-scale oil portraits. He produced many notable paintings—*The Flight into Egypt; Dolce far Niente; Old Fort, St. Lawrence River; The Village Gossips; The Admirer of Nature; The Twin Grandchildren; Old and Young; Going after Marshmallows; Solid Comfort; The Grandfather's Story; Playing at Dominoes; A View of Trenton Falls; The Toll Gate; After Work; The Orphaned Grandchild; After a Long Cruise.* Some of these were later displayed at the milestone 1934 International Exhibition of Fine and Applied Arts by Deaf Artists at the Roerich Museum in New York City.

Carlin's best-known work is his oil portrait, from life, of the aged and revered Laurent Clerc (*circa* 1860-66). This portrait, commissioned by undergraduates and alumni of Kentucky School for the Deaf, still hangs in a place of honor in its chapel. (Carlin was the only artist considered for the commission.)

In the early 1850s, Carlin began actively participating in Deaf-community affairs. He helped raise $6,000 to build St. Ann's Episcopal Church for the Deaf in New York City (1852). Founded by Rev. Thomas Gallaudet, this was the first church for deaf people in the States. Carlin was a member for 40 years. He was secretary of the committee in charge of financing a monument to T. H. Gallaudet in Hartford; he designed a bronze side panel for the column that shows Gallaudet teaching his first pupils fingerspelling. At its unveiling in 1858, he gave a signed oration. In 1864, he founded the Manhattan Literary Association of Deaf Mutes, to promote intellectual and social interaction among deaf scholars. From 1873 to 1881, he headed the committee to raise funds for the building of the Gallaudet Home for Aged and Infirm Deaf.

As the first published deaf poet in the States, Carlin inspired other deaf poets to write, publish their work, and succeed in literary endeavors—something considered impossible for deaf people to achieve. For many years, he had experimented with poetic expression, and finally learned to compose poems in "correct" meter and rhyme (quite a feat, considering that he had no knowledge—or memory—of pronunciation or accents). Some of these were printed in leading newspapers, and he was commended for his work by William Cullen Bryant, the eminent poet and editor of the **New York Post**. On this achievement, Luzerne Ray, the first editor of the **American Annals of the Deaf**, said, "We should as well expect a man born blind to paint a picture as a congenitally deaf man to write a poem."

As Domich noted:

> However, Mr. Carlin's writing was not confined to poetry alone. He was one of the most prolific writers of his day. One of his most important achievements in his line was the writing of a book entitled **The Scratchsides Family**, a book for children. He also wrote treatises on

architecture for the **Philadelphia Sunday Courier**, lectures on subjects ranging from geology to New York Central Park, columns in many of the leading papers for the deaf, and somewhat pugnacious letters to anyone who disagreed with his principles. He usually avoided using his own signature, preferring rather to use the pseudonym *Raphael Palette*. Many of his arguments with other writers of that day were caused by the sign language, for he contended that oralism and finger spelling were sufficient for the education of and communication with the deaf. The sign language was his anathema. However, as a lecturer before the deaf, he was in great demand; and despite his aversion to the sign language, he used it extremely well, and always chose interesting subjects which he described in a very simple, yet forceful, manner.

The largely self-educated Carlin recognized the value of higher education. As Domich noted: "He was active in influencing Edward Miner Gallaudet to found a college for the deaf." In 1854, Carlin published an article, "The National College for Mutes," in **The American Annals of the Deaf**. Ten years after Carlin published this article, the world's first liberal-arts college for the deaf was chartered, with E. M. Gallaudet as founder and first president—originally the Columbia Institution for the Deaf and Dumb, then National Deaf-Mute College, then Gallaudet College, now Gallaudet University.

At its opening ceremony, Carlin addressed the audience: "Mr. President, ladies and gentlemen: On this day, the 28th of June, 1864, a college for deaf-mutes is brought into existence. . . . Is it likely that colleges for deaf-mutes will ever produce mute statesmen, lawyers, and ministers of religion, orators, poets, and authors? The answer is: They will . . . I thank God for this privilege of witnessing the consummation of my wishes—a college for deafmutes—a subject which has for past years occupied my mind." In recognition of his services on behalf of the community, he became the first deaf recipient of an honorary degree (Master of Arts) granted by the new college. Amos Kendall, Postmaster General under Andrew Jackson and Martin Van Buren, who donated the original parcel of land for the new campus, presented Carlin with the degree.

On April 23, 1891, Carlin died of pneumonia. He was 73.

Laura Redden Searing: "Our life has much of sunshine." From an old engraving.
(Courtesy of Richard D. Reed/Missouri School for the Deaf)

CHAPTER 6

Laura Redden Searing

1840-1923

Literary patriot

There are but few instances of the deaf and deaf-dumb having attained literary eminence. It must be partly because the mind, in most cases, does not rise above the common level; and partly because the language of signs, from its peculiar structure, disqualifies them for expressing their thoughts in written language. How could we expect an English poet to excel in writing French rhymes? And thus a mute may be never so eloquent when expressing his thoughts in pantomime, but be utterly powerless to reproduce the same on paper.—Laura Redden, age 18

On August 5, 1995, a "Poet's Garden" was ceremoniously dedicated in City Park in Glyndon, Minnesota, organized by Minnesota Women's History Month. What made this a unique occasion was that the town Glyndon was named after "Howard Glyndon"—the pen name used by Laura Redden—a deaf journalist. She was the first deaf "career woman" in the States, and the first to succeed in the field of journalism and literature. And she became the first woman writer to have a town named after her during her lifetime. Ironically, for the better part of a century, this remarkable character was virtually forgotten.

Laura Catherine Redden was born on February 9, 1840, in Somerset County, Maryland. After her family had moved to St. Louis, Missouri, she was totally deafened at age 11 by cerebrospinal meningitis, which also affected her speech.

In 1855, she entered the Missouri Asylum for the Education of the Deaf and Dumb (now Missouri School for the Deaf) in Fulton. As Richard Reed, who later taught at MSD, notes: "While still a student at MSD, Laura demonstrated a remarkable literary talent. She was already writing essays and poetry on diverse topics that ranged from religion to politics and included nature and her own deafness."

She graduated on July 15, 1858. Her commencement speech, together with the farewell poem she composed for this occasion, were published in the **American Annals of the Deaf**. Says Reed: "Consider [this] address, written when she was 18. How perceptive she is in her comments on deafness, the sign language, and the contrast between being born deaf and losing one's hearing! Her writing flows like a clear, brisk stream, always sparkling, never sluggish. And this piece of writing was only the beginning."

After her graduation, Redden began a long and successful career as a journalist, biographer, and poet. And all this in an era when women were discouraged from pursuing journalistic careers. She first began writing for **The Presbyterian and Our Union**, a church newspaper published in St. Louis. In 1860, she began contributing poems and articles to the **St. Louis Republican**.

The War Between the States (a.k.a. "Civil War") was barely underway when Redden wrote a fervently patriotic poem, "Belle Missouri." Its 7 stanzas were set to music and became widely popular among pro-Union Missourians. Its first stanza:

> Arise and join the patriot train,
>   Belle Missouri! My Missouri!
> They should not plead and plead in vain,
>   Belle Missouri! My Missouri!
> The precious blood of all thy slain
>   Arises from each reeking plain.
> Wipe out this foul disloyal stain,
>   Belle Missouri! My Missouri!

Recognizing her writing and reporting skills, and despite the fact that she was a woman *and* deaf besides, the **St. Louis Republican** sent her to Washington, D.C. as a correspondent at the beginning of the Civil War. As Richard Reed notes: "Though she had not become deaf until age 11, her speech was not especially intelligible and she was a poor lipreader. In her exclusive interviews with hearing people, she relied exclusively on pad and pencil or slate and chalk!" To improve her speech and lipreading, she later attended the Clarke School for the Deaf at Northampton, Massachusetts, for two years. She also studied under Alexander Graham Bell in nearby Boston, and was able to develop a clear and pleasant speaking voice. However, she never mastered lipreading and continued to communicate with people, as well as do newspaper interviews, by writing. So wherever she went, she *always* kept a pad and pencil with her.

But Redden never wrote under her own byline. She evidently recognized that a man's name would make her writing more acceptable in a time when it wasn't considered appropriate for women's names to appear in public print. (Journalism was considered "man's work," and women weren't supposed to be engaging in it. At least not under their own names!) The pen name she chose was "Howard Glyndon." Says Reed: "The fact that 'Howard Glyndon' was actually a woman was largely known and accepted." It was no secret.

On at least one occasion, she interviewed President Abraham Lincoln. She went out to the battlefields and there interviewed both generals and soldiers, including General Ulysses S. Grant, "with whom she maintained a lengthy correspondence."

After the war, she lived in Europe for 4 years while continuing to serve as correspondent for the **St. Louis Republican**, and for the **New York Times** and the **New York Sun**. Her articles, written in an easy, informal style, covered a variety of topics—people, places, politics, and books.

After returning to the States in 1868, Redden joined the staff of the **New York Evening Mail** and settled in New York City. She also contributed to popular magazines, including **Harper's**, **Atlantic Monthly**, **Putnam's**, and **Galaxy**.

She published several books: **Notable Men of the House of Representatives** (1862); her first collection of poems, **Idyls of Battle and Poems of the Rebellion** (1865), and her second, **Sounds from Secret Chambers** (1874). **Notable Men**, a collection of mini-biographies, was admired for its clear style and vivid portrayal of personalities. Quoting a contemporary historian, Reed calls her "a keen observer of the Washington scene."

Her poems were featured in several anthologies of American literature edited by popular literary figures like John Greenleaf Whittier and William Cullen Bryant.

During these years, Redden maintained close ties with the Deaf community and had an active interest in its affairs. She contributed articles to **The Silent Worker**, the precursor of **The Deaf American**. She had many deaf friends. Many of her letters, treasured by her descendants, have survived.

Her literary fame was such that in 1872, "Glyndon" was chosen as the name of a newly-founded railroad town in northwestern Minnesota. It may have been Lumen Tenney, a "colonizing agent" for the Northern Pacific Railroad and a Union veteran of the Civil War, who made this choice. Glyndon is thought to be the only town in the nation named after a woman writer in her lifetime.

In 1876 she married Edward W. Searing, a New York attorney. They had one daughter, Elsa. When her health began to fail in 1886, Mrs. Searing moved to California with Elsa. One of her last poems, "The Hills of Santa Cruz," expressed her feelings for the picturesque seaside village where she lived. An excerpt:

> I've seen the far-off Apennines
>   Melt into dreamy skies;
> I've seen the peaks the Switzers love
>   In snowy grandeur rise;
> And many more, to which the world
>   Its praise cannot refuse
> But of them all, I love the best
>   The hills of Santa Cruz!
> Oh, how serenely grand they stand,
>   Beneath the morning sun!
> Oh, how divinely fair they are
>   When morn to noon hath run!
> How virginal their fastnesses,
>   Where no Bacchante woos
> The kisses of the grapes that grow
>   On the hills of Santa Cruz!

This poem greatly impressed Whittier, who grandly predicted that "it would cling to the Santa Cruz mountains forever" and immortalize them as Bret Harte's writings did for San Francisco. But poetic tastes have changed, and Searing's very 19th-century rhetorical style, replete with classical allusions, archaic usage, perfectly regular meter and rhyme, and other conventionalities, has long since fallen out of fashion. Nonetheless, her poetry can be enjoyed for its craftsmanship and beauty of expression.

She wrote poems for the dedication of Daniel Chester French's bronze statue of Thomas Hopkins Gallaudet and Alice Cogswell on Gallaudet College campus (June 26, 1889), and Douglas Tilden's *Admission Day* fountain in San Francisco (September 5, 1897).

After 1908, she stopped writing. Her last years were spent as a semi-invalid living with Elsa in San Mateo. In 1921, Elsa published a final collection of her mother's poems, **Echoes of Other Days**.

Laura Redden Searing died in Elsa's home on August 10, 1923, at the age of 83. She was included in the **Dictionary of American Biography** (1928). By the time the Depression began, however, her reputation had begun to slip into obscurity. She is still virtually forgotten as an American literary figure.

Deaf Heritage mentioned her. In 1984, through Gannon's efforts, the Dean's residence at Gallaudet College's former Northwest campus was named Searing House in her honor.

There are welcome signs of a revival of interest in Redden's writings. These have timeless insight, charm, and style:

> But yet, do not think that our lot is dark; that because the many glad sounds of earth fall not upon our ears, and no words of affection or endearment pass our lips, all sources of happiness are closed to us. Oh! no, no. Our God is a tender and merciful Father, and well has he provided for his "silent ones." We can read upon your faces the emotions of your minds as if they were written in a book. All the world of nature is open to our eager gaze; and the eye almost supplies the deficiencies of the ear. Our life has much of sunshine; and our Father, in his all seeing wisdom, has blessed the greater part of us with buoyant spirits and quick sympathies. We are much more inclined to enjoy the present moment, than to repine for the past or doubt the future.—"A Few Words About the Deaf and Dumb," in **American Annals of the Deaf**, Volume X (1858)

Top: Douglas Tilden in his studio with the plaster model of *The Bridge*, 1934. Bottom left: *The Bear Hunt*. Bottom right: *California Volunteers*. (Courtesy of the Historical Museum, California School for the Deaf)

CHAPTER 7

Douglas Tilden

1860-1935

"Michelangelo of the West"

Douglas Tilden was born in Chico, California, on May 1, 1860, the second of five children, into a prominent family. His father, William Peregrine Tilden, was a physician and state assemblyman; his mother, Catherine Hecox Tilden, was an amateur sculptor and author. Just before he turned 4, Douglas was deafened during a scarlet-fever epidemic. He never spoke again.

Luckily, the "California Institution for the Education and Care of the Indigent Deaf and Dumb, and the Blind" (now California School for the Deaf) had opened in a rented cottage in San Francisco the day Douglas was born. He was enrolled on January 25, 1866. In 1869, the school relocated to Berkeley, where it remained until it moved to Fremont in 1980. Douglas was an honor student, and participated in the Excelsior Debating Society—until he was expelled for arguing. He graduated from CSD in 1879.

He showed an early interest in art—modeling mud figures and carving wood—and art was an important part of the school curriculum. He also enjoyed hiking, camping, and boating with friends, exploring the Sierras and Yosemite Valley, and sketching.

Although he passed the University of California entrance exams, he didn't enroll; he wanted to be a mechanic. (There were no openings for deaf applicants.) Invited to return to CSD to teach, he accepted, and stayed there for 8 years. He worked diligently, kept notes on his methods, and began to contribute articles on education of the deaf to various deaf journals—notably **American Annals of the Deaf**. **Overland Monthly**, the West's leading magazine, published his insightful story, "The Artist's Testament," about the struggles of a young deaf artist, in 1888. In 1897, he won first prize of $100 in its short-story competition. He strongly advocated the combined method and wrote eloquently about sign language. Two of his prime concerns were art education and deaf education. To him, both were connected. "The ideology underlying art and the sign method are exactly the same," he wrote. "I see pictures mentally and think in gesture."

He helped found the California Association of the Deaf in 1905, and was active in Deaf affairs. (He was too quarrelsome to be a leader.)

During the summer of 1882, he spent a month studying drawing and painting at San Francisco School of Design. By the following summer, he discovered his vocation: sculpture. Visiting home, he saw one of his brothers modeling clay, and was fascinated. He learned the basics, bought a barrel of clay, then set up his first studio in a vacant laundry shed on CSD campus. He resumed teaching in the fall, and continued modeling clay in his spare time for 4 more years. He studied anatomy at Cooper Medical College in San Francisco and dreamed of going to Paris—the fine-arts capital of the world.

Like Rodin (whom he admired), he loved Dante's poetry. His first original sculpture—a handsome bas-relief plaque of a male nude (1886)—had a Dantean theme.

Impressed by his *Tired Wrestler* (a plaster statuette of a slumping male nude), CSD's Board of Trustees loaned him $500 to study art in New York, and gave him a $600 yearly stipend (a princely sum). In June 1887, he resigned from his teaching post. That September, he took a cross-country train to New York, where he spent the next 8 months getting a solid foundation in drawing at the National Academy of Design and Gotham Students' League.

On May 11, 1888, he embarked for Paris, and arrived 14 days later. One of the first things he did was visit the prestigious Salon des Artistes Français. He wasn't overly impressed. "For the first time in my life I became conscious of whatever strength there was in me. I looked over the sea of sculpture—eight hundred separate pieces—generally with one leg straight and the other leg bent with its foot resting on something. I could do as well—I would be a sculptor." He immediately began work on *The Baseball Player*, which was accepted for the 1889 Salon. To have an entry approved for exhibit at the Salon was a tremendous accomplishment—a ticket to glory, and unheard-of for a young American on his first try. *Tired Boxer*, his next sculpture, won "Honorable" at the 1890 Salon—the highest status achieved by an American. (Only one other American sculptor, Augustus Saint-Gaudens, had ever won Honorable at the Salon.) Then he began work on *The Bear Hunt*.

The Baseball Player was one of his most enduringly popular works. In September 1890, the bronze cast was shipped from Paris to New York, exhibited at the National Academy of Design, then sent to San Francisco and prominently displayed. William E. Brown, a wealthy art patron and executive of the Southern Pacific Railroad, bought it and presented it to the city. It was unveiled in Golden Gate Park on July 8, 1891.

Bear Hunt was exhibited at the 1892 Salon and at the 1893 Chicago World's Fair (Colombian Exposition), which commemorated the 400th anniversary of the discovery of America. This magnificent bronze is now on CSD's Fremont campus. In 1903, an 8-inch gold replica was presented to President Theodore Roosevelt as a souvenir of his visit to San Francisco.

In September 1893, Tilden received a disheartening letter from Brown, who was forced to discontinue his patronage. Faced with a cutoff of funds, Tilden sold off a few bronze replicas, finished a two-figure group, *Football Players*, exhibited it at the 1894 Salon, reluctantly packed up, and, on June 13, 1894, sailed for California, ending 6 fruitful years of study and growth in Paris. (*Football Players*—in bronze—was unveiled on the University of California-Berkeley campus in 1900.)

He taught San Francisco's first sculpture classes at the Mark Hopkins Institute, communicating in writing and pantomime—the first time a deaf teacher instructed hearing students. He became a full professor in Fall 1899; he resigned in 1901. The Bohemian Club—an exclusive artists' circle—awarded him the distinction of Honorary Membership.

On June 6, 1896, he married Elizabeth Delano Cole, the deaf adopted daughter of a prosperous Oakland businessman. Bessie and Douglas had two children, Gladys and Willoughby Lee. (Although initially happy, the marriage was a disaster; Bessie was emotionally unstable and made his life miserable. They ultimately divorced.)

Tilden was the first sculptor to focus on Californian themes—pioneers, Indians, Spanish-American War volunteers—and won international recognition. He was called "the silent genius;" "Michelangelo of the West." James Duval Phelan, another wealthy patron of the arts who served as Mayor of San Francisco and then as U.S. Senator (and was to be Tilden's close friend and benefactor the rest of his life), first commissioned him to create a monument commemorating California's admission to the United States on September 9, 1850. Both wanted to make San Francisco a new Athens. On September 5, 1897, *Admission Day* was unveiled in downtown San Francisco.

Mechanics (*Donahue Memorial Fountain*) commemorates the career of pioneer industrialist Peter Donahue, who operated the Pacific Coast's first iron foundry, Union Iron Works. It was dedicated in 1901, and miraculously withstood the earthquake and fire that devastated San Francisco on April 18, 1906. Old photographs show the fountain and its five figures, unscathed, pumping away with demonic energy, surrounded by rubble and the jagged shells of burnt-out buildings. The fountain is long since gone, but the *Mechanics* are still part of San Francisco's downtown scene. (*Admission Day* likewise survived the catastrophe, but *Tired Boxer*, in the lobby of the Olympia Club, was destroyed.)

California Volunteers, an expression of patriotic pride, was unveiled 4 months after the earthquake-fire, as part of San Francisco's redevelopment. Tilden was directing the placement of *Oregon Volunteers* in Portland when the earthquake struck San Francisco. *Father Junipero Serra*, honoring the 18th-century founder of San Francisco, was dedicated in Golden Gate Park on November 17, 1907—his last large-scale commission.

After San Francisco began rebuilding, Tilden completed several projects, most of which didn't go beyond the model stage because of a lack of funds. There were memorials, civic projects, and statuary groups for world's fairs. *The Bridge* (1926), for example, symbolizing the union of the East Bay (domestic life) and San Francisco (work), was intended for San Francisco's Telegraph Hill. A number of smaller works (such as bronze portrait medallions and tablets) were executed and are still in their original sites. All of these display Tilden's dynamism and grace.

In Fall 1918, he took a job in a nearby machine shop for a few years. "Odd to say, after more than thirty years I am taking up the work I wanted to do long ago." In 1924 he moved to Hollywood and obtained a well-paid temporary position sculpting dinosaurs and other extinct animals for historical and educational films— even *Lost World*, the first science-fiction movie (1925). He was there nearly a year.

His last years were marked by frustration, bitterness, and spells of poverty. He repeatedly tried to obtain a position at CSD. "No vacancies," he was told. No more deaf teachers were being hired. CSD had gone oral. Tilden was angry enough to try to get *Bear Hunt* transferred from CSD to the Bohemian Club. Nonetheless, he remained concerned about the students, visited them and talked about his experiences, and had them visit his studio.

He was excited about the proposed Golden Gate International Exhibition of 1939, and began designing a frieze, *Vision of the Plains*. It was to be his last project. On August 6, 1935, he was found lying face-down on the kitchen floor of his Berkeley studio—felled by a fatal heart attack. He had presumably been dead two days. Nearby were his tools and the clay model he had been working on.

In 1980, art historian Mildred Albronda published a monograph, **Douglas Tilden: Portrait of a Deaf Sculptor**, the first full-scale treatment of his life and work. After gaining access to a treasure-trove of new material (augmented by rediscoveries of long-lost Tilden works, including letters and writings), she published **Douglas Tilden: The Man and his Legacy**, in 1995—a strikingly beautiful coffee-table book and definitive biography.

Top left: Daisy Low presenting the Golden Eaglet. Top right: A late portrait. Bottom: Daisy (at right) with Guard of Honor of First Class Girl Scouts at the White House, June 21, 1917. (National Historic Preservation Center, Girl Scouts of the U.S.A.)

CHAPTER 8

Juliette Gordon Low

1860-1927

"The first and best Girl Scout of them all"

She was named after her grandmother, Juliette Magill Kinzie, a pioneer settler and historian of Chicago, but nobody ever called her "Juliette." Her lifelong nickname was "Daisy." She was born on Halloween, 1860, in her parents' elegant house in Savannah, Georgia, second of six children. In 1864, after Savannah surrendered to Union forces, the Gordon children, weak from starvation, were sent to their Kinzie grandparents in Chicago; she survived a near-fatal bout of "brain fever." She was "a born mimic" and "a perfect actress." And she loved being useful.

She had a cosmopolitan, boarding-school upbringing. Artistically gifted, she excelled in drawing, painting, and sculpting. Spelling was something she never mastered (and she was hopelessly inept with arithmetical matters), but her poems and letters show her flair for writing. She traveled extensively in the North and South, and made her first visit abroad in 1882.

Daisy's illogical stubbornness was partly to blame for her deafness. She believed in the far-fetched testimonials and cures touted in magazines and newspapers. If it was in print, it *had* to be true! Bothered by an earache (she evidently had an abscess or infection), she bullied a local doctor into injecting nitrite of silver into her left ear—because she had read that it was a sure-fire treatment for earache. It was a horrible mistake. Daisy endured agonizing pain as the nitrate "ate out the eardrum." She recovered, having lost most of the hearing in her left ear. She was 25.

Then came the freak mishap. On her wedding day about a year

later, she and the groom, William Low, were showered with handfuls of the traditional good-luck rice. Unnoticed, a grain of rice lodged in her good right ear. During her honeymoon she began feeling terrible pain. Another doctor discovered that the ear was badly inflamed. In removing the rice-grain, he apparently lacerated Daisy's eardrum. As a result, she lost all the hearing in her right ear. She remained severely deaf for the rest of her life.

She used ear trumpets, or an electric horn. This bulky and primitive instrument "helped her enormously," but emitted screaming feedback when improperly connected. (There's a funny story about her taking ten deaf Londoners and *their* instruments to front-row seats at a concert and affixing hers to the orchestra bar, whereupon it drove the orchestra to distraction.) Socializing was stressful. Since her near-total deafness made it difficult for her to participate in the give-and-take of a conversation, she did all the talking—and her listeners were fascinated. Asked how she always managed to be "the center of things wherever she was," she replied, "I got tired of straining to hear conversations that weren't particularly interesting anyway. I decided it was simpler to take things into my own hands!" Forced to rely on herself, she became more impulsive and eccentric. As her niece "Daisy Doots" Gordon Lawrence noted: "She quickly learned to turn her deaf ear to anything she did not wish to hear."

Still, she got involved in all manner of misunderstandings and miscommunications. At the first International Council of Girl Scouts and Girl Guides in London (1919), Daisy, representing the States, committed a gigantic blunder that she enjoyed retelling:

> One of the speakers was Miss Anstruther Thomson, for whom Daisy had great admiration, and to Daisy's dismay the audience was not applauding her. "I determined that I at least would show my appreciation, so, although I could not hear a word of what she was saying, I clapped and called, 'Hear, hear!' every time she paused. It was only afterward that I found her speech had been all about me and must have sounded like this: 'Mrs. Low is a very remarkable woman.' (Hear, Hear! from D. L.) 'It is a marvelous piece of work to have founded the Girl Scouts of the United States.' Loud applause from me, while the audience remained in stony silence!"

William Low, whom she married in 1886, was a dashing, handsome English playboy-heir, utterly without responsibility or character. The marriage proved a disaster. At first, though, they shared a lovely house in Savannah, then moved to England and lived the aristocratic life. In 1889, they bought their "fairy castle," Wellesbourne in Warwickshire. Daisy evidently had an early miscarriage. There were no children.

The breakup came in summer 1901. Before the divorce could be finalized, Low died. Daisy fought to gain a fair settlement for his sisters and herself, and got the Savannah house. She bought a house in London, and rented Lochs, a small house in the Scottish glens. In 1911 she spent several months in Paris, studying sculpting. Had she maintained her focus, she might well have become an internationally-renowned sculptor. Soon after her return to London, though, came the legendary "fateful encounter" that was to prove the turning point of her life. She was 51.

At a social gathering, she met Sir Robert Baden-Powell, hero of the siege of Mafeking (Boer War), who had already founded the Boy Scout movement in England. He, too, was a gifted sculptor and draftsman. Both shared an interest in pioneer lore. They had an amazing number of things in common, and became fast friends. The magnetic Baden-Powell inspired her to join the Girl Guides, the "counterpart" movement he and his sister Agnes had recently founded. In August 1911, Daisy formed a patrol (troop) of seven girls at Lochs, starting with delicious weekly teas—a great adventure—then introducing knot-tying, flag lore, knitting, cooking, first aid, and signaling. Then she helped them set up cottage industries. In London, she found a market for the finished yarn spun by her girls, and formed two more patrols, one in impoverished Lambeth. And then she returned to Savannah.

That evening, she telephoned Nina Pape, a distant cousin and principal of a local girls' school: "Come right over. I've got something for the girls of Savannah, and all America, and all the world, and we're going to start it tonight!"

Her enthusiasm was contagious. On March 12, 1912, 18 girls were formally enrolled in two patrols. (But Daisy entered the first name herself—"Daisy Doots" Gordon.) They met in the spacious carriage house in back of her garden. Across the street, she installed basketball and tennis courts in a vacant lot she owned. Soon there were six patrols, some small, some large. They used the English Girl Guides' handbook, worked on the tenderfoot and second-class requirements, formed a basketball league, and made their own uniforms. They learned survival skills; knotting; Indian, pioneer, and nature lore; first aid; cookery; hiked, camped, and played vigorous sports. (The name was changed to "Girl Scouts" in 1913.) Mothers who otherwise would not have permitted their daughters to participate in "unfeminine" activities allowed them to join Daisy's troops "since, though Daisy might be odd in some ways, she was a Gordon, and undeniably a lady."

Having established a local network, Daisy began planning a nationwide one. She opened the Girl Scout National Headquarters in 1913. She enlisted and recruited her family, friends, society matrons, and three First Ladies—Edith Wilson, Grace Coolidge, and Lou Henry Hoover. She cunningly used her deafness to benefit the cause. If an unwilling recruit protested, Daisy would simply *not hear*. And that was that.

She said: "We mustn't lose sight of the girls. The girls must always come first!" And: "The Angel Gabriel couldn't make them take up what they don't want." And: "Ask the girls." This was revolutionary thinking, since nobody had ever thought of asking the girls before.

Girl Scouts volunteered *en masse* during World War I, sold Liberty Bonds, assisted the Red Cross, tended vegetable gardens, made sandwiches for soldiers, and after women got the vote in 1920, watched babies in front of polling places while the mothers cast their ballots. By early 1916, some 7,000 had registered. The Girl Scout magazine, **The American Girl** (originally **The Rally**), was started in 1917 (it was to be published for 62 years). That year, Scouting was opened to disabled girls. In 1919 a troop was organized at Illinois School for the Deaf.

By that time, the organization had become too big to be handled solely by volunteers. Benefactors were found. Fundraising was implemented. Professionals were hired. At the National Convention in January 1920, Daisy resigned as president, and was thereafter known as "The Founder." Ann Hyde Choate, daughter of Daisy's old boarding-school friend Mary Gale Carter, became the second national president of the Girl Scouts.

Knowing that she had terminal cancer (which she kept secret from almost everyone), and determined to accomplish as much as she could in the time remaining to her, Daisy pushed ahead with her plan to hold the Fourth International Conference—delegates from every country where Girl Scouting had been established—in May 1926 at Camp Edith Macy on the Hudson River. It was the first International Conference held in the States. Lord and Lady Baden-Powell were there.

She spent her last days in Savannah surrounded by friends and family, maintaining her courage and wit to the end. There were flowers, letters and telegrams—the outpourings of love and esteem. Most cherished was a telegram from Choate and the National Board of the Girl Scouts: "You are not only the first Girl Scout, but the best Girl Scout of them all." There could be no higher praise.

She died on January 18, 1927. She was 66. In accordance with her request, she was buried in her beloved Girl Scout uniform, with the cherished telegram tucked in the breast pocket.

In 1944, a Liberty ship was named after her, and christened at Savannah. In 1948, a commemorative postage stamp was issued. In 1974, President Jimmy Carter unveiled a bronze bust of Daisy Low in the Georgia Hall of Fame. But her best memorial remains the Girl Scouts of the U.S.A., the largest voluntary organization in the world. Girl Scouting has undergone many changes since 1912, but the original ideals—promoting independence, good citizenship, community service, and a concern for the welfare of the earth and other people—remain the same. Daisy Low is a legendary figure in Girl Scout lore; stories are still told of her exploits. October 31 is celebrated by "her girls" as Founder's Day.

The most familiar image of William Ellsworth "Dummy" Hoy: an 1888 Old Judge cigarette card. Hoy was then a rookie with the Washington Senators. (Courtesy of National Baseball Museum)

CHAPTER 9

William E. "Dummy" Hoy

1862-1961

First deaf major-leaguer

William Ellsworth Hoy was born on May 23, 1862, on a farm in Houcktown, Ohio, a small village about 50 miles south of Toledo. At age 2 or 3 (the accounts differ), Will was deafened by "brain fever" (spinal meningitis). Until he was 10, he had no schooling, but was finally enrolled in the "the Deaf and Dumb Institute" in Columbus (now Ohio School for the Deaf). Making up for lost time, he completed 12 years' worth of schooling in 8 years.

OSD was the first school for the deaf to introduce baseball, around 1870, and Joseph "Dummy" Dundon, who graduated in 1878, became the first deaf professional baseball player as well as the first deaf person to officiate as umpire in a professional game. Hoy certainly knew Dundon. And he played and practiced.

He was trained in shoemaking, once the second most popular vocation for deaf boys (printing being the first). After graduating in 1879 as valedictorian of his class, he returned to his parents' farm, worked there, and set up his own shoe-repair shop. Business was especially slow in the summer, when most everyone would go barefoot—so there was plenty of time for baseball.

In those days, every town, no matter how small, had at least one amateur baseball team. Hoy and his three brothers joined the "Stonewall Jackson" club. For several years, he played on week-ends as a catcher against teams from neighboring towns and villages like Findlay and Elyria. Eventually, his sensational play-ing attracted the attention of players and promoters in nearby communities. He began to realize he was an outstanding player when was asked to play with Kenton against Urbana. He hit so well, scoring a home run and three singles, he decided he was good enough to try his luck in professional baseball.

The following spring, Hoy, now 24, made his move. He closed his shop, slipped away in the middle of the night, and boarded a train to Milwaukee, Wisconsin. He left without having told his strict Presbyterian parents, who would *not* take kindly to the prospect of any of their sons becoming professional ballplayers. (Professional baseball was a crude, scruffy, aggressive, rowdy setup.)

In 1886, Hoy began his professional career in Oshkosh, Wisconsin, for $75 a month. After making good with Oshkosh, he took a week off from the team, returned home, sold the shop, gained the blessing of his parents, and was in baseball for keeps.

They called him "Dummy"—a casually thoughtless nickname for *any* deaf player—and thus he is listed in the record books. He wasn't a bit embarrassed or apologetic about his deafness. Nor did he mind being called "Dummy." When he was 95, he wrote to **The Sporting News**: "Tell them to call me Dummy again, like they always did." A lifelong signer, he rarely used his voice. Although he could lipread quite nicely on occasion, he preferred using pad-and-pencil when communicating with hearing people.

When Hoy arrived, the Oshkosh team was doing badly. His excellent outfielding pulled it up during the second half of the season, leading to a late surge that clinched the league pennant. A story from Hoy's Oshkosh days tells how he accomplished the feat of catching a fly ball while balancing on a buggy shaft.

He taught his teammates fingerspelling and signs, and they found this useful on the field, devising a gestural code to avoid collisions during fly balls and flashing "secret" signals to each other. No overview of Hoy's career is complete without a mention of his role in developing the standard hand-and-arm signals (*strike*, *ball*, *safe*, and *out*) used by umpires throughout the world. These signals are so very much a part of the game that it's hard to imagine baseball without them. But when Hoy entered the leagues in 1886, there were no signals. Umpires shouted the calls, which he couldn't hear. It severely hampered his playing. It was to accommodate him, legend has it, that umpires first began using exaggerated arm signals to indicate balls and strikes.

In 1887 or so, the story goes, he asked the plate umpire to raise his right arm emphatically to signal a strike, his left arm for a ball. He probably penciled his request on a slip from the notepad he always carried; the umpire agreed to try it. Using signals freed them from having to shout. Hoy's batting performance improved dramatically. Moreover, the fans liked it, as the umpire's voice, no matter how loud, could not possibly carry far enough to reach everybody in the grandstands. A clear signal could, however, be seen from the furthest corner. Out of professional courtesy, the umpires began using hand signals in games where Hoy played. Eventually, they began to signal strikes and balls for *all* batters. Signaling became the standard procedure. As one writer put it: "Today, an umpire's gestures are a colorful part of any baseball game."

There are several contemporary references to the signals—the oldest being an 1888 newspaper article—and other evidence in favor of Hoy's claim. (The "safe" signal, for example, looks like an exaggerated American sign for *safe/free*. "Out" looks like the ASL *won't*.) These basic signs led to the development of the intricate secret-signaling systems used today.

Hoy was small, even by 19th-century standards—5' 4" or 5' 5" tall, weighing 145 to 155 pounds, which would put him among the lightest. But he had big, powerful hands "like bunches of bananas," and a pair of deadly arms. He was quick, too. In 1888, he led the National League in base-stealing.

Asked if he considered his deafness a handicap or asset during his career, he replied: "On the whole I found it no handicap. . . . Indeed, my deafness was often an asset. The yelling of the opposition was useless as far as I was concerned, and they soon found that out. As to the yelling of my own coaches, it meant nothing to me." Fans learned to cheer visually when Hoy made a spectacular play—which was often. According to an 1892 report: "When outfielder Hoy made a brilliant catch, the crowd arose 'en masse' and wildly waved hats and arms"—an early version of "Deaf applause."

Hoy played two seasons at Oshkosh, then was grabbed by the Washington at the end of his first year (1888). It was the start of his major-league career. By the end of his rookie year with Washington, Hoy led the National League in stolen bases—with an astounding 82. For the Senators, he set a fielding record that still stands. On June 19, 1889, he threw out three Indianapolis baserunners at home plate from the outfield—the first of only three outfielders in history to do so.

In 1890, Hoy joined the Buffalo Brotherhood team of the short-lived Players' League (1890). Buffalo was another loser, and Charlie Comiskey gave Hoy a try with the American Association's St. Louis Browns. It was Hoy's first experience with a team that *wasn't* in last place. The Browns finished a strong second; Hoy led the league in walks with 119 and led the Browns with 136 runs scored. But the American Association folded, so Hoy returned to Washington and put in two more seasons with the unlucky Senators. In 1894, he was sold to the Cincinnati Reds, then under Comiskey's management. There he played centerfield again as an outstanding flyhawk. The Cincinnati fans adored him. He was with the "Redlegs" four seasons, his longest stay with any team, and liked Cincinnati so much that he settled there during off-season.

In 1898, he was traded to the hapless Louisville Colonels shortly before they disbanded. He gave Louisville two of his finest seasons, batting .318 in 1898 (his best average in the majors) and .306 in 1899.

On May 1, 1901, Hoy hit the first grand-slam home run in the newly-formed American League. That year, he played in 130 games and hit .294 for the Chicago White Sox (under the management of Clark Griffith), and helped win the first AL pennant for them. He had 45 assists from the field—a record for any league.

He returned to the Reds for what was to be his last major-league season. On August 7, 1902, the Reds released Hoy.

After racking up 1,792 games in the major leagues and a .291 lifetime batting average, Hoy finished out his career in Los Angeles, in the Pacific Coast winter league, with an impressive 46 stolen bases and 413 putouts. He played in 211 games—the complete schedule. His very last play—a stunningly calculated 9th-inning catch in a thick gray San Francisco fog—clinched the 1903 pennant for his team.

Hoy married Anna Maria Lowery, also deaf, in 1898. They had three children: Carmen, Clover, and Carson.

In 1903, Hoy, now 42, bought a 60-acre dairy farm near Mount Healthy on the outskirts of Cincinnati. He operated it for 20 years, and sold it in 1924. He was a personnel director of Goodyear's several hundred deaf workers. He coached the Goodyear Silents baseball club from 1919 to 1920, when the Akron "deaf colony" was at its absolute peak and boasted outstanding sports clubs.

In 1951, Hoy was unanimously voted the first player to be enshrined in the AAAD Hall of Fame. AAAD began lobbying to get Hoy inducted into the National Baseball Hall of Fame in Cooperstown, New York, while he was still alive.

On October 7, 1961, Hoy tossed the first ball at Opening Day of the third World Series game in Crosley Field (Reds vs. Yankees). Shortly afterwards, he became ill and was hospitalized. On December 15, 1961, he died of a stroke. He was 99 years, 5 months, and 8 days old—just over 6 months shy of his hundredth birthday.

He was eulogized in publications across the country—newspapers and sports periodicals, hearing and Deaf.

The AAAD Committee for Dummy Hoy spearheaded a new campaign to get Hoy into the National Baseball Hall of Fame. Between 1989 and 1992, he was inducted into the Hancock Sports Hall of Fame in Findlay, Ohio, OSD's Hall of Fame, the Louisville Colonels Hall of Fame, and the Ohio Baseball Hall of Fame. On May 23, 1995, the mayors of Oshkosh and Cincinnati issued "Dummy Hoy Day" proclamations.

Not only did Hoy have the courage to break the communication barrier, but his deafness proved to be a tremendous asset to the sport of baseball. He left his permanent stamp on the game. His place in baseball history and lore is secure. Without "Dummy" Hoy, baseball would not be what it is today.

William Wolcott Beadell: "an excellent business man who has conducted his newspaper on a profitable basis." (Gallaudet University Archives)

CHAPTER 10

William W. Beadell

1865-1931

Originator of the "Want Ads"

How many people have read the classified section in the news-paper? Just about everyone? How many have benefited from reading the "Want Ads," which led them to a job, an apartment, an antique instrument, a used car, a kitchen set, a lawn mower, a breeder of Birmans or Scottish terriers? Hundreds of thousands—millions, perhaps? And how many others have made a tidy profit from advertising their products or services in this section? A similarly countless number? For this, they can give thanks to the man who first developed the "Want Ads" as a regular daily feature in his newspaper—William Wolcott Beadell.

Although he became totally deaf, Beadell enjoyed a successful career as editor and publisher of **The Observer**, a "mainstream" weekly newspaper in Arlington, New Jersey, recognized as one of the most successful of its kind in the East. He became known as a leading advocate of truthful journalism and his editorial writings were often quoted or reprinted in other newspapers. So strong was his dedication to his work that, during his 30 years as owner of **The Observer**, he was absent on only *two* publication days.

Beadell was born on December 31, 1865, in Dubuque, Iowa. Several years later, the family moved to LeMars, Iowa, where his father served as postmaster. (There were two brothers, Edward and George, and two sisters, Ella and Flora.) Spinal meningitis partially deafened him at age 11; his deafness later became total. Although he dropped out of high school, his mother taught him to become an expert lipreader.

He began his newspaper career while he was a teenager. He and a boyhood friend hung around the printing office where the friend's father published a newspaper, the LeMars **Sentinel**. Both boys began "sticking type" and learned to operate a printing press. After learning the printer's trade, he became a reporter for the **Sentinel**, then local editor.

Now 20, he decided to return to school, and applied for admission to Iowa School for the Deaf. However, they found the self-taught young man too advanced for the curriculum, so he applied for admission to Gallaudet College and was accepted. He graduated in 1891, the only member of his class to complete the course and earn a degree.

As a graduation gift, his father bought him a weekly newspaper in Yellow Creek, Illinois. The ambitious young editor wanted a more romantic name for the town—and for his paper. He influenced the citizens to change it to "Pearl City" after he learned that the creek was full of clams yielding freshwater pearls! Hence, **The Pearl City News**.

In 1895, Beadell married Luciana Chickering, the daughter of Professor J. W. Chickering of Gallaudet College, where the two had met. It was a happy marriage and a good partnership. Luciana served as bookkeeper for William's various newspapers, and as librarian for Arlington's circulating library, which was located at **The Observer's** office.

Beadell's **Pearl City News** improved in quality and interest, largely because of his shrewd management and superior editorial skills. A few years later, he sold **The Pearl City News** and took a teaching position at the Minnesota School for the Deaf. After a year, though, he returned to his first love, newspaper work. He decided to go East, where he felt he would have better opportunities. For the next 3 years, he served as managing editor of **The Register** in Middlebury, Vermont. He had almost completed arrangements to purchase **The Register**, but its owner "became involved in a personal controversy" with some local citizens and decided not to sell.

In 1900, Beadell, now 35, took the most important step in his life.

He purchased the Arlington, New Jersey **Observer**, which was struggling to compete with the big newspapers of nearby Jersey City, Newark, and New York. Again, he put his energy and ability to work, building up a rundown newspaper until it became profitable—and an important social and business presence in the closely-allied cities of Arlington and Kearney. "In spite of the close competition his printing office, run in conjunction with the news-paper, enjoyed a steady and profitable patronage," as a 1931 **Iowa Hawkeye** tribute put it. The roster of advertisers, subscribers, and customers increased.

Beadell's development of the "Want Ad" page became "one of the marvels of modern journalism." Editors' and publishers' maga-zines (trade journals) and newspapers "frequently engaged" him to write articles for their publications, explaining "his method of conducting the Classified Page of **The Observer**."

He also found a better method of distributing his newspaper, through "regular authorized newsboys" who established their own routes—franchises—and through newsdealers in Kearney, Arlington, and North Arlington. Sales were honestly reported; advertising agencies and bureaus knew that they could trust the circulation figures that Beadell quoted.

In contrast to the popular stereotype of the fire-breathing news-paper editor, Beadell was a "most considerate" employer, "never imposing or exacting in his demands." He made working condi-tions as pleasant as possible for his staff, and, insofar as he could, provided the most modern equipment and labor-saving devices.

A fellow journalist, Phil Durkem, shared his impressions of Beadell. The two had never met, but enjoyed a long correspon-dence. (Durkem's tribute was included in **The Observer's** 1931 memorial booklet.)

> I suspect that W.W.B.'s humor was unlimited. When I wrote from a Spanish-speaking island my reply came addressed to Señor Durkem, when from a French possession, I became Monsieur, when in Russia I was addressed as "Dear Durkemsky" and as "Dear Durkemovitch." When I wrote from New England W.W.B. "guessed;" when my letter was dated Miami W.W.B. "reckoned." (...)

The Observer had the distinction of being the only newspaper I knew in which editorial policy was not dictated by the business office. I wrote an article denouncing the corrupt practices of the Public Service Corporation and W.W.B. did not hesitate to print what I wrote, although he carried, every week, a large advertisement from that corporation; the same thing occurred with my article criticizing motion picture production, As I wrote at that the time, I doubted if any other paper of its type in the United States maintained so high a standard of integrity.

Beadell was "a leader in his field." Many of his editorials, reprinted in The Observer 25 years after they'd been written, were "just as applicable to local conditions" as they had been when first published.

He was loyal and generous, a good citizen (he voted Republican, was "broad-minded and favored clean politics"). As Daniel Van Winkle put it in his History of the Municipalities of Hudson County, New Jersey (1924):

Mr. Beadell is an excellent business man and has conducted his newspaper on a profitable basis. He is a strong writer, has the true journalist's instinct for news, and has made "The Observer" a valuable local medium, as well as a most interesting one. He is a member of the New York Press Club; the National Editorial Association; is a Presbyterian in his religious views, and a Republican in political faith.

He was also a member of the Historical Society of New Jersey. In the words of the Iowa Hawkeye: "His business associates and his neighbors held him in the highest respect and esteem."

Although not actively involved in Deaf affairs (his work kept him in Arlington and Kearney most of the time), Beadell took an interest in the Deaf community. He kept himself informed, and when called on, served its interests. He was a member of the New York Chapter of the Gallaudet College Alumni Association and the Alpha Chapter of the Kappa Gamma fraternity. He contributed generously to St. Ann's Episcopal Church for the Deaf in Manhattan as a member of the Men's Club. He waged an ongoing campaign to prove that deaf automobile drivers had a safety record as good or better than hearing drivers. As chief of the Automobile

Bureau of the National Association of the Deaf, he collected material and data that helped the NAD in fighting nationwide discrimination against deaf automobile drivers. In his own state, he influenced the Commissioner of the Motor Vehicle Department to revoke "the ruling of a hostile official" unfavorable to deaf drivers.

On Friday, July 3, 1931, Beadell took a Fourth-of-July-weekend automobile trip to Harpers Ferry, West Virginia. He returned on Monday "feeling somewhat indisposed, believing he had contracted a severe cold." Not until Thursday was a doctor summoned. Beadell was taken to West Hudson Hospital for an immediate operation for appendicitis. Although poisoned, he seemed to be recovering, resting comfortably. On Friday, he carefully read the new issue of **The Observer**; on Saturday, he seemed the same. On Sunday morning, July 12, he glanced over the headlines of **The New York Times**. At around 11 a.m., though, he suddenly lost consciousness. It was reported that in his delirium, he said, "I want to correct this proof." A half-hour later, he was dead.

His untimely death was widely mourned. A simple Presbyterian memorial service was held, followed by the reading of a favorite poem, Tennyson's "Crossing the Bar." He was buried in Rock Creek Cemetery in Washington, D.C. "A brief service of commitment in the sign language was performed at the grave." The staff of **The Observer** published a biographical booklet in memory of their "beloved Chief," who was one of the most prominent and respected citizens of Arlington.

Thomas Scott Marr in his studio. (Courtesy of Tennessee School for the Deaf)
Left: Sudekum Building, demolished 1992. Bottom: Nashville Post Office, "one of the
finest," and still in use. (© Gary Layda, Photographer, Metro Government of Nashville)

CHAPTER 11

Thomas Scott Marr

1866-1936

Nashville architect

Thomas Scott Marr was born into an eminent Nashville family on October 20, 1866, and, shortly afterwards, severely deafened by scarlet fever. His father, Thomas senior, a native of Warrenton, Virginia, was a banker and "highly esteemed by the community." His mother, Delia (Tarbox), was from New York. Three of his brothers later distinguished themselves in banking and medicine. When he was 6, he watched, fascinated, as stonemasons constructed the Old Federal Building on Eighth Avenue, and decided that he, too, would become an architect.

He could read and write before he started public school as a second-grader. Although he was bright, he made no progress there. He was held back in second grade for three years, given up as hopeless—a humiliating experience. Finally, when he was 11, his parents reluctantly enrolled him at Tennessee School for the Deaf in Knoxville. He was unable to do simple arithmetic. But with the encouragement of the principal, Thomas L. Moses, and a young teacher, Kate Ogden, he made rapid progress, mastered algebra and Latin, and became a top student.

In 1884, he entered Gallaudet College, and was given the first choice of rooms allotted to freshmen, an honor reserved for those who scored highest on the entrance exam. His roommate was a senior, Cadwallader Washburn, who later became internationally famous as a drypoint etcher. He was also friendly with Olof Hanson, who was to become an eminent architect himself. At Gallaudet, the only architecture-related course was "Mechanical

Drawing," and Marr's exceptional ability influenced his decision to become a draftsman. He excelled in mathematics and the sciences, and graduated with honors in 1889.

His first job, for $2.50 a week, was as an apprentice draftsman in the office of George W. Thompson, a well-known Nashville architect. Marr worked there for three years and then, seeking to improve his knowledge and prospects, took special architectural-study courses at Massachusetts Institute of Technology in Boston.

However, his stay at MIT was cut short after one year because of a sudden reversal in the Marr family's fortunes. In 1893, a financial panic swept the United States. Naturally, it affected the banking establishment as well as business, and Marr was forced to go back to work. When he returned to Nashville, he was welcomed back by his former employer, the senior partner of the architectural firm Thompson & Gibel. He worked there for several years, drawing a small salary because of poor economic conditions.

During these years as a struggling architect, he often experienced frustration and disillusion. As Mrs. J. B. Chandler noted in **The Silent Worker** (1929), "After five years he had saved up capital of $500 with which he opened an office of his own, paying $10 a month rent. For ten years he struggled with meager returns, often tempted to give up. He says he held on because he did not know what else to do, but his friends know it was grit and [tenacity]."

Because he was deaf and preferred not to speak, it was difficult to communicate with his clients. (He was said to be a fairly good speaker and skilled lipreader. He was, of course, a fluent signer.) Most of his early commissions were thus for private residences. But his work became respected for its high standards of quality and his integrity.

In 1904, Marr met an ambitious 13-year-old, Joseph W. Holman, who was selling the **Saturday Evening Post**. Seeing his eagerness to learn, Marr hired him as office boy, and taught him architecture and business management. After several years of apprenticeship, Holman was put to work representing the firm and soliciting contracts. Marr established a partnership with Holman in 1910. According to Mrs. Chandler, Holman "became such a valuable assistant that his fame spread to other architects. One big firm offered him a permanent position at $10,000 a year, but he refused to leave Mr. Marr. Needless to say, he has never regretted this decision."

Holman handled the business transactions. Marr, as senior partner, focused on the actual architectural designs, drew the plans, wrote specifications, and supervised draftspeople. During their 26-year partnership, Marr and Holman were commissioned to design a wide variety (and huge number) of buildings, including hospitals, schools, a county jail, and hotels. As the firm's reputation grew and the economy prospered, Marr's became a "phenomenally successful" architect who designed many public buildings in Nashville and elsewhere in Tennessee.

Among these were the Methodist Publishing House (Nashville, 1906), Morgan School in Petersburg, the Tennessee Boys' Reformatory School in Jordania, and the new Tennessee School for the Deaf campus (dedicated in November 1924). In Nashville, he designed the Post Office Building and three modern luxury hotels—the Noel, the James Robertson, and the Andrew Jackson. (The Noel Hotel, one of his most famous commissions, was renovated as the Union Planters Bank in 1973.) His designs for large apartment buildings included the Clifton and the West End Apartments.

As Judy P. Mannes notes in **GEDPD**:

> The Broadway National Bank (Nashville, 1910), the Cotton States Building (Nashville, 1920; demolished 1982), and the Sam Davis Hotel (Nashville, 1928) are examples of the firm's early commercial designs. Marr and Holman's use of arches, columns, pilasters, and other classical details reflects the taste of the period for the academic style. Marr and Holman's use of arches, columns, pilasters, and other classical details reflects the taste of the period for the academic style. Marr's Colonial Revival design for the Tennessee School for the Deaf was appropriate for an educational complex. Brentwood Hall (Nashville, 1920), an adaptation of Andrew Jackson's Greek Revival-style Hermitage (Nashville, 1834-1836), was one of their better-known domestic commissions.
>
> The absence of ornate neoclassical details in the lobby of the Commerce Union Bank (Nashville, 1920; demolished 1977) and the virtually unadorned limestone and brick exterior of the Noel Hotel foreshadowed the firm's best works in the 1930s. The Sudekum Building [Nashville,

1930-32, demolished 1992] and the United States Post Office [Nashville, 1934] are examples of Marr and Holman's competence with the new, streamlined esthetic of the Art Deco style. Although only 13 stories tall, the Sudekum Building clearly embraced the insistent verticality and stepped-back pyramidal massing of the great Art Deco skyscrapers of Manhattan's skyline. The $1,000,000 Post Office was the first federal building approved and constructed after Franklin D. Roosevelt entered the White House. Its sleek white marble exterior, stylized carvings, and vibrantly polychrome lobby made it and the Sudekum Building the two most modern buildings of their day in Nashville.

An article published in the **Nashville Banner** on November 18, 1934, the day the new Post Office held open house, conveys something of the admiration it inspired:

New Building One of Finest in Nashville

(...) When Nashvillians and visitors stop inside of the sturdy new Post Office Building, they will see lofty walls of Tennessee marble, broken occasionally by aluminum doors. Electrical fixtures are in expertly selected spots. Huge chandeliers provide light in addition to built-in wall lights. The exterior is finished in Georgia white marble and Minnesota granite and extends 182 feet from front to back and 250 feet in width. . . . The building cost approximately $1,000,000 and is one of the most modern in the South.

Although the Marr and Holman firm was primarily noted for its sleek, elegant Art Deco/Depression Moderne designs, Marr's work displayed his versatility. He designed the Warner Building, the Princess and the Knickerbocker theaters, the fireproof E.M. Bond Warehouses, an office building for the Ford Motor Company, and the War Memorial Building in Nashville, many buildings in Columbia, Clarksville, Fayetteville, Chattanooga, and Sewanee, and even a baseball grandstand in Toledo, Ohio. In 1935, Marr and Holman designed the Bedford County Courthouse (Shelbyville) in the stately Greek Revival style, with Corinthian columns and a cupola. Their design duplicated (as closely as possible) the previous 1873 building, which had been destroyed in 1934 by a lynch mob. (The handmade bricks of the 1873 building were salvaged and reused as facing for the new one.)

As the commissions kept coming in, Marr & Holman hired engineers to help handle the increasing workload. Several of these became well-known themselves, notably Richard S. Reynolds, who played an important role in Marr & Holman's success from 1923 on.

Marr never married, and never really retired. Even after his "retirement," he continued putting in a full day's work. He built a charming cottage with a long breezy porch, "Marr's Hill," in the resort town of Beersheba Springs, where he took short vacations. He was an avid reader and traveler, studying the details of buildings wherever he went.

Early in 1936, Marr & Holman was chosen by Governor Hill McAlister to draw the plans for the State Supreme Court Building. It was Marr's last design. On March 2, 1936, he died suddenly of a stroke. He was 69.

"A warm and generous friend," he was a philanthropist to the Deaf community. In 1931, he helped establish the Dixie Association Home for the Aged and Infirm Deaf in Moultrie, Florida. To his alma mater, TSD, he was a generous benefactor. In 1923, for example, he sent money to be used for the purchase of new basketball uniforms for its varsity team. According to TSD's **100th Anniversary Book**: "In October 1937, TSD received a sum of money from the Thomas S. Marr estate for a library fund. Upon his death, he left a legacy of $2,500 to the school for building up the inadequate library. As a lasting memorial to him, the school library became the 'Marr Memorial Library.'" Gallaudet College (which had awarded him an honorary Master of Science degree in 1924) received a $5,000 bequest in 1937 as the Thomas S. Marr Scholarship Fund.

One of the first technically-trained Southern architects, Marr helped shape Nashville's modern skyline. **The Nashville Tennessean** eulogized him as "this dean of Nashville architects," but neglected to mention the fact that he was deaf. (Marr himself considered the new TSD campus perhaps his proudest achievement.)

Holman continued the firm, but, as Mannes notes, "it moved away from the energetic Art Deco style that distinguished Marr and Holman design in the 1930s."

Cadwallader Washburn in his studio.
(Gallaudet University Archives)

CHAPTER 12

Cadwallader Washburn

1866-1965

Artist and adventurer

With a name like that, he had to be unusual. Frank G. Bowe summed him up nicely: "Internationally known etcher and painter, brash war correspondent, noted authority on insects, rival to Marco Polo as a world traveler and explorer, author of several articles, fluent 'speaker' of English, French, and Spanish; award-winner in architecture, oologist, printer, teacher, biographer, diplomat—a man more completely 'alive' in the full sense of the word is difficult to imagine."

Cadwallader Lincoln Washburn was born on October 31, 1866, into a prestigious and wealthy Minneapolis family. His father, Minnesota Senator William Drew Washburn, was a timber magnate and director of the Washburn-Pillsbury Flour Company, founded four railroads, and later became a U.S. Senator. (Ironically, he had voted against the establishment of Gallaudet College.) His mother, Elizabeth (Muzzy), "was a woman of exceptional courage and sympathy." Cad was devoted to her. According to Bowe: "Regardless of what part of the world he was in, he wrote her a letter every day." Three of his uncles—Cad was named after one of them—served as naval commanders, congressmen, statesmen, and ambassadors.

When he was 5, Cad was deafened by spinal meningitis. He regarded his deafness as "merely a slight inconvenience," and even noted, "The lack of hearing undoubtedly sharpened my sense of sight and awareness of color, form, and line." He communicated through sign and pad-and-pencil.

At Minnesota School for the Deaf in Faribault, where he graduated in 1884, he showed aptitude for printing (under the distinguished tutelage of Olof Hanson), drawing, and entomology. His
essays on spiders, bees, and caterpillars—which he illustrated—
were well received. Even though he was drawn to art, he remained
an enthusiastic student of nature. He pursued his scientific interests at Gallaudet College, graduating in 1890 as valedictorian. He
presented his senior dissertation, "The Working Mind of a Spi-
der," in sign on Commencement Day.

Believing that he should pursue a "compromise" career in architecture (and possibly influenced by Hanson), he enrolled at MIT,
where he won a First Award in Design. After one year, however,
he became "firmly committed to art," and embarked on a bohemian life—to his father's disapproval. The proper-Victorian Senator Washburn cabled a stern warning to Cad to return home
immediately or have his generous allowance cut off. As Donna
Chitwood notes, "Once he had set his heart and mind upon a career
as an artist, nothing could deter him—not even the threat of loss of
his allowance."

During the next few years, he studied art at New York City's Art
Students League, under Henry Siddons Mowbray. He also studied
and traveled with the distinguished painter William Merritt Chase.
(His New York roommate was Howard Chandler Christy, who
would later achieve fame as an illustrator.) In 1896, Washburn
accompanied Chase to Europe; he visited Spain, Holland, and
Morocco. In 1897, he studied with Joaquin Sorolla in Madrid,
becoming a favorite pupil, then, in 1898, with Albert Besnard in
Paris, assisting him in painting chapel murals, and exhibiting at
the Salon Elysée continuously from 1896 to 1903. Undaunted by
the prospect of starvation, Washburn took the risk of surviving on
his art. He economized, in Chitwood's words, by "living in a room
so tiny that he had to take down his easel whenever he wanted to
hang his sleeping hammock (the room was too small to accommodate a bed)." He also met Pablo Picasso. They dined together and
covered tablecloths with their sketches.

While visiting Venice in 1903, Washburn saw an exhibit of

drypoint etchings by the great American artist James McNeill Whistler, studied them carefully, and was inspired to shift his focus from oil painting to drypoint. (In drypoint, the design is scratched directly onto the copperplate with a needle [*stylus*]. Rough metal ridges left on either side of the furrows create a soft, fuzzy effect in the inked and printed lines.) Washburn returned to Paris, bought etching supplies and a small printing press, received some basic orientation from an American etcher there, and struggled to master the technique. Two months later, he produced his first drypoints, then took several more months to master printing. Washburn's drypoints, done without preliminary sketches, are notable for their dazzling technique, freshness, spontaneity, psychological insight, and verve. They've been favorably compared to Whistler's work—and Rembrandt's. By 1910, his drypoints had begun to gain him international fame. He ultimately acquired a reputation as the world's greatest living drypoint etcher.

Art, of course, was only one of Washburn's interests. He traveled widely, and with his brother, Colonel Stanley Washburn, served as a war correspondent for the **Chicago Daily News** during the Russo-Japanese War (1904-05).

In 1910, while he was studying architecture and culture in Mexico, revolution broke out. The Associated Press cabled him an assignment to interview Francisco Madero, the "notoriously secretive" revolutionary-president—a job no reporter had been able to accomplish. Washburn, who became coordinating correspondent for all U.S. reporters in Mexico, knew that he would need some sort of gimmick to gain access and get the interview. As Bowe put it:

> Utilizing a bit of Mexican psychology, Cadwallader purchased an impressive suit, complete with silk hat, spats, gloves and goldheaded cane. "I knew they were impressed with appearances," he later told William McGaffin of the **News**. "Then I went to the palace in this outfit, sent in my card and said I that was expected." His brash approach paid off handsomely. Whipping out his ever-present notepad, he questioned President Madero in fluent Spanish about his policy towards the States. Madero was so impressed that he dictated a 500-word statement for the **News**. Washburn was the last "outsider" to see Madero before [he] was assassinated [in 1913].

Bowe quotes another typical Washburn anecdote from William Holland. Cad was typing a dispatch to the **News** (possibly the one about Madero) in a Mexican railway station, "totally oblivious of a battle raging around the building," which got peppered with bullets. A man pushed Washburn to the floor. "Utterly outraged, Washburn wrote furiously on his pad, 'What is the meaning of this gross indignity?' The man tried to explain that there was a fierce battle raging outside. 'Nonsense,' Cadwallader scribbled, and resumed his typing."

When the political unrest worsened, he escaped on board the *Merida*, taking with him paintings and 50 copperplates, among other treasured possessions. But when, on May 12, 1912, the *Merida* was rammed by the *Admiral Farragut* and sank, Washburn lost them all. Even so, he was grateful to escape: "I thought of the many months of happy labor that were summed up on my copperplates and canvases and for a moment a regretful thought followed the lost ship. But day had come, two boats were on the horizon hurrying to our rescue, and I am sure that to the men, women and children, though shivering with cold and bereft of possessions, life seemed very good at that moment." In 1959, he told the **News**: "God will take care of me. He always has."

Washburn's interest in sketching rare birds and collecting their eggs brought him to the Marquesas Islands in the South Pacific on a field expedition in 1925, with a professor from the University of Minnesota who left almost immediately. Washburn stayed on. Leaving the main island, Hiva Oa, where Paul Gauguin is buried, he stopped on a nearby island where cannibals killed his native guide, leaving him stranded with his Belgian police dog, "Chief of Police." But he made friends with them, taught them signs, persuaded them to pose for him, etched a portrait of the chieftain, and was rewarded with a canoe. He and Chief escaped and survived 6 months until they were picked up by a French ship, which had been alerted to look out for him.

Drypoint etching remained Washburn's favorite medium for more than three decades. His output was phenomenal—some 970 portraits, architectural views, and landscapes. Asked how he found the time, he told the Toronto **Star**: "Simply because I never gave a fly an opportunity to light on me." He traveled to California in 1925, Tunisia in 1929, Paris in 1934, the Canary Islands in 1935. In 1937, eyestrain forced him to abandon etching. He returned to oil painting, but, as Chitwood notes, "his etchings remain his most distinctive legacy to the world." In 1934, he exhibited 15 dry-points—mostly foreign scenes—in the International Exhibition of Fine and Applied Arts by Deaf Artists at the Roerich Museum in New York City. The New York Public Library exhibited representative works in 1939. There were further exhibits in museums in San Francisco, MIT, and Bowdoin College Museum of Fine Arts in Brunswick, Maine, where he had a campus studio.

His works are at the Library of Congress, Corcoran Gallery of Art, Metropolitan Museum, British Museum, Victoria and Albert Museum, Musées de l'État Luxembourg, and the Bibliothèque Nationale in Paris. He received numerous honors and awards (e.g., Fellow of the American Geographic Society). In 1924, Gallaudet College awarded him an Honorary Doctor of Science degree; Bowdoin College, an Honorary Doctor of Humane Letters in 1947. Portraits show him in his academic robes or suit with a charming smile and mischievous twinkle in his eyes.

He never stayed in one place long enough to settle down. Nearly 77, he married Margaret Cowles Ohrt on October 17, 1943, and together they shared two more decades of travel and adventure. She also interpreted for him—Bowe describes Cad's style of signing as "delightfully idiosyncratic" but baffling to the uninitiated.

Despite his daring, even perilous, lifestyle and deceptively frail appearance, Washburn lived nearly a century. After retiring to South Livermore, Maine (his family's "vacation" home), he died on December 21, 1965, age 99. Newspapers eulogized him as "the dean of American etchers."

On May 18, 1969, Gallaudet College dedicated its Washburn Building. Gallaudet's Washburn Room was officially opened on June 18, 1976, during GCAA's reunion. Margaret Washburn donated the majority of the collection, comprising more than 80 splendid drypoints.

Luther Haden "Dummy" Taylor during his stint with the New York Giants,
circa 1902-1904. (© *The Sporting News*)

CHAPTER 13

Luther "Dummy" Taylor

1875-1958

Major-league pitcher

Luther Haden "Dummy" Taylor was the first—and so far the only—deaf pitcher to succeed in the major leagues. He was born deaf on February 21, 1875, in the small town of Oskaloosa, Kansas. In a 1952 **Silent Worker** article, Leonard Warshawsky recounted the story of how, as a boy, Luther was watering his father's horses one day when a "panicky" horse kicked him squarely in the face, "smashing his nose at the forehead." He was left with a permanently "hiked" upper lip (which looked cleft) and a bashed-in nose. Sportswriters later ridiculed him for his looks—"and he didn't seem to mind it at all!" The New Orleans **Times-Picayune** called him "the ugliest BUT the most colorful on the ball field beside John McGraw." He began playing baseball when he was 8. His original ambition was to be a boxer. "But Ma and Pa objected," he later said.

After graduating with honors from Kansas School for the Deaf in Olathe, he began playing in the "crack" semi-pro Nevada, Missouri club (Southern League) in 1896, then Lincoln and Mattoon (Illinois), Shreveport, and other clubs in the Central League. In 1900, he was with Albany in the New York State League, where he won 10 games against 8 losses. He was a gangly right-hander, 5' 11", around 155 pounds. (A fascinating quirk was his unorthodox "corkscrew" pitcher's windup and release.) His blazing fastball caught the attention of George Davis, manager and scout of the New York Giants, who purchased his contract on July 16, 1900. He played in 11 Giants games (4-3). In 1901, as the workhorse of the foundering team, he pitched 45 games. The Giants finished in seventh place, having won only 52 of its 137 games. Taylor had won just over one-third of them, with an 18-27 record. During his second year (1902), the Giants came in a dismal eighth.

In Winter 1901, lured by a bigger salary, Taylor jumped to the Cleveland Indians ("They were waving big money at us, you know"), but in early May 1902, the Giants sent catcher Frank Bowerman to persuade him to return. As Taylor later told **The Sporting News**: "Frank sat in the grandstand and every time I walked out to the mound and back to the bench he kept talking to me with his fingers. I kept shaking my head 'No,' but Frank kept boosting the money. Soon I nodded my head 'Yes,' and that night I was on my way back to New York with him." That season, he played in 23 games (8-14).

On May 26, 1902, "Dummy" Hoy, going to bat for the Reds, faced "Dummy" Taylor of the Giants. A Cincinnati sportswriter wrote that when Hoy came up to bat for the first time in the first inning, he greeted Taylor in Sign: "I'm glad to see you!"—and then cracked a hit to center. Taylor made sure that Hoy didn't steal any bases during the game, but Hoy got one run and two hits off him anyway. Taylor was unable to strike him out. Even so, the Giants won 5 to 3 with 5 runs in the 9th inning. It was the only time in major-league history that two deaf players faced each other, and it was to be their only such encounter. Hoy was nearing the end of his career while Taylor, 13 years his junior, had yet to reach his peak.

He stayed with the Giants when John J. McGraw (1873-1934), took over. (McGraw's nicknames were "Little Napoleon" and "Muggsy"—not necessarily meant affectionately. On the field, he was arrogant, ruthless, rowdy, an umpire-baiter, and plain mean. He was also, according to Charles C. Alexander, "the game's premier strategist and . . . an absolute genius at getting maximum performance from his players." Off the field, "he was "warm, friendly, and incorrigibly generous.")

When McGraw left the infamous Baltimore Orioles in mid-July 1902 to manage the Giants, he brought some star players with him. He found a team "in the cellar"—last place, to be exact, 25 games behind the top-ranked Pittsburgh Pirates. And he traded away or released every player on that dreadful team except the brilliant Christy "Big Six" Mathewson, Bowerman, and Taylor. In 1903, the Giants finished second. Taylor won 13 and lost 13.

In 1945, Taylor told **Baseball Magazine**:

> In the old days Hoy and I were called Dummy. It didn't hurt us. Made us fight harder. Nobody ever felt sorry for me, especially umpires who put me out of about fifty ball games. All I had to do was twirl my finger near my ear to indicate that they had wheels in their heads, and I got the afternoon off. One day I wrenched my neck and decided not to go to the Polo Grounds. I changed my mind the next morning and showed up at five minutes after nine-thirty, and Andrew Freedman [the owner] fined me forty dollars—ten percent of my month's pay.
>
> Being mute wasn't much of a handicap. John McGraw learned the sign language well and then made the whole New York team take it up. I always carried a pad and pencil, but never had to on the ball field. During my eight years with the Giants, every player learned to sign. Some of them were all thumbs, and [pitcher] Joe McGinnity was very careless with his spelling.

Like Hoy, Taylor was popular with the fans, and taught his teammates sign language. Unlike Hoy, he was something of a wiseguy, a prankster. (Occasionally, because he was deaf, he became the butt of his teammates' pranks.) He engaged in the time-honored (if not honorable) practice of taunting umpires—but in sign language. Supposedly, since *they* couldn't understand his signing, he didn't worry about being thrown out of the game. However, there are variant (and contradictory) tales about how Taylor engaged in umpire-baiting—unaware that the umpire (usually identified as Hank O'Day) knew what he was saying, and flabbergasted when he got punished. (O'Day had learned signing from a deaf relative.) One story, set in Cleveland in 1902, has Taylor mouthing insults to an umpire, who ejected him from the game. Afterwards, the umpire told reporters: "Even if I wasn't a good lip reader, I knew Taylor wasn't saying his prayers. For a guy who can't hear, he's picked up some nasty words. Why, he actually called me some names I'd never heard before."

In 1904, the Giants had the best pitching staff in the majors. They won 106 games, and its "Big Three" collected 89 of that total—

McGinnity (35 wins), Mathewson (33), and Taylor (21). In 1904 and 1905, the Giants won National League pennants. Taylor was a major cog in the machine. His best year was 1904 (21 wins and 15 losses). He followed that with 16 wins in 1905, 17 wins (against only 9 losses) in 1906, 11 in 1907, and 8 in 1908, his last season with the Giants. He missed his only chance to pitch in a World Series game in 1905 when it was rained out. (Mathewson rested that day, then returned next day to pitch his third straight World Series shutout against the Athletics.)

When he "had his stuff," it was tough trying to score runs against him. Runners who tried to steal second base were quickly picked off—Taylor could "hear" the pounding of their feet, even with his back turned. "The vibrations were very clear," he said.

During his 8-year career in the majors, Taylor played in 274 games. He won 116 and lost 106, for a .523 percentage. He pitched 160 complete games, with 767 strikeouts against 551 walks. He allowed an average of 2.75 runs per game and hurled 21 shutouts in which he didn't allow opponents a run. Judged by modern standards, this earned-run average (ERA) of 2.75 compares favorably with those of some of today's best and highest-paid pitchers. (If he were pitching today, he'd likely be earning a princely salary. In 1906, he earned $2,700.)

In 1909, when his arm went bad, Taylor left the Giants. His teammates presented him with a solid-gold medal studded with 20 diamonds. He returned to the minor leagues, where he was still able to compete successfully. From 1909 to 1912, he pitched for Buffalo, Montreal, and New Orleans (Eastern and Southern Leagues). In 1913, his arm gave out, ending his pitching career, but he played briefly for several other International Loop minor-league clubs in Montgomery, New Orleans, and Topeka before retiring as a player in 1914. From 1915 through 1920, he umpired games in Kansas, Iowa, Nebraska, and Illinois, for the House of David and Union Giants, and playoff tourneys in Council Bluffs.

From 1914 until 1923, Taylor worked as boys' supervisor and athletic coach at Kansas School for the Deaf (his *alma mater*), where, as Warshawsky noted, "he turned out powerful football and baseball teams, defeating such strong opponents such as Ottawa University, William Jewell College, Rockhurst College, and Baker University." (KSD named its gymnasium after him in 1961.) In 1923, he left KSD to coach at Iowa School for the Deaf, where his teams ran up outstanding records in both baseball and football. He was a peppery, cheerful, charismatic figure.

In 1933, Taylor began working at Illinois School for the Deaf in Jacksonville. There he discovered Dick Sipek and helped get him into the majors. (Sipek—the first deaf player to escape the "Dummy" nickname—outfielded for the Reds in 1945. He was the last deaf major-leaguer before Curtis Pride.)

Twice a widower, Taylor married Lina Belle Davis (also deaf), on August 29, 1942, in Akron. Shortly afterwards, on Labor Day Weekend, he and "Dummy" Hoy met again at the Ohio State Deaf Softball Tournament in Toledo (Toledo vs. Akron "Rubber City Silents"). To the fans' delight, they played as battery-mates (Taylor pitching, Hoy catching) in the opening game.

Taylor retired from ISD in 1949, having been House Father 18 years, but continued living in Jacksonville. He was occasionally publicized in newspapers and baseball magazines. In his interviews (conducted with pencil-and-paper), he enjoyed reminiscing about his old Giants teammates. He stayed active, working out regularly in the gym, boxing with anyone he could "coax to box with him." In 1936, the major leagues gave him a lifetime silver pass granting him free admission to all baseball games; he attended enthusiastically.

In 1952, he became the second player inducted into the AAAD Hall of Fame. That year, he was appointed a scout for the Giants. He continued umpiring semi-pro, sandlot, and college games in the Chicago area. **The Sporting News** reported that he quit baseball, "a game he loved more than anything else in his life," after umpiring the Illinois College-Principia game on April 14, 1956. He'd been active in baseball for 72 years.

He died on August 22, 1958, age 82, 11 days after suffering a mild heart attack, clear-minded and in "excellent spirits" to the end.

George Hyde, at home with a favorite pipe and book, July 22, 1951.
(**Omaha World-Herald**)

CHAPTER 14

George Hyde

1882-1968

Plains Indian historian

George E. Hyde was born in Omaha, Nebraska, on June 10, 1882, the only child of Lucinda (Reed) and George W. Hyde, a policeman. As a boy, he became friends with a son of E. L. Eaton, a photographer who had actually known George Custer, Buffalo Bill Cody, and the Brulé Sioux Chief Spotted Tail. In his attic, Eaton kept his collection of glass-plate negatives of these legendary Wild West characters, and Hyde was intrigued with them and inspired by the adventurous tales Eaton told.

As for school, he never liked it and kept running away. As he laughingly told reporter Philip Gurney in 1961, "But the teachers kept bringing me back, and I finally decided it was less trouble to stay there. . . . My teachers predicted I'd grow up to be a bartender." His formal education ended at 8th grade.

His early interest was kindled into passion during the 1898 Trans-Mississippi Exposition in Omaha—one of the greatest events in the city's history. (Geronimo himself was there.) By that time, Hyde had become profoundly deaf and had lost most of his eyesight. After meeting a few Indians who were attending, he was invited to their camps, and was enchanted. His career was a natural outgrowth of the friendships he made at the Exposition.

He remained semi-blind the rest of his life. Recognizing the limitations this put on him, but determined to succeed, he decided to become a historian concentrating on the subject he loved most. He later wrote: "I took up writing as about the only thing I could do, because I had sense enough to know that a man to write must have first hand information, and there was no subject as suitable as Indians, and I was in a position to get first hand information from several tribes." He equipped himself with strong corrective lenses and a high-powered magnifying glass, and laboriously read everything he could find on the subject.

In 1905, after a friend taught him how to type, he started a 12-year correspondence with George Bent, son of a pioneer "Anglo" settler and his Cheyenne wife, Owl Woman. This inspired his last book, **Life of George Bent Written from His Letters** (edited by Savoie Lottinville). Published posthumously in 1968, it was hailed by **The Saturday Review's** Oliver Knight as a "treasure."

Through Bent, George Bird Grinnell, an eminent ethnologist, found out about Hyde, visited him in 1912, and, recognizing his talent, employed him as research assistant. It was Hyde's first professional assignment. "I could only work half the time because of my blindness," he later noted. **The Fighting Cheyennes** (1915) was the result of this collaboration. But Hyde's contribution went beyond the mere gathering of information; he contributed greatly to Grinnell's early drafts. Much of the writing was his.

Technically, his responsibilities were to collect data—oral history and eyewitness testimony—from Cheyenne informants. He became expert at this, using an unconventional approach of letter-writing and notetaking. In doing so, he developed an elaborate network of Plains Indian friends who aided his research. Many of his informants became lifelong friends.

Historian John Dishon McDermott called **The Fighting Cheyennes** "one of the first [studies] to accept and utilize Indian sources." That Grinnell and Hyde went directly to the Cheyennes for information, rather than depend entirely on "official documents" found in libraries and archives, marked the beginning of a new approach to Native American research. No longer would the story be told by using second-and-thirdhand reports based on hearsay, colored by superstition, and distorted by prejudice. Lottinville, Director Emeritus of the University of Oklahoma Press, which published six of Hyde's books, said Hyde "made a signal contribution by recognizing the fact that there are always two sides to Indian-white conflicts, and that if history is to be told, it must not overlook, reject, or deny out of hand the Indian side."

Hyde's second collaboration, with George F. Will of North Dakota (with whom he corresponded for almost 50 years but never met), resulted in **Corn Among the Indians of the Upper Missouri** (1917), which described agricultural techniques and lore.

In 1920, because of increasing blindness, he moved in with his half-sister, Mabel L. Reed, a former actress and principal of the Webster and Central Grade schools. She took care of him, sharing her modest schoolteacher's income. He pounded out his books on an old typewriter whose keys he couldn't see. Reed checked the spelling as he went along and reviewed the final proofs. She told Gurney, "George has a stubborn mulishness that once he starts something, he finishes. It's a wonderful quality"—she laughed— "but it's sometimes hard to live with."

For a time, to augment his income, he operated a little second-hand bookstore from the house. It didn't bring in much. Neither, for that matter, did his works, although several of them won acclaim.

Gurney's 1961 article in the **Dundee and West Omaha Sun** described Hyde as "a recognized authority among scholars of Indian lore and historians of the early West," but "a man practically unknown in his native city." Since he couldn't travel (he very rarely left Omaha), and couldn't easily use library resources, Hyde relied on professional friendships, correspondence with experts, and the assistance of the Omaha Public Library staff. They would search for books and source materials, sometimes for weeks. Hyde gratefully acknowledged their efforts in the prefaces to **Indians of the Woodlands** and **Spotted Tail's Folk**. But the librarians' greatest reward was Hyde's friendship. They cherished his letters. He addressed them affectionately as "Dear girls," and showed humorous gallantry towards them: "If I write a diary I will not show it to you. Library girls are supposed to be top-drawer, morally, and my diary would not be fit reading."

In his 1975 tribute (in **Arizona and the West**), McDermott noted:

Through all the years of adversity, Hyde never despaired. He maintained a lively sense of humor, was always thoughtful and kindly,
and took a special pride in his appearance, wearing carefully tailored
clothes. Friends described him as 'a handsome, strong-looking man,'
about six feet in height, with an erect carriage and particularly
expressive hands. . . . He once said that he "didn't like skunks,
whether white or Indian" . . . Each December he made his uncertain
way down icy streets in Omaha to mail Christmas packages to Indian
boys and girls at the Rosebud Boarding School.

Ralph Smith wrote in the Omaha **World-Herald**: "George E.
Hyde said Saturday he would talk to a reporter about his new book
[**The Pawnee Indians**, 1951] on one condition . . . that the reporter
wouldn't do one of those things about fortitude triumphing over
great odds and that sort of tripe. 'No sob stuff,' he said firmly." As
Gurney observed:

Hyde has a keen sense of humor, a delightful wit, an unending supply
of stories of the Old West. But these are hard to project to other than
close friends because of the difficulty of conversation.

Questions to him must be written out and he then reads them through
a magnifying glass, word by laborious word. His thick-lensed spec-
tacles are not sufficient to read by, enable him only to differentiate
objects and to recognize people he sees often, and then only when they
get very close.

He speaks haltingly, but in a rich voice and not in the flat monotone
of a deaf person who has never heard speech. (...)

He also has a novel, his first, under consideration by a publisher. A
young Indian princess is the main character, and the yarn includes an
Indian nudist colony that the whites attempt to disturb. "I'll bet they'll
faint," the author says of the publishers, "when they find out I'm 78. But
I'll just tell them I'm in my second childhood."

He wrote three monographs for John VanMale's Old West series:
Rangers and Regulars, The Early Blackfeet and Their Neighbors
(both 1933), and **The Pawnee Indians** (1934), later expanded into
a full-length book (1951). **Indians of the High Plains** (1959) and
Indians of the Woodlands (1962) traced the general sweep of
Indian migrations and conquests across the continent, and were
unfavorably reviewed by anthropologists who faulted Hyde's
lack of field experience.

His masterpiece was his trilogy on the Sioux, which McDermott calls "his major contribution to Western history . . . the most thorough study ever done on a Plains Indian tribe." The trilogy—**Red Cloud's Folk** (1937), **A Sioux Chronicle** (1956), and **Spotted Tail's Folk** (1961)—is epic in scope, tracing the history of the Sioux from 1660 to the massacre at Wounded Knee, South Dakota, on December 29, 1890, then back to the assassination of Spotted Tail in 1881. It's thoroughly detailed, but written in a brisk, lively style.

Spotted Tail's Folk is considered his finest book, his depiction of Spotted Tail boldly revisionary. As historian Merrill J. Mattes summarized it: "Chief Spotted Tail was almost alone in his ability to transcend the stone-age mentality of his race, to perceive the hopelessness of the Indian cause in the face of white greed and trickery, and to make a dignified and honorable adjustment to history." According to Gurney, Hyde spent 30 years gathering the material and 10 years working on the book. Mattes praised its "solid scholarship, spiced with satire and wry humor."

As McDermott put it: "The choice of history as a profession for a man who was deaf and partially blind is unusual. That he excelled at his craft is notable. That he became an Olympian in his field is truly remarkable."

Hyde died of cancer on February 2, 1968. He was 85. Eleven days before he died, he bade farewell to his "dear girls": "George is gone. The poor blighter got lost in all this gloom and we may never be amused, or enraged, by his antics again." He bequeathed royalties from 10 of his 11 books to the Omaha Public Library.

Notably modest, he shunned publicity. A "sidelight" in **Contemporary Authors** (1962) is illuminating: "Concerning the sparse information he provided about himself, Hyde said simply: 'I am an old man, and too busy to fill out forms.'" One of Hyde's publishers lamented that "he would rather write about Indians than himself!" However, he had definite opinions about the merit of his work: "I don't care what the run of newspaper reviewers say—they don't know one blessed thing about my Indians, and their views don't matter a hoot." He was confident that his work would stand the test of time. So far, it has.

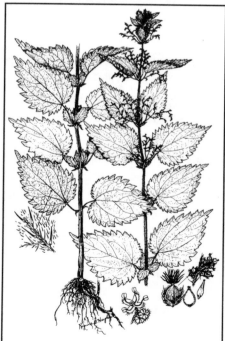

"I don't believe in retirement." Regina Olson Hughes at work in the Smithsonian. (Gallaudet University Archives.) Hughes' pen-and-ink drawings of stinging nettle (left) and ivyleaf morning glory (right), originally for the USDA. (Dover Publications.)

CHAPTER 15

Regina Olson Hughes

1895-1993

Botanical artist

Regina Mary Olson was born on February 1, 1895, in Herman, Nebraska, just west of the Missouri River and about 30 miles north of Omaha. Her parents, Johana and Gilbert, had come from Wisconsin in covered-wagon days, long before Nebraska was a state. "I could draw before I could write," she later said. "I would draw all over my schoolbooks, and Papa would have to pay for my books." Her parents provided private art tutoring for her. "I have sold watercolors since I was in grade school," she later told **Gallaudet Today**. She was always fascinated by plants, and had a passion for flowers—particularly orchids. When she was 10, she began losing her hearing (possibly from scarlet fever), and by the time she was 14, had become deaf. Although she had attended public schools, she decided to go to Gallaudet College, where she received her Bachelor's in Art in 1918, and her Master's in 1920.

She said, "In 1918, when I graduated from Gallaudet, deaf people were looked down upon. We were treated like children." But she never backed down from a challenge. After she graduated, she called on Nebraska Senator Gilbert Hitchcock, founder of the Omaha **World-Herald** and a friend of her father's, and asked if he could help her find a political job. He told her, "Nice girls don't work. You go home and stay with your papa and meet a nice man, and he'll take care of you." She was notably "unimpressed" with this advice. Instead of a political career, she found a job as translator in the State Department, and also at the departments of War and Commerce. She was fluent in four foreign languages: French,

Spanish, Portuguese, and Italian. (Later, she tackled technical Latin and learned some German, Norse, and Romanian.) Her most prestigious assignment was translating during the Conference on Limitation of Armament in Washington, after the Armistice.

In 1923, she married Frederick H. Hughes, Gallaudet's legendary Deaf economics professor, theater enthusiast, and football coach. As Professor Hughes' wife, she developed close connections to the Gallaudet community. Bob Panara recalls:

> When I was a student at Gallaudet—and, later, on the Faculty—she was not the kind whom you would call "an extrovert;" not even "socially inclined." She led a quiet life, seldom was seen in public except for Drama Club performances, Faculty socials, special events. Otherwise, I hardly ever saw her. But I remember her as a very lovely woman; short of stature, like Freddie, quiet, smiling faintly but seeming like her mind was elsewhere (most likely on her work at the U.S. Department of Agriculture). [She was] unassuming, [liked] privacy, and [was] content (and happy) to let her husband lead the way and enjoy the spotlight.

For 30 years, until Professor Hughes died of a heart attack in 1956, she lived on Kendall Green in House Two—right next to House One, where the president lived. She stayed at home for a few years, gardening, then, in 1930, went to work at the U.S. Department of Agriculture, first as a research clerk, then as a scientific illustrator and translator. She took compulsory retirement from the USDA in March 1969, then started a second career at the Smithsonian Institution, painting orchids and bromeliads for Dr. Robert W. Read, Curator in the Smithsonian's Department of Botany, and continuing as a contract illustrator for scientists at both the USDA and the Smithsonian. When some of the contracts ran out of money, as Dr. Read's did, she continued to work 5 days a week as a volunteer. She told Dr. Read, "Don't worry about the money— just keep me busy." "And I did," he says.

She depended largely on lipreading for everyday communication. But if a matter involved business or money, she demanded that it be written down. "When you are deaf, you learn to distinguish between people who are saying something that you want to hear and people who are just talking."

Primarily self-taught, she worked in several media: watercolor, oils, gouache, and pencil. But she's best known for her strikingly beautiful, precise, and intricate depictions of weeds, orchids, and exotic species. Armed with a high-power Swiss microscope, pen, ink, and paper, she produced thousands upon thousands of scientifically accurate and detailed illustrations of plants for the USDA. It was painstaking work, but never boring; she found it challenging. "The most complicated seed that I know of is the radish." She noted, "Many of my drawings are in the public domain now and they turn up like old friends. A couple of weeks ago, there was one in the **Post**. I've seen them on pesticide labels and many other places, from a small-town newspaper in Montana to the **New York Times**." Highly regarded by her colleagues, she was a member of the Guild of Natural Science Illustrators. At the Smithsonian's Department of Botany, she worked closely with botanists and taxonomists. Her work appeared in numerous botanical papers.

In collaboration with Dr. Read, Hughes illustrated the collection of living orchids in the National Orchid Collection. A collection of 40 meticulous watercolors of orchids were exhibited in the Rotunda Gallery of the Smithsonian's National Museum of Natural History in 1982: "Artist and Botanist—A Collaboration." She was the first deaf artist to have a solo show at the Smithsonian. In Fall 1986, she had three overlapping Smithsonian exhibitions—at Selby Botanical Garden in Sarasota, Florida, the Eastern Orchid Congress in Alexandria, Virginia, and at Gallaudet University. (Dr. Read arranged several of these exhibits.) Others exhibits were at the National Arboretum (1968) and National Agricultural Library (1972). Her drawings and paintings are in the collections of several other museums and galleries, including Maryland's Brookside Gardens, the Hunt Institute for Botanical Documentation at Carnegie-Mellon University in Pittsburgh, and Gallaudet.

Her many publications include **Journal of the Bromeliad Society, Grassland Seeds** (1957); **Vetches of the United States— Native, Naturalized, and Cultivated** (1960); **Identification of Crop and Weed Seeds** (1963); **The Agave Family in Sonora** (1972); **Aquatic and Wetland Plants of the Southwestern United States** (1972); **Economically Important Foreign Weeds** (1977, containing over 6,000 of her illustrations along with plant descriptions); **The Genera of the Eupatorieae (Asteraceae)** (1987); and **Caryopsis Morphology and Classification in the Triticeae (Pooideae: Poaceae)** (1993). **Selected Weeds of the United States**, originally published by the USDA in 1970, was reissued by Dover Publications in 1971 as **Common Weeds of the United States**. Hughes' name doesn't appear in the title page or text, but her signature can be seen on the illustrations themselves. There are 222 full-page, meticulously detailed pen-and-ink drawings, multiple views of the plant with details of the flowers and seeds. Her drawings and elegant compositions bring out the essential beauty of the nastiest, most commonplace weeds.

Art, flowers, and language were three of her lifelong passions. Travel was her fourth. She traveled extensively, bringing along plenty of sketchbooks, making detailed notes on what she saw. These sketches became the basis for many flower studies and paintings. "I have sketchbooks full of drawings that will eventually become paintings," she said. "Unnumbered others remain to me as treasures of the mind." She also wrote and published poetry in several magazines.

What she did, she did with zest, precision, and style. Dr. Read, who calls himself "a true admirer," describes her as "that marvelous, positively brilliant woman." Staff Illustrator Alice Tangerini, another Smithsonian colleague, provides a glimpse of Hughes' flamboyant side:

"Regina Hughes and I shared an office in the Botany Department for almost 20 years. She was doing contract work for both the Smithsonian and USDA botanists when I came on staff in 1972. . . .

Regina had a sporty side to her life; she drive a 1960 Thunderbird to work everyday. The car's interior was done in turquoise leather—presumably to match an outfit she had at the time. She made her own clothing, mostly silk suits in bright orchid-like colors, and which was augmented by beautiful custom-designed jewelry. She traveled abroad, taking summer art courses with Temple University (Western Europe, the Greek Islands, and Asia Minor, 1964 and 1968), University of Utah (Eastern and Western Europe, 1965), and University of Oklahoma (Egypt, Greece, Persia, India, and Nepal, 1966).

Regina would often bring in some of her paintings from her travels to the office. She told many stories of those travels, including purchasing various gemstones to bring back to the U.S. for setting in rings. She had two matching rings, large black star sapphires surrounded by five rows of diamonds—they were quite impressive. When I asked how she came by two such enormous rings, she told me she had the first one designed after purchasing the sapphire on a trip to India. Then she made a trip to Thailand and bought another star sapphire. She brought it to the same jeweler to have it set exactly the same as the previous one. The jeweler tried to dissuade her, saying it would not be in good taste. She replied, "I don't want it to be in good taste; I want it to knock your eyes out." The jeweler did as she requested.

Still, Hughes was unpretentious, and when honors were bestowed on her, tended to downplay her achievements. She received USDA's Superior Service Award for botanical illustration and technical translation in 1962, an honorary Doctor of Humane Letters from Gallaudet (1967), and its Amos Kendall Award in 1981. She was named Woman of the Year by the Gallaudet sorority Phi Kappa Zeta (1970) and "Artist of the Year" by the Chevy Chase Branch of the National League of American Pen Women (1980).

In 1980, Dr. Read named a species of bromeliad, newly discovered in Brazil, after her: *Billbergia reginae*. Because of her many drawings that appeared in **The Genera Eupatorieae (Asteraceae)**, the authors, Robert M. King and Harold Robinson, named a member of the Asteraceae (the daisy family) after her in 1981: *Hughesia reginae*. As the citation for the Kendall Award noted, this was "a very singular honor." It is exceptionally rare for someone to have both a genus *and* species named after her.

Says Alice Tangerini: "She worked here [the Smithsonian] until 1990, but at that point her eyes were giving her too much trouble to continue drawing. She also lost confidence in her ability to drive and gave up her beloved Thunderbird." In 1991, **Gallaudet Today** commented: "Her work is much sought after by scientists who have not allowed her to retire—not that she would be content to do so." When she was 92 (and still working 5 days a week), she told Cate Peterson of the Omaha **World-Herald**, "I don't believe in retirement. I hope to die with a brush in my hand."

She came close. On August 12, 1993, she died of heart failure at her Washington apartment, aged 98.

Top: Two portraits of David Peikoff. Bottom: Working on another successful fundraising effort—this one for the statue of Edward Miner Gallaudet on the Kendall Green mall (1965), shown in the illustration behind him. (Courtesy of Polly Peikoff)

CHAPTER 16

David Peikoff

1900-1995

Canadian-U.S. Deaf Rights advocate

David Peikoff was born on March 21, 1900, in Yanoschina, Poltava Province, Russia, "battleground of the Czars." He was fifth of 15 children. When he was 5, he decided that the time had come to begin school. He secretly followed his older brothers and sisters as they walked to school on winter day. No one realized that he was following them. Before he could reach the school, he got lost in a violent snowstorm. By the time he was found buried in snow, he was frozen, unconscious, and nearly dead. He remained hospitalized for 6 months, ill with "brain fever" (spinal meningitis), which left him profoundly deaf.

In 1906, the family, eager to escape Czarist persecution of Jews, emigrated to Canada and settled on a farm at Bird's Hill, near Winnipeg, Manitoba. That September, David began school at the Manitoba Institution for the Education of the Deaf and Dumb (now Manitoba School for the Deaf) in Winnipeg. (D.W. McDermid, the school's superintendent, had learned about David and persuaded his parents to enroll him.) Although he arrived without knowing a word of English, he was a bright student. As Mel Williams noted:

> A puny little boy, but devilishly active, he was soon in the thick of competition in sports and in every school activity. From a stunted growth he sprang up like a weed and in the environment of signs and finger spelling his mastery of English sped apace, with the result that in a province-wide essay competition sponsored by the Winnipeg **Free Press** he won top honors.

Later, though, he became bored—as he put it, he "got fed up with reviewing the same lessons for two years in a row!" He left school on his 17th birthday. His father took him to Chicago and enrolled him in the Mergenthaler Linotype School. He became a master printer, and worked as a Linotypist at the Winnipeg **Telegram**, then, after it folded, the **Free Press**.

A fellow printer, an older deaf man, thought David was wasting his life in a print shop, told him about Gallaudet College, and convinced him that he should go there. At that time, none of the provinces provided financial support for their deaf college-bound students. There were no scholarships, no VR funding. Nevertheless, Peikoff went to Washington and entered Gallaudet in Fall 1924. At 24, he was the oldest prep student in his class.

Williams described him as "a tempest on the campus." To pay for tuition and other expenses, he worked evenings at **The Washington Post**. "A fleet runner," he participated in track-and-field and varsity football until he was badly injured, then became team manager. He was an active member of the Ballard Literary Society and performed in several Saturday Night Dramatic Club presentations. **The Metropolitan Gallaudetian** noted that "during his senior year [he] held just about every office of importance"—Head Senior, Grand Rajah (president) of the Kappa Gamma fraternity, editor of **The Year Book** (forerunner of **The Tower Clock**), and editor-in-chief of the campus newspaper, **The Buff and Blue**. He took additional journalism classes at George Washington University, and received his B.A. in English and Journalism from Gallaudet in 1929.

It was at Gallaudet that Peikoff began his remarkable career as a "one-man fundraising committee." He established the McDermid Scholarship Fund (in honor of the father-son administrators at the Winnipeg School for the Deaf) to enable other deaf students from Canada's western provinces to attend Gallaudet. (It later merged with the Canadian Deaf Scholarship Fund.) In 1950, he persuaded the trustees of the Joseph Atkinson Foundation (which memorialized the publisher of the **Toronto Star**) to provide grants to Gallaudet-bound students from Ontario.

As for his Canadian career, he co-founded the Western Canada Association of the Deaf in 1923. (He was already actively involved in the Winnipeg Association of the Deaf.) In June 1923, he was elected WCAD's first president and also chaired its Labour Welfare of the Deaf Committee. He served as president of the Ontario Association of the Deaf from 1938 to 1956; he launched and edited **The OAD News** in 1941.

He also served as president of Toronto Division #98 of the "Frat," which elected him second grand vice-president (1943-1947) and chief agent in Canada (1959-1960). He served on the Gallaudet College Alumni Association (GCAA) Board of Directors for 15 years (1939-1954) and as president for 7 years (1954-1961); he was a key figure in the NAD from 1949 to 1960, mainly as a fundraiser.

In 1940, he became one of the Canadian Hearing Society's two deaf charter members. Later that year, however, the disillusioned deaf members left and formed the Canadian Association of the Deaf (CAD). Peikoff served as CAD's executive secretary, and chaired its Canadian Scholarship Fund, from 1940 to 1960. Says Dr. Clifton F. Carbin, author of **Deaf Heritage in Canada**: "Peikoff was the driving force behind the creation of the CAD and one of its most dynamic leaders.... The CAD made Peikoff a life member, presented him with a special award in 1972 for his 50 years of service to the Deaf community, and inducted him into its Hall of Fame in 1994."

Mel Williams aptly described Peikoff as a "champion of champions." As he wrote in a 1951 **Silent Worker** article: "In 1930 Dave started a tour of the continent working at his linotyping trade from Hartford to Halifax, then westward to [the coast]. It was during his sojourn in Vancouver that Dave emerged as a fighting deaf leader." The Provincial Government was threatening to prohibit all deaf citizens from driving motor vehicles. The WCAD asked Peikoff to launch a campaign to reverse this ban. He published dozens of "fighting letters" in area newspapers "as he sought to swing public support to his cause." He carried on a vigorous letter-debate with the immovable Police Commissioner. Noted Williams: "In 1931, a showdown battle took place between the Police Commissioner and a deputation of the WCAD resulting in the

Attorney General of [British Columbia] rescinding the discriminatory edict."

In his "passionate and articulate" letters and articles, Peikoff argued persuasively on behalf of deaf Canadians. A strong supporter of Deaf teachers, he vehemently opposed the rigid pure-oral method. What he had to say about education is still pertinent. In 1932, addressing the WCAD's 4th Triennial Convention, he argued that the "objective of education for the deaf is not to develop speech alone, but to produce well-adjusted deaf adults, capable of enjoying life and functioning as a taxpayer, not a tax consumer."

He met Pauline Pearl ("Polly") Nathanson, an alumna of the Manitoba School for the Deaf, KDES, and Gallaudet ('36), at a WCAD convention in Winnipeg. They were married soon afterwards, on November 6, 1932. "Her energy is boundless," noted **The Silent Worker** in 1963. They had two hearing daughters, Myrna Lou and Joyce. From 1932 to 1936, they lived in Winnipeg, where David co-owned a print shop. In 1936, they moved to Toronto, where they lived for the next 24 years. Polly was a homemaker and a legendary hostess; David was service and production manager for his father-in-law's bedding-and-sofa factory. During World War II, he worked as a job-placement officer, finding jobs for over 200 deaf workers.

In 1961, GCAA launched its Centennial Fund drive, and persuaded Peikoff to chair it. The Peikoffs returned to the Metro Washington area, where David established Gallaudet's first Alumni Office. After the drive, he became Gallaudet's Director of Development, and raised more than $1,000,000—which Jack Gannon calls "an amount never before dreamed of by an organization of the deaf, much less attempted." For the rest of his life—even after he retired in 1970 and suffered a stroke in 1971—Peikoff continued volunteering for the Alumni Association.

In 1974, Peikoff and Wallace D. Edington ('15), compiled the first **Gallaudet Almanac**. In 1979, David and Polly Peikoff became honorary co-chairs of a nationwide campaign to raise $1.3 million to restore "Ole Jim," Gallaudet's original campus gymnasium and a much-loved landmark (built 1880-81), as Alumni House. They assisted Alan B. Crammatte ('32) and his wife Florence ('35), national chairs for this fundraiser. In June 1982, "Ole Jim" was officially opened as the Alumni House. Afterwards, the Peikoffs were "regular fixtures there," volunteering to help Gallaudet maintain contact with its alumni and the alumni with each other.

Gallaudet bestowed two honorary degrees on Peikoff: a Master of Arts in 1950 and a Doctor of Laws in 1957. His many other U.S. and Canadian awards and honors included the Gallaudet College Alumni Association's Laurent Clerc Award for "outstanding social contributions by a deaf person" in 1970. One of GCAA's fellowship funds was named after him. As Dr. Carbin notes, "In 1971, he became the first North American recipient of the Gold Medal of Honour presented by the British Deaf and Dumb Association (now the British Deaf Association), in recognition of the many years of service he had contributed to deaf people in Canada and the United States. He was inducted into the National Fraternal Society of the Deaf Hall of Fame in 1973, the Canadian Cultural Society of the Deaf Hall of Fame in 1976, and the National Congress of Jewish Deaf Hall of Fame in 1986." And in 1987, the University of Alberta in Edmonton established the David Peikoff Chair of Deafness Studies, the first endowed-professor position in the world honoring a Deaf person.

On January 28, 1995, David Peikoff died in his sleep at his home in Laurel Maryland, a little short of his 95th birthday. Several Canadian schools for the deaf flew their flags at half-mast in his honor, or issued official statements. Said Dr. Carbin: "Those of us who knew him personally felt a combination of pride and sadness—pride to have been acquainted with a man whose life had been devoted to the Deaf community, and sadness to think that his guiding light had been extinguished."

A memorial service was held at Gallaudet on February 2. At its February 9 meeting, the Board of Trustees voted unanimously to rename Alumni House "Peikoff Alumni House" (P.A.H.) in honor of David and Polly Peikoff. (PAH! is an ASL expression roughly equivalent to "We made it!" or "Victory!") When Polly was informed, she was overjoyed, and her eyes filled with tears.

LeRoy Colombo, in his favorite element: swimming (top) and sailing (bottom).
(Rosenberg Library, Galveston, Texas)

CHAPTER 17

LeRoy Colombo

1905-1974

"World's Greatest Lifeguard"

Fate plays strange tricks on us. Consider LeRoy Colombo and his contemporary, Johnny Weissmuller. Both of them were champion long-distance swimmers, tall and tanned, with the handsome faces and bodies of Greek gods. One became a Hollywood star in the popular "Tarzan" movies—twelve of them. The other is comparatively obscure. As Hollywood's Tarzan, Weissmuller is still famous. Colombo, profoundly deaf, was never Hollywood material. Yet his deafness made him all the more determined to excel as a swimmer and be of service to those in need. So well did he succeed that not only was he the first deaf but the world's greatest lifeguard, officially credited with saving *907* lives. By any reckoning, that's an incredible number.

He was born on December 23, 1905, in Galveston, Texas, the island city on the Gulf of Mexico. When he was 7, an attack of spinal meningitis deafened him and paralyzed his legs. Recovery was slow and painful. His brothers Nick and Cinto gave him the only physical therapy he ever received. Every day, they dragged him up and down the alley behind their house, trying to make him walk again. The rough-and-tumble sessions worked. When LeRoy regained some strength in his legs, Nick and Cinto began taking him to the beach. He quickly learned to swim and felt more at home in water than on land. Gradually, he regained full strength.

Now 8, LeRoy was enrolled in a local public school. Unable to keep up with the others, he dropped out several months later. He used to come back from a day in the surf to face the fury of his

Italian-born mother, who feared for his life (and whose pleas to stay away from the beach were useless). When he was 10, he entered Texas School for the Deaf in Austin, where he learned speechreading and sign language. He also perfected his swimming in the school's indoor pool, where he practiced daily for hours, building up his body and stamina.

He was forced to leave school 6 years later when his father died. By that time, he had become an expert swimmer. As **The Deaf American** put it: "Swimming was one recreation [he] could afford and he spent most of his free time in the water." Galveston beachgoers started noticing him because he could swim for hours on end.

Finally, Cinto asked the exclusive Surf Toboggan Club if LeRoy, now 18, could become a member. To qualify, LeRoy had to pass a test in which he would have to swim continuously for 3 hours without stopping or floating on his back. He passed the test with ease and became the first deaf person to join the STC. He became one of its stars. That same year, he also became a full-fledged Life Guard for the City of Galveston.

One year later, he took on another challenge. This was more of a showdown. He competed against Herbert Bernau, Jr., the Amateur Athletic Union's national endurance champion—the man who could swim longer than anyone else without stopping. LeRoy Colombo beat him. The next year—Labor Day, 1925—the two men had a rematch in a 10-mile race. Fourteen swimmers started; only two—Colombo and Bernau—crossed the finish line. And again, Colombo won. He beat Bernau by a full mile, setting a new record for Galveston by completing the race in 6 hours and 55 minutes.

Another Labor Day, LeRoy and Cinto took first- and second-place honors in a 15-mile marathon race, during which all the contestants had to struggle against strong ocean currents, changing tides, and stinging jellyfish. Of six starters, the Colombo brothers were the only ones to finish. (Bernau dropped out after 8 hours because of cramps.) LeRoy was timed at 11 hours and 30 minutes, beating Cinto by 3-1/2 hours.

When he was 23, LeRoy swam 30 miles in 16 hours and 24

minutes. Between the 1929 and 1939, he won all the distance races held in the Gulf of Mexico.

In 1926, he competed in a 10-mile race in the Mississippi River off St. Louis. He dislocated a shoulder after the eighth mile and swam the last two miles with one arm. He didn't win that one, but he finished. Johnny Weissmuller, freestyle champion and 5-time Olympic gold medalist, was also in that race—and didn't finish.

As a dashing young man—"a regular Jean Lafitte with the ladies"—Colombo worked part-time as a bouncer in nightclubs.

During all these years, he was also doing a great service to humanity—saving lives. He knew "where the treacherous currents and undertows are—around the piers and rock groins." Beginning the summer when he was 12 and rescued a drowning boy, he regularly made headlines in the Galveston newspapers.

In 1966, Harold Scarlett wrote a poignant "Spotlight" profile for the **Houston Post** of the heroic, grizzled, good-humored "beach bum":

> [Broadway celebrities] Phil Harris and Alice Faye, Ben Bernie and Henry Busse—they aren't around any more to kid with Colombo. But most of the old regulars along the beach know Leroy. Millionaires, gamblers, prostitutes, street cleaners—they know and respect Leroy.
>
> They know about how the tugboat *Propeller* exploded in flames in 1928, how Colombo made the front pages by swimming beneath burning oil and rescuing two crewmen.
>
> They know how he once rescued a fireman trapped on top of a burning building, how he got a city commendation for his courage.
>
> They remember how he won the $500 purse in a five-mile race in 1937, then dived back into the water, still fresh as a daisy, to retrieve a purse a woman had dropped in the excitement.
>
> They remember how, even after World War II when he was getting along in years, Colombo regularly won five-mile races by training on cigars and beer.
>
> They know, if they are really close to him, that Colombo has almost drowned 16 times himself while trying to rescue others. The last time was last summer, when a foundering youth got a panic armlock around Colombo's throat. But Colombo worked free and saved him.

There seemed to be something supernatural about his ability, as these two quotes from **The Deaf American's** tribute suggest:

Galveston Police Chief D. K. Lack said, "He saved more people than I ever heard of or knew. He was one of the greatest lifeguards that ever lived. I know where he saved three people at one time, and once, four. He could sense anything going on in the water and see it before anyone else could. He's a legend in the city of Galveston."

[Faith Colombo, Nick's wife, added], "He had a sixth sense about saving lives. . . . He would work on a person and bring him back to life after others gave up. He would ride in the ambulance to the hospital and bring them back. It was a God-given sense. From the time he started until the time he retired, he saved over a thousand people."

During his 40 years as a lifeguard, he saved 907 lives—an achievement formerly listed in the **Guinness Book of World Records**. (He also brought back 24 who couldn't be saved.) A passage in **Deaf Heritage**, however, provides an ironic insight into the psychology of heroism:

A reporter once asked Colombo if he had ever received an award for saving a life. "Yes," Colombo responded. A grateful owner gave him $25.00 when he saved a dog from drowning. What about people, were they appreciative? No, responded Colombo. They were embarrassed and they even crossed the street to avoid passing him face to face.

This is elaborated in Scarlett's article:

In his years on the beach, Colombo has seen some strange values placed on human life.

Once, he says, he plucked two drowning girls from the surf. Their father went off, promising to bring Colombo a case of beer for his trouble. The father returned with two cans. Two girls saved, two cans of beer.

In the depression, he saved a 15-year-old newsboy. A newspaper story about the rescue noted that bystanders took up a collection for Colombo. The collection totaled $1.

The lifeguard's salary for saving lives used to be 75¢ cents an hour. Now he gets a dollar an hour for patrolling Termini Beach between 53rd and 61st Streets. (He pads out his income by renting beach umbrellas and floats, and by making homely souvenir ash trays out of sea shells he collects.)

Colombo says no rescued bather ever gave him a nickel as a reward.

One little old lady, he says, once gave him $30 for retrieving her false teeth, which she had lost in the surf. Another woman gave him $25 for rescuing her poodle.

"I spend the $25 on whisky for beach boys," Colombo recalled.

"Even at 60, an age when most men think twice about mowing the lawn, Colombo is happily savoring another summer of hard swimming," Scarlett wrote.

Despite the poor pay, the grizzled old lifeguard keeps on dragging the gaspers out of the waves. (...) [He] has no philosophy, no mystic dedication about giving life back to hundreds of people. Ask him about that part of it, and he just shrugs. Sometimes he must wonder to himself if some of them are worth saving. But he keeps on bringing them in. He says he will go on doing it "as long as I live."

He was forced to retire at 62 because of a heart condition, but continued to hang around with old friends and characters on Galveston Beach. (Scarlett: "To augment his croaky voice, Colombo communicates—fluently—with his quick hands, his mobile face, his whole body. He is an expert pantomimist with a salty humor.") The lure of the sea was irresistible, and he found swimming easier than walking. As Jane Kenamore, then Archivist at Galveston's Rosenberg Library, attested in 1979, "he was still swimming a mile a day in the Gulf (summer and winter!) up until a few weeks before he died."

That happened on July 12, 1974. According to **The Deaf American**, "the thousands of young swimmers who crowd Galveston Island's pleasure beaches hardly noticed his passing; but oldtimers on the Gulf, veteran sports writers and the deaf community paid tribute to an authentic hero."

His death didn't go totally unnoticed, nor was he completely forgotten. Senator A. R. Schwartz of Galveston introduced a resolution honoring him in the Texas legislature, and its members stood for a moment of silence. In many parts of the state, the Texas flag was lowered at half-mast. The citizens of Galveston erected a landmark with a plaque on the beach he had patrolled. It commemorates LeRoy Colombo's dedication to duty and his peerless record of saving the lives of 907 persons.

Bottom left: Hillis Arnold. Top: Arnold with his altar-panel *I am the Vine, You are the Branches* (partial view), completed 1966. Bottom right: In his studio.
(Courtesy of Caroline Becher)

CHAPTER 18

Hillis Arnold

1906-1988

Midwestern sculptor

Hillis Arnold was born on July 10, 1906, on a farm in North Dakota's Golden Valley, near Beach. Meda and Algie Arnold were schoolteachers-turned-homesteaders. There was an older brother, Don, and a black spaniel, Gypsy. Hillis was profoundly deafened by spinal meningitis when he was around 6 months old, and had no recollection of sound.

Although she knew of no suitable oral school in North Dakota, Meda had some familiarity with oral education. She corresponded with the "Home for the Training of Little Deaf Children" in Philadelphia, worked with Hillis tirelessly, and taught him to speak and lipread. She later wrote: "He early showed skill with his hands. By the time he was three he was cutting paper, drawing with a pencil and modeling with clay. Sometimes he drew pictures in the mud with a little pointed stick. He loved to cut long trains out of newspapers. He discovered that if he cut them on a fold they would stand up." He himself recalled:

> I was about 7 or 8 years old. We had a terrible rainstorm and the cows were up to their knees in mud. I found it fascinating to [stand on the back porch and] watch them trying to pull themselves from the mud and stooped down and began playing with the mud. When my mother came over to see what I was doing, she saw I was making a cow—or a replica of a cow—in the mud. She immediately bought me some modeling clay, and from then, I was an artist and on my way.

After the Arnolds moved to Minneapolis, repeated crop failures forced them to return to in North Dakota. Hillis spent a year with

Minnie and Walter Howe of Milwaukee, who gave him intensive speech training, then returned to the farm, where he learned to drive the horse-teams and work in the fields. When he was 12, they moved back to Minneapolis. He attended Minneapolis Day School for the Deaf for 6 years, then Minneapolis Central High School, graduating with honors in 1928, and likewise earned a B.A. *cum laude* from University of Minnesota in 1933. (Ironically, the dean had been reluctant to admit him because he was deaf.) He attended Minneapolis School of Fine Arts on a 2-year full scholarship, then Cranbrook Academy of Art in Bloomfield Hills, Michigan, and Chicago Institute of Art.

In Summer 1935, while Arnold was still a student at Minneapolis School, he and Meda visited Cranbrook, where he met the renowned Swedish-born expressionist sculptor Carl Milles, who recognized his talent and commissioned his assistance on several projects, including the famed *Meeting of the Waters* fountain in Union Station Park, St. Louis, completed around 1940. It symbolized the union of the Missouri and Mississippi.) Arnold settled in Kirkwood, a St. Louis suburb. (In 1951, he married Eulalia "Lee" Guebert, a nurse, in Red Bud. They had two daughters, Katherine and Caroline.)

In 1938, on Milles' recommendation, Arnold took a position as professor of sculpture and ceramics at Monticello College, a prestigious private junior college for women in Godfrey, Illinois (now Lewis & Clark Community College). He was to remain a "talented and devoted member of the Monticello faculty" for 34 years, "an unforgettable force on the lives of the thousands of students who have been privileged to study under him." He was friendly, warm, unaffected, and funny, with an uncanny talent for mimicry.

"Communication with my students has never been a serious problem," he said. "At our first meeting I tell the students that by the end of the first or second week I will be able to read their lips if they move their lips a bit slower, and that they will understand me as they get used to my way of speaking." To sharpen his communication skills, he took night classes in advanced lipreading and speech at Central Institute for the Deaf in nearby St. Louis.

Although he never learned fingerspelling or sign, his speech was "easy to read," even by other deaf people.

His position at Monticello gave Arnold the opportunity to do what he liked best—teaching and freelancing. Over the next half-century, he emerged as one of the most productive sculptors in the Midwest, and one of the most versatile anywhere, working in every possible medium—including new and unexplored. As Nancy Wahonick noted in **December Rose**:

> "Arnold's art is scattered in museums, shopping centers, office buildings, colleges, churches, national parks and private collections from coast to coast. (...) He works in many media and there is no single "Hillis Arnold" look.
>
> He is equally at home working with marble, aluminum, terra cotta (which many of his smaller pieces tend to be), plastics, wood (he is especially partial to 'finding' animals and human forms in the grain of beautiful woods), bronze, welded copper, brass plaster with gold leaf, and even fiberglass. (...)
>
> Often Arnold will order a new material when he hears of one. When he received a can of polyester resin from a chemical company while he was in the middle of another project, he set the can aside. When he finally opened it some months later, he discovered the material had hardened and taken on a remarkable blue coloring. He looked at the hardened material, useless for the purpose he intended, and he "saw" a shape, which he carefully carved. The resulting sculpture, "Angel," has received numerous awards and was one of the works chosen by the United States Information Agency for exhibits held in Europe and the Soviet Union.

He developed his basic approach in the 1930s: simplified forms. Each commissioned work was adapted to the theme, setting, and viewers. His sculptures ranged from small, intimate ceramic sketches to monumental public pieces. They could be witty and whimsical (*Cat*), austerely moving (*Abraham and Isaac*), or ultra-modern (*The Lord is My Shepherd*). He made many miniature portrait heads, donating the proceeds to charity. His smaller works were exhibited at museums, galleries, colleges, and fairs, and received numerous awards. In 1960 he was awarded the presti-gious title of Live Fellow of the International Institute of Arts and Letters, which recognized him as one of the finest sculptors in the

States. According to Wahonick, he "[shrugged] off the awards;" he evidently considered his work only "good."

His works were often symbolic. At Monticello, he created an 18' corten-steel sculpture of a tree, *New Heritage* (1969—also called the "Olin Statue" after the benefactors it was dedicated to), symbolizing the process of growth and education. The roots and sturdy trunk represented the intellectual strength of faculty, alumnae, and trustees; the leaves, graduating students; the new growth emerging from the leafy arc and "nurtured and supported by the past and present," future generations.

Two works are in downtown St. Louis. One is the *World War II Memorial* in Aloe Plaza. The imposing 32' limestone shaft depicts soldiers and sailors on either side—leaving home, in combat, and emerging from death. For the Jefferson National Expansion Museum underneath the Gateway Arch, he carved a great walnut American eagle with 5' wingspan, symbolizing *Manifest Destiny*.

Arnold estimated that 75% of his work had a religious theme. Cardinal Joseph Ritter purchased two sculptures for his private residence in LaDue, a St. Louis suburb. An abstract interpretation of *The Lord Is My Shepherd*, carved of Georgia marble and set on a tall pedestal in the garden, was designed to be seen from all sides, and each angle shows a different attribute—judgement, admiration, or protection. A 2-1/2' statue of *Abraham and Isaac*, of polychromed mahogany, was carved for the Cardinal's chapel. It was one of 16 U.S. works chosen for the International Biennale of Contemporary Christian Art in Salzburg, Austria (1948), and was then displayed at the national exhibit of the Religious Art Center of America, in Latrobe, Pennsylvania. A 16' limestone statue, *Mother Ann and Child Mary*, above the entrance of St. Ann's Catholic Church in Normandy (another St. Louis suburb), was featured in **TIME** and **LIFE**. Arnold's resplendent 8' bronze doors for the Normandy Presbyterian Church won second place at the annual convention of the Church Architectural Guild of America. He created a striking 15' x 5' burnished-copper reredos (altar-panel) for Grace Episcopal Church in Kirkwood (*I am the Vine, You are the Branches*, 1966), representing the Eucharist as a fish-shaped chalice and a broken loaf of bread in the center surrounded by a symbolic vine, flower, and leaf. It took a year to finish and, as Arnold said, "from 15,00 to 20,000 hammer blows just to make each of the 12 figures on the screen."

A few of his sculptures have "deaf" themes. For CID, he sculpted *The Learners* of white Tennessee marble, depicting a teacher/ mother practicing vocalizations with a deaf child. The smooth, rounded abstractions and interlocking forms (which resemble *The Lord is My Shepherd*) communicate tenderness, and invite touch. It's displayed in the lobby of the school building. *Deaf Given a Voice* reflects his belief in Total Communication; it incorporates an eye (since deaf people rely in visual skills) and an arm with mobile fingers (representing signing).

Arnold made bold use of innovative techniques and media— e.g., plastic aluminum. One notable commission was the 9' statue of Christ for the Gustavus Adolphus Church in St. Paul, Minnesota. For LaDue Junior High School, he created companion statues of Mark Twain's immortal characters, Tom Sawyer and Huckleberry Finn.

In May 1972, he retired from Monticello, but continued to work in his Kirkwood studio. As an art reviewer noted in the St. Louis **Post-Dispatch**: "Arnold at 77 is still working on commissions, still full of the enthusiasm of an artist, the delight taken in observation. 'Because I am deaf,' Arnold said, 'I am a better observer.'" One of his last works (1987) was a striking patinated-terracotta bust of the martyred Abolitionist newspaper editor Elijah P. Lovejoy, donated to the Alton Museum of History and Art to commemorate the sesquicentennial of Lovejoy's death.

He died at home on November 18, 1988, after a bout with cancer.

Although most of his works were one-of-a-kind, shortly before his death he began making limited-edition cast-bronzes. He told Wahonick: "Art is not something that has anything to do with age. I was an artist at 7 years of age—and I am still an artist today. I am still trying new materials, working on new ideas, and developing new projects. Art never ends. It goes on communicating—with us or without us."

Frances Woods and Billy Bray, the Wonder Dancers.
(Courtesy of Esther and Anthony Caliguire)

CHAPTER 19

Frances Woods

1907-

The Wonder Dancer

The overhead lights dim. The nightclub patrons, seated at their tables, stop talking. The orchestra strikes up; the spotlight is switched on. It focuses on "The Wonder Dancers." The man is tall, dark, and handsome, Valentinoesque, and the woman is a golden beauty whose radiance outshines the gilt sequins of her gown. As they swing and sway to the rhythm of the rhumba, they are so picture-perfect that it's almost like looking at a scene from a Ginger Rogers-Fred Astaire movie.

A quick look at the printed program, however, reminds the audience that they are being entertained by one of the most unusual dance teams ever seen—Frances Woods and Billy Bray. They are unique because Frances Woods cannot hear a single note of music; she is totally deaf. But her whole body is alive with music. She can feel the cadence through vibrations in the air and on the polished wooden floor, and even when dancing on a marble floor, she can sense the flow and beat of rhythm through her fingertips.

When Esther Richina Thomas was born 3 months premature on March 21, 1907, in Girard, Ohio, they didn't expect her to live. She weighed only 1-1/4 pounds. Her head was the size of an English walnut. It was later discovered that she was born without eardrums. But she survived, and grew up to be strong and athletic.

During the summer of 1924, she met Anthony Caliguire, a dashing young steelworker-dancer from Pennsylvania who looked like Rudolph Valentino and was a colorful character himself. Tony moonlighted by teaching dance classes, and Esther's parents thought she'd benefit from learning how to dance. Although Tony was initially reluctant, he agreed to teach her. He studied basic sign language at OSD, and was impressed by Esther's strength and fearlessness. He learned how to sign; she learned how to dance.

In his crudely-written but often exciting self-published autobiography, **The Wonder Dancers Woods & Bray** (1974), Caliguire describes their early days:

> When I met Frances in 1924, she was going to the Deaf Mute School in Columbus, Ohio. In her school days, she played center in the basketball team, and her team won five years in a row.
>
> We used to dance and rehearse in her father's garage. She took her dancing lessons when she was home on vacation. So in 1924 and 1925 we practiced. We won many awards when she came home, and we went to dances. All the while, no one knew that she was a deaf mute. Well, to make a long story short, Frances graduated in June of 1926. By this time we were very much in love. I asked her parents for her hand. Her mother consented immediately, but her father was tough. He was rather reluctant and would rather see her married to one of her own kind. Another deaf mute. But he gave in and Frances and I got married September 5, 1926.

As a husband-and-wife team, Tony and Esther worked hard to develop a variety of dance acts and routines in preparation for their professional career. With great patience and skill, he taught her by playing the piano and getting her to feel the difference between 4/4 time and 3/4 time. Then he would teach her the dance steps to follow the particular rhythm.

Esther helped Tony improve his fingerspelling and signing, and he helped greatly to improve her speechreading skills. He also became her interpreter, so they were able to interact freely and communicate with both the deaf and hearing.

Their first engagement was at Pittsburgh's Nixon Café, and they appeared there annually until it closed in 1951. At first, they were known as "The Dancing DeSondos." In 1928, Charles B. Maddock, director and producer at R.K.O., gave them the stage names of "Frances Woods" and "Billy Bray." Not long afterwards, they caught the eye of Robert L. Ripley, who included them in his "Ripley's Believe It Or Not!" syndicated-cartoon feature and dubbed them "The Wonder Dancers." That's how they were billed thereafter. (Today, life-size wax figures of The Wonder Dancers are in the Ripley Museum.)

Success didn't come easily. Their early years in show business were a struggle. First came the infamous stock-market crash of 1929 and onset of the Great Depression. Millions of people were unemployed, money was very scarce, and the entertainment business suffered. Woods and Bray practically lived out of a single suitcase and were often down to their last dollar. Bray recounts how they "saved a buck by not eating in restaurants"—they bought a frying pan, climbed on a chair, and used the gaslight fixtures still common in second- and third-class hotels to fry eggs or grill sandwiches. "It was crude, but it was workable."

The dance routines were strenuous, demanding tremendous physical strength and endurance as much as skill. The nightclubs were hot; the spotlights could be blinding. On several occasions, they got hurt. Once Bray injured his neck but continued to perform despite excruciating pain. ("All acts go on and do their work regardless of how they feel.") Once, while being held by one wrist and ankle and whirled like a roller skater, Woods flew out of Bray's sweat-slippery hands, slid across the stage, and fell headlong into the bass drum. Bray, suddenly caught off-balance, followed her. Woods sustained broken ribs from another "acrobatic" fall. Splinters from sliding on a rough dance floor when Bray threw her down during the Apache. And a badly gashed head when Bray, blinded by an unaccustomed 3,000-watt carbon spotlight, spun her too close to a mirrored pillar and shattered it. They coped with illness, obnoxious customers, and mistreatment. In 1937, they were marooned in Louisville, Kentucky during a catastrophic flood.

Like good troupers, however, they scraped through, kept their act together, and their suitcases packed. Their big break came in the early 1930s when R.K.O. Productions booked "The Wonder Dancers" to perform in vaudeville acts. One of their specialties was the "Adagio," an exciting dance number that included acrobatic feats of the kind seen in circuses. Another was the "Apache," a combination of dance and mime.

The Apache, a French routine, dramatizes man's cruelty to woman. At the end, the male "stabs" the female partner with a rubber stiletto, then carries her offstage. Bray recalls: "Ours was so outstanding and mean-looking that after the dance we didn't get much applause. Some were throwing beer and whiskey bottles at me! So I was dodging bottles and glasses. I said to Frances, 'Honey, we must change the finish of our dance, or I am going to get killed!' I taught her how to carry me offstage at the end of the dance. She had a little gun in her skirt (a .22 caliber pistol, loaded with blanks), and before I could knife her, she shot me twice. I staggered and fell forward. She bent down and put me on her shoulder and carried me off." (Bray weighed 150 pounds.) "That was a show-stopper!" They got thunderous applause.

Although they were famed for their Adagio and Apache, Woods and Bray developed a versatile program that included all the popular dances of the times—the Fox Trot, the Waltz, the Tango, the Rhumba, and the Samba. For each of these dances, Woods, a skilled seamstress, designed and made *all* her own costumes— "elaborate gowns that can stand a lot of punishment." In 1974, Bray reported that Woods had just finished a dress with 26,000 sequins, each sewn on by hand.

In a 1980 newspaper article, Joan Cochran commented:

> But these were learning and growing years in which they developed their Apache Dance—their greatest all-time success. Frances' blond, pastel prettiness and Bray's dark machismo lent an added piquancy to this stylized version of seamy Paris nightlife.
>
> Through the Thirties and Forties they appeared in most of the major nightclubs and hotels. They were accompanied by all the great "big bands"—Wayne King, Ted Weems, Cab Calloway, Ben Bernie, Eddie Duchin, Anson Weeks, Bob Crosby, Will Osborne, Horace Heidt, Henry Busse, and Paul Whiteman. They performed at the Edgewater Beach Hotel in Chicago on the occasion of Lawrence Welk's first major engagement. Welk, to this day, credits Bray with helping him to become the fine dancer he is.
>
> Extended engagements at the Shoreham in Washington made them favorites with the government social set. They made many friends among the great. This added impetus to fame and fortune led to several appearances at the Palladium in London.

When they played the Roosevelt Theatre in Oakland, California, deaf people came in from across the state and presented Woods with huge baskets of flowers at each performance. "I never saw so many beautiful roses in my life." The ushers could hardly carry them.

In the '50s, they opened a dance studio in Youngstown, Ohio. At first, they taught ballet, modern, jazz, acrobatic, and tap dancing; later they narrowed the focus to ballroom dancing for adults. They spent summers entertaining audiences at the Northernaire Hotel in Three Lakes, Wisconsin, their winters teaching dance. Many honors came to them, but their greatest satisfaction was in cheering and inspiring others. Nothing delighted them more than giving dance lessons to local schoolchildren or entertaining disabled and elderly people, especially those in nursing homes.

For this, they were honored at the Governor's Awards Banquet on February 9, 1978, which recognized Ohioans whose careers have benefitted humanity and brought honor to the state.

This astounding duo were still dancing into their eighties. By that time, they'd been together for more than 70 years—and, to look at them, audiences and reporters found it hard to believe. Frances Woods ultimately developed a heart problem that necessitated her wearing a pacemaker (the electronic device that regulates heartbeat). She first had one implanted in 1968, when she was 61, and 17 years later was dancing to the rhythm of her fourth one—and still going strong.

As a concession to their advanced ages (and wary of pulling one of the pacemaker's electrodes), they discontinued the "Adagio" (which involved Bray's lifting Woods into the air, shoulder-high), but not their ballroom routines—Rhumba, Tango, Waltz, Samba, Cha-cha-cha, and the Dance of Love. "Upbeat and energetic" as always, Woods and Bray remained active, giving dance concerts at local nursing homes and hospitals.

According to a 1993 newspaper report: "Bray said they read each other's minds. They know, without a word, what the other is thinking."

The secret of their longevity? Dance!

Ernest Marshall with one of his reels.
(© George Potanovic, Jr.)

CHAPTER 20

Ernest Marshall

1910-

Filmmaker

I remember when I was very small, a young boy, my father bought me a hand-cranked projector that I wanted. Then I acquired some 35-mm film scraps and cuttings from theatrical movies. Great fun! My heart was poured into film work—I found my interest.
*Around 1928, talking movies—"talkies"—began to replace silent movies. Up to that time, everybody enjoyed silent movies. There were many good ones—lots of variety, and those wonderful dialogue frames. Talkies changed all that. Equality was swept away. Vitaphone's Al Jolson—famous for his blackface routine, singing "Mammy"—started the trend with **The Jazz Singer**, released in 1927. Whoosh! Suddenly, everything changed! Silents became obsolete. Talkies became the rage. More and more talkies were made. Deaf people felt disappointed, saddened—they were pushed right out.—adapted from "The Projectionist," Ernest Marshall's autobiographical video*

The coming of the "talkies" coincided with the advent of the Great Depression. But the "talkies" takeover also coincided with the introduction of the Cine-Kodak movie camera for amateurs. Ernest Marshall, a pioneering by-the-Deaf, for-the-Deaf filmmaker, seized the opportunity.

He was born on January 2, 1910, in Poughkeepsie, New York, an only child, third-generation Deaf. He "grew up watching [his] parents conversing in ASL." In 1917, he entered New York Institution for the Instruction of the Deaf and Dumb (renamed New York School for the Deaf in 1933), popularly known as "Fanwood."

His parents signed him fairy tales, which he shared with the other boys at Fanwood. He became a master storyteller, later performing at Deaf literary meetings and conventions. He recalls that after he lectured on astronomy, "Frederick Hughes, the theatrical coach at Gallaudet College, told me I was good enough to be a teacher!"

Fanwood was the first military school for the deaf. Ernest joined the band as fifer, later drummer, lieutenant, and band leader. They even gave a half-hour recital on radio! (He was also active in the drama club and sports, winning several bicycle races.)

He was valedictorian of his class (1931). The Great Depression was in full force; unemployment was high. After depending on his father several years, he finally landed a job at Manhattan's Mid-City Hotel as an interior decorator. He worked there 38 years until he retired in 1974.

In 1938, he arranged a 5th-anniversary dinner for two old classmates. There he met his "best beloved," Alida Purdy, an alumna of St. Joseph School for the Deaf (the Bronx). At their second meeting, a Union League of the Deaf social, they began their courtship, and were married on August 31, 1939.

Marshall participated in local Deaf-theater groups. In 1955, he and Philip Hanover founded the relatively long-lived Metropolitan Dramatic Club of the Deaf, with a troupe of over a dozen performers. He wrote, directed, and performed in *Satan and the Miser*, which played twice in Brooklyn and New Jersey that year.

He then combined his dramatic talents with his old interest in photography and movies. The Cine-Kodak 16mm system appeared in 1923, the Standard-8 system in 1932, and Kodachrome in 1935—all geared towards amateur filmmakers. He decided to produce a filmplay with a deaf cast, rounded up some old Fanwood friends, rehearsed for several months, and in 1937, released his first film, *It is Too Late* (14 minutes). Using ASL, it mimicked the old silent movies with their melodramatic acting and tearjerker plots. Deaf audiences, tired of having nothing but stageplays to watch, loved it. "They were thrilled to see movies with deaf actors. I first showed it at St. Ann's Church for the Deaf in New York City—40¢ admission. I didn't care about the money. I just wanted to entertain deaf people."

Marshall produced a total of 11 films—7 feature films and 4

shorts. He directed most of them. He called his production company "Independent Theatrical and Cinema Club of the Deaf." Independent it certainly was. There was no financial backing, no NTD-type grants. "I got the money from my own pocket. The clubs agreed to split the proceeds 50-50 with me. Attendees paid $1 as a donation for the 'film fund,' not for admission. I made only a small profit to cover expenses such as rolls of film and travel."

When he arranged a screening in a Deaf club, he almost never shipped his films—which were his *originals*—he brought them with him, as a precaution against mishandling and damage. He took excellent care of them. (Over 50 years after its first showing, *It Is Too Late* was still in good condition.) Moreover, he enjoyed traveling and socializing with new audiences—something he'd miss out on if he simply sent the films.

Emerson Romero (1900-1972), cousin of the Hollywood actor Caesar Romero, had been a silent-film comedian. He and Marshall became close friends. Romero gave Marshall helpful tips on filmmaking and directed one of his best productions, *A Cake of Soap* (1960, 9 minutes), a hilarious adaptation of a Saki short story.

In 1956, Marshall directed *The Confession* (15 minutes). Adapted from a story by Guy de Maupassant, it carried Marshall's first dialogue subtitles (for the benefit of oral-deaf and hard-of-hearing viewers who might have difficulty following the signs). Subtitles were also used in *The Debt*, *The Dream*, and *Sorrowful Approach*.)

Marshall and two others performed in *The Face on the Barroom Floor* (1959, based on the sentimental Gay Nineties song). This film had a problem with synchronization—"the captions didn't match with the actors' signs—even though the actors were very good." Dissatisfied, he removed it from circulation.

Since Marshall and the other performers lived away from each other, he preferred scripts with only a few characters; this made direction much easier. *The Debt* (1959) was adapted from Anton Chekhov's *The Boor* by Dr. LeRoy Subit, who played Ivan Borisovitch. *The Neighbor* (1962, 16 minutes) was likewise adapted from another Chekhov play, *The Proposal*. Both plays have only three characters.

At 55 minutes, *The Debt* is Marshall's longest feature film, and the only one in Technicolor. Over 400 subtitles (neatly hand-lettered by Marshall) were superimposed. It featured Kathleen Fettin as the spirited but stubborn widow, Natayla Gayef, Subit as a landowner trying to collect a debt, and Frank Heintz as Natayla's faithful old servant, Yasha. Amazingly, this film was made before William Stokoe published **Sign Language Structure**, but it shows what a powerful medium ASL could be.

The Dream (1961, 33 minutes) was a unique experimental pro-duction—a film with a deaf cast portraying hearing characters! No signing was used. ("I wanted to do something different.") Marshall chose performers with extensive oral training (especially those from P.S. 47). Filming, done only during evenings and weekends, took 6 months to complete. He added captions but *The Dream* remained unpopular with Deaf viewers, who preferred signed films. (The cast had a great time.)

Marshall's final film, *Sorrowful Approach* (1962, 15 minutes) was directed by Kathleen Fettin, one of his best actresses. (Thus, *Sorrowful Approach* is the first known feature film to be directed by a Deaf woman.) Marshall later told Melinda Weinrib that he was pleased with Fettin's work as a director.

Then there was his "live film." Sometime in the 1950s, the American Athletic Association of the Deaf sponsored a nation-wide basketball tournament, and for its "Entertainment Night," under the auspices of the Union League, requested a special show. The audience was elated with the one he created, which combined cleverly-synchronized live and film performances of Marshall and an actress.

From 1931 until 1994, Marshall was a skilled and dedicated projectionist for New York-area Deaf clubs and organizations. A captioned Hollywood or subtitled foreign film was a weekly or monthly tradition, and a main attraction. As Weinrib notes, after the Captioned Films for the Deaf distribution program was launched in 1959, "Marshall extended his filmmaking interests and became a film programmer. He took responsibility for the New York City area and showed the captioned films on loan throughout the Deaf community." He arranged a total of 2,042 screenings around the city. Nothing could stop him.

Along the way, he acquired other films now of interest to Deaf historians. As a projectionist, he had access to a variety of material—including other Deaf filmmakers' works—and made authorized copies that he later donated to the Veditz Collection in Gallaudet University Archives. Besides producing feature films, Marshall, like his contemporary Charles Krauel, filmed Deaf-club outings, weddings, and boat-rides sponsored by the Union League Ladies' Auxiliary. These events attracted hundreds of Deaf members and friends, and the films are a priceless record of old-fashioned ASL celebrations.

After *A Sorrowful Approach*, Marshall stopped making films, largely because of the increasing expense. He continued to travel and show his films. In 1964, he and Alida celebrated their 25th wedding anniversary with a cross-country train trip. He contacted 8 Deaf clubs and brought *The Debt*, *The Neighbor*, and *A Cake of Soap*.

Marshall has received many honors and awards; his favorite is the Gallaudet University Alumni Association's 1988 Laurent Clerc Award "for outstanding social contributions by a deaf person in the interest of Deaf people."

By contemporary cinematic standards, Marshall's films would be considered primitive, but they are still enjoyable. They document the artistic use of an everyday language that hadn't yet been recognized as a language.

Marshall wasn't the only independent Deaf feature-filmmaker, but he was an imaginative and innovative one. He was quite possibly the first to produce an ASL feature film and to use subtitles; he was the first to give a deaf woman the opportunity to direct a film; he had a deaf cast playing hearing characters; he devised a magically synchronized interactive film/live performance. And he preserved his work and helped preserve that of other deaf filmmakers. His films are not only entertaining, they are valuable artistic, cultural, and linguistic documents, providing insight into the Deaf experience.

"At the hub of the VR movement:" three views of Boyce R. Williams.
(Courtesy of George Kosovich/RSA)

CHAPTER 21

Boyce R. Williams

1910-

Vocational Rehabilitation specialist

Boyce Robert Williams was born on August 29, 1910, in Racine, Wisconsin. An outstanding athlete, captain of the Racine High School football squad, he dreamed of joining the Green Bay Packers. When he was 17, he contracted spinal meningitis, which totally deafened him. (Ironically enough, he was from a dynasty of physicians.)

He recovered, returned to Racine High in February 1928, and graduated in June. Not knowing what to do next, he felt lonely and depressed. Dr. Williams suggested that he go to Wisconsin School for the Deaf to further his education. He later told Frank G. Bowe: "I had passed that school many times when we went to play ball. I was under the impression that it was an asylum for the mentally ill. It looked about the same. It is much improved today. But I would not have gone to the school under any conditions. In February [1929], a field worker came along to see me—my father had arranged it. She wanted me to go to the school in Delavan and I said 'Not a chance.' Then she told me that they had a fine basketball team. And oh, that was *different!* . . . And that was what really hooked me, and nothing else."

At WSD, he learned sign language. He also developed an awareness of the communication problems that many deaf people experience in and outside of school. In Fall 1929, after 4 months at WSD, he entered Gallaudet College, where he advanced rapidly (he skipped two years) and was an outstanding football player.

Williams graduated with a B.A. in Mathematics in 1932, the peak of the Great Depression, but managed to get a teaching position in WSD's Intermediate Department. He had already learned about the bleak realities of life for deaf people, unemployed and unemployable. In 1935, he transferred to the high school at Indiana School for the Deaf.

In 1936, he married Hilda Tillinghast, a hearing ISD teacher who represented the third generation of a family of teachers and administrators who had pioneered in the founding of several schools for the deaf in the United States and Canada. They had three sons, Boyce, Jr., John, and Thomas.

In 1937, Williams became Director of Vocational Training at ISD, a position he held until 1945. He took summer courses at Marquette University, and received his Master's in Education from Columbia University in 1940. (He survived there by borrowing classmates' notes, extensive reading, independent study, and after-class "bull sessions" with professors.)

The Vocational Rehabilitation Act Amendments of 1943 had broadened the original program established in 1920, authorizing new services to eliminate or lessen disabilities. In 1945, the Office of Vocational Rehabilitation, in the Federal Security Agency, Washington, D.C., was looking for someone to establish the foundation of a VR program for deaf and hard-of-hearing people. (A discriminatory hearing requirement had just been eliminated.) Williams' background at ISD made him a strong candidate, and he was hired.

He began his career with the OVR on August 1, 1945; it was to last 38 years. Starting as Consultant for the Deaf, the Hard of Hearing, and the Speech Impaired, he advanced to the position of Chief (Director), Deafness and Communicative Disorders Branch. (OVR was renamed Rehabilitation Services Administration, in the Department of Health, Education, and Welfare, in August 1967.)

As he wrote: "The VR movement, although 25 years old when I began in 1945, had just really caught on nationally through its dramatic contributions to the war effort by training thousands and thousands of severely disabled people for war production, including deaf people. Industry finally learned that properly trained and placed disabled people were superior employees."

His first 10 years of service with the federal VR office and the state VR agencies were "important learning experiences." At that time, these programs were on a much smaller scale, so most of his work was committed to activities other than national-program development. Even then, however, Williams pioneered initiatives that promoted deaf rehabilitation. He worked hard to convince the state agencies that deaf clients must be served by counselors able to communicate in sign language, and that training services be especially adapted to deaf clients' needs. He pushed for sign-fluent counselors. As a result, each state ultimately hired a number of counselors serving Deaf clients exclusively. He wrote: "Cooperative agreements were developed with all of the program-oriented organizations in the broad field of communicative disorders, including the NAD." Also CEASD, CAID, the American Hearing Society, and FRAT.

Williams was greatly aided in advancing VR program development for deaf people by two events. First, in 1950, Dr. Mary E. Switzer, whom Edna Paananen-Adler calls "a great humanist and visionary," became Commissioner of OVR. A staunch supporter of the Deaf and hard-of-hearing, Dr. Switzer provided the kind of enlightened, dynamic leadership that often gave high priority to their needs. Recognizing that VR could be the means to implement Williams' goals, she became "an active partner" in his plans. Notes Adler: "She was to work closely with him for over 15 years, a golden period in which many . . . programs [benefiting] deaf people emerged. These include the National Theatre of the Deaf, the Registry of Interpreters for the Deaf, Captioned Films for the Deaf, the Communicative Skills Program, the National Leadership Training Program on Deafness, and a network of postsecondary programs especially for deaf persons, including NTID."

Second, in 1954, new amendments to the Vocational Rehabilitation Act provided for innovative projects and long- and short-term programs to meet the needs of "severely disabled and low-functioning deaf people," and authorized research, demonstrations, and training activities. Paananen-Adler notes:

Mention should be made of the critically-needed promotion that Williams provided, eventually leading to the network of mental-health programs, community-service programs, and postsecondary programs that deaf and hard-of-hearing people have access to today. Williams engineered over 100 national workshops in his drive to promote, develop, and establish programs needed by deaf and hard-of-hearing children and adults. In doing this important work, he saw to it that deaf people were fully involved in decision-making and planning along with normally-hearing people. Deaf people recall those early workshops as "walking in trails of glory."

"One of the most rewarding parts of my career work has been the rapid materialization of effective deaf leadership," Williams said. In 1960, CSUN (then San Fernando Valley State College) received a planning grant from OVR to design a graduate-level National Leadership Training Program in the Area of the Deaf, which was implemented two years later under the dynamic leadership of Dr. Ray L. Jones, Director. Professionals in the field of deafness (teachers, rehabilitation counselors, school counselors) received the training necessary to develop leadership skills and move into administrative positions. This comprehensive 8-month course of study included a variety of practical field experiences and led to a Master's in Education, Administration and Supervision. NLTP graduates became program coordinators, supervisors, school principals, and superintendents throughout the nation. (The NLTP was axed by the Nixon Administration as part its budget cuts.)

At a 1970 testimonial dinner honoring Williams on his 25 years of government service, Joseph Hunt, then Deputy Commissioner of RSA, said, "It was indeed a great day for the deaf and hard-of-hearing when Boyce came out of the West to give inspiring leadership. Today, we see the fruits of his work—in firm relationships, expansion of state operations, training, research, and demonstrations. And perhaps the greatest of all achievements: hope for thousands of people in our country, who had no reason to hope before." NAD President Robert G. Sanderson said, "He has provided the push, shove, and boot that has brought the needs of deaf persons to the attention of the decision-makers and the persons who serve."

For 38 years, Boyce Williams had, as he said, "personally been at the hub of the national rehabilitation movement." Directly, and indirectly, his programs proved of benefit to persons with disabilities throughout the world, and his example inspired and encouraged deaf persons aspiring to leadership positions in all walks of life. He retired from RSA in August 1983.

His appointment to Gallaudet's 1983-84 Powrie Vaux Doctor Chair of Deaf Studies capped a distinguished career. This, according to Adler, "provided him the opportunity to write the history of the vocational-rehabilitation movement as it pertained to deafness and deaf people, covering a period of over 40 years." It's being prepared for publication.

Williams served enthusiastically on virtually every executive board of deaf-related consumer and professional organizations. He was president of the GCAA, president of the Commission on Social Rehabilitation of the World Federation of the Deaf, Vice President of the Professional Rehabilitation Workers for the Adult Deaf, and a consultant to numerous organizations serving the blind, deaf-blind, and disabled. He was the first Gallaudet alumnus appointed to the college's Board of Directors and served as the first chairman of Gallaudet's Board of Fellows.

In 1958, he received an Honorary Doctor of Laws from Gallaudet, and in 1972, an Honorary Doctor of Humane Letters from Carthage College in Wisconsin. His list of awards and honors is (to put it briefly) lengthy. These include a clutch of Distinguished Service Awards (DHEW, CSUN's Daniel T. Cloud Leadership Award, CEASD, CAID, NAD, ICED, National Rehabilitation Association, GCAA, Wisconsin Association of the Deaf). He was named Man of the Year by the Gallaudet fraternities Kappa Gamma and Alpha Sigma Phi, and served on the President's Committee on Employment of the Handicapped. During Eighteenth Annual Deaf Heritage Week (1991), the District of Columbia Public Library included a salute to Williams (who was still living in Washington) by Dr. Victor Galloway, RSA Program Specialist.

And Stephen P. Quigley, Institute for Research on Exceptional Children, University of Illinois, Urbana, Williams' longtime colleague, said: "We shall not see a man like him again in our time."

Top left: Cal Rodgers, 1911. (Courtesy of National Air and Space Museum; thanks to Henry Kisor.) Top right: Nellie Zabel Willhite. (Courtesy of Marilynn Madison.) Bottom: Rhulin Thomas (with family) receives his gold medal. (King Memorial Library.)

CHAPTER 22

Cal Rodgers 1879-1912
Nellie Z. Willhite 1892-1991
Rhulin Thomas 1910-

Three pioneer aviators

Calbraith Perry Rodgers made the first transcontinental flight in 1911, piloting a Wright biplane, the *Vin Fiz*, from the Atlantic to the Pacific Coast.

Adventure was in his blood. He was the great-grandnephew of Captain Oliver Hazard Perry, hero of the War of 1812, and great-grandson of Commodore Matthew Calbraith Perry, who opened Japan to the West in 1854.

Scarlet fever deafened him when he was 6. Biographer Eileen Lebow describes him as "almost totally deaf." Henry Kisor says that "records of the time say he understood less than half of what was said to him, and that his own speech was hard to understand. Moreover, he was very shy and taciturn, and avoided social events whenever he could. Possibly he could have been classified as severely hard-of-hearing. But he experienced what we do, and I consider him one of us." Because he had no connection with the Deaf community, his achievements weren't listed in "Deaf" records. Indeed, he was all but forgotten after his early death.

In June 1911, Rodgers went to Dayton, Ohio, where Wilbur and Orville Wright operated an aircraft factory and flight-training school. He eagerly learned how to fly, bought a Wright Model B biplane, got his pilot's license, and competed in the International Aviation Meet in Chicago, where he won the endurance prize ($11,000). By then, he had decided to try for the Hearst prize.

On October 10, 1910, newspaper tycoon William Randolph Hearst announced a $50,000 prize to the first person who flew from coast to coast. The offer, open to everyone, was good for a year. There were a few conditions: the flyer could make as many stops and repairs as needed, but had to use the same plane. A stop had to be made in Chicago. And the flight had to be completed in 30 days.

The Armour Company of Chicago (of meat-packing fame) agreed to sponsor Rodgers' flight. In turn, he would promote Armour's new grape soft drink, "Vin Fiz." He'd be paid for each mile and provided with a special 3-car train. It included a "hangar car"—an aircraft-repair shop on rails—and a crew of four expert mechanics. A new Wright EX Flyer was built for Rodgers (with a 35-horse-power, 4-cylinder, water-cooled engine), named the *Vin Fiz Flyer*, and made into a "flying billboard" advertising "VIN FIZ/THE IDEAL GRAPE DRINK." Box-kite-like and bicycle-sprocketed, the *Vin Fiz* was a fragile, unstable contraption of wood, metal, wire, and rubberized fabric. It had to be repaired daily.

On September 17, 1911, only 41 days after he received his pilot's license, Rodgers took off from the Sheepshead Bay racetrack.

Flying was hazardous, painful work. It demanded tremendous skill, concentration, endurance. And luck. Fearless, handsome, a strapping 6' 4", 200 pounds, Rodgers was an "iron man." The *Vin Fiz* offered no protection from the elements. Storms tossed it around like a feather. The chill could be extreme; numb hands made steering difficult. The constant clattering roar of the motor temporarily deafened *hearing* pilots.

He followed the "iron compass"—the railroads. The roof of the special was marked with white canvas strips so he could find it easily. Cousin John Rodgers—himself a pioneering Navy flyer—kept Cal supplied with maps. Occasionally, though, he got lost. Wherever he landed, he attracted crowds, most of whom had never seen an "aeroplane" before.

By the time Rodgers reached Missouri, the one-year limit for the Hearst prize expired. The prize was withdrawn. There would be no extension. But he pushed on: "I'm going to do this whether I get $50,000 or 50¢ or nothing. I am going to cross this continent simply to be the first to cross in an aeroplane."

He and his dedicated crew coped with all sorts of problems—a leaking oil tank, blown cylinders, drenched magnetos, snapped bracing wires, splintered propellers, a broken fuel-feed line, engine failures, even complete wrecks. The *Vin Fiz* crashed no fewer than 12 times. By the time Rodgers completed his pioneering cross-country flight (4,231 miles), the only original pieces of equipment left were two wing struts, engine drip pan, and vertical rudder.

On November 5, 1911, Rodgers brought the battered *Vin Fiz* down in Tournament Park, Pasadena, to a hero's welcome. Next day, trying to reach the Pacific, he crashed near Compton and was injured. On December 10, with a crutch strapped to the lower wing, he triumphantly steered the *Vin Fiz* to Long Beach and dipped its wheels into the Pacific. He'd made it.

Four months later, on April 3, 1912, his luck ran out. While making a trial run in his Model B at Long Beach—very near where he had completed his flight—he suddenly lost control. As bathers watched in horror, the plane plunged into the surf. Pinned in the twisted wreckage, Rogers was killed on impact. A seagull had flown into the plane, jamming the rudder.

The restored *Vin Fiz* is now proudly displayed in the Smithsonian's National Air and Space Museum. Lebow's 1989 biography signaled a revival of interest in Rodgers' neglected feat. In Summer 1995, Kisor retraced Rodgers' flight for **The Flight of the *Gin Fizz***.

Eleanor Zabel Willhite is recognized as the first Deaf pilot to earn a license. Born on a farm in Box Elder, South Dakota, on November 22, 1892, she was deafened by measles at age 4, and attended South Dakota School for the Deaf. She was working as a typist in Pierre when she became interested in flying. Even though female pilots were still rare and deaf pilots supposedly nonexistent, she enrolled in an aviation school, 13th in a class of 18, and after

13 hours of instruction, made her first solo flight on January 13, 1928. (13 was a lucky number for her!)

Her father, Charley "Pard" Zabel, bought her an open-cockpit Alexander Eagle Rock OX-5 biplane, which she named *Pard* in his honor. She later said, "Even though I could barely hear the engine roar, I could sure tell right away if anything was wrong—just from the vibrations." She barnstormed—participated in air shows and races, traveled to county fairs, gave rides, and had a good time. At one local air show around 1930, "They were hiring stunt pilots to thrill the crowd. The pay was $50, and I wanted to earn some money. The air-show manager pretty much told me to get lost." After a male pilot did some simple stunts, Willhite climbed into the *Pard* and executed rolls, spins, loops, and dives that made the crowd gasp. The manager angrily demanded: "Why didn't you tell me you could do all that?" Willhite replied: "I did that just to limber up. Wait until you see my act." She left him gaping.

Willhite, who worked as a commercial pilot until 1944, was the first woman to earn a pilot's license in South Dakota, and founded the state chapter of the Ninety-Nines, the group of pioneering women flyers of which she was a charter member and Amelia Earhart was president. "Something of a folk heroine in her day," she died at age 98 in Sioux Falls. *Pard* is now displayed at the Southern Museum of Flight in Birmingham, Alabama.

Her example inspired other deaf people in the States and Canada to earn pilot's licenses and fly their own planes. It wasn't always smooth going. But by 1996, the International Deaf Pilots Association (founded in 1994) could boast 56 members, more than half of the total number of deaf pilots operating in the States.

Rhulin A. Thomas achieved a modest measure of fame in 1947 when he made a solo coast-to-coast flight.

Born on a farm in Arkansas, July 29, 1910, he was profoundly deafened at age 2 by diphtheria. After graduating from Missouri School for the Deaf in 1930, he attended Gallaudet College for a year. For a while, he worked as a printer's apprentice, then secured a job as a Linotypist for the **Washington Evening Star**. In 1946, during his spare time, he took lessons at the Maryland Aviation, and received a pilot's license. After saving up, he bought his own monoplane, a single-engine, 65-horsepower Piper Cub.

Soon afterwards, Thomas decided to fly solo across the United States—a 3,000-mile flight. He knew it could be dangerous. Unable to use a land-to-air radio, he would have no way of knowing if he was approaching a bad storm until he was caught in it. Anyway, he had two good reasons for trying: he wanted to prove that a deaf pilot *could* fly across the continent alone—without radio. And he hoped to reach California in time to greet George Truman and Cliff Evans, who had just accomplished a first by flying "tandem" around the world in two Piper Cubs. Truman had taught Thomas how to fly. (They'd passed a pad and pencil back and forth.)

On October 26, 1947, Thomas took off from Rehoboth Beach, Delaware. He survived terrifying electrical storms in Indiana and Missouri. Once, he lost his way during a storm and ran out of gas. His engine stalled, and he made a forced landing on a farm. Often, his Cub was buffeted by strong headwinds. At Banning Pass at 9,500 feet in the San Bernadino Mountains—notorious as a "pilots' graveyard"—treacherous downdrafts sent him on a "rollercoaster ride." He finally sighted the Pacific on November 7 and touched down at Van Nuys Airport, Los Angeles—in time to greet Truman and Evans upon the completion of their own record-making flight.

Through the efforts of Max Mossel, a teacher at MSD, the Missouri Association of the Deaf, and the NAD, arrangements were made to have Thomas' achievement honored. On September 30, 1948, at a White House ceremony, Major General Harry H. Vaughan, military aide to President Harry Truman, presented Thomas with a handsome gold commemorative medal studded with three diamonds and inscribed: "FIRST DEAF SOLO TO FLY THE CONTINENT." Thomas said: "Thank you for this honor. I appreciate it and greatly appreciate, too, that the United States, our free nation, gives to the deaf equal opportunity to get not only education but higher education, licenses to fly airplanes and to drive cars, employment in the work of their choice, and all the rights and privileges of citizenship."

"The heart and soul of the Deaf Olympic movement." Art Kruger, raising money for the U.S. Team's trip to the 1981 WGD in Köln. (Chuck Liddy, **Morganton News Herald**, 1981)

CHAPTER 23

Art Kruger

1911-1992

"The Father of AAAD"

Sports have long been a vital part of American Deaf culture. In schools for the deaf, *all* children get a chance to participate. Many become outstanding athletes. Unfortunately, opportunities for the deaf in organized sports have long been limited, especially after high school.

Art Kruger devoted his life to enhancing opportunities for Deaf athletes to participate in, and experience the thrill of, national and international competition, and to promoting Deaf sports in general. He has been called the "architect," "guiding light," "father," and "wizard" of the American Athletic Association of the Deaf, which he co-founded in 1945, and which has grown into a coast-to-coast network of over 180 clubs. His dedication to the AAAD spanned nearly half a century. In 1981, Charlie Atkinson, Sports Editor of the **Morganton News Herald**, called him "the heart and soul of the Deaf Olympic movement."

Born in Philadelphia on March 6, 1911, Arthur Abraham Kruger lived a "regular" life until he was 3, when a fire destroyed his family's apartment. His sister rescued him and threw him into a fireman's net. He was deafened during the fire or the fall—he was never sure exactly how.

He attended the Home for Training in Speech for Deaf Children in Bala, Pennsylvania, Philadelphia's McIntyre Grammar School and Northeast High School, spent two years at the Mt. Airy School for the Deaf, then enrolled at Gallaudet College in 1928.

A "short and scrappy" character, he was "too small and too light for most sports," so when he wasn't busy studying, working, or socializing, he focused on managing, scheduling, record-keeping, and reporting Gallaudet's athletic activities. He had an extraordinary memory for sports.

When, in 1931, J. Frederick ("Jimmy") Meagher (a popular Deaf columnist and sportswriter who originated the All-American Schools for the Deaf Basketball Selections) published his own choices in the **Deaf-Mute's Journal** and invited readers who thought otherwise to respond, Kruger took up the challenge. He wrote to Meagher, criticizing some of the choices and proposing a few of his own. It was obvious to Meagher, the editors, and the readers of the **Journal** that Kruger knew his subject. His letter launched a career. (And a long friendship with Jimmy Meagher.) Later, Kruger wrote for the **Journal** and other publications such as **The Silent Broadcaster**, and, in 1949, became Sports Editor of **The Silent Worker/Deaf American**, selecting his own All-American deaf football and basketball teams, bringing recognition to many deserving young athletes and their coaches, and chronicling Deaf achievements in sports.

In 1932, the U.S. was caught in the stranglehold of the Great Depression. Unemployment was widespread; fear was epidemic. Undaunted (and probably because he didn't have much else to do anyway), after his junior year at Gally, Kruger took his tattered travel bag and hitchhiked across America, taking in the splendor of the land and the variety of its people. As George B. Elliott later wrote, "Art, being Art, made many friends on this trip . . . articles were written about him in numerous papers . . . they all hailed the courage and humor he displayed." He then returned to Gallaudet that September to start his senior year, and continued to organize sporting events.

Marriage (to Eva Siegal, a Fanwood alumna), a job, and a home in New York followed his graduation from Gallaudet in 1933. In 1938, he organized his first national tournament—of schools for the deaf, hosted by Fanwood. Then he turned his attention to deaf clubs. In 1940, with very little financial support, he organized a deaf-club regional-basketball tourney in New York City.

The Krugers moved to Akron, Ohio, during World War II, and Art worked in the war plants. As catastrophic as the World Wars were, they ironically benefited the Deaf community. Deaf citizens, unable to enlist, found more jobs than ever during the wars and were finally able to prove their worth to employers previously reluctant to hire them. Akron, with its large manufacturing industry, became a Deaf mecca. Goodyear and Firestone organized campaigns to attract more deaf workers, and Firestone even established a Deaf colony, complete with recreational facilities. Deaf-club sports flourished as workers organized athletic competitions.

As incomes increased, members could afford larger contributions to the clubs. The growing treasuries provided the funds necessary for a national tournament. Kruger, together with Edward C. Carney, Alexander Fleischman, Thomas Elliott, and other Deaf-sports enthusiasts, founded the AAAD (originally called the American Athletic Union of the Deaf). On April 14, 1945, the First National Club of the Deaf Basketball Tournament, sponsored by the Akron Club, was held in the Goodyear Gymnasium, with none other than Art Kruger as chairman of the coordinating committee. Five teams from across the country participated. (Buffalo beat Akron.) The Akron tourney launched the AAAD with—of course—Art Kruger as its first president. (After serving as president 2 years, he was secretary-treasurer for 7.)

Almost single-handedly, Kruger took on the task of building the AAAD into the well-structured organization it is today. (It was once half-jokingly known as "Art Kruger's Folly.") His experience at Gallaudet helped him make decisions requiring quick thinking. He drafted laws and procedures, and established a network of 7 regional affiliates, with the AAAD serving as the governing body. Rules and regulations were drawn up to safeguard and enhance the quality of play for both players and spectators. Participation in international Deaf athletic competition also became a goal.

After the war ended, the Krugers moved to Los Angeles, the nation's new "boom town." Art headed the Materials Department at the Western Costume Corporation, which **Deaf Heritage** describes as "a firm owned by six major movie producers and the largest costume firm in Hollywood," working there for 30 years until his retirement in 1975. (The Krugers then moved to Virginia, later Maryland.) In his free time, with imagination and dedication, he continued to build the AAAD.

And while he guided the AAAD, Kruger also spearheaded the World Games for the Deaf U.S. Committee. The WGD had been launched back in 1924 in Paris, when Kruger was 13. But because of lack of leadership, organization, and funding, no representatives from the States were sent for over a decade. Even then, the number was small—only two U.S. athletes competed in the 1935 WGD in London. But with Kruger at the helm, things changed. After he became Team Director, 40 Deaf U.S. athletes participated in the 1957 WGD in Milan. The U.S. contingent won 23 medals during that competition; 7 were gold. Kruger continued as Team Director for the 1961 WGD (Helsinki), and for the 1965 WGD (Washington, D.C.). From 1966 until 1982, he chaired the AAAD/WGD Committee.

All the while, through numberless hours of sheer hard work and dedication to the cause, he labored to raise the necessary funds to support U.S. WGD teams. In the States, Deaf athletes are sponsored or funded by private contributions from individuals and businesses, and the costs have steadily increased to keep pace with inflation and the expanding teams. During his long association with the AAAD, Kruger raised a total of over a million dollars. (He raised a record $730,731.51 to send an entourage of 213 athletes, coaches, and officials to the 1981 WGD in Cologne. After the U.S. Olympic team boycotted the 1980 Moscow Olympics, Kruger tried to get some of the unused funds—around $75,000—for his Deaf athletes. The U.S. Olympic Committee refused.) As Ronald Sutcliffe wrote in **Dee Cee Eyes**: "He did it alone, without the luxuries that we enjoy today: TTY, FAX, e-mail, computers, and photocopiers. He pounded his old Underwood typewriter throughout his tenure with the AAAD. He wrote to each athlete and their parents, coaches, sponsors, and all other parties to raise sufficient funds for the team." At the '81 WGD, the U.S. team placed first in collecting medals, a total of 111.

After he stepped down as Chairman on May 1, 1982, he continued his active participation in the AAAD as Chairman Emeritus. He was responsible for the U.S. Alpine-skiing team that competed in Madonna di Campiglio, Italy, in 1983. From 1957 to 1983, he helped send a total of 12 teams to the summer and winter WGD.

As President of the Pan-American Games for the Deaf Federation (1975), he helped improve organization of sports in Central and South American countries.

And he organized the first National Deaf Games Tryouts, which helped improve the quality of the U.S. WGD teams. This involved 3 weeks of training at North Carolina School for the Deaf in Morganton.

Kruger's unequaled service to Deaf athletics was, of course, officially—and widely—recognized. In 1954, he was the first person chosen for the AAAD Hall of Fame in the "Leader/Sports Writer" category. In 1973, he was inducted into the Helms Foundation Hall of Fame (founded by Paul Hoy Helms, "Dummy" Hoy's nephew). At the '81 WGD, the Comité International des Sports des Sourds (CISS), which coordinates the WGD, awarded Kruger its Gold Medal of Gratitude for his "tireless and unselfish service to the deaf athletics." He received Gallaudet's prestigious Powrie Vaux Doctor Medallion for International Service in 1976, AAAD's S. Robey Burns Sportsman of the Year Award (given in honor of another Deaf-sports pioneer) in 1978, and GCAA's Edward Miner Gallaudet International Award ("for promoting the well-being of deaf people of the world") in 1980. In 1982, he received an Honorary Doctor of Pedagogy degree from Hofstra University. After he signed his commencement address, he received a "tumultuous" standing ovation.

He continued to serve the cause of national and international Deaf sports until his death on March 10, 1992, from heart failure.

President Larry Fleischer says, "He is revered—not only because he was one of the founders of the AAAD, but because of his hard work, dedication, and loyalty to the AAAD since its inception. Without any dispute, he belongs on the AAAD Scroll in the galaxy of giants."

Top: Robert Weitbrecht with his ham-radio setup. (Courtesy of Colleen Lane, Ultratec.) Bottom: The three creators of the TTY coupler (from left): Weitbrecht, Dr. James C. Marsters, and Andrew Saks. (Courtesy of Mrs. Jean Saks; thanks to Dr. Harry G. Lang)

CHAPTER 24

Robert H. Weitbrecht

1920-1983

Physicist and inventor

Robert H. Weitbrecht was born profoundly deaf in Orange, California, on April 11, 1920, and grew up on an orange farm. As soon as they realized he was deaf, his parents enrolled him in a correspondence course and began teaching him to speechread. A few years later, he was placed in a small private school for deaf children. But when his teacher left to take a public-school post, he and a fellow student were tutored in reading and speech by a retired teacher.

It wasn't all tedium, of course. He was taken to orange- and lemon-packing houses, beet fields, rope factories, wineries, and dairies. These trips sparked his interest in science—particularly electrical equipment—as he examined milking machines, generators, and separators, then wrote class papers about them.

After his teacher died in 1931, his parents unsuccessfully sought a replacement, then enrolled him in public school. Although he managed to keep up academically with his hearing classmates, Bob hated being the butt of their teasing and cruel jokes. He became increasingly rebellious.

Luckily, he had a stable family life. On clear nights, the family took walks together and stargazed. Bob soon became fascinated with astronomy, which became a lifelong passion. Armed with a sky-map and a small telescope, he studied the constellations with his parents, speechread them by flashlight, and learned the names and positions of the stars. Wrapped in a blanket, he would sit up late, alone, waiting to see a meteor streak across the sky. In 1930, when he was 10, he wrote a class composition about a solar eclipse. And when he was 18, he won the Bausch and Lomb Honorary Science Award for the reflecting telescope he constructed. He designed the mounting himself in the high-school machine shop; it used an old Ford axle and a 6-inch Pyrex disk for a mirror.

After graduating with honors in science from Santa Ana Junior College, he enrolled in the University of California at Berkeley, which had a small Astronomy Department. Finally, he found an academic environment where he fitted in comfortably. He made friends among the faculty and students. With the help of a modest scholarship and a number of odd jobs, he worked his way through. He worked and studied with another deaf student, who taught him sign language. But aside from occasional notes borrowed from classmates, he received no support services. In 1942, he received his Bachelor's in Astronomy with honors.

World War II had begun, and he chose to remain at Berkeley. From 1942 to 1945, he worked as a physicist on the Manhattan Project at UCB's Radiation Laboratory ("Cyclotron Hill"), under the direction of the distinguished nuclear physicist, Professor Ernest Orlando Lawrence, co-inventor of the cyclotron, the first high-energy particle accelerator ("atom-splitter"). He spent many nights in the observatory studying double stars and planets.

He worked at UC's Aeromedical Laboratory from 1945 to 1947, then as an electronics scientist at the U. S. Naval Air Missile Test Center in Point Mugu, California (1947-1951), where he helped develop precision timing and number-coding systems and designed radar systems, electronic optical devices for cameras, and also developed the "WWV" Radio Time Signal used worldwide today. For this, the U. S. Navy awarded him a Superior Accomplishment Award in 1949.

From 1951 to 1957, he was a Research Associate at Yerkes Observatory, University of Chicago. While earning a Master's in Astronomy there, he helped develop photoelectric guiding systems and photometers. He received his M.S. in 1952.

Returning to California, he worked at Stanford Research Institute's Communications Laboratory from 1958 to 1969. There, he designed a precision astrometric camera system for the Lick Observatory—the first electronically-guided camera in the world. He also worked for NASA on an earth-satellite (ECHO) project.

He received his amateur-radio license in 1936, and used amplified Morse Code to communicate. In 1951 he petitioned the Federal Communications Commission to open low-frequency amateur-radio bands to Radio Teletype (RTTY). This resulted in FCC Docket No. 10073, which opened bands to RTTY in 1953. Subsequently, he was active in research and development of anti-fade systems for improved RTTY reception.

In 1964, Dr. James C. Marsters, a deaf orthodontist in Pasadena, sent Weitbrecht a TeleType Model 32ASR and asked him to set up a system so they could communicate with each other. Because Marsters didn't have a ham-radio license, they decided to use the telephone-line system. They both formed a partnership with Andrew Saks, a deaf mechanical engineer-businessman.

During his spare time, Weitbrecht began working on the acoustic coupler or terminal unit (TU). This enabled typewritten communication over telephone lines, using TTYs. The first public demonstration of experimental TUs was staged in June 1964 in Salt Lake City, by the Communications Committee, Oral Deaf Adults Section, Alexander Graham Bell Association for the Deaf (AGBAD).

After a year of continued development and testing via long-distance-telephone lines, using old TeleTypes, Weitbrecht acquired a patent and formed the R. H. Weitbrecht Company to manufacture TUs. In 1969, he left Stanford Research Institute and, in partnership with Saks and Marsters, launched a new business venture, the Applied Communications Corporation (APCOM). As experimental physicist, he continued developing new signaling and auto-answer devices. APCOM began manufacturing TUs under the trademark "Phonetype." Marsters had inspired Weitbrecht to develop the TU; Saks helped him market it. None profited financially from it, however.

From 1980 to 1982, Weitbrecht worked as a member of the Ultratec engineering team. Weitbrecht Communications was founded in 1982 as a descendant of APCOM. Now located in Santa

Monica, it's a major distributor of TTYs and assistive devices.

Martin L. A. Sternberg, who used a TTY at Red Cross' New York City headquarters in 1943, long before they became available to the Deaf community, recalls:

> The AT&T equipment was on the TWX (teletypewriter exchange) system, a leased wire available to large users like the Associated Press, the FBI, the Stock Exchange. How could an individual, Deaf or hearing, afford to pay the hefty monthly access charges?
>
> It remained for Dr. Robert Weitbrecht, a brilliant deaf physicist in California, with the encouragement of my good friend Dr. James Marsters, an equally brilliant deaf California orthodontist and gadget guru, to bring this about.
>
> Weitbrecht had been told that the equipment was available to all, Deaf and hearing, on payment of the TWX monthly fee. All TTY lines went through them, and these lines were the property of AT&T and only available on lease.
>
> Weitbrecht was able to put together a coupling device, to pick up the clickety-clack signals emitted by the TTY and, instead of these signals going out on the TWX line, they would go out on the regular phone lines, to be counted as an ordinary telephone call. This coupler, which Weitbrecht patented, was initially a simple, home-made plywood box with listener and transmitter devices. It became the forerunner of today's modem, used so often in computers to network them. The Internet would be impossible without a modem.
>
> And so Robert Weitbrecht had achieved what the gigantic AT&T system, with its access to vast laboratories and testing sites, had declared unachievable. He had circumvented the TWX system, and had plugged into the regular telephone lines. In chagrin, AT&T reluctantly began to release old Model 15's and other equipment from dead storage, and allowed Deaf people to acquire them, usually for a token fee, but with several provisos. They would do their own cleaning up, lubrication, parts replacement, transportation from storage site, maintenance, and, quaintest of all, they would sign a form saying they would not compete with commercial AT&T users, who relied on the TWX system. This last proviso, which I signed, was designed to appease angry commercial customers who, as far as I know, never materialized.
>
> This proviso was shortly rescinded, as totally unenforceable.

In 1968, American Telephone & Telegraph Company (AT&T) agreed to release surplus TTYs to the Teletypewriters for the Deaf Distribution Committee of Indianapolis, Indiana, a nonprofit organization founded by deaf leaders representing opposite poles—H. Latham Breunig, then Executive Director of AGBAD, his wife

Nancy, and Jess M. Smith, President of NAD and editor of **The Deaf American**. Teletypewriters for the Deaf (TDI), as it was renamed in 1969, was responsible for refurbishing and distributing the TTYs. Only 25 TTY stations were in operation throughout the U.S.A. in 1968. But slowly, steadily, interest—and demand— grew. The proliferation of TTYs began to revolutionize the way deaf people lived and communicated. By the end of 1982, there were over 150,000 TTYs in the United States—mostly in deaf people's homes, but also in public places such as airline-reservation desks, police departments, hospitals, schools, and businesses. Then came the inevitable: the increasing demand for TTYs outstripped the dwindling supply of old machines. New companies began developing and manufacturing compact lightweight TTYs.

In 1979, TDI changed its name to Telecommunications for the Deaf, Inc., reflecting its expanded scope. The passage of the ADA in 1990 led to a boom in the use of TTYs and relay services, which are now available in every state 24 hours a day, 7 days a week. Title IV of the ADA took effect in July 1993, and the number of businesses, agencies and facilities with TTYs continues to grow.

Weitbrecht lived to see the beginning of the revolution. For his work on the TU and his contributions to the deaf community, he received a Citation for Meritorious Service from the President's Committee on Employment of the Handicapped (1969); GCAA's Laurent Clerc Award (1971); AGBAD's Honors Citation for Distinguished Service to the Deaf (1971); an honorary Doctor of Science degree from Gallaudet College (1974); a Certificate of Achievement from Johns Hopkins University (1981); and an honorary membership in Telephone Pioneers of America.

On May 19, 1983, Weitbrecht was taking an evening walk with his dog Mickey near his home in Redwood City. Crossing the street in a pedestrian zone, he was struck by a car. Twelve days later, on May 30, he died of head injuries without having regained consciousness. The community mourned its loss.

The TTY, no less than the telephone, has become an indispensable part of millions of lives. One could say that it all began in 1964 with the brilliant invention by Weitbrecht, Saks, and Marsters.

Multiple portrait of Fred Schreiber by William Bruce Sparks.
(Courtesy of Mr. Sparks)

CHAPTER 26

Frederick C. Schreiber

1922-1979

Humanitarian, leader, and advocate

Frederick Carl Schreiber was born in Brooklyn, New York, on February 1, 1922, to Helen and Louis Schreiber, middle-class Russian-Jewish immigrants. He had an older brother and younger sister. At age 6, he was profoundly deafened by four successive bouts of spinal meningitis. Left with severe spinal curvature, he was temporarily encased in a plaster cast from neck to knees, attended "a school for crippled children," and wore a brace for 3 years. He finally returned to public school—unaware that he was deaf.

In 1932, at age 10, he was enrolled in Lexington School for the Deaf (then rigorously oral), and learned fingerspelling. (He later recalled how he and his classmates, fearful of being caught and punished for violating the prohibition against signing on the premises, had been forced to "hide out" in the dorm lavatory when they wanted to talk to each other.) At 13, he was transferred to Fanwood, then a boys' military-style academy. The combined method was used there. Eager to escape the tedium, he tried— unsuccessfully—to leave when he was 14, took the college-preparatory program, and was accepted at Gallaudet in September 1937, when he was only 15. (Eager to convince the ladies he was 21, he attempted to grow a beard. The wispy results inspired his namesign.)

Under President Percival Hall, Gallaudet accepted only the "intellectual elite." Fewer than 200 students were enrolled. Fred thrived. He was popular, active in sports, and wrote a humorous column, "The Hurdy Gurdy," for **The Buff and Blue**. He majored in Chemistry—not that he was planning to become a chemist; he simply saw it as the least unappealing option.

He graduated from Gallaudet in 1942. World War II had begun; he went to Akron, where he worked as a machine operator at the Firestone Company. Confronting the prejudice that existed even in a "progressive" company, he became what he called a "gate-crasher"—the first deaf machine-shop inspector. His area became the most productive.

He married Kathleen ("Kit") Bedard in 1944. An alumna of Minnesota School for the Deaf, she was one of the students he tutored at Gallaudet in 1941. After his graduation, they had gone separate ways and, a few years later, met again. They had four children: Beverly, Louis, Stephen, and Elizabeth.

In 1947, Fred took a teaching position at Texas School for the Deaf. He lasted a year—he quarreled with administrators about discrimination against deaf faculty—and returned to New York City, where he joined the International Typographer's Union and worked as a printer. He moonlighted for the New York Department of Vocational Rehabilitation as a part-time tutor of illiterate and immigrant deaf clients.

Fred attended his first NAD convention in 1949, which voted to eliminate racial barriers to membership, considered a motion to establish a permanent home office, and revived its magazine, **The Silent Worker** (which had ceased publication in 1929). He recognized the importance of these changes. He was active in the affairs of the Brooklyn Association of the Deaf, where he removed the longstanding "gender barrier" by opening regular membership, and full participation, to women. In 1950, he was elected president of the Hebrew Association of the Deaf—at 28, its youngest ever.

In 1952, he relocated himself, then his family, to Washington, D.C. For several years he worked as a printer for **The Washington Evening Star**, then (until 1966) as a compositor in the U.S. Government Printing Office. He joined District of Columbia Club of the Deaf and Maryland Association of the Deaf; he helped found District of Columbia Association of the Deaf, his "vehicle to power." In 1960, NAD restructured into a federation of state associations. In 1961, Fred headed the "Fort Monroe Conference" on deafness rehabilitation, and pushed for "a more active NAD." He became Executive Director of DCCD, revitalizing it into a model community center. He also founded and edited its monthly publication, **Dee Cee Eyes** (1961; still going strong).

At the 1964 convention, Fred successfully campaigned to have NAD's home office relocated from Berkeley to Washington. It was part of his plan to rebuild NAD into an aggressive, visible, national consumer organization and effective lobbyist. He was also elected as Secretary-Treasurer, "an unpaid position second in power only to the presidency." That October, NAD rented an office suite on Eye Street, Northwest.

All this Fred had done voluntarily while holding down a full-time night job as a printer. When the position of Executive Secretary (later "Executive Director") was approved at the 1966 convention, the Executive Committee unanimously chose Fred. The catch to this "full-time position" was that, in effect, he had to find his own salary. It represented a 50% cut from what he'd been earning at the Government Printing Office, but he accepted the challenge.

Fred's accomplishments thereafter were extraordinary, bordering on incredible. His goal was to make NAD solvent—and strong. He understood its members' longtime refusal to accept an extra income-tax exemption such as Congress had granted blind citizens. He spent a major portion of his time meeting formally and informally with government officials, serving on committees, testifying before Congress and state legislatures, appearing at functions and banquets, and even being interviewed on TV (PBS' *Nova*, for example). He served as Vice President of the World Federation of the Deaf and traveled extensively to other countries.

Dr. Jerome D. Schein, Director of New York University's Deafness Research and Training Center, hearing, was Fred's chief consultant in grantsmanship. Fred lobbied successfully with various federal agencies and obtained several grants that helped enrich the meager NAD treasury. From the U.S. Office of Education, he won a long-term contract for the evaluation and selection of Captioned Films for the Deaf. From the Vocational Rehabilitation Administration, he secured contracts to start a continuing-education program in Washington and establish nationwide sign-language classes for hearing adults (Communicative Skills Program), and the National Consortium of Programs Training Sign Language Instructors. He negotiated contracts with the Defense Department's Office of Civil Defense to make air-raid warnings accessible to deaf people, and with the Labor Department's Job Corps to try to get deaf youth accepted. NAD received a grant to undertake a national census of the deaf, using a rigorously scientific approach. **The Deaf Population of the United States**, an exhaustive—and authoritative—study undertaken by Schein and Marcus Delk, was published by NAD in 1974. One significant finding was that previous government figures, relying on guess-work, vastly underestimated the deaf population. Instead of 200,000, there were at least 410,000. Fred obtained a federal grant to hire more personnel to manage the business affairs of the newly-established (1964) Registry of Interpreters for the Deaf, which NAD helped organize.

To Fred, communication was of paramount importance. The revived **Silent Worker** became the quarterly **Deaf American** in 1964. Fred's "Home Office Notes" were distinguished by his vivid style, honesty, and openness. He discussed office goings-on, national concerns, events, issues, plans, hopes, and frustrations. NAD, he argued, belonged to all deaf people; all were welcome to visit the Home Office. He founded the **NAD Broadcaster**, a monthly tabloid for all members, first published in May 1979, and **Interstate**, an upper-level-membership newsletter.

Fred wanted NAD to own real estate. In 1971, NAD purchased Halex House, a modern 3-story, 21,500-square-foot building in Silver Spring, Maryland, for $535,000. The staff was increased to 28 full-time and 11 part-time employees in 1972. A gala dedication ceremony was held in 1973.

In early 1977, Fred met with Schein, Edward C. Carney, and Elmer Bartels, head of the Massachusetts Rehabilitation Commission, about a proposal for a Deaf-run rehabilitation center in

Boston, agreed, and enlisted the support of Jack Levesque, President of the Massachusetts State Association of the Deaf. On November 20, 1977, Deafness Evaluation and Adjustment Facility (DEAF, Inc.), held open house. The facility was named the Frederick C. Schreiber Center. Fred was "speechless" when he saw it.

Fred was friendly-looking, earthy, warm, funny, compassionate, and generous. He was absentminded and rumpled. He was a visionary, and a shrewd, practical thinker. He loved roses, books, song (he loved to sing—off-key), and people. He had the gift of making each person he met feel like a dear friend. Since he had spent most of his life among other deaf people from all walks of life, he *knew* the Deaf community. He rejected no one. His writings embrace all the major concerns of the Deaf community: communication, education, employment, rehabilitation, social work, interpreting, research, consumerism. He advocated Total Communication; he felt that, for deaf children, easy communication was more important than speech training. He reassured parents; he criticized the failures of deaf education and low expectations, as well as the prejudice against sign language and the stereotypical insistence that deaf people learn to fit into the hearing world. He supported early intervention, but urged audiologists to *learn* about the Deaf community.

On September 5, 1979, while Fred was recuperating from gallstone surgery, his weakened heart collapsed, and he died.

Among his many honors were CSUN's Daniel T. Cloud Leadership Award (1973); WFD's International Solidarity Medal, 1st Class; IAPD's Special Award (1975); and an Honorary Doctor of Laws from Gallaudet College (1977). GCAA's Laurent Clerc Award was presented posthumously in 1980. Scholarships, a fund, and the Golden Rose Award were established in his memory.

In 1981, NAD published Schein's tribute, **A Rose for Tomorrow: Biography of Frederick C. Schreiber**. As Schein wrote in his preface: "He was a builder, a creator, a man who added good to the world he found. He altered the flow of history; he changed for the better the society in which he lived." Says Jack Gannon: "He was a giant."

Dr. Donald L. Ballantyne: hard work and self-reliance.
(Courtesy of Dr. Ballantyne)

CHAPTER 26

Donald L. Ballantyne

1922-

Medical scientist

On June 7, 1979, during the morning rush hour, 17-year-old Renee Katz, a talented flutist at Manhattan's High School of Music and Art, was attacked in the crowded 50th Street subway station and pushed off the platform as the E train came in. She fell underneath. Her right hand was sliced off as she tried to roll away. Quick work by the police and a team of ambulance medics saved Katz's life. They also recovered her severed hand, packed it in ice, and rushed to Bellevue Hospital, where the hand was reattached to her wrist by microsurgery.

Microsurgery is performed by specially-trained doctors using powerful Zeiss microscopes with foot-controlled "zoom" systems that magnify the operating field 6 to 36 times. Using microscopes, surgeons can reattach severed limbs and fingers, restore sight to eyes clouded by diabetic hemorrhaging, remove tumors, and redirect blood flow in the brain to save stroke victims.

It took two teams of surgeons 16 hours to reattach Katz's hand— one team working on the wrist-stump, the other with the severed hand. (After 6 more operations and hundreds of hours of therapy, Katz regained partial use of her right hand. Her career as a flutist was over. But she became a occupational therapist herself—moonlighting as a cabaret singer.) The chief surgeon was Dr. William W. Shaw, Chief of Bellevue's Reconstructive Plastic Surgery Service.

The story, publicized in the New York newspapers throughout the summer of 1979, had all the lurid fascination of a tabloid-television episode. Yet the story-behind-the-story was in itself fascinating. Few media-watchers realized that it was a deaf scientist, Dr. Donald L. Ballantyne, who was in charge of the training program designed for use in microvascular and microneurological applications, which Dr. Shaw had taken "and passed with excellent proficiency."

Donald L. Ballantyne, Jr., was born in Beijing (Peking), China, on November 8, 1922. His mother, Gladys, was Australian; his American father managed an international East Asian bank. He was born with *pylorus stenosis* (stomach obstruction) and soon underwent stomach surgery. While recovering, he contracted pneumonia; the high fever deafened him. "Only the most heroic efforts saved him," Gladys later said. Ultimately, his deafness was diagnosed. Unwilling to send him to a school for the deaf, Gladys attended classes, read up on oral education until she'd mastered the subject, and taught her son to speak and lipread.

Because of the elder Donald's shifting bank assignments, the family was constantly on the move—Hong Kong, Shanghai, Peking, Hong Kong, Tientsin, Hong Kong. "Often we had to travel on antiquated Chinese tugs, junks, or tramp ships crowded with coolie soldiers who had no consideration for foreigners. Once, on the [frozen] Yangtze River, we had to lie flat on the deck of an old 1500-ton boat to escape the cross-fire of opposing Chinese and Japanese [troops].

"I was enrolled in various schools, too numerous to recall—French, German, Italian, Chinese, English, American, religious, or public. Don't ask me how I ever managed to receive an education during those years, but nevertheless I *did* learn." He acquired a working knowledge of Latin, German, French, and Russian.

"For several years I had very little free time and little vacation." Every afternoon, when he returned home from school, Gladys drilled him in speech and lipreading. "Even the servants, coolies, and amahs were required to talk to me continuously, and no gestures. Likewise, all of my parents' friends and my own. Talk! Talk! Talk! My father always ordered me to read the newspapers or books [aloud] to him, constantly correcting my [pronunciation]. To top it off, private tutors [came] in the afternoons and evenings [and kept] hammering me. Even [they] instructed their own children to correct my speech." He found foreigners easier to lipread than Americans—and even interpreted for his father's Chinese customers by lipreading them. (Despite all the drills and tutoring, he managed to find time for swimming, horseback riding, golfing, and having good times with his friends.)

He was dissatisfied with the patchwork schooling he'd been getting—and there were no prospects for higher education in East Asia. In 1936, when he was 13, Donald was enrolled at Archmere Academy, a Catholic private school in Claremont, Delaware. Parting from his parents was wrenching, but Gladys promised that he could come back to Hong Kong every summer. It was a good decision. He developed self-confidence and self-discipline. "By traveling thousands of miles alone, I had to find my way around, talk to and lipread people of different countries on trains, ships, and ashore." Each summer, he took a train to the West Coast and shipped to Hong Kong alone, then back to Archmere. "Those trips were the only free times I ever had and I took every opportunity." On August 30, 1937, he was returning East on board the *S.S. President Hoover* when it was bombed near Shanghai by the Chinese Air Force, mistaking it for a Japanese troop ship. (The Sino-Japanese War had just begun.) "[A] bomb hit the [adjacent] cabin and I thought someone was knocking on my door very hard, so I opened the door and no one was there. It happened three times!"

At Archmere, he learned to play "the famous three"—football, baseball, and basketball. His parents provided him with yet another private tutor. "I had no rest." Even though he excelled academically, what with his parents' drills and the tutoring, he found Archmere too easy. "I wasn't learning anything new."

After 3 years there, he transferred to Canterbury Prep in New Milford, Connecticut, one of the nation's toughest. He was the first deaf student enrolled there. No more private tutors. "I was thoroughly happy to have some freedom for the first time." He became "one of the best swimmers on the varsity team." When he graduated in 1941, Gladys was there. Her hard work had paid off.

He applied to Lehigh University and was accepted—then told

that he first had to attend a school for the deaf for one year. (He was furious.) He visited Princeton University, met with the Dean of Freshmen, and was quickly accepted—its first deaf student. (On December 7, 1941, Pearl Harbor was attacked, and on Christmas Day, Ballantyne's father was taken prisoner of war by the Japanese in Hong Kong. Ballantyne was so upset that he flunked one of his courses—Biology.) He had the best note-taking classmates make carbon copies of their notes for him, and did extensive outside reading. He graduated from Princeton in 1945, after only 3-1/2 years, with an A.B. in Chemistry.

"For a year, I attended Columbia as a graduate student in biochemistry, which soon bored me, even though I still had high marks. Although I was a pre-med student with high grades at Princeton, no medical school would accept me because of my deafness." So he transferred to Catholic University in Washington, D.C., where he received his Master's in Biology (with minors in Botany and Biochemistry) in 1948, and his Ph.D. in Biology in 1952.

In 1946, while studying for his M.S. and Ph.D., he took a part-time job at Gallaudet College as an instructor of organic and physical chemistries. He met his first deaf "others," learned ASL, and coached the men's and women's swimming teams.

He was also courting Mary Lou Stevens, a student at Duke University in Durham, North Carolina. In Summer 1949, he attended UC Berkeley to study French (to fulfill the Ph.D. language requirement). Stevens and Ballantyne were married in 1952, shortly after he received his Ph.D. and she her B.A. They had three children—Patricia, Leigh, and Paul.

Dr. Ballantyne began his professional career in 1951 as a research assistant in parasitology with Squibb Laboratories in New Brunswick, New Jersey. "I [then] worked at the Illinois State Psychopathic Institute, evaluating [the effects of] parasites in pregnant women. It was dangerous work, so dangerous that when my wife was going to have her first baby, I was happy to get out." In 1954, Dr. John Marquis Converse, founder and director of the Institute of Reconstructive Plastic Surgery at New York University Medical Center, invited Ballantyne to join. He worked there more than 35 years, becoming Professor of Experimental Surgery, Director of the Microsurgery Training Program, and Chief of Microsurgical Research Laboratories.

Microsurgical techniques, which revolutionized medical care, were first introduced in the States during the 1960s. As they became more and more widespread, Ballantyne acquired an international reputation as a "master teacher." Because of his superb lipreading skills, he was responsible for teaching the principles and methods of plastic and microvascular surgery to many foreign students, residents, fellows, and visiting physicians, surgeons, and professors. He also taught at numerous other hospitals, universities, and research centers in the States and Europe.

Ballantyne co-authored (with Converse) **Experimental Skin Grafts and Transplantation Immunity** (1979) and (with others) **Microvascular Surgery: A Laboratory Manual** (1981) and **Organized Bibliography of the Microsurgical Literature** (1985). He also collaborated with Converse and others on over 120 medical articles on a variety of tissue grafts in various animal species; revascularization of grafts; transplantation immunity; preservation of grafts in cold storage; and microvascular flaps and surgery. He presented several papers at medical meetings and also lectured on medical careers and related issues. He urged deaf medical students to work hard and cultivate self-reliance: "You must know what you have to do without relying upon the interpreter."

He was a member of many scientific and medical organizations. A charter member of the American Professional Society of the Deaf, he served as its president from 1976 to 1988. In June 1979, Ballantyne became the first recipient of Gallaudet's Amos Kendall Award, which is presented to a deaf person for notable excellence in a professional field not related to deafness. In March 1981, he became NTID's first Edmund Lyon Memorial Lecturer. In 1983, he received the Outstanding Achievement Award in the Field of Medical Research from the Catholic University of America Alumni Association.

He retired in October 1990 and was designated Professor Emeritus of Surgery by the President of NYU.

Roy Kay Holcomb: "Because of my own very difficult communication problems I knew that there had to be a better way." (Courtesy of the Holcomb family)

CHAPTER 27

Roy Kay Holcomb

1923-

"The Father of Total Communication"

Roy Kay Holcomb was born near Alexander, Texas, on July 24, 1923, the eldest of Alice Vera Thedford and Charles Colby Holcomb's eight children. (Alice and Charles were farm laborers who lived in a shack—no electricity or running water—and earned $1 a day hoeing and picking cotton. But they were a cheerful and loving family.) At the local schoolhouse, Roy kept repeating first grade, but nobody realized he was severely deaf until he was 9.

Roy's plight was discussed at a town meeting. His teacher donated $5, and arrangements were made with some local sheriffs, bound for a convention in Austin, to drop Roy off at Texas School for the Deaf.

At the rigorously oral TSD, Roy got his first taste of life outside poverty. He struggled to catch up, loved reading, and worked hard. He was renowned for his athletic prowess—his namesign was "R"-on-the-chest, a play on "fine." After graduating in 1942, he entered Gallaudet College on a full scholarship. Basketball was his great love—he was the Bisons' leading scorer. Otherwise, he was a mediocre student, working part-time to support his family. He worked two summers in war-defense plants, then, after World War II ended, at a resort hotel in Lake Placid, New York.

"The most exciting championship in Gallaudet history" occurred in 1943, when the Bisons, then in eighth—and last—place, participated in the Mason-Dixon Conference Basketball Tournament in Baltimore. The Bisons scored a thrilling victory over top-rated Randolph-Macon (48-37), proceeded to beat American University as well, then scored a 2-point victory over University of Delaware (42-40). The Bison five (Paul Baldridge, Roy Holcomb, Don Padden, Earl Roberts, and Hal Weingold) who had played throughout those three games were dubbed "The Five Iron Men."

There was time for socializing, sundaes at a nearby drugstore soda-fountain, and romance. At the 1946 Spring Intramural Basketball Tournament in Ole Jim (he couldn't play since he was on the varsity team), Roy struck up a friendship with Marjoriebell ("Mabs") Stakley of Akron (OSD '43). Unlike Roy, she was from a "Deaf dynasty." They were classmates, but didn't start their courtship until their junior year. They graduated in 1947.

After receiving a teaching/coaching offer from South Dakota School for the Deaf, Roy asked the superintendent for permission to marry Mabs. Permission granted, they were wed in Akron in September 1947, and both taught at SDSD for 8 years.

During summers, they drove around, visiting schools for the deaf. Roy contributed a series of articles on 50 schools to **The Silent Worker** (April 1951 through June 1963). "Clubs of the Deaf" appeared in December 1951 and May 1952, and later, 8 installments of "Children of Deaf Parents."

In 1955, "after 8 years of *frolicking*," Roy and Mabs moved to Knoxville to teach at Tennessee School for the Deaf. The University of Tennessee was nearby. "We decided to further our studies in Special Education. There were no support services in those days but we managed to get through." Friendly classmates let the Holcombs copy their notes. In August 1957, they received their first Master's degrees. A year later, Roy earned an M.S. in Guidance, becoming TSD's first guidance director. Their sons Sam and Tom, both deaf, were born in Knoxville.

In 1961, they moved to Indianapolis in 1961 to teach at Indiana School for the Deaf (which offered better educational opportunities for their boys), and took extension courses at Ball State University in Muncie, where Roy earned his third Master's—in Sociology (1966). He became involved in ISD's Parent Association and "decided to start one on a national scale." Although "in the past, 'parents' was a dirty word to many Deaf people, Roy found that they could be a big asset to our needs politically." At the 1965 Convention of American Instructors of the Deaf (CAID), Roy first proposed a Parent Section. After CAID confirmed the need for, and interest in, such an organization, a motion was passed at the 1967 meeting formally proposing a parents' affiliate group, and Roy was appointed Chairman of the National Parents Group Planning Committee. Its first meeting was held at CSD-Berkeley in June 1969. The new group was endorsed by the NAD, which underwrote its newsletter, **The Endeavor**. Originally "International Association of Parents of the Deaf," it's now called the American Society for Deaf Children.

Even with three Master's degrees, Roy was frustrated by his inability to secure an administrative post because he was deaf. He was also discouraged by the restrictions that oralism imposed on young deaf children. He later wrote: "Long before [I went] to California, the education of the deaf had been very much on my mind. Because of my own very difficult communication problems I knew that there had to be a better way." He envisioned an all-inclusive approach involving all modes of communication—signing, fingerspelling, oral, aural—to meet the individual needs of each child. There would be no barriers in the classroom.

Roy wasn't the first to use a combined approach. In the early 1960s, Dorothy Schifflet, a teacher in the Anaheim Union High School District, disillusioned by the lack of progress her own deaf children, Robin and Maureen, were making under the oral system, switched to a combined system (signing and fingerspelling, supplemented by speech), with partial mainstreaming, and began using it with the other deaf junior- and senior-high students she was teaching. Even if he didn't actually initiate it, though, Roy popularized the concept of Total Communication and brought sign language to very young children, even toddlers.

Seeking to improve his administrative credentials, Roy attended the 8-month NLTP at CSUN with Mabs, and received his fourth Master's degree—in Administration and Supervision—in 1968. (It was Mabs' second.) He had drawn up plans for a combined approach at ISD in 1967. At CSUN, with the support of his professors and fellow students, these were developed and refined.

"There were no takers for my services as an administrator except for one small program in Santa Ana, California," Roy wryly noted. In Fall 1968, he became the first area supervisor of this program, which operated out of 5 classrooms in the James Madison Elementary School, serving 34 deaf children among an enrollment of 800 hearing students. ("The reputation of the program left much to be desired.") He immediately introduced combined communication at all age levels there, and in 1969, began using the catchy term "Total Communication." (He was inspired by a huge banner he'd seen in front of a supermarket, proclaiming "Total Discounts!") He also began hiring deaf teachers and set up sign-language classes for the entire community—students, siblings, teachers, and especially parents, who were encouraged to learn sign language as soon as their children were diagnosed as deaf—a revolutionary idea. Interpreting services were provided for deaf students taking mainstreamed classes and participating in schoolwide activities (e.g., student government). Many families moved to Santa Ana to enroll their deaf children there. In 1973, the James Madison Total Communication Program was moved to a new building adjacent to Taft Elementary School. By that time, it had grown to 100 students. Visitors came from other cities across and outside the States to observe and copy it.

Roy wasn't satisfied with the success of the Santa Ana program. He wanted to break the stranglehold of oralism on the education of deaf children everywhere. In Summer 1970, he addressed the general body of the International Congress on Education of the Deaf (ICED) in Stockholm, Sweden, and got a standing ovation. He gave talks on TC to parents, teachers, and administrators, and assisted many schools in making the transition to a signing environment. Maryland School for the Deaf was probably the first residential school to adopt the TC philosophy. Pioneering TC programs were implemented there and other progressive schools for the deaf—Delaware, California, and Indiana. The NAD and many other Deaf organizations endorsed TC. By the time Roy presented "The Present Status of Total Communication" at the

1975 ICED, it had become the fastest-growing movement in the history of education of the deaf. By 1976, more deaf children were learning via TC than by any other means of communication.

At its 48th Meeting on May 5, 1976, CEASD officially adopted this definition: "Total Communication is a philosophy requiring the incorporation of appropriate aural, manual, and oral modes of communication in order to insure effective communication with and among hearing-impaired persons." By bringing sign language back into the classroom, TC represented a break with the rigid oral/aural method that had been dominating education of the deaf since the late 19th century. There has been ongoing controversy as to just what TC is and isn't, how well it works, the role of ASL in TC, and if the Bilingual-Bicultural approach, which uses ASL to teach English, is better. Likewise, there is bitter controversy about the merits and demerits of mainstreaming.

"In 1973, feeling that my work in Santa Ana was mostly completed, I accepted a new challenge." Roy became Director of the Margaret S. Sterck School for the Hearing Impaired in Newark, Delaware. In 1977, the Holcombs moved back to California—first Santa Clara, then Fremont. Mabs taught at Ohlone College; Roy became Director of the Santa Clara County Hearing Impaired Program, commuting to San Jose until Proposition 13 eliminated his position. He accepted an offer from CSD to coordinate the Community Services for the Deaf at Berkeley, then Fremont when CSD moved there in 1980. He was Coordinator of the Continuing Education Program at CSD-Fremont until 1985, when Parkinson's disease forced him to retire.

Roy received CSUN's Daniel T. Cloud Leadership Award in 1975, a Doctor of Laws, Honoris Causa, from Gallaudet College in 1976, and ASDC's Pioneer Award in 1977. His students remember him as a warm, funny, friendly character. Wanting to give hearing people a better understanding of the "Deaf experience," he published three books of quips, anecdotes, and whimsical observations—**Hazards of Deafness** (1977), **Silence is Golden, Sometimes** (1979), and **Deaf Culture: Our Way** (1995). Although gravely ill, both Roy and Mabs continued their interest in Deaf affairs.

Top left: Peggie Parsons, Canberra, Australia, June 1976. Top right: with the birds in Venice's Piazza San Marco, 1965. Bottom right: on the Great Wall outside Beijing, 1986. (Courtesy of Peggie Parsons/Gallaudet University Archives)

CHAPTER 28

Frances "Peggie" Parsons

1923-

"Ambassador of Total Communication"

Stubbornness is a flaw in my character that I have developed to near perfection in my 60-some years on this planet.—Peggie Parsons, **I Didn't Hear the Dragon Roar**

Frances Margaret Parsons—known as "Peggie"—was born prematurely on September 25, 1923, on a ranch in El Cajon (near San Diego), California, daughter of Hester (Tancré), high-school principal/teacher/writer, and Harold Parsons, rancher. She wasn't expected to live, but Harold nurtured her through the first crucial weeks. "I slept in a cigar-box crib with cotton balls between my legs for diapers. Perhaps I lost my hearing from that time." She quips: "My mother didn't realize I was deaf until I was 5 years old—she thought I was just stubborn!"

Peggie was first sent to an oral school where she "learned nothing." In 1931, when she was 7, she transferred to the progressive California School for the Deaf in Berkeley, where she learned sign language, fingerspelling, reading, and writing. CSD "helped me catch up on all that I had missed by the time I was 10." Refuting the common notion that signing interferes with the acquisition of speech, she notes that her own speech became intelligible after she learned sign. (She originally had a bit of residual hearing.) There were sessions with Hester, too, and private tutors. "Books were my comfort."

In 1935, hoping to escape the Great Depression, Hester arranged for the family to move to Tahiti, returning in 1941. It was there that

Peggie began her habit of carrying a journal to spontaneously record her experiences. Her first book, **Sound of the Stars**, based on her Tahitian journal, was published in 1971.

She attended Gallaudet from 1943 to 1945, and was a champion varsity swimmer, working summers (1942-45) as a welder in aviation plants. She got married in 1945 and divorced in 1964; she has two daughters, Vincette Dee Versaggi and Valerie ("Bunny") West, and four cherished grandchildren—Michael, Matthew, Vinetia, and Stephenie. She worked as a statistician for Naval Electronic Laboratory from 1955 to 1960, then as keypunch operator for Convair Astro (1961-63). Shortly before her divorce was finalized, she re-enrolled at Gallaudet. She graduated in 1967 with a B.A. in History of Art. She received her M.A. from University of Maryland in 1972, and completed postgraduate coursework (ABD) at George Washington University in 1982.

She was a divorcée in her forties with two teenaged daughters when she began another career—as an art historian. For 19 years, she taught History of Art at Gallaudet, first as instructor (1968-76), then assistant professor (1976-84), finally associate professor (1984-1988). She gained an intimate knowledge of deaf people's written-English skills and their relationship to their "communicative backgrounds." From 1989 to 1993, she worked as Coordinator of International History Collections at Gallaudet.

Recognizing the difficulties deaf students have with reading and writing, Peggie adopted a dynamic, imaginative approach—donning a long white pleated dress and assigning names to its parts corresponding to a chart of a fluted Doric column (base, capital), for example. "I practically bedecked myself with *loads* of bracelets, rings, and beads to represent Flamboyant Gothic!" She taught her students to have "listening eyes." They considered her a tough but exciting teacher. At Gallaudet, she gained insight into the social development, culture, and leadership capabilities of deaf people. This experience had great impact and influence on her.

Her most famous role is that of global traveler, "ambassador of Total Communication," and "Gallaudet's World Ambassador." As she explained in a 1977 article:

My own work as an "ambassador" for Total Communication began in 1971. On my vacation from teaching at Gallaudet I had been persuaded by Mervin Garretson, then the Executive Director of COSD, to travel to Argentina to teach sign language and speak with deaf people about their problems and needs. I felt comfortable about this assignment because I speak Spanish; in addition, I have suffered from considerable wanderlust all my life. I was especially eager to go because I would have the opportunity to spread the use of sign language . . . the mother tongue of the deaf.

In some ways I feel that my life began at 43 when I started traveling in Europe during my summer vacations from my job as an art-history professor. But 5 years later my life changed even more drastically after a visit to a school in Buenos Aires, Argentina, that specialized in training deaf children orally. A teacher there twisted a little girl's tongue with a pair of metal tongs and explained that what she was doing would correct the child's pronunciation—never mind the girl's tears. Since then I have been a 'goodwill ambassador' and a world citizen, visiting schools all over the world and explaining the need for the right kind of education for the deaf children.

As a frequent traveler, I have faithfully written in my journal, even when I had to brace it on my lap while on trains, airplanes, and boats, or in hostels, restaurants, and parks. China was the most challenging place to travel. I found that great, isolated country so fascinating and so frustrating for me because of my age, my deafness, and my sex. My lengthy journal wound up as the book **I Didn't Hear the Dragon Roar**. I hope my writing will inspire [and encourage] others.

During her long stint at Gallaudet, her vacation time was given to working with international professionals in education of the deaf and contacting deaf adults at clubs and organizations. As the United States' most active unofficial ambassador to the global Deaf Community, she's visited countless schools for the deaf, teacher-training colleges, Deaf clubs and organizations, hospitals, city halls, ministries of education. She made two major global tours in 1974 and 1976. Her message? "The happiness of the children should come first, their education second, and only then their speech. But many educators consider their speech first, then their education, and their happiness not at all." She campaigned—successfully—for TC "in Commonwealth countries where the deaf suffered horribly under the ironclad oralism originated by Manchester University in England," and encouraged teachers, administrators, governmental authorities, and politicians to recognize sign language in schools for the deaf. She has taught 500 basic "English Signs as a First or Second Language" in South America, Caribbean Islands, Central and Southeast Asia, and Africa.

No matter where she's gone, she's able to communicate with other deaf people in local gestures or "home signs." "We know what it is like to be deaf, from our own experience," she says. When she gave an illustrated lecture in Bombay, she was grieved that the ones she most wanted to reach—parents of deaf children—didn't come to hear her speak.

She has seen the benefits of TC in her own work. At an oralist school in Malaysia, she conducted an experiment. The principal arranged to have half of the class taught orally (as usual) but the other half with TC. At the end of 7 months, the orally-taught students had vocabularies of about 20 words; the TC group, 500 words.

She was instrumental in developing a deaf Peace Corps program in the Philippines in 1974. She served as the Peace Corps' first deaf participant-traveler in East Asia, Kenya, and the Seychelles, and as a cross-cultural trainer and recruiter. Predictably, she influenced many deaf schoolchildren and college students throughout the United States to volunteer likewise. Wherever she has gone, she's encouraged students and teachers to come to Gallaudet. Dozens have—and some ended up in her classes!

In 1976, the prime ministers of India (Indira Gandhi), Iran (Hoveya), and Malaysia (Matathir), and other notables personally thanked her for her contributions to Deaf education in their countries. She's received numerous honors and awards from diverse organizations in Washington, D.C., the States, and abroad. She's lectured nationally and internationally, written and published extensively about education, sign language, her professional work, and her "freelance" adventures as a world traveler. Her work has been widely acclaimed worldwide through newspapers, magazines, radio, and TV. **People Weekly** ran an article in its "Teacher" category in May 1976 ("The deaf of the world find a vigorous champion in Frances Parsons"); she appeared on PBS' *Nova* in 1978, **The World Who's Who of Women**, 1992-93, and **Contemporary Authors** (1993).

As a spokeswoman for DOH (deaf children of hearing parents), she's expressed concern about an ASL-as-first-language policy. She has taken the politically-unpopular stance that the "combined method" (successfully used before hearing aids were popularized) is the most preferable for deaf children of English-oriented hearing parents to use in the classroom. She respects ASL for Deaf adults or school peers, but doesn't advocate ASL as a mandatory first language for everyone. She and other advocates prefer "English signs" (they dislike the term "Pidgin Sign English") and employ American signs in English order with or without speech. Due to dire misunderstanding, she has thus become the target for extremist hostility. (ASL has its militants.)

She has helped many people (deaf and hearing) get awards, honors, grants, jobs, and admission to postgraduate and doctoral programs. In 1980, she established the Frances Parsons International Endowment to assist in the teaching of English as a second language, using "English signs," to deaf and hard-of-hearing students worldwide. This endowment enables students, teachers on sabbatical, and retirees to spend about 10 months teaching English in a foreign country. Three have already gone to France, Malaysia, and Thailand.

I Didn't Hear the Dragon Roar, her remarkable account of her 3-month solo journey through China (Hong Kong to Kathmandu, Nepal, May through August 1986), was published in 1988 by Gallaudet University Press.

As few of us can ever hope to do, Peggie Parsons has seen firsthand how deaf children and adults actually live, how they're treated, and what their prospects are in their native cultures. And she has fought unrelentingly on their behalf, encouraged them to come to Gallaudet, and established better relations between the States and the global Deaf community. In 1976, a Bombay newspaper described her as an "indomitable crusader for the deaf." She says simply, "The deaf all over the world are my children."

Martin L. A. Sternberg: "My exciting and eventful life has kept me young and alert."
(Courtesy of Dr. Sternberg)

CHAPTER 29

Martin L.A. Sternberg

1925-

Scholar and ASL lexicographer

As Martin Leo Altar Sternberg says, "Looking back on my life, I am amazed when I see how many truly epoch-making events in the field of deafness I have witnessed and participated in. At times I imagine myself hovering in a time machine over an incredibly rich landscape of 'firsts.' I cannot imagine a more serendipitous time for a Deaf person to be alive than right now."

He was born on January 10, 1925, in New York City, "in the midst of what, in retrospect, was the Dark Ages for Deaf people." He had three sisters. "My grandmother predicted a career as a concert pianist or a symphony-orchestra conductor for me. I never shared my secret ambition with her—to be a different kind of conductor, a trolley-car conductor!"

Meningitis deafened him at age 7. "My family was devastated; I was only puzzled and confused. I took instantly to lipreading. Mom and Dad had both nurtured in me the desire and the expectation that my hearing would soon return completely. I was a mixed-up child."

He attended P.S. 47, New York City's only public school for deaf children. "I proved to be a case study in maladjustment. Even though it was an oral school, I was offended and perplexed when I observed other children using signs. I did not even learn fingerspelling until years later and, unbelievable as this may seem, I did not learn Sign until I was 24! The outward manifestation of deafness—signing—to me meant surrender to a lifetime of deafness. Denying deafness was keeping one's foot in the door for the time one would hear again. And so I grew up 'neither fish nor fowl.'"

After completing 8th grade at "47," he attended Townsend Harris, a "prestigious and ferociously competitive [prep] school for intellectually gifted [boys], now defunct. It was Dad who pushed me in; yet another form of his constant denial of my deafness. I was good as the best of them, and the deafness counted for nothing at all, so he said. At Townsend Harris, modeled after the strictest of German gymnasia, I studied Latin and Spanish, in addition to the usual academic high-school subjects. Among the many graduates were Dr. Jonas Salk, inventor of the polio vaccine, actor Edward G. Robinson, and George W. Goethals, builder of the Panama Canal. Much later I learned I was the first and only Deaf student in the entire history of that school. Graduation from Harris meant automatic, exam-free admission to the City College of New York—'the poor man's Harvard.'"

In 1943, as an after-school volunteer at the American Red Cross's Manhattan headquarters, became quite possibly the first deaf person to operate a TTY. ("I could handle all four TTYs almost simultaneously, sitting in a low-slung chair with ball-bearing wheels, and sliding to and fro on the linoleum floor.") He was on duty the day an airplane crashed into the Empire State Building.

"For a Deaf person, it was a deeply exciting experience. I developed a network of operator 'contacts' all over the country, and we exchanged weather information, local news, and occasionally personal talk."

At City, he struggled to survive. "No Office of Disabled Students, no interpreters, no note-takers, seldom would a student even let me copy notes, so viciously competitive was that place. It was all 'swim or sink,' and the mortality rate was a shocking 50%. It was a rare professor who even remembered I was Deaf, and I shudder when I recall how lonely I was, going home daily on the subway to a quick supper followed by 8 hours of homework. My most vivid memories: Latin declensions and conjugations; struggling with algebra, my poorest subject. Friends? Social activities? Nothing but a large void."

He not only survived, but excelled, taking Special Graduation Honors in English in 1949. "I received an interesting offer from President Elstad of Gallaudet College. For serving as an instructor in English and for setting up [the new] Office of Public Relations, I could get my room and board at Gallaudet while studying for my Master's [in Communication at American University]. No salary! But I considered it a good deal, for it would mean I'd be at least partially independent.

"I'll never forget my first day teaching at Gallaudet. It was an elective course in Shakespeare, for juniors and seniors. I was 24, younger than several of my students." *And* an oralist. The atmosphere was tense.

"I started off. No signs. Only mouthing of words, with a little awkward fingerspelling here and there. Surprise! Shock! Consternation! Snickers, laughter, hysteria soon ensued. In the midst of all this, in walked the department chairman. He had been resentful about my hire, for I had been invited by [Elstad], and not by him. He sat himself down in the back row, arms folded, head shaking disapprovingly. It was the longest class hour in my entire life, When it ended, finally, he marched over and, with a finger waving under my nose, warned me to either learn Sign, fast, or look for a new job!

"Fortunately, a very elderly and lonely professor, ready for retirement, came to me and offered to give me private ASL lessons daily after school. I snatched at the offer, and for several years I was her daily pupil. I did not know who she was until long afterwards. The name Elizabeth Peet meant nothing at that time." That name is now legendary in Gallaudet history. "She had been taught ASL by her mother, Mary Toles Peet, a noted Deaf poet. Her father, Isaac Lewis Peet, and her grandfather, Harvey Prindle Peet, both hearing, had both been superintendents of Fanwood. Elizabeth, herself hearing, had thus grown up on the Fanwood campus, and at Gallaudet she had served for many years under the presidency of Edward Miner Gallaudet himself. At Gallaudet she rose to Professor of Romance Philology and Dean of Women, serving for 50 years before she retired. Her teachers and sign-language models were her mother and President Gallaudet, and they were absolutely the best. Elizabeth in her time was generally considered the most fluent and graceful ASL communicator in the nation. She became the standard against which others would be measured. How lucky I was to have her, quirks and all, as my private tutor!

"It was Elizabeth Peet who first inspired me to produce my **American Sign Language: A Comprehensive Dictionary**, a labor of love that took 19 years in the pre-computer era, with index cards, individual hand drawings, and the rest. It finally came out in 1981, having taken my publishers, HarperCollins, 4 years to edit and design, after the manuscript was delivered. My only regret: Elizabeth Peet did not live to see this work. There are now two paperback offshoots, both popular and widely used; and a very recent newcomer: **American Sign Language Dictionary on CD-ROM**, which has treated quite a stir." It won the 1995 Software Publishers Association's prestigious Codies Award for Excellence in Software. "[It's] held in the same esteem as a National Book Award or a Pulitzer Prize in print publishing."

The **ASL Dictionary** contains 5,340 signs and is considered the definitive work (and a monumental achievement). Sternberg wants to update it to include new signs that have come into currency since 1981.

In 1962, he "accepted an assistant professorship at New York University. Things were cooking there. Dr. Edna Levine, a noted psychologist, had just begun a program in deafness there, and asked me to come on board. I taught the nation's first course in ASL for academic credit. I stayed for a good many years, earning a doctorate in Deafness Rehabilitation under Dr. Levine's successor, Dr. Jerome D. Schein, who had molded the Levine program into the nationally renowned NYU Deafness Research & Training Center, which in turn became a model for the whole country. I was poised now to make some strategically important and innovative contributions. The revolutionary 1960s had made their impact, with President Lyndon Johnson's signing of the Civil Rights Act of 1964, [which inspired] all minority groups.

"Communicative equality became a buzzword, for it implied

many changes and innovations. I became a charter member of the newly formed Registry of Interpreters for the Deaf, meeting in Muncie, Indiana. Interestingly, this Registry was first proposed by an oralist member of this pioneer group. It was to be merely a listing of members of the RID, but interpreter evaluation and certification soon [became] an important goal. I took and passed the first interpreter-evaluation program and test, in Memphis, soon after. I organized and conducted the nation's very first interpreter-training program, at NYU, together with Dr. Schein and Dr. Carol Tipton. Called 'the Dirty Dozen' because there were twelve pioneering candidates, this program, under a Federal grant, had enormous implications for the future. Today, all interpreter-training programs are modeled after this one. Concurrently with this training, Dr. Tipton, Dr. Schein, and I wrote the nation's first **Interpreter Training: A Curriculum Guide**.

"In the '60s, too, some great pioneering activity was being carried out toward recognizing ASL as a true language in its own right. William Stokoe was at the forefront of this. In the same period, the National Theatre of the Deaf was formed, to provide a showcase, not just for Deaf performing talent, but to show the visual beauty and the possibilities of ASL as a communicative mode. Indeed, the NTD can arguably be considered the single most influential ASL advocate in history." Sternberg tutored Anne Bancroft in sign language for her role as Anne Sullivan in the original Broadway production of *The Miracle Worker*, "which led to her abiding interest in deafness in the performing arts, which in turn resulted in the founding of the NTD. So many wonderful things happened during those crucial 10 years that made up the '60s!

"Yes, I have had a thrilling and fulfilling life. But wait, I'm not quite ready yet to kick off. I may be 70+, yes, but my exciting and eventful life has kept me young and alert. I'm still teaching—part-time—at Adelphi and Hofstra Universities on Long Island. Still planning for the future. Still dreaming up new projects. Why not?"

Top: "MMM" with Senator Tom Harkin (D-Iowa), at a meeting in Santa Monica on the ADA's first anniversary, 1991. Bottom: At a rally in front of Kern County Court House on March 8, 1995. (Courtesy of Marge Klugman/**GLAD News**)

CHAPTER 30

Marcella M. Meyer

1925-

Chief Executive Officer of GLAD

"MMM," as she is widely known, was born Marcella Mae Gulick on May 14, 1925, in Kansas City, Missouri. She was deafened by scarlet fever at age 6, and attended "regular" public schools there—Madison (now Troost) School (an oral program) and Central High School.

"My parents had a restaurant and filling station in their later (retirement) years but the family, especially the women on my mother's side, have always dabbled in the restaurant business. My father was a jack-of-all-trades prior to his retirement from the Chevrolet plant. They then retired to a small town in Missouri where they farmed for a while, then opened their restaurant."

From 1941 to 1970, Meyer held a variety of jobs, including clerical, tutoring, and manufacturing electrical components. She also worked in her family's restaurant business. She relocated to California in 1966. "I have some [CSU-LA] college credits but no degree, but I do have a Lifetime Credential for Adult Education."

From 1970 to 1974, she was Assistant to the Coordinator of Special Services to the Hearing-Impaired, La Puente Valley Vocational School. She served in several capacities, primarily as a counselor-tutor to deaf students seeking high-school diplomas. She also developed a testing system for placing deaf students in the appropriate grade level.

Founded in Los Angeles in August, 1969, the Greater Los Angeles Council on Deafness, Inc.—better known as GLAD—has become one of the best-known Deaf organizations in the country, perhaps the most powerful. And GLAD has been, from the start, linked with MMM. Her career is, so to speak, the story of GLAD's evolution, growth, and remarkable success.

What attracted her to a public-service/community-advocacy career? "I fell into it," she says. "I had my own experiences in discrimination in employment, especially when it came to using the telephone (remember, this was before TDDs or relay services were around). From those experiences I became very vocal regarding civil rights for the deaf and hard-of-hearing community. Also, when the National Leadership Training Program at CSUN established GLAD in 1969, I became very involved in the organization and another project came out of the NLTP, which was to provide direct services to the deaf community. I volunteered my services for one year, then the program was funded for 3 years by he Department of Rehabilitation and later GLAD's program was funded through a line item in the State budget, and is to this day."

In 1974, working as a full-time volunteer in cooperation with INFO LINE—Information and Referral Service of Los Angeles County—Meyer established the GLAD-INFO office to provide deaf and hard-of-hearing clients with information-and-referral services, walk-in and via TTY line. She was instrumental in writing a proposal that resulted in GLAD-INFO receiving an Innovation and Expansion grant, enabling deaf people to receive free interpreting services.

From 1975 to September 1998, Meyer was Chief Executive Officer of GLAD, a United Way organization serving as an umbrella agency for some 53 deafness-related organizations and agencies and a diverse deaf/hearing membership of 1,500. She administered a total of 13 outreach offices: GLAD-INFO, Interpreter Referral Program, Information and Referral Services, Advocacy. Employment, Tobacco Control Program, Family Health Education, and AIDS Education/Services for the Deaf.

As a service agency, GLAD provides a wide array of support services for the Deaf and hard-of-hearing community: peer counseling, advocacy, community-education activity, work with law-enforcement agencies, lobbying (and even filing lawsuits) for the civil rights of deaf citizens. GLAD also links the community with traditional social-service agencies, insuring full accessibility. These services are provided to all clients, whatever their preferred mode of communication, age, onset or level of deafness, or additional disability. GLAD even acts as a consultant to TV and movie producers for productions involving deaf characters.

GLAD publishes an annual resource directory for the southern California area, and a glossy quarterly newsletter, **The GLAD News**. It also operates a bookstore that stocks media on sign-language and deafness, signaling devices, and telecommunications equipment.

With an administrative center in Los Angeles, and 5 regional outreach offices—Bakersfield, and Orange, Riverside, Ventura, and San Bernardino counties, and an affiliate office in Buena Park—GLAD covers a lot of ground. GLAD's staff now numbers more than 60. As a matter of policy, GLAD ensures that its staff (both deaf and hearing) are able to communicate with all recipients of their services, whatever their mode—ASL, oral, gesticulation, pidgin, whatever else may be required—so that the entire communication spectrum is covered, with no gaps. GLAD doesn't just serve the Deaf community; deaf and hard-of-hearing people are involved at all levels, including the top. In accordance with its philosophy of self-determination, both the president and vice-president of GLAD *must* be deaf; so are most of its board of directors. Deaf leadership is a reality here.

GLAD's first headquarters were on Westmoreland Avenue in Los Angeles, In early 1994, GLAD relocated to spacious new quarters on Laverna Avenue in Eagle Rock, on the outskirts of Los Angeles. "[The old headquarters] were adequate for the time (1979) but by the '90s we had outgrown that facility because we were not able to expand into other fields such as more health services." A ribbon-cutting ceremony was held on February 3, 1994. "The Eagle Rock move was to a much safer and relaxing environment away from the hustle-and-bustle of downtown Los Angeles. The new facility will fulfill the need for expanded services, low-income housing, and meeting place for the community, which has been sorely lacking in recent years."

The timing of the move, so to speak, was perfect. Ten days later, on the morning of January 17, 1994 (4:31 a.m., Pacific time), the San Fernando Valley, which has perhaps the nation's largest Deaf community, was rocked by an earthquake, magnitude 6.8 on the Richter scale. The epicenter was located near CSUN. Northridge, Reseda, and North Hollywood were badly hit. Sixteen people died when their apartment building collapsed, but there were no deaf fatalities. Damage was estimated from $13 to $30 billion. As Marge Klugman, **GLAD News** Editor, noted: "GLAD immediately geared itself for emergency services." An emergency shelter was set up in one of the bungalows on the GLAD compound. GLAD's LifeSigns emergency-interpreting services responded to many requests; Red Cross volunteers brought in several deaf people for direct communication assistance. GLAD staff helped families move belongs from condemned houses into storage.

Says Meyer: "My most memorable experiences are too many to mention. Some are getting line items in the State budget and other funds. Also, the big move to our new facilities was very thrilling, not to mention a week later we had the big earthquake. What was so exciting about this is that we had everything in place to help the deaf community, even to the point of giving housing to misplaced persons temporarily. Also court cases we won: right to sit on a jury, police-brutality case, our litigation against PBS for open-captioning. (We lost that case, but it resulted in some landmark guidelines for PBS stations.) Many more experiences too numerous to mention.

"GLAD has had a big impact on both the deaf and hearing communities. We have helped many deaf persons to become full participants in society by advocating for equal access to the workplace as well as access to other services. GLAD has made a big impact on the hearing community by providing information and referral about resources available to them regarding their deaf children, adults, and people who are recently-deafened. We have also made an impact on education for the deaf, [and] were involved in developing legislation that gave the deaf child a Bill of Rights."

Meyer is a divorcée with three daughters, Jamie, Coleen, and Michele. "My 'proudest achievements' have been my three daughters who have produced me 5 grandchildren and 4 great-grandchildren. All daughters are in the helping profession, two of them with deaf services and the other with elderly and disabled. My second-proudest achievement is the acquisition of the Eagle Rock property and being able to obtain the funds to pay off the mortgage within one year."

A member of several local and state Deaf organizations, Meyer has served as a Board member of INFO LINE (1976-1980), Southeast Council on Alcoholism and Drug Problems, Inc. (1990-92), Deaf West Theatre, and TRIPOD (both currently); GLAD's representative on the American Coalition of Citizens with Disabilities (1977-1983); on NAD's Legislative Committee (1980-84); as President of the California Association of the Deaf (1985-89), as a delegate to the California Democratic Convention (January 1987), and, since 1989, as Commissioner of the Los Angeles City Commission on Disabilities. She has served on numerous advisory boards, participated in several major conferences, and conducted workshops and given keynote presentations on a variety of topics, including interpreter evaluation, leadership, community service, and the political process. In 1985, she sponsored and chaired the first National Deaf Women's Conference in Santa Monica, which led to the establishment of Deaf Women United. She was Honorary Co-Chair of the 1995 CAD Convention in Fresno. She's been honored for her efforts on behalf of the Deaf community—the Distinguished Service Award from CSUN's National Center on Deafness (1979) and NAD's Randall McLellan National Leadership Award (1990), for example.

Meyer has a reputation for being opinionated and aggressive. But she wants this to be known: "'That I am not the ogre that some people make me out to be, that I am a very approachable person, friendly, helpful, and always willing to help in any legitimate cause for deafness.' If my advocacy has pictured me differently, there is not much I can do about it, as I plan to continue to be very vocal on important issues."

Man with a mission: Andrew Foster.
(Gallaudet University Archives)

CHAPTER 31

Andrew Foster

1925-1987

Missionary and educator

The son of a coal miner, Andrew Jackson Foster was born on June 27, 1925, in Birmingham, Alabama. At age 11, while attending public school in the suburban steel-mill town of Fairfield, he was totally deafened by spinal meningitis.

For several years, he attended the Alabama School for Colored Deaf in Talladega. In 1942, when he was 17, his family moved to Detroit, Michigan. World War II had begun, the United States had entered it, and the war industries were booming. Foster worked in a factory that produced military equipment, and spent his evenings studying.

Around that time, he went to a lecture given by a missionary who described his experiences with a neglected population: deaf Jamaicans. Foster was moved and inspired to consider an evangelical career.

After World War II ended, Foster resumed his schooling. Eric Malzkuhn ("Malz"), Gallaudet College's much-loved Deaf storyteller, teacher, and Drama Club enthusiast, was then working as a VR counselor in Michigan. He later recalled their first meeting in 1947: "He was 22 and I was 25. He was just as smart as I was—if not smarter." Malz encouraged Foster to continue his education and apply to Gallaudet.

Initially, Foster pursued a business career. He received a Diploma in Accountancy and Business Administration from the Detroit Institute of Commerce in 1950, and, through correspondence courses, a high-school diploma from the American School in

Chicago in 1951.

That year, Foster, now 26, became the first black person to gain entrance to Gallaudet College in its 87-year history. He was a determined and dedicated young man. Getting in was the first his many pioneering achievements. Succeeding was next. As Gallaudet's first and only black student, he found himself under intense scrutiny. Everyone on Kendall Green, it seemed, was watching his behavior and progress. But he proved equal to the challenge. He had confidence, a winning smile, and a lively sense of humor. He began making friends. He impressed his teachers and classmates with his intelligence and stamina.

During his three years in Washington, he found his vocation. In his spare time, he would often go to Washington's rough-and-tough inner-city neighborhoods where he sought out young deaf blacks who needed encouragement, inspiration, guidance. Education of the deaf had long been segregated, although sweeping changes were soon to come. Very, very few deaf blacks had received a decent education that prepared them for any kind of professional career.

While working on their behalf, Foster learned that, in all of Africa—an entire continent—there were only 12 schools serving deaf children. He thus began think about bringing education and the Gospel to the deaf population there. Unknown numbers of them were illiterate, languageless, isolated. Remembering the plea for help made by the missionary in Detroit, Foster decided to devote his career to improving the lot of deaf people in Africa.

During his stint at Gallaudet, he took summer coursework at Hampton Institute in Virginia. He earned a B.A. in Education in 3 years, becoming Gallaudet's first black graduate in 1954.

Abandoning his earlier plans to pursue a business career, he now focused on education and missionary studies. He earned a Master's in Special Education from Eastern Michigan University in 1955, and, in 1956, a degree in Christian Missions from Seattle Pacific College. His schooling was—for the time being, anyway—complete.

In 1956, with the assistance of friends and church groups in

Detroit, and with the encouragement of Gallaudet President Leonard M. Elstad, Foster organized the Christian Mission for Deaf Africans, initially based in Detroit. Its goal was to bring regular and Christian education to all deaf Africans, whose numbers were estimated at 250,000. Under its sponsorship, he embarked on his solitary mission.

With ambitious faith, Foster arrived in Accra, Ghana, in 1957. A newly-independent nation, Ghana had no programs, no schools, no classrooms, no teachers for deaf people. (The situation was reminiscent of the United States at the beginning of the 19th century.) He encountered official resistance—the government claimed that there weren't enough deaf children to justify his attempts. Erroneous judgement.

After months of hard work, Foster rounded up 53 deaf people and set up a makeshift program in a rented Presbyterian public-school building. Classes for children met from 4 to 5 in the afternoon, and for adults, 6 to 7 in the evening. Foster juggled many different tasks and roles, serving as primary teacher, evangelist, administrator, and public-relations specialist. It was a Herculean task, but he proved he had the expertise, the stamina, the patience, and the sheer determination to prevail.

By 1959, his school had 25 boarding students, another 20 day students, and a waiting list of over 100. Foster trained 7 assistants to help educate all these students. Within 5 years there were 113 students, and a waiting list of over 300. The two pilot programs developed into the Ghana Mission School for Deaf Children and the Ghana Mission Center for Deaf Youths and Adults, both of which were ultimately accredited and funded by the Ghanaian government, which also asked him to investigate, and make recommendations for establishing, a comprehensive rehabilitation program for all disabled Ghanaians.

These were extremely busy years for Foster, who periodically returned to the United States to give fundraising speeches—then went back to work.

Motivated by his success in Ghana, Foster trained teachers of the deaf in Nigeria, where he established three more Christian Mission

Schools for the Deaf—at Ibadan (1960), Kaduna (1962), and Enugu (1962).

Returning to Detroit, he took postgraduate coursework at Wayne State University to better prepare himself to train teachers, and studied evangelical work at Detroit Bible College.

In 1961, he married Berta Zuther, a deaf woman who shared his zeal for missionary work and became a dedicated partner. They raised five children. Together they devised a master plan to launch a chain of satellite schools and programs for the deaf in Africa. As co-founders, they opened up schools in Abidjan (Ivory Coast); Lome (Togo); Moundou (Chad); Dakar (Senegal); Cotonou (Benin); Bangul (Central African Empire); Kumba (Cameroon); and in Gabon, Kenya, Niger, Sierra Leone, Upper Volta, and Zaire. They also founded the African Bible College for the Deaf. For each of these schools, Foster served on the Board of Governors.

In 1965, he was honored for his pioneering achievements by being elected President of the Council for the Education and Welfare of the Deaf in Africa. This multinational cabinet was the first of its kind in all of Africa. But civil war and political unrest made it short-lived.

In 1970, Gallaudet College awarded Foster a Doctor of Humane Letters degree, *honoris causa*. (Needless to say, he was the first black person to receive an honorary degree from Gallaudet.) The administration cited him as a model for those black Africans, deaf and hearing, who had studied at Gallaudet and later returned to their homelands to assist in the education and rehabilitation of the deaf. In 1975, he received the Gallaudet College Alumni Association Award "for promoting the well-being of deaf people of the world." In 1980, Western Michigan University named him an Outstanding Alumnus. He was also voted Seattle Pacific University's runner-up "Alumnus of the Year."

Although Berta Foster was diagnosed with cancer around that time, she successfully underwent treatment. The family lived in Ibadan, Nigeria.

Foster established a record 20 to 22 schools for the deaf. In addition to the schools, he established many churches, Sunday schools, camps, and programs. By training promising deaf Africans, he enabled many to attend Gallaudet and return as leaders and agents of change. By 1974, there were more than 70 schools for the deaf in Africa—a sixfold increase over the 12 that existed in the early '50s.

Foster continued his fundraising/speaking tours, in 47 states, across Canada, in Mexico, the Caribbean Islands, nearly all of Western Europe, and 25 African countries. During the next 10 years, while continuing his missionary work, he established and taught intensive teacher-training courses (in English and French) in several countries.

On December 3, 1987, Foster accepted an empty seat in a chartered Cessna airplane carrying 12 others to Kenya. For 20 minutes, the plane struggled to gain altitude. Eyewitnesses saw the doomed passengers frantically waving, then tossing their briefcases from the windows—their identities, at least, would not be lost. The plane finally crashed into a mountainous area near the town of Gisney in Rwanda, killing all those aboard.

In accordance with Foster's wishes, his body was buried in Rwanda.

On January 26, 1988, a memorial service for Foster was held in Gallaudet's Chapel Hall. Many old friends and co-workers gathered to pay tribute, including Rev. Clifford Bruffey, his old Gallaudet roommate; and Dr. Gilbert Delgado, a classmate. Malz recalled their early friendship in Michigan. Al Couthen represented the National Black Deaf Advocates, which established an annual memorial award in Foster's name. Also there were representatives of the "second generation" of Foster's students at Gallaudet. Gabriel Adepoju, a former student and co-worker (who later taught English at Gallaudet), summed it up tellingly: "Andrew Foster is to Africa what Thomas Hopkins Gallaudet is to the United States of America."

Three portraits of Mac Norwood.
(Courtesy of Marjorie Norwood)

CHAPTER 32

Malcolm J. Norwood

1927-1989

"The Father of Closed-Captioning"

On September 2, 1958, President Eisenhower signed into law P.L. 89-905, creating the Captioned Films for the Deaf Program. From its modest beginning as a tiny agency in the Bureau of Education for the Handicapped, U.S. Office of Education, Department of Health, Education and Welfare, it greatly expanded in size and function over the years. Its title changed from Media Services and Captioned Films for the Deaf (1970) to Captioned Films and Telecommunications for the Deaf (1975) to Captioning and Adaptation Branch to reflect its evolving role. In 1981, its captioned services were further expanded to include the special-education needs of other disabled groups.

Dr. Malcolm J. Norwood was actively involved in all of its aspects. The first deaf professional to work in the Department of Education and the first to head a major program there, he was Chief of Media Services and Captioned Films for the Deaf from 1972 until his retirement in 1988. It is for his pioneering work on captioning films and TV programs that he is best known. Although he wasn't the first deaf person to experiment with captioned media (that distinction goes to Emerson Romero, who worked with Ernest Marshall), he popularized it. He was in the forefront of almost every research-and-development program related to captioned media for the deaf, and was the first to envision the possibilities of closed-captioned television. His persistent efforts in this direction led to the creation of the captioning industry. For this, he's honored as "The Father of Captioning."

"Mac," as he was affectionately known, was born on March 16, 1927, in Hartford, Connecticut. At age 5, he was deafened by consecutive attacks of measles and scarlet fever. Unaware that schools for the deaf existed, his mother enrolled him in public school. Ironically enough, the American School for the Deaf, founded more than a century before, was flourishing in nearby West Hartford.

Through the first five grades, Mac experienced the usual agonizing frustrations. Fortunately, a school nurse (whom he called his "Irish angel") visited his mother one evening and urged her to send him to ASD. Luckily, she agreed. "For the first time since my deafness, communication became free and easy," he later said. In 1943, when he was 16, he graduated with honors.

At Gallaudet College, he discovered the nonfiction books by Richard Halliburton (the real-life Indiana Jones)—exciting tales of travel and adventure in far-off places. To prepare for his own future voyages, Mac joined the varsity track and cross-country teams. He became editor of **The Buff and Blue** in his senior year, and had a role in the Drama Club's production of Gilbert and Sullivan's comic opera *The Mikado*—the closest he could get to geishas and Japan!

After graduating from Gallaudet in 1949, he taught at Texas School for the Deaf. The following year, he returned to ASD, where he taught for the next two years. He married Marjorie Hale, a former student, in 1952, and accepted a position at West Virginia School for the Deaf and Blind as Director of Curriculum, supervising teacher of the high-school program, and coach of a championship basketball team.

According to **Deaf Heritage**, while at WVSDB, Mac "built up a large collection of filmstrips and was an early advocate of their use. He had also made it a regular practice to order captioned foreign films for the students." He established a budget to encourage his teachers to rent old silent films and use them in their classes. During summer vacation, he attended classes at the University of Hartford, and received his Master's in Education in 1957.

When CFD was established as a federal agency in 1959, Dr. John

A. Gough, an experienced teacher of the deaf who had served as principal of KDES and chairman of Gallaudet's Department of Education, was chosen to direct it. Some of Gallaudet's teachers-in-training had been farmed out for practicum at WVSDB, which was how Gough came to know about Mac Norwood and his interest in media. In 1960, Gough hired Mac as a program specialist and research assistant.

P.L. 87-715, which President Kennedy signed into law in 1962, expanded the tiny, ill-funded CFD program to include both educational and "fun" films, and provided for "acquisition and adaptation, research and development, production, distribution, and training." Four regional media-distribution centers and 60 educational-film depositories were set up. "Annual workshops and institutes to introduce and train teachers in the use of media and other instructional materials were held around the country."

Mac was given the responsibility of acquiring films for CFD. He negotiated the leasing and captioning of educational and Hollywood feature films. These were made available on free loan to schools for the deaf and other registered groups of deaf people. At a nominal cost—the price of return postage—a different captioned film could be enjoyed each week. As the acquisition of new films increased, so did the number of registered consumers.

In 1965, an amendment, P.L. 89-258, provided CFD with an annual budget of $3 million and the opportunity to promote deaf awareness through outreach activities, and to initiate research. Materials and services also became available to parents, social and rehabilitation workers, and employers. CFD now loaned out instructional sign-language, fingerspelling, lipreading, and cued-speech films, even auditory-training recordings.

When Gough retired in 1970, he was succeeded by Dr. Gilbert Delgado. But when Delgado left CFD in 1972 to become dean of Gallaudet's Graduate School, Mac took over full responsibility for the program. (Its annual budget was now $19 million.) As Chief of Media Services and Captioned Films Branch, he pioneered the breakthrough into closed-captioned television programming.

Enthusiastic about the potential impact of TV on the Deaf community (education and entertainment-wise), Mac had begun exploring the possibilities of captioning TV programs in the late 1960s. Hearing viewers overwhelmingly rejected open captions. Commercial networks were unwilling to take the risk. An alternative was to produce *closed* captions—visible only to those who wanted them. In 1970, BEH contracted with WGBH-TV, Boston's PBS affiliate, to produce a demonstration captioned program for use by PBS. WGBH engineers built the first caption computer. Captioning was previewed at a conference in 1971, and soon afterwards, the National Bureau of Standards (NBS) and ABC-TV demonstrated that Line 21 of the vertical blanking interval of the TV signal could be used to transmit captions. In March 1972, WGBH's new Caption Center broadcast its first captioned program: Julia Child's *The French Chef*. It was a hit. In December 1973, *The Captioned ABC News* debuted on PBS, giving deaf viewers equal access to the news for the first time. That year, closed-captions were encoded and broadcast for the first time on Line 21.

Mac and Marjorie lived in New Carrollton, Maryland; they had five children—Mac, Jr., Montgomery, Maureen, and twins Marsha and Martha. What with his family and Deaf-community activity, Mac somehow found time to pursue doctoral studies at the University of Maryland. His dissertation compared deaf viewers' comprehension of captioned and signed newscasts. He received his Ed.D. in Instructional Technology in 1976.

Through a joint undertaking by MS-CFD, PBS, and NBS, a prototype decoder was developed by NBS. After years of further development, testing, and evaluation, it was finally mass-produced and marketed. The TeleCaption "black-box" decoder was relatively lightweight and portable, and attached to any television set to display closed-captioned programming. There was also a color TeleCaption set with a built-in decoder.

Mac had already arranged for the establishment and funding of the nonprofit National Captioning Institute (NCI), to provide the actual captioning services. In December, 1976, the FCC agreed to reserve Line 21 for transmission of closed-captions. PBS and other broadcasters now had authority to televise closed-captions.

In 1972, he was asked to serve as liaison officer between the Bureau of Education for the Handicapped and the newly-established NTID. He served on the advisory committees of several schools for the deaf, the Maryland Association of the Deaf, and the State Advisory Board for Mental Hygiene for the Hearing-Impaired. His honors and awards include Distinguished Service Awards from HEW and NAD, IAPD's Special Service Award, the Certificate of National Recognition from the Association for Special Education, and GUAA's 1988 Alice Cogswell Award.

On a balmy April night during his freshman year at Gallaudet, Mac, acting on a lark, had climbed to the top of Chapel Hall and turned the hands of the great Tower Clock one hour *backwards*. For this, he was suspended from college for a year. In 1972, Gallaudet awarded him an honorary Doctor of Laws (LL.D.). His citation included a touch of humor: "Although as a student, Malcolm J. Norwood, '49, turned the Tower Clock back one hour, he is forgiven. He has been turning time forward ever since."

In January 1988, Mac retired as Branch Chief, and was succeeded by Ernie Hairston.

On March 22, 1989, Mac died of a heart attack. Larry Goldberg, Director of The Caption Center, said, "Whenever advances were made in media accessibility for people with hearing impairments, Mac was there: the captioned-films program of the sixties; The Caption Center's open-captioning of **The French Chef** and **The Captioned ABC Evening News** in the seventies; the development of Line-21 closed-captioning and the National Captioning Institute; the growth of network captioning from 10% of prime-time to 98%—none of these things would have been possible without Mac's guidance."

In 1990, NCI established the Mac Norwood Memorial Award scholarships for deaf students pursuing media-communication/technology careers. The Television Decoder Circuitry Act of 1990, which became Federal law, mandated built-in circuitry (the "decoder chip") to display closed-captions in *all* television sets with screens 13" and up, manufactured for sale in the United States, as of July 1, 1993. Doubtless, Mac would have been delighted.

Top sequence: Bernard Bragg performing in his one-man show in Tokyo. (Courtesy of Asaka Yonichi.) Bottom left: In Deaf West Theatre's *A Christmas Carol*. Bottom right: A formal portrait.

CHAPTER 33

Bernard Bragg

1928-

"Prince of Players"

He has been called the "Prince of Deaf Players." He can rightly claim to be the first professional Deaf performer. As such, he has opened the doors of opportunity to countless others. His influence on many of the finest Deaf actors, storytellers, mimes, and poets today is immeasurable.

Bernard Nathan Bragg was born in Brooklyn, New York, on September 27, 1928, the only child of Jennie and Wolf Bragg, both Deaf. (Wolf was a talented actor who managed and directed a small Deaf amateur-theater group, but because of the lack of professional opportunities, could only perform at Deaf-club gatherings on weekends.) Bernard attended Fanwood, where, in his junior year, he met a new teacher, Bob Panara, whose influence was contagious. He not only was a dramatic signer, he had a genuine love and enthusiasm for literature. Bragg—already a skilled mime and signer—was enthralled by the "colorful and exciting" way Panara acted out quotations, poems, and characterizations. Sign language, he saw, could be a rich, inspiring, and powerful artistic medium. When Panara produced *A Christmas Carol*, he chose Bragg to co-direct it and play Scrooge. Active in the Drama Club, Bragg was also a top student and cadet captain. He graduated in 1947.

At Gallaudet, he met Drama Club director-teacher Frederick Hughes, and got leading roles in Molière's *The Miser, The Bourgeois Gentleman*, and *Tartuffe*. (He was voted "Best Actor of the Year" twice.) Panara had left Fanwood to teach at Gallaudet, so he and Bragg continued their friendship. (Bragg was one of many Deaf achievers for whom Panara was a model and mentor.)

After graduating from Gallaudet in 1952, Bragg taught English at the progressive California School for the Deaf in Berkeley. He attended night school at San Francisco State College, majoring in Education and minoring in Drama. But he was restless and hungry. In February 1956, when the famed French mime Marcel Marceau made his American debut in San Francisco, Bragg made his move. After the performance, Bragg returned to the empty theater and found Marceau, who invited him to perform (which he did, right there) and then invited him to study, free, at his school in Paris (which he also did, that summer).

Back in Berkeley, he teamed briefly with Joe Velez, a gifted mime and actor himself, doing NAD-fundraiser variety shows, then went solo, performing for the first time at a convention of teachers of the deaf in Knoxville. An invitation to perform in Miami led to one in Puerto Rico. Good publicity led to a weekend job at The Backstage, a San Francisco nightclub, where he was written up in **LIFE**. He then did mime improvisations at various theaters, nightclubs, and private parties. He was "well received everywhere." At one of these parties he met Janet Mason, who worked at the local NET (National Educational Television Network, now PBS) station, KQED. She offered him a weekly job there, so he "did not have to give up teaching."

Bragg "acted out Aesop's fables and fairy tales in mime." After KQED received "a flood of calls from children asking where 'the quiet man' was," he was offered his own weekly TV show—*The Quiet Man*. This innovative program aired from 1957 through 1963. He "worked with a superb team that enjoyed experimentation and creative use of the camera."

In addition to fables, he did improvisations and specials. Two such favorites were *A Christmas Carol* and *Hamlet*; he mimed *all* the characters. In *Hamlet*, he stayed in one place—"I kept myself within an imaginary film frame and switched from one character to another with lightning speed. It was here that I perfected my 'Visual Vernacular' technique." This blends theatrical ASL with cinematic devices—long-shots, close-ups, slow-motion, zooming, high and low angles, and crosscuts. It's now widely used, along with another of Bragg's innovations: sign mime.

On national NET, "I taught elements of pantomime as well as performed stories in mime under the overall title '*What's New*.' Unfortunately, all tapes were destroyed because they were black-and-white. Aw, shucks!"

Still teaching at CSD, he performed "throughout the country and abroad, attaining both national and worldwide recognition." Panara called him "the Houdini of pantomime."

As early as 1961, Bragg had received an offer from Raymond Levy, a "Broadway angel," to help establish a national theater of the deaf—a dream he had cherished all his life and shared with Hughes and Panara. Broadway actress Anne Bancroft and NYU psychologist Dr. Edna Simon Levine, who had good connections to the theater community, had tried to get a government grant for such a theater and been turned down, but hadn't given up trying. In June 1966, Bragg received a fateful invitation from David Hays, a Broadway set and lighting designer and a vice-president of the Eugene O'Neill Theatre Center in Waterford, Connecticut. This led to the founding of the National Theatre of the Deaf in 1967. Bragg was the first Deaf actor Hays approached; he asked Bragg to choose other Deaf performers for NTD's very first effort, **NBC Experiment in Television with the National Theatre of the Deaf** (1967). The actors and actresses chosen—including Phyllis Frelich, Audree Norton, Gil Eastman, June Eastman, Howard Palmer, Nanette Fabray, and Lou Fant—"subsequently became the core of the NTD ensemble."

The Alexander Graham Bell Association for the Deaf tried—unsuccessfully—to prevent the program from being broadcast, and issued a statement criticizing NBC for promoting sign language on TV. But NTD got the support of teachers of the deaf across the States. And its new grant proposal was approved by the U.S. Department of Health, Education, and Welfare, "owing largely to its sympathetic consideration by a key official, Mary Switzer." NTD's first production—a one-act adaptation of Puccini's satiric opera, *Gianni Schicchi*, with several other pieces—was a rousing success. "And the rest is history."

NTD participated in a theater festival in Belgrade, Yugoslavia, during the 1969 WGD. At that time, the Moscow Theatre of Mimicry and Gesture was the only other professional theater of the deaf. An exchange of actors having been arranged, Bragg went to Moscow, worked with the deaf actors, learned Russian Sign Language, and appeared as Hermes in one of their productions, Aeschylus' *Prometheus Unbound*.

After 10 years with NTD, Bragg took a year-long sabbatical. This included "a 6-month tour as the American goodwill ambassador to deaf and hearing people in 25 countries," sponsored by the U.S. State Department, NTD, NAD, Ford Foundation, and International Theatre Institute, "performing one-man shows and giving workshops and lectures."

After returning to the States, Bragg decided it was time to leave NTD, although he continued as a lecturer in its Professional School for Deaf Theatre (the famed "Summer Program").

For two years, Bragg worked closely with scriptwriter Michael Bortman on a new project—a TV-movie with a Deaf theme. Both sought authenticity.

And Your Name Is Jonah was another "first of its kind"—the first TV-movie to portray Deaf culture with some accuracy, and with Deaf performers playing all the Deaf characters. There was even a scene in a Deaf club, affording a glimpse of this secret world on prime-time TV. *Jonah* was about a young deaf boy who is misdiagnosed as mentally retarded and whose anguished parents finally venture into the Deaf community for support. It was realistic, touching, and memorable, with fine performances by 9-year-old Jeff Bravin in the title role, and Sally Struthers and James Woods as his parents. Bragg, who was technical-production advisor and special coach for Jeff, also played Paul, a Deaf man who counsels and comforts Jonah's mother. *Jonah* aired on CBS in January 1979, predating 1985's *Love is Never Silent* by several years.

Bragg collaborated with Gene Bergman, an old Gallaudet friend, on a full-length ASL play, *Tales from a Clubroom*. It's set in that once-familiar but now-vanishing institution, the Deaf club, and peopled with recognizable Deaf-club types. It premiered at the 1980 NAD Centennial Convention in Cincinnati, Ohio.

For 15 years (1979-94), Bragg was Visiting Professor and artist-in-residence at Gallaudet University.

Signs of Silence, a biography by Helen Powers, was published in 1972. Bragg's autobiography, **Lessons in Laughter** (1989, written in collaboration with Gene Bergman), contains many vivid stories, funny and sad. (The title is an ironic reference to a "neurotically squeamish" teacher at Fanwood who disliked the sound of deaf children's laughter and drilled his students to laugh "properly.") It's already been translated into Japanese. In 1994, Deaf Life Press published **Meeting Halfway in American Sign Language: A Common Ground for Effective Communication Among Deaf and Hearing People**, which Bragg co-wrote with Jack R. Olson of Montana State University. Bragg also wrote several articles for NAD Monographs, among other publications.

Because of the intense chemistry between the performer and audience that's missing with videotaped and filmed work, Bragg prefers live stage to TV and film. (He continues to tour internationally with his one-man show, gives workshops, directs, and has performed at Deaf West Theatre.) Nothing gives him more joy than watching his audiences' faces light up, seeing them react to the "thoughts, ideas, feelings" he conveys onstage. When Bragg interacts with his audience, communication barriers are eliminated through artistry. And often, as Powers observed, members of the audience are so moved, they want to tell him how they feel, and go to his dressing room—and the communication barriers are there again. They don't know Sign and he can't magically understand their clumsy gestures. "Nor could they understand my speech. Swans walk clumsily on land."

He has won numerous awards for his work, including the International Medal from the World Federation of the Deaf for his service to the deaf of the world. Shortly after the DPN revolution, he received an honorary doctorate from Gallaudet University.

"My life speaks for itself," he says.

Top right: Morris Broderson. (© Mariana Cook, 1979.) Top left: *Eli and Friends*, 1993; oil, 36" x 36". Bottom right: *Flowering of the East II*, 1981; watercolor, 40" x 30". Bottom left: *Memories*, 1989; oil, 45" x 36". (Courtesy of Joan Ankrum.)

CHAPTER 34

Morris Broderson

1928-

Artist

Morris Broderson was born deaf on November 4, 1928, in Los Angeles. His first form of expression was "home sign"—impromptu gestures. He says: "At the Berkeley School for the Deaf [CSD], where I was a boarding student from ages 7 to 10, I learned to express myself in sign language." He uses speech, lipreading, and pen-and-pad when communicating with hearing people.

He started drawing—on a school blackboard—when he was 7. That was for fun. When he was 14, he began drawing seriously. Visiting his aunt, Joan Ankrum, he did a pencil sketch of her playing the piano. She later wrote: "It was not just a child's drawing. It had great lines, authority, imagination. I was very excited. . . . I felt compelled to take immediate action."

Because he was deaf, she couldn't "find a suitable teacher," so she worked with him for about a year. To guide him, she gave him a book of Leonardo da Vinci's drawings and Kimon Nicolaïdes' **The Natural Way to Draw**. Broderson won an art scholarship to the Pasadena Art Museum, where he studied life drawing with Francis de Erdely, a dynamic artist-teacher recently arrived from Hungary—"a volcano of a man," as Ankrum describes him. De Erdely was so impressed by Broderson's work that when he became associate professor of art at University of Southern California, Broderson was enrolled as a special student at his insistence. Broderson recalls: "I was strictly disciplined and not allowed to use color until I had proven my skill in drawing." These were rewarding and happy years for him.

He "concluded his studies at USC when he was 19, and continued as a private student for a few months with de Erdely, as Ankrum explains: "Although deeply grateful to his teacher, [he] reached a point of acute awareness of the need to break away from de Erdely's strong influence." As Broderson put it: "I said, 'I'm free now, but I'm not Broderson yet.' I wanted to find myself, what I liked." He enrolled in the short-lived Jepson Art Institute in Los Angeles, where he studied with William Brice and Howard Warshaw. (Rico Lebrun, an influential figurative artist, was director.) After the school closed in 1950, he "began working alone, experimenting with form and making technical discoveries in searching for new ideas in the use of silk screen and mixed media," and further developing his nonconformist romanticism. There was nothing of the then-fashionable abstract expressionism in his work. It "did not suit his personal vision."

For several years he worked as a janitor at local race tracks, and in a photographer's darkroom. He rented a small house—some of the doorways were widened to accommodate his largest canvases—and worked in his free time, especially at night.

He had his first solo show—mixed-media paintings—at Dixi Hall Studio in Laguna Beach when he was 28. "[This marked] the beginning of my career as a recognized serious artist."

But he underwent a period of emotional turmoil, struggling with alcoholism and depression. He stopped painting for 2 years. ("I painted in my sleep," he later said.)

After he brought the alcoholism under control, and began painting again, his work gained national recognition. A 1957 solo show at the Stanford Museum of Art led to a show at the Santa Barbara Museum of Art the following year. Ankrum notes: "His paintings won purchase awards at the Municipal Gallery in Los Angeles and the Los Angeles County Museum of Art in 1958 and 1960, and his work was included in important shows." In 1960, his *Chicken Market* was included in the Whitney Museum's "Young America" exhibition. Joseph H. Hirshhorn took notice of Broderson's work and immediately bought three paintings for his great collection. He became "a major collector of Broderson's work during the ensuing years, and his sustained belief in the importance of his work gave Morris great encouragement and support."

Up to that time, Broderson had no gallery representation, so Ankrum and William Challee opened the Ankrum Gallery in Los Angeles. "Our first project was the organization of a major Broderson exhibition for the M. H. de Young Memorial Museum in San Francisco, which opened in December 1960." Broderson spent the winter in Europe, soaking up inspiration, then mounted an exhibit of new works for the Ankrum Gallery's debut in March 1961. In 1963, after "an enriching visit to Japan," he was invited to become a permanent member of the famed Downtown Gallery in New York, and had a 10-year-retrospective exhibit. After its founder, Edith Halpert, died, he joined Staempfli Gallery, also in New York. Other galleries in cities across the nation followed suit. By the time he was 35, he'd had eight solo shows.

Ultimately, he set up his own studio in another house where he lived alone, letting Ankrum handle all the business aspects. (After she closed the Ankrum Gallery in 1989, she continued to represent him.) Oblivious to artistic fashions and trends, he followed his own course. His work—figurative, lyrical, and humanistic—contrasted sharply with the splattery abstracts then in vogue.

Diane Casella Hines, whose perceptive cover story on Broderson appeared in the October 1980 issue of **American Artist**, noted:

> Entering Morris Broderson's apartment studio is like "entering" one of his paintings. A stone Ming head, a Japanese No doll, an intricate wall hanging from India, an elaborately embroidered ceremonial robe—all the objects are seen in the artist's intimate still lifes and interiors, and in his daily surroundings, as well. But the paintings are much more than realistic transcriptions of his environment. They are the synthesis of a unique vision derived from deep emotions, expressed through a masterful draftsmanship.
>
> Although every artist possesses such vision to some degree, Broderson's vision seems further reaching. The timeless quality of his work sets it apart from art fashion.

Hines observed that he worked large, often on several paintings at once, alternating back and forth between watercolor and oil.

(Some of his largest, most intricate works were done in water-color.) To guarantee absolute "fidelity and brilliance of color," his windowless studio was brightly lit in full-spectrum light.

Broderson's oils, watercolors, pastels, and lithographs are marked by a brilliance of technique, color, emotional intensity, and mystery. Many are dreamlike. Seemingly unrelated objects are unified "through exquisite use of color and elegance of composition," as Hines noted. There are intricate patterns and textures: embroideries, Renaissance and Chinese brocades, porcelain, lace, cascades of flowers, a jumble of floral patterns.

His subjects are drawn from varied sources—observation, history, Catholic liturgy, personal symbolism. A Tijuana bullfight, noted Hines, inspired "a series of powerful, allegorical paintings." He was particularly fascinated by Kabuki, the Japanese theater form that evolved from life-size puppets and is characterized by extremely stylized gestures and expressions. (*The Rape*, which won the 1963 Whitney Annual Award, incorporated Kabuki figures and sign language.) Agnes de Mille's ballet about Lizzie Borden, *Fall River Legend*, inspired several haunting paintings. Broderson read Anne Frank's diary when he was 14—his introduction to the Holocaust. Deeply moved, he did a series of paintings of her. Many of his works show "exquisitely modeled," sculpturesque single figures posed against a simplified background or tapestry-like backdrop. Recurrent motifs include queenly or childlike Madonnas, sometimes pregnant; the crucifixion, flowers, still lifes. Images of death, but also a celebration of beauty and hope.

It's an art of stillness, isolation, and, yes, silence. Critics have long discussed the relationship of Broderson's deafness to his art. As John Canaday put it in 1978: "If Morris Broderson had not been deaf, he might have been a second-generation abstract expressionist in 1960, which would have deprived us of a quiet individualist in a time of noisy conformity . . . Broderson's deafness [must] be recognized. The only danger would be to attach too much importance to it, for it's only one of the many things that have gone into making him the artist he is."

A few self-portraits allude to deafness (e.g., *Self Portrait with*

Hearing Aid, 1993). Some of his paintings have "Deaf" themes; several incorporate fingerspelling, like passages of visual poetry (*Lament for Ignacio Sanchez II* [1966]; *Lizzie's Dream* [1966]; *Tribute to Winslow Homer* [1968]). Broderson's fingerspelled title was used in the poster and program for the original Broadway production of ***Children of a Lesser God***.

A favorite theme is *The Sound of Flowers*. As **TIME** noted in 1960: "Once a friend told him of having seen a small child wandering through a field 'listening to the sound of flowers.' Says Broderson: 'This is a theme I'll be working on for the rest of my life. To me it is a beautiful thought.'"

His paintings are now in the permanent collections of the Hirshhorn Museum and Sculpture Garden, National Museum of American Art, the Smithsonian, Gallaudet University (Washington, D.C.); Williams College of Art (Williamstown, Massachusetts); Museum of Fine Arts (Boston); Yale University (New Haven); Guggenheim Museum, Whitney Museum of American Art (New York); NTID/RIT; Palmer Museum at Pennsylvania State University; University of South Florida (Tampa); Kalamazoo Institute of Art; Loyola University (Chicago); Joslyn Art Museum (Omaha); Marion Koogler McNay Art Institute (San Antonio); James A. Michener Collection at University of Texas (Austin); Phoenix Art Museum; San Diego Museum of Art; Laguna Museum of Art; Santa Barbara Museum of Art; Bakersfield Museum of Art; Fresno Museum of Art; M. H. de Young Memorial Museum; San Francisco Museum of Modern Art; Stanford University Museum of Art; and Israel Museum (Jerusalem). This is a *partial* list.

He's known as a shy, private man. "You have to have first the heart, then the head, then the hands," he's said. "There is a statement that Winslow Homer made in his autobiography: 'The life that I have chosen gives me my full hours of enjoyment.... The sun will not rise, or set, without my notice and thanks.' It's just the way I feel about my work. My paintings are about life: war and peace, joy and pain, and the renewal of life realized in nature, as an expression of hope. . . . I want to make my paintings lovable, beautiful. I like to make peace."

Top: Frank R. Turk in his office. Bottom: With Andrew Bottoms of Charlotte, North Carolina, a 7th-grader at NCSD, Morganton. (Courtesy of Dr. Turk)

CHAPTER 35

Frank R. Turk

1929-

Teacher, adminstrator, and leader

To those who have had the pleasure of meeting him, Frank Turk is an energetic, small, but powerfully-built man. (His sign-name denotes his distinctive features—"nose-ears-crewcut.") Powerful in a quiet way. The term "driving force" comes to mind, but he doesn't like being in the spotlight. He defines leadership as "the art of getting things done through the work of others." He prefers actions to words. And he's utterly dedicated to Deaf and hard-of-hearing people in whatever he pursues. Very no-nonsense, but with warmth and a sense of humor. Much loved by young people and widely respected by all, he has also stood squarely in the center of controversy.

Frank Robert Turk was born on September 22, 1929, in Hibbing, Minnesota. Deafened at age 4 by spinal meningitis, he attended Minnesota School for the Deaf in Faribault, graduating in 1947. One of his mentors was Dr. Wesley Lauritsen—himself deaf—teacher, editor of the school magazine (**The Companion**), and athletic director at MSAD for 42 years. Turk adopted Lauritsen's motto: "Good work is never lost." It has shaped his own opinions and behavior. He says, "The purpose of life is work and the purpose of work is personal growth. When we work, we get to know what we are, what we can do, and what we may be able to be in becoming all that we are meant to be."

At Gallaudet College, Turk excelled in wrestling and football. After receiving his Bachelor's in Education in 1952, he taught Physical Education there and at KDES. He obtained his Master's in

Guidance Counseling/Physical Education from University of Maryland in 1969. He was Dean of Men in the Gallaudet Preparatory Department and Assistant Professor of Physical Education from 1965 to 1971, and from 1971 to 1980, Youth Relations Director at the Office of Alumni/Public Relations. Later he became Director and Assistant Dean of College Student Life, and in 1985, Dean of Pre-College Student Life (at MSSD). In 1983 he received his doctorate (Ed.D.) in Counseling/Student Development with Educational Administration as supporting field, from American University in Washington, D.C., the third deaf Minnesotan to earn a doctorate. In between those dates and diplomas was a lot of hard work. And one accomplishment after another.

He married his childhood sweetheart, Marilyn Zahrbock (an alumna of MSD), in 1981. It was the second marriage for both. He says: "My biggest reward in life is the intimacy, trust, and security of my friendship with my wife, Marilyn."

In 1964, **LIFE** published a short article, "Saturday's Silent Heroes," about the Gallaudet Bisons football team under Coach Turk's energetic leadership and inspiration. Turk was quoted thus: "A football field is one of the few places left in a deaf boy's life that demands the very best the boy has within him. Too many deaf people seek a soft way to circumvent a tough situation. Football does not teach short cuts." He never believed in taking shortcuts. He says, "We cheat ourselves when we avoid the necessity for hard work, struggle, and sacrifice, our three most outstanding of all lifelong teachers!"

He is especially proud of his 14-year stint, from 1966 to 1980, as national director of the Junior National Association of the Deaf (Jr. NAD). He established over 80 chapters across the country, and, with Gary Olsen (later NAD Executive Director), co-founded the NAD Youth Leadership Camp program. In 1970 Turk and Donald Padden, an old friend from Minnesota, purchased a lovely 40-acre tract, Swan Lake Lodge, near Pengilly, Minnesota. Until 1988, it was YLC home base.

Turk has also served as a board member of many organizations, including NAD, Maryland Association of the Deaf, National Committee on Scouting for the Handicapped, and Youth Section of the President's Committee on Employment of the Handicapped. He has written numerous publications on Deaf education and youth leadership, such as "The Deaf Child is a Person," "Deaf Youth and Self-Discipline," "Deaf Youth Leadership," and "Student Development: An Innovative and Collaborative Approach." And he's earned an impressive batch of honors and awards—e.g., from the NAD and state affiliates, FRAT, National Cued Speech Association, and SHHH. In 1985 he was inducted into the AAAD Hall of Fame; in 1995, into Gallaudet's newly-established Athletic Hall of Fame. He received GCAA's Laurent Clerc Award in 1975 in recognition of his "dynamic and innovative" leadership in Jr. NAD, and for excellence as an outstanding teacher, counselor, athletic coach, and dean.

His most disappointing experiences have been: (1) failure to meet the deadline—by just two weeks—to complete the requirements of the doctoral degree that would have qualified him for the then-vacant position of Director of the School of Preparatory Studies at Gallaudet in 1982. (2) In 1984, he was not offered the superintendency of Washington State School for the Deaf although his name was recommended to the state officials with a committee vote of 8-2. And (3) surrender of ownership of the Swan Lake Lodge property, for financial reasons.

In March 1988, he played an prominent role in the DPN movement at Gallaudet University. He was one of three staff members elected to serve on the 16-member DPN Council, which operated and managed the week-long protest. "The protest experience taught deaf and hard-of-hearing students the need and value of being assertive. During that week, student empowerment was significant. It had never been stronger, more important, or more effective."

In 1989, after 37 years of distinguished service at Gallaudet, Dr. Turk became Superintendent of South Dakota School for the Deaf. He was the school's first deaf superintendent—the first time a sign-language-dependent, non-speaking deaf person had become superintendent of a school for the deaf.

"Among the many positive things that took place during my superintendency of the school was my intensive work with the Communication Services for the Deaf headed by Ben Soukup [later NAD President]. Whatever political skills and sophistication you see in me, I learned from that incredible man and friend of mine. He taught me the simple methods of converting seemingly-impossible goals into accomplished ones, and much more. SDSD benefitted much from this simple yet effective team effort at the Legislature."

In October 1991, Turk took over directorship of the North Carolina Department of Human Resources' newly-established Division of Services for the Deaf and the Hard of Hearing (DSDHH), His responsibilities involved "cradle-to-grave" programs and services for North Carolina's 650,000 deaf and hard-of-hearing people, including three residential schools for the deaf (NCSD in Raleigh, Eastern in Wilson, and Central in Greensboro), 26 preschool satellite centers, and six regional resources centers for adult services.

A tireless advocate and a dynamic leader, Turk set about turning DSDHH into a model statewide agency. He established numerous task forces, forums, and action committees—e.g., the Annual Statewide Conference on Deafness and Hearing Loss, Statewide Parents Education and Advocacy for Kids (SPEAK), DSDHH's quarterly **Insider** newsletter, and co-founded the 1992 Task Force on Quality Assurance for Deaf and Hard of Hearing North Carolinians. The annual budget jumped from $22,800,000 in 1991 to $37,848,500 in 1996. The quantity and quality of statewide programs and services have increased accordingly.

In 1992, Turk was voted Outstanding Person of the Year by the North Carolina Association of the Deaf. In 1993, he was chosen as the state's Manager of the Year by the N.C. State Government Chapter of the National Management Association. In the nomination form for that award, the DSDHH staff wrote: "With an endless amount of energy, Dr. Turk works at all hours, often taking his work home with him to develop and perfect his ideas. The staff at DSDHH have come to respect and admire his whirlwind approach, uncompromising principles, and undying perseverance."

In 1993, he was elected president of TDI, and his 2-year stint brought new policies, an updated mission statement, accountability, measurability, and other positive changes.

Turk is well-known nationally for his leadership and sponsorship of all-level conferences in the areas of education, parenting skills, leadership, and student development. Of note: *National Jr. NAD Conference* (Washington, D.C., 1968), *Youth Leadership Conference* (Indianapolis, 1968), *National Conference on Student Development* (Rochester, 1987), *National Conference on Quality Education of Deaf Children* (Sioux Falls, 1990), *Statewide Conference for Deaf and Hard of Hearing People* (Raleigh, 1995). In August 1994, he originated the innovative Middlers Leadership and Literacy Camp for outstanding middle-school deaf and hard-of-hearing students in North Carolina. "The future of Deaf America is in the hands of those young people; hence, my first and foremost commitment has always been and always will be to them." The MLLC was so successful that it's being held annually each summer with line-item funding, and may be carried over to other states.

In late 1994, CNCSD/Greensboro was threatened by statewide budget cuts. But this time, Turk, who had fought to keep it open two years previously, now supported a plan to consolidate its staff and resources with Morganton and Wilson, which, he argued, would benefit the community in the long run. It was one of the biggest challenges he ever faced.

But the school was saved. As a result of the Greensboro crisis—which Turk calls "a blessing in disguise"—the state legislature allocated additional funding for all three schools.

"I can honestly say I have done what I thought was right for all deaf and hard-of-hearing children. I have simply never chosen the adult side, only the children's side. To be on the inside of that is not always comfortable. In fact, the politics and parental issues were a bit more intense than I had anticipated. But I never lost any sleep throughout all that. Not even to this day."

Lowell Myers and Donald Lang: a most extraordinary case.
(Courtesy of Mr. Myers)

CHAPTER 36

Lowell Myers

1930-

Attorney at Law

Lowell Myers is the best-known deaf lawyer in the country, with a reputation as a tough, shrewd advocate and formidable opponent. Over the years, he has taken on a variety of cases, winning many that were considered "impossible to win." His brilliant defense of Donald Lang, a languageless deaf man accused of murdering two prostitutes (and ultimately convicted of the second murder) made legal history, and inspired a best-selling book and a TV-movie. Myers also wrote **The Law and the Deaf**, a now-standard work, and was instrumental in getting sign-language interpreters into the civil courtroom—a right most of us now take for granted.

He was born to Deaf parents on January 26, 1930, in Los Angeles. His father, Joseph, had attended Illinois School for the Deaf at Jacksonville; his mother, Annie, Bell School for the Deaf in Chicago. "I started going deaf when I was about 12 years old and by the time I was 17 my hearing was totally gone." By then, the family had moved to Chicago, where Joseph worked as a printer.

Myers attended public schools, including Lake View High. He earned a B.S. in Accounting from Roosevelt University in Chicago (1951), and a Master's in Business Administration from University of Chicago. He became a Certified Public Accountant and worked for the Illinois Department of Revenue as an auditor and investigator. He chose accounting because he "thought it would be a good field for a deaf person. It was interesting work. I might spend a week working on nightclubs, and the next week I might be investigating a railroad, and after that it might be a steel-mill—one type of business after another. It was a good way to get a background in the business world."

This work "had a lot of legal matters connected with it and I was working with lawyers all the time. I got interested in law and applied for admission in the night school at the John Marshall Law School, in Chicago."

Not surprisingly, he had a rough time getting in. "The dean of the school told me that no deaf person had been admitted to any law school in the United States for over 50 years. He said that it was a very tough program and that sometimes 80% of the class would fail. He said, 'A deaf person couldn't possibly do it. I think you would be wasting your time.' I said, 'I've got the time. Let's try it out.'" He was admitted. "At the end of the first semester I was second in the class." No interpreters were provided, and since he "couldn't afford to hire one," he managed without. Instead, he made arrangements with classmates to copy their notes.

For 4 years, he worked as a State investigator by day and attended law school at night. "When I graduated [in 1956], there were only 20 people left in the class. Out of the 80 people who had started, 60 were gone. I graduated second in the class, out of 20." He now had a Juris Doctor (J.D.) degree. That year, he was admitted to the Illinois Bar and licensed to practice law. (In 1979, the John Marshall Law School honored him as a "Distinguished Alumnus.")

Quitting his Department of Revenue job, he worked for Sears, Roebuck and Co. as a tax attorney. He also started a part-time practice as a general attorney. (By this time, he had married and was ready to start a family. His daughter Lynda, who's deaf, became a social worker; his son Benjamin, a lawyer.) "At that time, I was the only lawyer in the state of Illinois who knew sign language, so a lot of the judges started assigning cases to me involving deaf people." As his reputation grew, so did his practice—with hearing as well as deaf clients. He handled all kinds of cases—"the entire range of humanity."

An expert on Biblical law, he has used the Jewish Scriptures (a.k.a. "Old Testament") as an up-to-date legal resource, and has "a whole library of books on that subject. The judges and the juries have a lot of respect for the Bible. They pay attention." The Bible "gives a fascinating viewpoint into human nature, and into the fundamental problems that people have. You see the same problems repeated over and over again, generation after generation." Example: Cain and Abel, the first murder recorded in the Book of Genesis. It was motivated by jealousy. So are a large proportion of murders today. "Cain is still around. He has changed his name, and he uses a gun now instead of a rock, but he is still very much with us. Jealousy can be a terrible thing."

After a deaf door-to-door saleswoman entered a large public building, overlooked a warning sign, got off on the "wrong" floor, and was attacked and badly injured by an enormous police dog, Myers sued the company operating the building. It was insured by the famed Lloyds of London, which hired "one of the biggest law firms" to fight the suit. They argued that the saleswoman was trespassing and deserved no compensation. Myers cited Mosaic law to prove that the owner of a vicious animal is legally responsible for injuries it inflicts—even on a trespasser. "I won the case in the high court. The judges were not going to change a rule of law that has existed for 3,000 years."

In 1965, Donald Lang, a young black laborer from the Chicago slums, was arrested for the murder of a prostitute. He couldn't communicate in sign language, speak, or lipread, nor did he know how to read or write, so he couldn't explain what had happened, answer questions, or defend himself.

Even though Lang had no money, Myers accepted the case immediately because he knew what would happen to Lang if he didn't. (He ultimately received $1,000 from the State for his defense of Lang, which averaged out to a mere $2 per hour.) Believing that Lang had been unjustly accused, Myers tried to prove that he was the victim of circumstantial evidence. The case made the front pages of the Chicago newspapers, and in May 1970, it went to the Illinois Supreme Court. Finally, in February 1971, the charges against Lang were dropped and he was released.

But 6 months later, Lang was accused of another murder—almost a carbon copy of the first one. Once again he was convicted, mostly on grounds of circumstantial evidence, and again Myers defended Lang—brilliantly. Although Lang was found guilty and sentenced to prison, the decision was reversed on appeal in 1975, because he was still unable to communicate and thus couldn't be guaranteed a fair trial. He was sent to a state hospital and enrolled in a special-educational program to learn the communication skills necessary to defend himself when he would be found competent to stand retrial—if that day ever came. (Says Myers: "Donald still has not learned sign language, and still cannot communicate. Apparently, he has a 'block' for language, which is very sad.")

In 1974, Ernest Tidyman published **Dummy**, an absorbing account of the Lang case. It became a best-seller. In 1979, the TV-movie version (also written by Tidyman) premiered on CBS, with fine performances by Paul Sorvino as Myers and LeVar Burton as Lang, and got excellent reviews.

Lang was only one of the thousands of deaf people Myers defended and assisted. With Myers' help, the legal system became more aware of the problems and needs of deaf people, and more responsive.

Early in his career, Myers recognized the vital need for having interpreters in courtroom situations involving deaf persons. He demonstrated this point in the Donald Lang case. Even though his speechreading skills are exceptional, he employed his own sister, Jean Myers Markin (who also signs) as an oral interpreter.

In 1965, Myers wrote the first statute providing for the payment of sign-language interpreters by the state in civil-court (private) cases. "It was always the law in every state that a deaf person was entitled to a free interpreter in a criminal case." But not for *civil* cases. "I believed that the law could provide a free interpreter in a civil case, provided that [it] was written properly." He drafted a law "and had it passed by the Illinois legislature. I got about 130 members of the House of Representatives to co-sponsor the bill. That was more co-sponsors than any other bill had for many years. The law was passed and the Governor signed it.

"But then we ran into trouble." State officials and lawyers for Cook County claimed that the law was unconstitutional. He took the case, *Myers v. County of Cook*, to the Illinois Supreme Court, which upheld the validity of the law. He won. "Then I wrote letters to all of the State Associations of the Deaf in the United States, and told them exactly what to do to get the same law passed in their states. Today, most states have this law, copied from the Illinois law. Getting free interpreters gave deaf people a much better chance of getting justice in the court system."

He's written several books, notably **The Law and the Deaf** (1964), the first of its kind and a standard resource/text for interpreters, VR counselors, and others training for careers with Deaf clients. He also wrote a children's version, and a book about police brutality covering Illinois and federal laws.

Along the way, Myers became a millionaire. "Actually, I never paid much attention to money. If a case was interesting I would take it, regardless of payment. But I started winning some big cases, and some of them were cases that other lawyers had turned down as being impossible to win."

Being wealthy "doesn't make much difference in my personal life. You can only eat three meals a day. You can only sleep in one bed at a time. But money can make a big difference in handling legal cases." Lack of money can prevent a lawyer from handling cases properly—"being able to afford hiring investigators, experts, or court reporters. It limits his freedom of action. On the other hand, if money is no problem, then the lawyer is free to handle the case the best way. If expenses are involved, he just goes ahead without having to worry about how to pay for them. Money is important because it gives you time. It gives you courage and independence. It makes you free to do what is right."

On the key to success, he quotes a favorite source: "The Bible says: 'Whatever you turn your hand to do, you should do it with all your power and all your might' [Ecclesiastes 9:10]. The Bible is an old book, but that is still pretty good advice!" And he says bluntly, with a trace of wry humor: "My clients like me and my opponents dislike me—which is just the way it should be!"

Bill Schyman of DePaul University's Blue Demons. The Chicago papers named him
DePaul's "Most Exciting Player" when he was a junior. (Courtesy of Mr. Schyman)

CHAPTER 37

William Schyman

1930-

Pro basketball player

Bill Schyman has had a lifelong love affair with basketball—which he turned into a career. He made his way from neighborhood courts and school teams, through three fabulous years with a Division One varsity team, into the prestigious ranks of the National Basketball Association (NBA). He was the first deaf athlete to play big-time college-varsity *and* professional basketball.

He was born deaf on February 14, 1930, in Chicago. His parents, unaware that there were any schools for the deaf in the state, sent him to public school. By the time Bill was 12, he "was a very tall and awkward kid who could not speak well." The other kids shunned him. But once they noticed what a basketball player he was becoming, they began inviting him to join in their pick-up games. He became a fanatic, spending all of his free time on the courts. "Many, many times I would never come home for lunch or supper, so my mother brought me sandwiches and milk."

He attended Lane Tech High in Chicago, but was unable to make the varsity team until his junior year; he played occasionally as a sub. He finally made the starting lineup as a senior, helping his team to a winning season and the playoffs by scoring a team-high average of 29 points per game. "As a result, I was the top scorer in Illinois and part of the All-State First Team."

His prowess that year—1949—attracted the college scouts. DePaul, Loyola, Notre Dame, and University of Illinois offered him scholarships. "I picked DePaul because I wanted to be close to my mother's home cooking and everyone in Chicago knew me."

He never regretted the choice, as it was there that he met Ray Meyer, the famed coach of DePaul's basketball team, the "Blue Demons," and the man most responsible for developing him into a first-rate player. Meyer emphasized "hard defense" and rebounding—intimidation "under the boards." He forced Schyman to work constantly at sharpening his game to perfection. After an undefeated season his first year at DePaul with the freshman team, Schyman moved into Meyer's awesome varsity team, the only sophomore that year to make the starting lineup. His aggressiveness and hefty 6' 5", 200-pound frame earned him the nickname "Moose" and the reputation of "most feared player" on the Blue Demons.

They played all their home games to a packed 20,000+-seat Chicago Stadium. Schyman was always in the spotlight because of his unique situation—he was the first deaf player to make it as a starter on a top college-varsity-basketball team. Although his deafness didn't prevent him from becoming a star, it did cause some difficulties—such as the game against Oklahoma. With 5 seconds remaining and Oklahoma leading by only one point, Schyman grabbed a rebound. Thinking that the referee had blown his whistle to end the game, he gave him the ball. That was a tough one to lose.

Schyman enjoyed three outstanding varsity years with DePaul. In his junior year, he was named "Most Exciting Player" by the Chicago newspapers. And during his senior year, DePaul had one of its finest seasons, placing in the Top 20 week after week. At the Christmas Holiday Tournament, against unbeaten and #1-ranked LaSalle at a sold-out Madison Square Garden, DePaul stunned everyone by upsetting LaSalle. And at the rematch in February, DePaul beat LaSalle again as Schyman scored 14 points and muscled down 20 rebounds. LaSalle's record that year (1952-53) was 26-2. DePaul had played "spoiler" to what would have been an otherwise perfect year for LaSalle. The Blue Demons themselves placed third that year in the NCAA playoffs.

During his senior year, Schyman was drafted by the Baltimore Bullets. He was eager to sign the contract but waited until he returned from the Maccabiah Games in Tel Aviv, Israel, where, as captain, he led the USA team to a gold-medal victory over the Israelis. Signing the contract *before* participating in the Maccabiah would have resulted in a loss of amateur status and automatic disqualification. "I was selected as captain of the USA team due to my aggressive style during practice at training camp in New York," he recalls. It was his "first taste of international basketball. After winning the gold medal, I urged my teammates to donate our practice uniforms and sneakers to the Israel BB Team—[they were] overwhelmed with our gesture. They invited us to their club for the last-night party, an experience I will always cherish."

So, after returning from Israel and graduating from DePaul with a B.S. in Psychology in 1953, Schyman joined the NBA Baltimore Bullets and became the first deaf player to make it to the "big leagues" of basketball. Unfortunately, after a few months, the financially shaky Baltimore franchise folded.

But Schyman's NBA career was saved. "The late Abe Saperstein, owner of the Harlem Globetrotters, picked up my contract and I played for the Washington Generals and Boston Whirlwinds." Schyman initially enjoyed traveling to countries such as Canada, France, England, Ireland, and Israel. He always played against the same team—the razzle-dazzle, comical Globetrotters. Life as a Whirlwind was exhausting. (He also played for the Philadelphia Spas in the old Eastern Professional League.) One recollection:

Back in the late '50s, when I was playing professionally for the Philadelphia Spas, we had a game against the Harlem Globetrotters at the Los Angeles Coliseum. Picture this: the arena is packed, excitement is high, and during the first half, we are playing against the Globetrotters in a regular game. We're playing well, dribbling, shooting, rebounding; we are dazzling everyone, including ourselves, with our skill, our finesse, our total mastery of the game. Then comes the second half.

Many people may or may not know this, but when playing against the Globetrotters, the first half of the game is played fairly, but the second half of the game is show. The Spas had to become the straight men for the antics of the Globetrotters. We would pull back and let the Globetrotters work their legend-ary magic on the crowd. Normally, this was fine with me. But this was not a normal game.

Somewhere, in the throngs of people, sat a young actress (my date) whom I desperately wanted to impress. I suppose I had already caught her eye, but I wanted her to see what the women in the crowd would be missing. I got my chance. Leon Hillard was doing his dribbling for the awestruck crowd— everyone knew it was impossible for anyone to steal the ball from him, once he got his hands on it. Everyone but me, that is. I was clever, I watched, I waited, and just at the right moment—I was off. In a flash of motion. He never saw me coming. I grabbed the ball, dribbled downcourt, and made a textbook lay-up. The crowd, as the saying goes, roared.

Needless to say, I finished up the game on a cloud, happy, carefree, and confident. Nothing could have dampened my triumph. I was the King of the Court. But even a king can wear an uneasy crown.

In the locker room, after the game, my teammates and I were celebrating. I think all of them secretly envied me only because they had grown tired of playing supporting actors to the leads. Our celebrating died the second Abe Saperstein strode into the room. I remember two distinct things about that moment: one, it got very quiet very suddenly, and two, a large finger pointing inches from my nose. "I'm fining you $500 for that cute little stunt you pulled. And if you ever do it again, you're off the team!" I never did it again.

After 3 years playing pro, "I retired from pro basketball; I was tired of traveling every night and playing in different cities for 7 consecutive months."

Schyman returned to Chicago, where he worked for IBM. But it wasn't long before he was back on the courts, this time with an AAAD club. He says: "I am deeply indebted to the late Lenny Warshawsky, retired NFSD executive officer and leader in the Chicago Deaf Community. We met by chance while I was shopping in Marshall Field's. He tried to explain [about] the AAAD. At that time, I had no notion there were [other] deaf basketball players and teams in the country. I was recognized as the only deaf college player in the NCAA Division One and, as far as I know, [no other] deaf players have achieved this."

Joining the Chicago Deaf Club was his first experience with other deaf players. Predictably, Schyman, a skilled NBA veteran, led his Chicago team, and later deaf teams from Washington and Buffalo, to AAAD championships.

He found romance as well. "It was my great fortune to be involved in the AAAD, and I made my debut as a player for the

Chicago Deaf Club in the 1958 AAAD Tournament at DePaul U. This is where I had the incredible fortune to meet the only love of my life, Helen Daniels of Philadelphia. She asked for my autograph, and after a year of chasing and wooing her, we were married on February 14, 1959. Thank you, AAAD!"

While he was practicing with the Chicago Deaf Club in preparation for the 1961 World Games for the Deaf (erroneously but commonly known as the "Deaf Olympics"), Schyman was offered a coaching position at Gallaudet. He accepted and coached the 1962-63 Gallaudet team to its first winning season in over 50 years. "Dr. Leonard Elstad, President of Gallaudet College, offered me a position there. In a few years I became head basketball coach. My experience with playing in the AAAD helped me approach the game of coaching Deaf college players. My debut as a coach was successful; we posted an 11-9 record-winning season for the first time in the history of sports at Gallaudet. Van Nevel, Jim Bittner, Kevin Milligan, Harvey Goodstein, James Barnett, Gerry Cooper, and Jim Reineck were among the greatest bunch of players ever assembled. Colleges that always beat Gallaudet were not used to being defeated by us, and consequently, refused to play Gallaudet the following season. Gallaudet was no longer a sure-win tally or doormat." He coached at Gallaudet for 5 years and earned a Master's in Education at American University before accepting a teaching position at a Maryland high school.

Other accomplishments include coaching USA basketball teams to gold medals in the 1965 and 1981 WGD and refereeing varsity high-school-basketball games. He owned and operated Pine Lake Camp for the Deaf in the Poconos (for summer sports instruction). In 1979, he was inducted into the AAAD Hall of Fame.

He says: "Many people have come up to me and said, 'Bill, you are lucky to be so tall; that's why you can dominate the game of basketball.' My answer to that is 'No way. Luck had nothing to do with it.' I have dedicated my life to basketball—trained hard every day of the year—played every day of the year in rain or snow. I slept with my basketball in bed. I *earned* everything that I have. Basketball has opened the world to me."

Top: With his aggressive style, Eugene "Silent" Hairston was a top-ranked middleweight contender and a crowd-pleaser. Bottom left: In a classic fighting pose. (Both **New York Post**.) Bottom right: After retirement, with a young athlete. (Courtesy of Mr. Hairston.)

CHAPTER 38

Eugene Hairston

1930-

Pro boxer

Eugene "Silent" Hairston was one of the most successful deaf boxers (amateur *or* professional) in history. As an amateur, he compiled a stunning record of 60 wins and only 1 loss. As a professional, his record was an impressive 45 wins (24 by knock-out), 13 losses, and 5 draws. At the peak of his career—1951—he was considered by many boxing experts and fans to be one of the few middleweights with a chance of beating the great Sugar Ray Robinson for the World Middleweight Championship.

His story is a tale of sheer determination. Some people thought that because of his deafness, the odds were heavily against him. But he proved them all wrong.

Eugene Hairston was born in Harlem on July 23, 1930. Deafened by spinal meningitis at the age of one, he attended P.S. 47, Manhattan's only public school for the deaf. Gene's father, a house painter, hoped that he would become an artist because he had shown a real talent for drawing at school. But Gene's boyhood idol was the great Joe Louis, and he often dreamed about becoming a boxer himself.

Gene had to quit school at 15 to help support his brothers and sisters. After working at various jobs—parking cars, pin-spotting in bowling alleys, shining shoes—he decided to turn his dream into reality. One morning in 1945, he showed up at a Bronx gym, the Tremont Athletic Club—the place where fighters trained. Having arrived before it opened, Gene waited for the owners, Mike and Joe Miele, Italian-American brothers. When they finally appeared, Hairston quickly handed them a piece of paper on which he'd written: *I want to fight.* Then he performed a fast and furious shadow-boxing routine. The Mieles were skeptical. *This deaf kid wants to be a boxer?* They refused to allow him to practice there. Undaunted, every day, for 6 months, he re-enacted the ritual of waiting at the club for the Miele brothers and then shadow-boxing for them when they arrived.

His persistence paid off. The Mieles finally agreed to let him box a few rounds with some amateurs. Gene looked so strong and impressive in the ring—he outlasted four opponents—that the Mieles decided to give him a chance. Mike became Gene's manager and Joe his trainer. They used body English and speech, gesticulating instructions to him between rounds and supplementing this with well-formed words that he could lipread.

Guided by the expertise of the Miele brothers, Hairston quickly made his mark in the amateur-boxing ranks. In 1947, he captured two prestigious titles: New York Golden Gloves Champion, 137 lb. Open Division; and Chicago Intercity Golden Gloves (147 lb.) Welterweight Champion. After 61 amateur bouts, Hairston had lost only one!

That summer, the Miele brothers, recognizing that Hairston possessed tremendous potential, entered him into the professional ranks. Amazingly, the young rookie won his first 16 professional fights—the first four by knockouts.

Everyone began noticing him. Fans applauded his courage and determination, while network television began broadcasting his fights—he appeared 13 times on national TV. "Silent" Hairston was making himself heard—and seen.

He was also changing the boxing scene. Because he couldn't hear the time-keeper's bell that signaled the end of a round, the New York Boxing Commission installed flashing red lights on each of the four ring posts in Madison Square Garden. This not only enabled Hairston to see when a round was over, it benefited hearing boxers who couldn't hear the bell because of the noisy crowds. These flashing lights were also installed on the ring posts of many other arenas, and have become standard equipment.

With his exciting, aggressive style, Hairston was a crowd-pleaser. Unlike many boxers who favor one hand, he was a hard hitter with both fists. But he did have a favorite punch—the "one-two," left jab and right cross. His ability to hit hard enabled him to tire an opponent with constant body punches. Then, when the opponent let down his guard, Hairston would attack with that "one-two" combination.

During his professional career (1947-1953), Hairston fought many of the leading middleweight contenders of the world. Four of the more famous ones were Kid Gavilan, Johnny Bratton, Paul Pender, and Paddy Young. Hairston did very well against them. On October 30, 1950, he defeated Gavilan in a 10-round bout. Gavilan later became the 1951 Welterweight Champion of the World. In another contest, Hairston beat Young on a TKO (technical knock-out) after just two rounds. And on April 30, 1951, Hairston KO'd Pender, who later became the 1960 and '62 Middleweight Champ.

The Ring ("New Faces," May 1948) described him as a young fighter "with a devastating right and better-than-average boxing ability who should make the grade." He did. In its April 1951 issue, **The Ring** listed him as the second-leading middleweight contender in the world! **Ebony** gave him star billing in a feature story (*circa* 1951) and called him "the only fighter with a chance against the now-legendary Sugar Ray Robinson."

By the time "The Deaf Wonder" fought former Middleweight Champ Jake "Bronx Bull" La Motta, on March 5, 1952, he had fought in 58 matches and lost only 10. **The Ring** had been ranking Hairston as one of the top middleweight contenders for two straight years.

The confrontation with La Motta was—of course—dramatic. The setting was sold-out 10,000-seat Olympia Stadium in Detroit, with national TV exposure. La Motta was desperately in need of a victory. He had lost his Middleweight title to Sugar Ray Robinson 18 months before and had been doing poorly ever since. The critics said he was "washed-up," finished. La Motta promised his father that if he lost the fight to Hairston, he would quit.

Still, he was the crowd's sentimental choice. They didn't want to see him quit, so they were cheering for him to win. Hairston couldn't hear those cheers when the ex-champ's name was announced, but he surely felt the pressure—and the stress. He would *have* to win if he hoped to get a chance at fighting Robinson for the title. So the ring was set. Two careers were on the line: the promising young Hairston versus the old, fading, and perhaps finished La Motta. The ropes of the Olympia Stadium ring weren't the only things that were stretched taut that night.

Hairston followed Mike Miele's advice throughout the fight by trying to wear down La Motta with body punches. And, when the opportunity came, Hairston would deploy his old favorite, the one-two. He landed quite a few of them during the bout. To Hairston's credit, he had La Motta reeling a few times. Nobody had ever knocked out the "Bronx Bull," and nobody ever knocked him off his feet—before or after.

The fight went the full 10 rounds. Although the referee awarded the win to Hairston, the two judges ruled it a *draw*. Under Michigan rules, it was called a draw by split decision.

But La Motta never forgot that fight. He mentioned his two bouts against "Silent" Hairston in his best-selling autobiography, **Raging Bull** (1970). (The film version, directed by Martin Scorsese, became one of the best movies of 1980—a classic.) In his book, La Motta devotes a single sentence to Hairston: "I fought Eugene Hairston in Detroit and it was called a draw, so I fought him again [May 21, 1952], and again I won easily." (Yes—if you count a 10th-round win an easy victory.)

Hairston never did get the chance to fight Sugar Ray Robinson, nor did he ever realize his dream of becoming a champion. Fate dealt him an unlucky punch. The draw with La Motta gave Robinson the option of defending his title against Carl "Bobo" Olson. In a last-ditch attempt at getting a match with Robinson, Hairston challenged Olson to a bout on August 27, 1952. Hairston lost on a TKO. A severe gash above his right eyebrow caused nerve damage, making the eyelid droop and permanently blurring his vision. Because the injury was serious, the New York State Athletic Commission suspended Hairston's boxing license. Soon other states followed the New York ruling.

Refusing to give up, Hairston went to Paris, where, on November 3, 1952, he fought against European middleweight champion Charley Humez. (He later told **The Ring**, "That fight was the brightest moment in boxing for me because the people of France treated me as royalty.") But after losing a 10-round decision, and unsuccessfully trying to get his license reinstated, Hairston knew it was time to quit. He was 22.

When he quit boxing, he left with pride. Not once in his career had he ever asked for special rules because of his deafness, nor was he ever involved in any "fixes" or scandals of the kind that have hurt the reputations of many boxers. As the first deaf black prizefighter, he left his mark in the annals of boxing.

According to **The Ring**: "Boxing afforded Gene celebrity status, including flashy clothes, specially-built autos, and the means to transform his parents' home into a 12-room mansion." Having retired, he enjoyed "a peaceful life with his wife, Aline, and a job with UPS," in its Metro New York District mailroom. He also worked "with youths in P.A.L., refereeing matches, acting as a second, and judging fights."

A great favorite with deaf fight fans, he received many ovations and honors, which he cherishes with mementos from his fighting days—his gold satin robe, photos, and writeups. Proudly displayed is a black marble statue inscribed "Eugene Silent Hairston, 1951 Welterweight Contender. From the Scranton Association of the Deaf." In 1975, he was feted at an elaborate luncheon and received a plaque commemorating his induction into the AAAD Hall of Fame. In 1983, he was the guest of honor at the Annual Banquet of the NTID Student Congress, where his story was the subject of a special television program produced there.

Top: Dr. Gertrude S. Galloway with students at the Marie Katzenbach School
for the Deaf. (© New Jersey Newsphotos) Bottom: With student Stephon Williams
at MKSD, 1990. (© George Holsey/**The Baltimore Sun**)

CHAPTER 39

Gertrude Scott Galloway

1930-

Administrator and Deaf women's advocate

Gertrude Scott Galloway (commonly known simply as "Gertie") was born into a Deaf family on November 12, 1930, and grew up in Washington, D.C.

"My parents, and my maternal grandmother, graduated from Virginia School for the Deaf and the Blind, and my maternal grandfather, from Fanwood. (Incidentally, my mother had seven siblings, all deaf.) My Deaf family used ASL all the time; in fact, Mother told me that I used my first sign—"milk"—when I was 10 months old. This was because I had an older brother and sister to communicate with. Father always promoted leadership in the family and advocated for our rights. He was a very good provider, working at the Government Printing Office, and during the Depression, he was one of very few people on our block who were still working. Father had natural talents for leadership, but he put his family first.

"I was enrolled at Kendall School [at age 6] since it was the only school available for deaf children. Coming from three generations of deaf relatives, signing was my only mode of communication, so when I attended Kendall School, which practiced the oral philosophy, it was rather frustrating for me. At the time, ASL was not accepted. My English was not that good and I became very self-conscious. I was constantly criticized."

There were some positive aspects, though. "Although Kendall School [was oral], we were allowed to use sign language outside of the classrooms, for which I am grateful. I also appreciated the opportunity to learn to speak. Because I was doing very well academically, the principal and my parents felt that I could afford some of the classroom activities for individual speech training.

"I would like to attribute my 'training' for leadership to the Kendall School. Although we lived only 6 blocks from the school, I stayed in the residential program 5 days a week. It was [there] I learned and practiced leadership with other girls during the afternoons after school. Of course, it was a big 'trial-and-error' experience for me, but the experience was very rewarding."

She entered Gallaudet College when she was 15. "I took entrance exams [during my] junior year, and because I passed, was accepted without graduating. However, I [returned to Kendall School] the following June to receive my diploma."

At Gallaudet, she was an excellent student and starred in many Drama Club productions; she even co-starred with Bernard Bragg.

She received a B.A. in Deaf Education from Gallaudet in 1951, but got married immediately afterwards and worked occasionally as an auditor, keypunch operator, and substitute teacher while putting her husband through graduate school and raising two daughters, Dawn and Shayne, and a son, Vance.

In 1970, after a divorce she describes as "devastating," Galloway and her children left Rochester, New York, and moved to Frederick, Maryland, whose small-town atmosphere made her feel safe. One position was open at Maryland School for the Deaf—teaching math—and she took it. Encouraged by her close friend, McCay Vernon, a psychologist and advocate, she also began working on her Master's in Education at Western Maryland University in Westminster, which had an innovative teacher-training program for deaf students. She received her M.Ed. in 1972, and began work on her doctoral dissertation at Gallaudet. Meanwhile, she taught sign language as a part-time lecturer at Hood College in Frederick; sign language, psychology, and women's issues at WMC.

"My experience at MSD was very interesting and at some times scary, because I was adjusting to [the] new role of a single parent. Dr. Dave Denton was instrumental in starting me out as an administrator of an educational program. First of all, he had enough confidence in me to hire me for a teaching position without ever meeting me, and secondly, he offered me an assistant principal's position when the Columbia campus was established." That was in 1973. She held the post of Assistant Principal until 1990. She was instrumental in establishing elementary and multi-handicapped programs there.

Working full-time, she completed coursework for her doctorate at Gallaudet. In 1980, she became the first woman to serve as President of the NAD (1980-82)—in itself, a full-time job. She pushed to establish a stronger political network, improve access to TV, increase the role of Deaf women in the organization, and address the issues associated PL 94-142 (now called the Individuals with Disabilities Education Act) and Section 504 of the Rehabilitation Act of 1973.

She's written, with characteristic humor: "Becoming the first woman to assume the presidency of the NAD was the biggest highlight of my tenure. It became a very interesting challenge because as I accepted the presidency, I was approached by several persons who questioned my ability to preside [over] a meeting with many strong men. My favorite saying: 'When I first became the president of the NAD, I did consider burning my bra and getting rid of all men [on] the NAD Board, but on second thought, I decided not to because I depended on both for support.' Another exciting challenge was entering the NAD's second century."

After Line-21 closed-captioning debuted in 1980, CBS didn't join the other networks in captioning any of its programming, because it was pushing for its own system, Teletext. "We were fed up with CBS for postponing captioning, and decided to have a nationwide protest rally. The whole project was well-coordinated and the rally was held simultaneously all over the country, which brought a lot of attention to our concern. Surprisingly, we received a lot of support from other organizations and people. I never forgot the time when a person from The Caption Center came to speak to us during one of our Board meetings and confessed that the rally contributed largely to CBS' giving in and captioning some programs [in 1983], especially *Dallas*."

She also served as vice-president and president of the Maryland Association of the Deaf (1975-77), president of the Free State Chapter of GCAA, Frederick (1972-74); and vice-president of GCAA (1973-79). She chaired the Volunteer Committee at WFD's Seventh World Congress in 1975. She was one of the 13 teachers and administrators chosen for the prestigious National Commission on the Education of the Deaf (COED, 1986-88); she chaired the Pre-College Committee. In March 1991, she also chaired the National Commission on Equal Educational Opportunities for Deaf Children. In all of her official capacities, she was a vigorous advocate for the rights of Deaf women and children. She gave many presentations on education, sexism, and Deaf women.

In 1989, Richard G. Bozza, Superintendent of the Marie H. Katzenbach School for the Deaf in West Trenton, New Jersey, resigned to head another school district. A year-long search for a replacement was launched. Galloway won the post over 47 other applicants from across the nation.

On January 2, 1991, she officially became the ninth, and first deaf, superintendent in the school's 107-year history, and the first woman superintendent of a residential school for the deaf in the States. (But not the last!) When she took her first tour of the MKSD campus in December 1990, the first thing the students asked her was "Are you deaf?"

She was the first MKSD superintendent who could communicate directly with the students. She established warm rapport not with them and the staff. She regularly visited the classrooms. She was approachable, open to all. A 1991 article in the Newark **Star-Ledger** described how one student, whose own hearing mother didn't know sign language, told her, "I wish you were my mother." She herself said, "They identify with me." She set about making MKSD a model of excellence, "a pioneer in deaf education."

In May 1993, Galloway received her Ph.D. in Special Education Administration. Matriculating for a doctorate at Gallaudet, she says, "certainly prepared me well for the job. My experience at MKSD has been a very positive one. I did have some rough times, but this is to be expected for an administrator of a school with 250 students and located on 120 acres. I had the fortune of inheriting efficient and dedicated staff, which made my job very easy."

In 1994, she was voted President-Elect of the Conference of Educational Administrators Serving the Deaf (CEASD)—not the first deaf person to do so (Dr. Robert Davila holds that distinction)—but the first woman. "I am truly honored by that accomplishment." She began "learning the ropes" and preparing for the "enormous responsibility" of heading CEASD while running MKSD. She officially took over as President in 1996.

On July 19, 1995, Galloway received Western Maryland College's prestigious Bailer Award for her "significant contribution to the field of education." (It memorializes Joseph R. Bailer, the former chairman of WMC's Education Department, director of the graduate program, and creator of the Program in Deafness.) The citation was delivered by her old teacher and mentor, Dr. Vernon:

> "[She] has achieved even more than Dr. Bailer imagined any graduate would when he started deaf education at WMC over 25 years ago.
>
> (...) In 1970, Dr. Galloway suddenly found herself divorced with three small school-aged children, no job, and no profession. It was during the next 25 years of her life up to the present that Dr. Galloway accomplished professionally the amazing achievements for which we are here tonight to honor her (...)
>
> On [her] résumé are pages of achievements on state, national, and international levels, documenting the offices she has held and honors she has been awarded. To me, her Presidency of the National Association of the Deaf, her Superintendency of the Katzenbach School, her earned doctorate, and her overall contributions to deaf people are the main reasons we are honoring her tonight. Dr. Bailer, were he alive, would be as honored, as all of us are, to recognize the greatness personified in the achievements of Dr. Galloway."

She's a strong supporter of ASL in the classroom, Total Communication, and the Bilingual-Bicultural approach—whatever works. "Being an educator myself, I feel that the most important issue is quality educational programs for deaf children. As the COED report [**Toward Equality: Education of the Deaf**] pointed out in 1988, the education for deaf children was not satisfactory. NAD has worked with NASDSE, CEASD, CAID, AGB, and other organizations in developing guidelines to help school districts to better understand the needs of deaf children. Even this is not enough."

Douglas J. N. Burke, "a true champion." Top left: At Minnesota School for the Deaf, *circa* 1940; top right; at Rochester, 1960; bottom left: at Texas, 1970; bottom right; *circa* 1979. (Courtesy of Beatrice Burke)

CHAPTER 40

Douglas J. N. Burke

1931-1988

Founder of SouthWest Collegiate Institute for the Deaf

Douglas John Nicholas Burke was born on a farm in Avon, Minnesota (near Minneapolis), on November 11, 1931, and severely deafened by scarlet fever when he was 2 years old. For 6 years, he struggled through St. Ann's Public School—and tried to win acceptance by being the class prankster. When he was 11, Dr. Leonard M. Elstad, then Superintendent of Minnesota School for the Deaf (and later Gallaudet College's third president), having heard about Doug's plight, visited the farm, talked with the family, and encouragingly told Doug that he'd be attending MSD in the fall and that he'd like it there. Dr. Elstad was right. At MSD, Doug (Class of 1950) was a football and basketball star.

One of his teachers at Gallaudet College was Bob Panara, who recalls him as "every inch 'the Greek Apollo'—a football hero who was also President of the Student [Body] Government, and who excelled as a promoter and director in drama." He was twice named Football Player of the Year, and also played on the basketball, wrestling, and track squads. He became what he called a "theater nut," inspired by his schoolmate Bernard Bragg. In his senior year, Burke directed *Macbeth*, the first full-length Shakespeare play ever produced at Gallaudet. It was an early step toward his lifelong commitment to advancing Deaf cultural arts. He graduated in 1955 with a B.A. in English. At that point, he wasn't sure what career to pursue.

At Gallaudet, he met Beatrice Maestas ('58), alumna of New Mexico School for the Deaf. They were married on July 19, 1958, and had three children, Stephen, Theresa, and Patrick (all hearing).

His first job (1955-57) was counselor at California School for the Deaf, Berkeley. He returned to the Washington area, worked as Curriculum Director/Instructor and Director of Volunteer Services Programs at Children's Convalescent Hospital (1958-61), then as counseling specialist for the District of Columbia Department of Vocational Rehabilitation.

Still unsure about a career, Burke did graduate work in 1962 at Catholic University of America, in Psychiatric Social Work, Philosophy, and Guidance and Counseling. At which point, Alan B. Crammatte and Boyce Williams encouraged Burke to apply for a fellowship to the National Leadership Training Program at CSUN. There he finally realized that he had a gift for organization and administration. He received an M.A. in Educational Administration and Supervision (with emphasis on schools for the deaf) from CSUN in 1965. From 1965 to 1968, he served as Curriculum Coordinator for DC-DVRS, administering a continuing/vocational-ed program for deaf people, as Research Coordinator, and as Administrative Coordinator, founded its Comprehensive Services Unit for the deaf. From February 1968 through September 1969, he worked as Coordinator of Student Admissions and Planning (i.e., "Program Sampling") at NTID, then being established by Dr. Robert Frisina. Recognizing his need for doctoral-level training, he left NTID to begin work on his doctorate (1985) in Educational Administration and Supervision at University of Rochester.

He established and co-founded numerous guilds, programs, and organizations in Washington, Rochester, and Texas. Among these was the D.C. Club of the Deaf Dramatics Guild, which evolved into the Frederick H. Hughes Memorial Theatre of the Deaf. (His play, *The Good Peddler*, was produced at the DCCD in 1961.)

Recognizing the wealth and diversity of Deaf talent and the scarcity of opportunities to display it, Burke established the National Cultural Program under NAD's sponsorship in 1964 to provide fine and performing Deaf artists with opportunities to compete on local, state, and national levels. National Cultural Tournaments—talent competitions—were held during NAD Conventions in 1968, 1970, 1972, and 1974. After the 1976 Convention, due to waning interest, the Cultural Program was discontinued. But the National Cultural Committee's last (and most enduring) project, conceived by Burke and announced at the 1970 Convention, was the Miss Deaf America Pageant.

As chairman of the Cultural Committee, Burke helped launch the National Theatre of the Deaf. The DCCD Dramatics Guild was a treasury of Deaf talent, and a grant proposal to finance a national tour was submitted to the newly-formed National Council on the Arts during the Johnson administration. The Council turned down the proposal twice, but the NTD did become a reality, through another track—Dr. Mary E. Switzer, RSA Commissioner.

By now, Burke was not only an energetic and creative networker, but a seasoned teacher, administrator, and counselor of deaf students. In 1974, he took the position of Educational Program Director in the Division of Services for the Deaf, West Texas-Panhandle Region of the Texas Education Agency in El Paso. He was promoted to Superintendent in 1977. In 1975, he'd begun exploring the possibility of starting a new college serving deaf students—those who weren't considered Gallaudet, NTID, or CSUN material, as well as those who wanted to attend a Deaf college nearer than the "Big Three," which had limited enrollment and long waiting lists. Programs set up for deaf students at "hearing" colleges were often inadequate; the dropout rate could be as high as 75% to 85%. A local Deaf college would do much to solve these problems.

In early 1979, Burke learned about Webb Air Force Base in Big Spring (halfway between the Fort Worth/Dallas Metroplex and El Paso), which had closed in 1977. It was a good site for such a college, and the timing was right. Burke and others enlisted support from citizens, businesspeople, educators, administrators, legislators, Howard College, and the Deaf community (led by Jerry Hassell, then president of Texas Association of the Deaf). The hard work—a year of meetings, studies, and miles of travel—began.

Many Big Spring residents, deaf Texans, and parents of deaf students liked the idea and supported the project. A formal "feasibility study" showed that there *was* a need for a Deaf college, not only for Texas, but for the immediate 8-state area (Arizona, New Mexico, Colorado, Kansas, Missouri, Oklahoma, Louisiana, and Arkansas). On November 6, 1979, the Howard County Junior College District Board of Trustees voted unanimously to establish SouthWest Collegiate Institute for the Deaf as a part of Howard College in Big Spring. In 1980, the 57 acres of federally-owned property were deeded to HC for 30 years for the purpose of establishing a college for the deaf. The final obstacle was obtaining state funding for the project.

SWCID was formally established in September 1980; Burke was hired to design and launch the college. That the SWCID proposal won in such a short time was close to miraculous. Indeed, Burke felt certain that "God is watching over SWCID."

Classes began August 25, 1980, with 27 students enrolled in the prep and college programs. Despite the short time between getting funding and opening, SWCID attracted a staff that Burke called the best of any deaf-oriented program in the country. Official dedication, ribbon-cutting, and open-house ceremonies were held on November 7, 1980.

As SWCID's first Executive Director, Burke was the first deaf person in history to head a college—and the only deaf person to found a college for the deaf. Burke masterminded the whole concept—acquiring, designing, equipping, and staffing SWCID's unique liberal-arts and vocational-technical program. Panara calls SWCID "the crown jewel of his life's work."

Not quite two years after SWCID's founding, Burke was unjustly "terminated." Beatrice Burke explains:

> The HC administrator wanted to move SWCID to HC campus in order to move HC's Allied Health program to SWCID's campus. Doug fought to prevent this move—he pointed out that the federal property was specifically for the establishment of a college for the DEAF. Doug refused to make any compromise that would deprive the deaf of a sound education; he wanted SWCID to maintain its image/identity.

After widespread protest from the Deaf community, SWCID's

Board reinstated him—to a newly-created position, Director of SWCID Transitional Planning and Development. He served on SWCID's administration until Fall 1983, when he began working as Assistant (State) Director for Programs at Texas Commission for the Deaf in Austin. He was stricken with cancer and then with severe rheumatoid arthritis, which forced him into retirement in October 1984. Initially hoping that he might recover, he was eager to return to SWCID, which he called his "unfinished symphony."

Instead, he endured a long, agonizing, and crippling terminal illness. During its course, Burke, a fervent Catholic, wrote over 500 religious sonnets—more than any other deaf poet in history writing in the English language. They're meditations on spiritual self-discovery, suffering, love, nature, and God's workings, some whimsical, some deeply mystical. (He had been the first deaf leader in the Church's Cursillo spiritual-renewal movement.) Two collections of sonnets—**Love's Source of Grace** and **Wings into Eternity**—were published posthumously.

During his career, he received fellowships from CSUN (1965), Gallaudet (1970 and '71), and UR (1969 and '70). His many honors included Gallaudet's Olof Hanson Award for Leadership (1955), NAD's Knight of the Flying Fingers (1970), Texas Rehabilitation Commission's State Merit Award (1979), Personalities of the South Award (1981), TAD's Distinguished Service Award (1981), and El Paso Center for the Deaf's Outstanding Hearing Impaired Individual Award (1981). In 1986, SWCID's main dormitory was renovated and named Burke Hall in his honor. To his delight, the 1988 Miss Deaf America Pageant was dedicated to him.

He died of complications of terminal illness on September 27, 1988, age 56, at his home in Big Spring. As Beatrice Burke recalls:

Douglas was bigger than life—a true champion who was always willing to take risks in order to make life better for the Deaf. Not only was Douglas a great leader, he was also a wonderful father, friend, and husband; he served as a great role model to all who had known him, especially our 3 children. . . . I asked him if he would have undertaken the task of such a magnitude— establishing a college—if he had known it'd cost him his health and eventually his life. Without any hesitation, he answered, "Oh, yes, I would!"

T. J. O'Rourke, holding a copy of the best-selling **A Basic Course in American Sign Language**, celebrating its 25th printing in 1991. (Robert Burke, courtesy of T.J. Publishers, Inc.)

CHAPTER 41

T. J. O'Rourke

1932-1992

Publisher and advocate

"T.J. O'Rourke was an original," says Frank G. Bowe, professor and fellow Deaf-rights activist. "He loved language and, in fact, his favorite activity was writing songs and poems—both seemingly odd for a Deaf person, but both expressions of language that love led him, too, to be a leader in sign language and one of the major figures in the development of linguistics of sign language." He enjoyed a distinguished and wide-ranging career. He was a sign-language authority, author, veteran Deaf-rights advocate, closed-caption lobbyist, and entrepreneur.

Terrence James O'Rourke—everyone called him "T.J."—was born in Bellingham, Washington, on April 17, 1932. Ten days before his 11th birthday, he was deafened by spinal meningitis. Signing came as naturally to him as speaking and singing had. He graduated from California School for the Deaf in Berkeley in 1948, and attended Gallaudet College, majoring in Education and minoring in English. During his senior year, he edited **The Buff and Blue** and its literary issue. He graduated in 1953. (Later, he served as managing editor of the **Gallaudet Alumni Bulletin** and editor of **Gallaudet Centennial Newsletter**.)

He did postgraduate work at Catholic University in Washington, D.C. (1963-64, and in the doctoral-studies program in English at University of Maryland (1965-67). He taught various high-school subjects at North Dakota School for the Deaf (1953-56) and North Carolina School for the Deaf (1956-60), and was an instructor at Kendall Demonstration Elementary School (KDES, 1960-62). From

1962 to 1968, he was a professor in Gallaudet's English Department. "I've always been fascinated by languages and the connection between English and sign language," he told Erika Kotite of **Entrepreneur Magazine** in 1991. When he began teaching at schools for the deaf, he was frustrated by the lack of "good teaching materials. "There didn't seem to be much about how to teach sign language, or anything discussing deafness at all, for that matter," he told Kotite. Unable to find it, he began preparing his own.

T.J. was actively involved in the NAD (he served as Associate Executive Director from 1976 to 1978). In 1967, the Department of Health, Education, and Welfare awarded NAD a grant to start a series of pilot sign-language classes—the Communicative Skills Program (CSP). From 1968 to 1978, O'Rourke served as National Director of CSP. He spearheaded the establishment of sign-language programs in schools, colleges, and agencies across the nation, which led to formal recognition of ASL as a foreign language. He likewise encouraged and participated in formal neurolinguistic research of ASL at the Salk Institute in La Jolla, California.

He wrote the nation's all-time best-selling sign-language text, **A Basic Course in Manual Communication**. NAD published the first edition in 1970. It could be used with "supplemental teaching aids"—overhead-projector transparencies and 2" slides. By 1991, it had sold more than 3 million copies. In 1975, through CSP, he founded the Sign Instructors Guidance Network (SIGN), which later became the independent American Sign Language Teachers Association. In 1977, CSP organized the first National Symposium on Sign Language Research and Teaching.

O'Rourke left CSP in 1978 to start his own publishing business. He was president, then chairman of the board, of T.J. Publishers, Inc., in Silver Spring, Maryland, which specializes in ASL and Deaf Culture books and instructional multi-media. According to Kotite's April 1991 **Entrepreneur** article:

> [L]ike most entrepreneurial ventures, O'Rourke's company began as a tiny self-publishing operation run by himself and his assistant, Angela Thames. . . . [Its first book], **A Basic Vocabulary: American Sign Language for Parents and Children** [1978], didn't do well at first, and

O'Rourke was forced to take another job for a year and a half until sales picked up. He also experienced difficulties with bankers who didn't take him seriously at first. "And when they did give me a loan, sometimes I felt like a charity case," O'Rourke says. His extensive experience with NAD gave him the credibility he needed to get a loan, and his second self-published book, A **Basic Course in American Sign Language**, which he co-wrote with Tom Humphries and Carol Padden, became a standard textbook for the teaching of sign language.

Humphries, Padden, and O'Rourke's **A Basic Course in American Sign Language** (1980), lavishly illustrated with Frank Allen Paul's crisp frame-by-frame drawings of eight native-ASL models, not only became a standard ASL textbook but a best-seller. By 1991, it had reached its 25th printing. In February 1991, T.J. published a version *en español*: **Un Curso Básico de Lenguaje Americano de Señas**, translated by Lourdes Rubio, edited by Gilbert L. Delgado, and dedicated to Robert Davila. By then, T.J. had "a backlist of 20 to 25 book titles, 10 employees and about 50,000 customers. Projected 1991 income [was] more than $2 million."

In 1980, T.J. also published Dennis Cokely and Charlotte Baker's ASL textbook/videotape series, the first systematic multimedia ASL curriculum.

O'Rourke edited many publications, e.g., **Psycholinguistics and Total Communication: The State of the Art** (1972). He also co-edited **A Free Hand: Enfranchising Education of the Deaf**, which addresses many questions regarding the language and communication needs of deaf children, and was released posthumously.

He was not only an internationally-recognized expert on sign language but a long-time organizer and activist for the civil rights of deaf people. He played an active role in securing the long-awaited enactment of Section 504 regulations, the breakthrough legislation guaranteeing equal rights for disabled Americans. In 1977, he helped organize a 10-city takeover of the national and regional headquarters of the Department of Health, Education, and Welfare. He led the Washington sit-in where demonstrators held the office of HEW Secretary Joseph A. Califano. These high-profile demonstrations prompted enactment of Section 504. (Dr.

Bowe, who also took an active role in the Washington sit-in, described his adventures in **Changing the Rules**, published by T.J. in 1986.) From 1978 to 1980, O'Rourke served on the Executive Committee of the President's Committee on Employment of the Handicapped (now President's Committee on Employment of People with Disabilities [PCEPD]). He was a board member of the American Coalition of Citizens with Disabilities, serving as both First Vice President (1977-78) and President (1978-82).

He actively participated in symposia and conferences relating to Deaf issues, nationally and internationally (e.g., with the World Federation of the Deaf). He testified before numerous Congressional House and Senate committees regarding the rights of the disabled, and worked internationally as a consultant in the field of sign-language education.

He was a pioneering TV-captioning advocate, too. In the early 1980s, there were a smattering of closed-captioned TV programs. Television producers and networks were reluctant to caption more programs until there was a significant audience. O'Rourke was the first deaf person to underwrite the cost of captioning an entire television show (*The Perry Como Christmas Special*, 1982), and encouraged other viewers to follow his lead. He felt that participation from the deaf and hard-of-hearing community would encourage the TV industry to caption more programs, regardless of the size of the caption-viewing audience. In 1983, he founded the Caption Club, a voluntary organization supporting the efforts of the National Captioning Institute (NCI). Caption Club became a vehicle through which caption viewers could "lobby" the TV industry for more captioned programming. His efforts succeeded. During its first decade (more than 14,000 persons and organizations having joined), Caption Club partially funded nearly 170 television series and, by Fall 1989, was instrumental in getting the entire prime-time network lineup on captioned.

O'Rourke received numerous awards from organizations, including NAD, NCI, Registry of Interpreters for the Deaf, and the Texas Association of the Deaf. He was listed in **Who's Who in Maryland, The World Who's Who of Authors, The Dictionary of**

International Biography, and **Contemporary Authors**, and cited in **Deaf Heritage**.

Ultimately, Thames took over as president of T.J. Publishers and ran the Silver Spring office, which left O'Rourke free to spend more time at his second home in El Paso, Texas, "developing materials and working with publishing colleagues." This arrangement allowed him to focus on writing "without the constant interruptions of a busy office."

On January 10, 1992, O'Rourke died of heart failure at his Silver Spring home. He was a few months short of his 60th birthday. He was survived by his wife, Robin Byers; a daughter, Kathleen O'Rourke-King of Mt. Airy, Maryland; two sons, Michael Kevin O'Rourke and Terrence Patrick O'Rourke of Dallas, Texas; and two grandsons, Shawn O'Rourke and P.J. O'Rourke King.

His death stunned and saddened the Deaf community. Said librarian and fellow Deaf advocate Alice Hagemeyer, "It was my good fortune to work with Terrence J. O'Rourke the past few years. T.J. was a relentless crusader for what he believed to be right. He left an indelible imprint on American history and the life of the deaf community throughout the nation and the world. We feel a keen sense of loss in his passing."

Soon after O'Rourke's death, NCI announced that a number of classic musicals on videocassette would be captioned in his memory. In Fall 1993, Caption Club celebrated its 10th anniversary.

Portrait of a Deaf Irish-American: Terrence James O'Rourke, a video tribute produced by America's Disability Channel and The Silent Network (now Kaleidoscope), premiered at the 1992 Annual Meeting of the PCEPD, and has been aired in the States and on BBC.

T.J. Publishers continues to publish and distribute books and other Deaf Studies media. ASL has been formally recognized in several states and numerous colleges and universities. We now have the ADA—an outgrowth of Section 504—TV sets with built-in caption-decoder chips, more captioning, and more awareness.

ASL instruction, civil rights, captioning—what T.J. O'Rourke achieved touches the lives of all Deaf people here—and beyond.

Top left: Dr. Robert R. Davila. Top right: Testifying before Congress. Bottom: Vice President Dan Quayle (left) swears in Dr. Robert Davila as the Assistant Secretary of OSERS, at the White House, July 21, 1989. (Courtesy of Dr. Davila)

CHAPTER 42

Robert Davila

1932-

Highest-ranking government official

"From migrant worker to presidential appointee, Robert Davila epitomizes courage and academic excellence."—Dr. Rex Cottle, President of Lamar University, introducing Dr. Davila's commencement address, August 14, 1993

April 25, 1989, was a very good day for the Deaf community. On that day, President George Bush announced his intention to nominate Dr. Robert R. Davila for the post of Assistant Secretary of the Office of Special Education and Rehabilitation Services in the Department of Education (OSERS), pending Senate confirmation. Dr. Davila, considered a "sure bet," then collected endorsements from Congressional representatives and a wide variety of disability groups. The Senate unanimously confirmed Dr. Davila's appointment in July, and on July 21 he was sworn in at the White House, before family and friends, as the new head of OSERS. (He replaced Madeline Will.) This was the highest position a deaf person had ever held in the federal government.

OSERS directly and indirectly affects just about every disabled and deaf person in the country. It's the federal office that oversees special education and Vocational Rehabilitation programs. As head of OSERS, Dr. Davila directed a $5.4 billion annual budget and had authority for federal involvement in the education and rehabilitation of the U.S.A.'s 36 million persons with disabilities. Although most direct control over education falls to state and local agencies, OSERS monitors all programs to make sure they comply with federal regulations. OSERS directly supervises a dozen programs, including Gallaudet University and NTID. Davila's post was considered to be one of "the most difficult jobs in our nation's education"—if not *the* toughest!

Davila was born on July 19, 1932, in San Diego, California, one of seven children of migrant Mexican farmworkers. Spanish was his first language. When he was 6, his father had a fatal heart attack while working in a fruit orchard, leaving his mother to raise the family. When he was 8, he was totally deafened by spinal meningitis. His mother sent him, by himself, 500 miles away to the California School for the Deaf at Berkeley. No one there spoke Spanish, so he quickly learned ASL—and English. As Gallaudet University's **Progress Report** later put it: "That feat would not be easily duplicated by a child with intact hearing; for the profoundly deaf Robert Davila, it was no less than astonishing."

He says, "I have never dwelt on these aspects of my early life as disadvantages. In fact, my humble beginnings were actually a motivating force that inspired me to succeed in whatever I attempted. I have built on my background in formulating my life's work. Access to a quality education has made all the difference. I was able to get into a good program almost immediately after losing my hearing. I encountered teachers and staff who took a personal interest in me and assisted me in many ways. Without a quality education I could never have achieved what I have."

An extraordinary student, he made rapid progress. At 16, he entered Gallaudet, graduating in 1953. (**The Tower Clock** made a prophetic comment: "Loves to shoot the breeze about matters pertaining to education of the deaf.") He continued his education in graduate schools "that had rarely, if ever, seen a deaf student" before, "and which offered no interpreters, no notetakers—in short, no supports." He comments: "It was not a question of 'managing.' In those days that was the only way to do it. The problem was, of course, that very few profoundly deaf persons attended graduate school in those days; the support services just didn't exist. Even the graduate programs at Gallaudet excluded deaf students. I wasn't trying to prove anything in graduate school, it was simply the only way to go."

He began his career in special education as a math teacher at Fanwood. He taught math, social studies, and English there for 14 years, and later became the first deaf member of its Board of Trustees. In 1972, he received his Ph.D. in Educational Technology from Syracuse University, becoming one of the select group of deaf people with earned doctorates. In 1990, he said: "The term 'educational technology' encompasses those innovations that couple advances in technology with the learning process. Technology can be a great equalizer in the education process. I am still very much interested in this field, but I am also excited to work with the broad range of technology projects that are funded by OSERS. Self-paced computer-learning programs, distance learning, environmental controls, augmentative communications devices, and job-site modifications using robotics, are making a real difference in the lives of people with disabilities. We are working with the states to see that all types of technological devices are made more readily available to people with disabilities. This will be a time of challenge and opportunity."

In 1974, he was appointed Director of KDES. In 1978, he was promoted to the position of Vice President for Pre-College Programs, where, until his OSERS appointment, he directed both KDES and MSSD. "I was a Vice-President of the University with administrative responsibility for the Pre-College Programs. My biggest challenge in my last position at Gallaudet was trying to get my colleagues in other schools and programs committed to their own school's renewal."

Davila served on the Central Administration Management Team (an interim administrative committee) during the epic DPN protest at Gallaudet University. He was the only senior administrator who was given full access to his duties and to the campus during the strike. During the upheaval, he was on campus most of the time, trying to ensure that MSSD and KDES students were getting essential services.

When he was appointed to the OSERS post, he declared that he was thrilled by the challenge. "I have always had a desire to serve my country in a position where my training, experience, and personal attributes would be useful to other Americans with disabilities, their families, and advocates. I was a product of special education and I am grateful for the support and assistance I received throughout my life."

After taking office, Davila was a visible and respected leader and advocate, guiding OSERS through some far-reaching changes that had been set in motion—such as the reauthorization of PL 94-142 (the "mainstreaming law"); differing interpretations of its most controversial provision, LRE ("least restrictive environment"); and the passage of the ADA. ("I have a number of priorities, but one important one is to strive for improved quality of educational outcomes. . . . Many young persons in need of special education are still 'falling through the cracks.'") He worked not only on behalf of deaf students in the States, but all students with disabilities; he was considered a fair-minded administrator who preferred to take each case on an individual basis, getting all sides before making a decision. "I am for the appropriate placement that is determined for each child on the basis of identified needs. This is what PL 94-142 mandates, and this is what we must do. . . . The law itself has assured all children with disabilities of a free and appropriate education. We need now to emphasize the appropriateness."

The Washington Post credited him with improving morale among OSERS' 400 employees, and noted that he taught sign language to everyone on his personal staff. "I may be gone by the time I finish, but I'm getting there."

In November 1992, George Bush lost his bid for re-election. President-elect Bill Clinton appointed a new cabinet. Ironically, Davila's successor at OSERS, Judith Heumann, was an implacable foe of separate schooling, which she publicly called "immoral."

Davila returned to Fanwood—this time as Headmaster (superintendent). He was able to resume working directly with students—something he missed at OSERS. He began working on behalf of the growing nationwide Black and Hispanic student population.

He remains a leading figure in the Deaf/Hispanic communities. Wherever you find people discussing special education and the rights of deaf and disabled people, chances are he'll be mentioned—or he'll be there. A popular keynote speaker, he's participated in numerous worldwide conferences, and written many reports for educational journals. He served as the first deaf president of the three top professional deaf-education organizations: CEASD, CAID, and CED. He's been active in the NAD, and a veteran member of the Council for Exceptional Children.

On May 29, 1990, he delivered the commencement address at Hunter College, New York City, and was awarded an honorary Doctor of Humane Letters degree. "This was a high point of my professional and personal life. Hunter is the prestigious institution where I earned my Master's degree. To be recognized in this manner is a tremendous achievement for anyone. As a deaf person, I am tremendously proud of this achievement." Other honorary degrees were bestowed by RIT (1991), Stonehill College (1991), and Gallaudet (1996). He was also inducted into the National Hall of Fame for Persons with Disabilities in 1987; to Hunter's Alumni Hall of Fame in 1988; and was honored as Syracuse University's Alumni of the Year in 1987.

In May 1996, he was appointed NTID Director, the first deaf person to hold this post since NTID's founding in 1968.

He says: "I think it is wrong for a disability to be the primary determinant of what someone can or cannot do. It is important for deaf people to understand that one is limited solely by his or her dreams and ambitions, not by a loss of hearing. I am proud of my academic accomplishments as well as of my record of service. When we can highlight the accomplishments and successes of persons with disabilities, we do much to eradicate the negative attitudes the create obstacles to progress."

Davila married Donna Lou Ekstrom of Seattle on August 8, 1953. (She's the daughter of deaf parents and had three deaf sisters.) They have two sons, Brian and Brent, both in construction management and engineering. For relaxation, Davila favors golf and tennis. He is also an avid sports fan, although he laments that his favored teams "never win anything." His passion, however, is his grandchildren—twin girls and a boy.

Alice L. Hagemeyer giving a FOLDA presentation. (Courtesy of Ms. Hagemeyer)

CHAPTER 43

Alice L. Hagemeyer

1934-

"Librarian for the Deaf Community"

Deaf people have traditionally not used the library; they have a very bad memory connected with the use of libraries. Libraries were used as punishment: you did wrong, you [got sent] to the library, and so we got the image it was not a good place.—Alice L. Hagemeyer

Traditionally, deaf people have shunned libraries. At the same time, many librarians and library administrators have been all too unaware of the needs of deaf and hard-of-hearing consumers, their hearing family members, and the professionals who serve them, and uninformed about the riches of the deaf community—its history, culture, and language.

Somebody had to do something. It was a deaf librarian.

For 34 years, Alice Lougee Hagemeyer worked for the District of Columbia Public Library (DCPL). She's cited in **Deaf Heritage** as one of the earliest organizers of a Deaf Awareness Week (now known as Deaf Heritage Week). In 1976 she began serving as "Librarian for the Deaf Community." In 1986, she founded Friends of Libraries for Deaf Action (FOLDA). Her goal was twofold: to encourage better understanding of the deaf community in the library community and general public while increasing the deaf community's awareness of and access to the services available in the public-library system.

Alice Lougee was born on February 22, 1934, "in a small farmhouse, located in the western part of Nebraska near a small town named Mitchell. My sister was 15 months my senior. Our brother arrived 7 years later. Our parents moved a lot, from one farm to another farm when we were small. We lived for 7 years in Guernsey, Wyoming, where our Dad worked as a miner; later he started a small dairy business. Unfortunately, he became sick and was unable to work and we had to move again, this time to Morrill, Nebraska, to be near my grandparents. Our Dad died when I was 14. Our mother had always been a housekeeper throughout our lives.

When she was 3-1/2, she was severely deafened by spinal meningitis. "Although I have no memories of what it was like to hear, I do recall a battle upon my returning home from the hospital as I struggled to control my balance while walking. My grandma also had spinal meningitis at the same time I did, and we shared the same room at the hospital." But her hearing and balance were unaffected.

When Alice was 5-1/2 years old, her parents took her to the Nebraska School for the Deaf in Omaha, over 500 miles away. NSD was still rigidly oral. No one was allowed to use sign language in the classroom. But Alice learned it "outside" from older students and the Deaf adults who worked there. "At home, during summer and Christmastime, I communicated with my family by use of paper and pencil, gestures and homemade signs. I also sometimes read their lips. They understood my speech most of the time because I had learned to speak before my illness. Although my speech may not be clear today, some people are used to my voice. My family followed the advice of the school that they should not learn sign language but encourage me to use speech all the time. Nevertheless, I am proud to say that today all the children of my sister and brother have learned sign language.

"Ironically, I never went to a public library until the summer of my junior year at the high school. One Deaf teacher who knew about my interest in attending Gallaudet College made out a list of books and encouraged me to borrow books from the library. Unfortunately, for some reason, I did not feel comfortable reading them at home by myself so I returned all the books back to the library. [Neither of] my parents read books and I didn't think they had ever entered a public library. They enjoyed the radio and there were newspapers and magazines lying around the house, so I read everything that was available. There was no TV at that time.

"During my time, there was no school librarian [at NSD]; there was a poor collection of books. The bookmobile came to our school once in a while, which was very good. However, school administrators, counselors, [and] teachers had not set good examples for us about how people can be independent in using the community resources for information on *any* subject after they left the school and were on their own.

"Library Science was my undergraduate major at Gallaudet. It was then a popular major for many Gallaudet students until the early 1970s, when a decision was made to discontinue it. Many Deaf students were disappointed, but 'Library Science' as an undergraduate major in any other college was unheard of; it's supposed to be for Master's. It was a wise decision.

"After graduation from Gallaudet in 1957, I worked for the D.C. Public Library, first as a clerk and then as a preliminary cataloger. I earned my Master's in Library and Information Science from the University of Maryland in 1976. During that time, my two hearing library colleagues at DCPL and I worked together to create a new position for a full-time librarian to serve the deaf community, in which role I was to serve 15 years. It was while at Gallaudet that I first developed a keen interest in books on all subjects and the function of a library, but it was at the University of Maryland that I first developed my passion for promoting both deaf and library awareness in the public."

On August 10, 1958, Alice Lougee married her Gallaudet classmate Ted Hagemeyer, an alumnus of Indiana School for the Deaf. "Thirteen years later, within 3 months—between December 2, 1971 and February 21, 1972—we were blessed with two children—David, a 5-1/2-year-old Deaf Canadian boy whom we adopted, and Noreen, our birth daughter."

At DCPL, Hagemeyer's two main targets were people's lack of awareness about deaf issues *and* Deaf people's lack of enthusiasm for libraries. She notes that the ASL sign for *public library* isn't *city library* but *hearing library*. "When I first became a librarian, I remembered one friend telling me that he had no interest in using a library and he tried to convince me that many others would not either. I said, 'Well, give me a little time; the DCPL has been in existence since 1896 and now we finally made it accessible to deaf people.' And I continued, 'If deaf people do not use their library, that will be their loss because I would *still* be at the DCPL earning their tax money!' I am proud that my friend is now a good user of the library."

During the first full week of December 1974, Hagemeyer launched Deaf Awareness Week at DCPL. It featured presentations by Deaf speakers. Other libraries followed suit, and ultimately the American Library Association (ALA) established a deaf unit. In recognition of her leadership in this area, the NAD gave her its President's Award at its Centennial Convention in 1980.

Hagemeyer wanted a national library-outreach program. Deaf organizations gave "verbal support" to the idea, but as far as taking an active role in promoting library outreach to the deaf community, had other priorities. In January 1986, Hagemeyer and volunteers Raymond Baker, Dorothy Casterline, and Bernard Sussman at DCPL, formed a new organization—Friends of Libraries for Deaf Action (FOLDA). It was "devoted to improving accessibility and services at libraries, and to encouraging the use of library services by deaf people." NAD provided office space. Merv Garretson, then interim director of the NAD, helped prepare a FOLDA "manifesto," "One for All; All for One." Copies were distributed to each state library, state deaf associations, and any organization or person who requested it.

Hagemeyer created **The Red Notebook** so the Martin Luther King Memorial Library (DCPL's main facility) and all branches "would have a 'first-stop information' resource that would provide unbiased information for all groups within the deaf community. People in other places heard about it and suggested that we also make it available to libraries outside of the D.C. The NAD agreed to become the only source to sell them.

"In 1994, FOLDA became an official NAD section, now known as FOLDA-USA. One of its goals is to motivate the deaf community in becoming involved in local friends-of-libraries activities. TDI maintains FOLDA-USA's registry list of libraries, nonprofit and for-profit organizations, and individuals who own a copy of **The Red Notebook**; FOLDA-USA sends them two free updates each year."

Hagemeyer has been an active member of the ALA since 1976, having been involved in various committees related to organizational structure, programming, publication, legislation, and services to people with disabilities and cultural groups. She was a Delegate-at-Large at the first and second White House Conferences on Library and Information Services (1979 and 1991).

Her many awards and honors include Phi Kappa Zeta Sorority's Woman of the Year Award (1988), GUAA's Alice Cogswell Award (1990), and the Exceptional Service Award (also 1990) from the Association of Specialized and Cooperative Agencies, a division of the ALA. She was selected the University of Maryland College of Library and Information Science Alumnus of the Year in 1987.

At the end of December 1991, Hagemeyer retired from DCPL, and began a new career as a library consultant. (Janice Rosen, DCPL employee through a Library Services and Construction grant, succeeded her.)

Hagemeyer notes that there are currently a handful of deaf librarians and paraprofessionals around the country, who mostly work at academic, school, and special libraries. Quite a few work for the public-library system—notably Susan Cohen in Montgomery County, Maryland, and Anne Feiler in the Chicago area.

Libraries are a powerful medium that can change people's lives. Recently, **Guidelines for Library and Information Services for the American Deaf Community** was published by the Association of Specialized and Cooperative Library Agencies, a division of ALA. Alice Hagemeyer's name has become synonymous with deaf/library advocacy. She says, "I hope soon I will be confronted with the question, 'Why do so many deaf people *like* libraries?'"

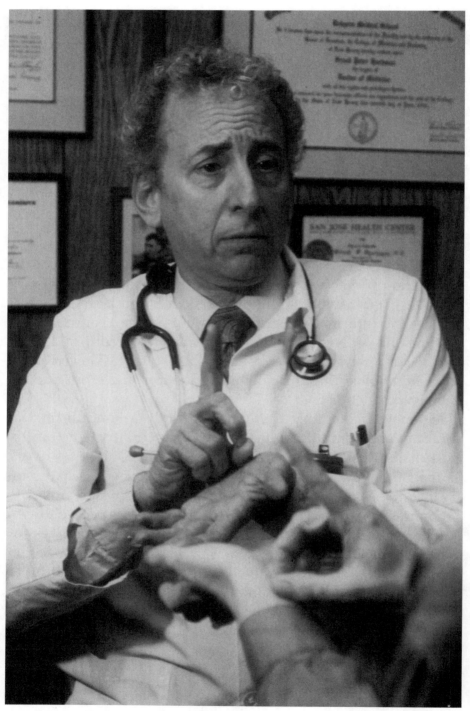

Dr. Frank P. Hochman with a patient. (Both are making the sign for "doctor.")
(© John A. Ramos/**The Argus**, Fremont, California)

CHAPTER 44

Frank Peter Hochman

1935-

Pioneering physician/surgeon

Frank Peter Hochman was the first born-deaf American to complete medical training and earn a degree—that is, to become a physician. He was born on December 26, 1935, in New York City—congenitally and severely deaf. "My parents went through the almost-traditional pilgrimage of going from doctor to clinic to hospital seeking a 'cure' or 'treatment' for my deafness. After three years of this without any success, they finally accepted my deafness as permanent and took me to a speech clinic, National School for Speech Disorders, from the time I was 3 until my second year at P.S. 47. For many deaf children, speech therapy is worthless, but in my rare case, it proved invaluable. My speech is easily (so I have been told) understood but many people upon first meeting me think I have an 'accent' which is usually guessed to be British or Middle European."

He entered "47" when he was 5. "I always wanted to become a physician, even [then]. This quixotic ambition of mine either amused or dismayed my teachers. At that time academic careers were frowned upon for deaf children and Medicine was not even remotely considered.

"My 9 years at '47' were mixed. I chafed under the strict oral program as I was repeatedly punished for signing. My parents were frequently called to come to school to be told how horrible a child I was for signing. I did, however, have a few truly caring and dedicated teachers and wonderful classmates—I still have contact with many of them.

"When time came to graduate, my advisor told my parents that I should attend the New York High School of Printing. Since I wanted to attend Stuyvesant High School for academically accelerated boys (possibly the best high school in the country), my parents questioned that recommendation. 'He spells well,' was the reason given to them. Stuyvesant was already receptive to the idea of deaf students, having accepted one the previous year [1949].

"Since I don't hear too well, I didn't follow the advice of my advisors at '47' and took the entrance examination for Stuyvesant and was accepted. This was truly a quantum leap in education. To keep up academically after a 9-year educational slumber in '47,' I had to read assignments/homework about 6-7 hours a day *after* school and much more on the weekends. The teachers at Stuyvesant did not 'feel sorry' for me. They just made me work harder and longer than I ever imagined possible. The education I received there well prepared me for everything and anything that followed.

"When it was time to graduate from Stuyvesant I wanted to go to a college with a good premedical reputation. My advisor told my parents, 'Send him to an engineering school.' When they asked why, they were told, 'Because he's good at math and science.' Again, too many hearing people were not hearing me."

At City College of New York, Hochman took courses in biology, chemistry, and physics, and received his B.S. in Biology in 1958. (He'd taken additional courses to qualify as a chemist.) At which point he wanted to enter medical school—a natural enough progression, but one that he was prevented from taking. Even though he'd been working nearly 40 hours a week as a lab technician at New York's Mount Sinai, Beth Israel, and the Veterans Administration hospitals while taking at least 20 credits each semester, no medical school would even grant him an interview. None wanted him. His advisors "laughed sadly and said that no medical school would take a deaf student. I made the mistake this time of listening (for the time being, anyway) to the advisors and did not apply to medical school, but instead went into medical research and working in and eventually directing clinical laboratories."

From 1966 to 1969, he was Chemist with Food and Drugs

Laboratory of the City of New York Department of Health, Supervisor of its Dairy Division, and Supervisor of its Narcotics Detection Unit. He almost didn't get this job. Despite finishing first on the written exam, the New York Department of Public Health rejected him because he was deaf. After threatening to initiate legal proceedings against the City of New York, he got the job.

He worked as Chief Technologist at St. Joseph's Hospital, research biochemist at Kingsbrook Chronic Disease Medical Center, and as Chief Medical Technologist at Trafalgar Hospital, all in New York; Brooklyn Jewish Geriatric Hospital; and Somerset Hospital in Somerville, New Jersey (1969-1972).

During the late 1960s, medical schools, responding to the pressure of social change, began admitting non-traditional applicants. Hochman noticed "all these 'undesirables'—women, blacks, people over 30, Hispanics"—getting into medical school. "In 1971 I decided to apply and took my MCATs (Medical College Admissions Tests) in which I did very well, despite having graduated from college 18 years before. I must have made some good impressions because I had no trouble getting several acceptances to medical schools. (It sounds egotistical, but there was no way they were going to say no. My MCAT scores were in the high 90s.)"

In 1972, Hochman, age 37, entered Rutgers Medical School/College of Medicine and Dentistry in Piscataway, New Jersey. "I was the oldest medical student in America—more of a curiosity piece than a celebrity.

"Still, I would not begin to imply that medical schools, hospitals, and physicians in general were all open to the idea of Deaf physicians and medical students. Quite a few of them needed some degree of 're-education.' I never cease to be amazed, even today, at my colleagues who refer to their 'deaf and dumb' or 'deaf-mute' patients. Oralism, too, is usually the only method of deaf education that most doctors know of. Too many are not aware of the role of sign language in the education of the deaf. This is important because 90% of deaf children have hearing parents and these parents listen to their often poorly informed physicians."

At medical school, he became more assertive—and fought ignorance with humor. "After many months of my fellow students and my instructors forgetting my deafness and not facing me when talking, I finally had a card printed up." It looked like a deaf peddler's card with a manual-alphabet chart, but instead of the usual pity-grabbing text (*I am a deaf-mute. I am selling this card for a living. Pay whatever you wish. Thank you*), read: *Dear Doctor: I am a deaf medical student who is anxious to learn from you—so if you continue to speak softly and do not look in my direction so that I may lipread you— I may end up selling these cards for a living. Thank you.* Anyone caught by me talking and not facing me was awarded one of these. Almost none of the students or physicians 'got it'!!! Some of those who had the experience of receiving a deaf-panhandler card got the point."

He completed his M.M.S. coursework in 1974 and his M.D. in 1976. After graduating, he served a 3-year residency in Family Practice at San Francisco General Hospital/UC-SF; and San Jose Hospital & Health Center/Stanford Medical School.

As Lori Eickmann of **San Jose Mercury News** put it: "With his doctorate in medicine firmly in place behind his name, he settled in the East Bay to serve the large deaf community attracted by the California School for the Deaf in Fremont." In addition to his own private practice, he was physician for CSDF from 1979 to 1992. (He also chaired the Department of Family Medicine in Fremont's Washington Hospital in 1990.) Most of his patients are hearing; about 10% are Deaf. They feel comfortable with him, and his deafness is even a plus—he pays particular attention to what they're saying, and has rare empathy. He communicates by signing and speechreading, and uses light-flashers and a vibrating beeper to notify him of incoming TTY calls. He's able to hear limited frequencies with a powerful hearing aid and a specially amplified stethoscope hooked up to an oscilloscope to display heartbeats. "I probably make fewer mistakes than a hearing person. A doctor with normal hearing assumes he hears something. I assume I don't. I'm much more careful."

Dr. Hochman and his second wife, Ann Dexheimer, who's progressively deafened and has taught at Ohlone College and MSD-Frederick (now at CSD), have two children, Noah and Lauren, both hearing. (He also has two, Adam and Marc, from his first marriage, to Sheila Elsbach.)

A popular speaker, he's presented numerous lectures and workshops on deaf-related medical issues (e.g., carpal-tunnel syndrome) and his own experiences to various groups around the nation. In April 1986, he received NTID's Edmund Lyon Memorial Lectureship Award. He's visited Gallaudet "many times" to encourage students to enter the medical profession. He tells audiences that while the barriers of attitude are still formidable, deaf students can succeed—with hard work, good grades, determination, and a measure of luck. "You don't get anything by not trying," he says. "Beware of the 'Can't Cant's.' These are experts in deafness who will always tell you things that you 'can't' do. Pay no attention to them. They 'can't' help it.

"I [have long] believed and still believe that most educational programs for the Deaf do not give or demand what is and will be needed of Deaf children to succeed in life. We still have far too much paternalism in dealing the Deaf. That means with children and adults alike. Too many of my Deaf adult patients have little or no conception of health care, medications, lab and X-ray tests, etc.

"Since I am the first graduate of a Deaf school to become a physician, I have always felt a strong obligation to aid and assist other Deaf who want to enter Medicine to do so. I have been able to help quite a few Deaf students enter medical school. We have also had Deaf (as well as hearing) medical students and residents do some of their training in my office; I demonstrate the coping strategies I use. I have also assisted several medical schools in enabling them to accommodate their Deaf medical students. Physicians (including those who are losing or have lost their hearing later in life) and medical students from all over the world correspond with me for advice and suggestions to help in coping with deafness. I have started an organization for this purpose, the Society of Hearing Impaired Physicians (SHIP). This takes up much of my 'extra time.' Helping all these people attain and retain their goals as physicians despite deafness has been very gratifying. In the words of Theodore Herzl: 'If you will it, it is no dream.'"

Jack R. Gannon in front of the Tower Clock of Chapel Hall, holding a copy of **Deaf Heritage**. (Courtesy of Gallaudet University Photography Department)

CHAPTER 45

Jack R. Gannon

1936-

Author and historian of the Deaf Community

Jack Randle Gannon was born on November 23, 1936, in West Plains, Missouri. "That little town is in the heart of the Ozark Mountains in southern Missouri, very close to the Arkansas border. I have always been very proud of my 'hillbilly' heritage.

"I was deafened [at age 8, by spinal meningitis] during World War II, when my family was residing in Richmond, California. My parents were working at the shipyards in that area, doing their share to aid America's war efforts. I attended some day schools and finally gained admittance to California School for the Deaf in Berkeley. (There was a waiting list at that time.) I was there about a year. When the war ended, and the shipyards starting laying off people, my family returned to Missouri. The following fall, 1946, I enrolled at Missouri School for the Deaf in Fulton.

"I did not relish the idea of leaving home and going away to school. I was literally taken from a simple, quiet, rural life in the Ozark Mountains and thrust into a busy, modern world with huge brick buildings and indoor plumbing. As I grew older I came to love and appreciate the school, my teachers, my houseparents, and my schoolmates. Today I feel very grateful for what these people have done for me. My years at MSD were very rewarding. Those were years of exposure to some of the nation's finest deaf teachers, and that experience gave me the opportunity to establish my identity, to develop my interest in writing, to gain basic leadership skills, to discover a sense of belonging." He graduated in 1954.

"Two teachers at MSD, in particular, influenced my interest in writing. One was Grover C. Farquhar, a 1913 graduate of Gallaudet, who was my high-school literature teacher and editor of **The Missouri Record**. The other was G. Dewey Coats (Gallaudet '22), principal of the Vocational Department and a national leader. Both loved to write and that love 'rubbed off' on me.

"My transition to Gallaudet College changed my life. I had the good fortune to further develop my interest in writing under the tutelage of Edward L. Scouten, Alan B. Crammatte, and Robert F. Panara. I was involved in just about every publication then in existence on the campus and was editor-in-chief of **The Buff and Blue** and the 1959 **Tower Clock**. I was also placed in leadership situations where I had the opportunity to further develop my people skills.

"In addition to my love for writing, I have a strong background in printing. For a long time it was my goal to own my own weekly newspaper. I majored in Education and trained to be a teacher. My goal of going into the newspaper business got a little sidetracked after I became a teacher!" He did graduate work at Omaha University and Ball State University.

During his first year at Gallaudet, Jack met Rosalyn Lee of Winston-Salem, North Carolina. "We were classmates and started going together during the spring of our Prep year. Our courtship lasted through college and we were married 5 days after graduation (June 6, 1959). I feel very fortunate to have found that young lady! I still haven't gotten over the bonus I got when we traded marriage vows some 36 years ago." They have a son, Jeff, and a daughter, Christy.

From 1959 to 1968, Jack taught graphic arts and coached football and basketball at Nebraska School for the Deaf in Omaha. In 1967, he was honored as "Coach of the Year" by Omaha's WOW-TV after his 8-man football team completed an undefeated season, the first in NSD's history. "Football was my favorite sport, and I was very fortunate to conclude my coaching career on such a positive note with an undefeated season! Teaching was a wonderful experience and I enjoyed it immensely. It was fun and a challenge to work with young people and help shape their lives as my own life had been shaped by my deaf and hearing teachers." (Rosalyn taught art there, and was the girls' physical-education teacher and volleyball coach. Later, she taught sign language in Gallaudet's Pre-College Program.)

In 1968, the Gannons returned to Gallaudet, where Jack became the first full-time Executive Secretary of the Gallaudet College Alumni Association (1968-1989). "This was a newly-created position; I was hired to set up and run Gallaudet's first budgeted Alumni Office." He held this position, he notes proudly, "for nearly a quarter of a century. I also had the title of Director of Alumni Relations (1968-71); I was the alumni liaison on campus and represented the best interests of both the University and the alumni. I was responsible for working with all Gallaudet alumni, whether or not they were members of the GCAA. These two jobs were separate, yet they overlapped in many ways. Through the years, my job title changed as my work responsibilities increased." He was Director of Alumni and Public Relations (1971-84), then Executive Director of Alumni Relations and Advancement (1984-89). In 1989 he succeeded Mervin D. Garretson as Special Assistant to the President for Advocacy. ("And as I tell friends, I have been sloshing around in his B-I-G shoes ever since.") For 7 years, Gannon worked closely with Dr. I. King Jordan, helping him coordinate his overwhelming responsibilities. In February 1996, Gannon announced that he would retire in December.

He's been actively involved with the NAD, WFD, and other organizations. He was one of the founders of the Deaf History International organization, established in Frankfurt, Germany, in 1991. ("President John Hay of Scotland calls me the 'midwife' of DHI!") One of Gallaudet's leadership trainers in its joint Deaf Leadership Training Program with NAD, he participated three times as a trainer in the Swiss LTP between 1987 and 1992.

Gannon is perhaps best known as a historian and writer. He edited **The Gallaudet Almanac** (GCAA, 1974), a compendium of facts and information about the college, alumni rosters, memorials and buildings, the Hall of Fame, and sports lore. His monumental, acclaimed work, **Deaf Heritage, A Narrative History of Deaf**

America, was published in 1981, a joint project of the NAD and Gallaudet. It has been described as "the 'Roots' of the Deaf Community," the most comprehensive history of deaf people written to date. "I never actually 'set out to be a historian.' I consider myself first of all a writer. It just happened that I had the opportunity to write a history of Deaf America, and what an experience it was!

"I owe many people for their help and support. Dr. Mervin D. Garretson and Rosalyn, in particular, contributed more to the success of that book than anyone else. Rosalyn was responsible for the photographs and did the layout. Mervin was the best 'feedbacker' a writer could ever have! How did I feel when it was done? I felt like I had just given birth to an elephant!"

Richly illustrated with photographs, engravings, paintings, and cartoons, with chronological narrative, personal spotlights, anecdotes, and overviews of each decade, **Deaf Heritage** is an entertaining and enlightening omnibus of material on an overlooked American minority culture. It includes information on Deaf America's schools for the deaf, higher education, communication, sports, religion, the arts, law, politics, telecommunications, the Little Paper Family, mass media, and controversies. It also disproved a then-prevalent stereotype: that deaf people have never written/cannot write their own history. **Deaf Heritage** was the first major deaf-written Deaf history. It's still popular as a reference work and Deaf Studies textbook. A workbook followed in 1984. It was the brainchild of Felicia Mode Alexander, a teacher at a school for deaf children in Massachusetts.

"Today, as a result of the book's popularity, many people recognize me and I get those funny glances or stares or people nod at me in acknowledgement of who I am. Some walk right up to me and ask, 'Are you Jack Gannon?' It's a funny feeling, and I sometimes feel awkward about the attention, but of course, it's appreciated."

As for DPN advocacy, in 1981, Jack and Rosalyn compiled a list of 94 deaf professionals with earned doctorates—simple proof that "there were many academically qualified deaf persons 'out there' worthy of consideration for the president's position." During DPN week, Jack recorded the day-to-day and hour-to-hour developments. This became **The Week the World Heard Gallaudet**, a handsome photo-chronicle/keepsake of the DPN protest, published in 1989 by Gallaudet University Press. **Like Deaf Heritage**, it's been selling nicely. "I still get requests to give presentations, respond to questions, or to be interviewed because of my two books."

He was one of three co-authors of a history of the WFD, slated for publication in 1996. Another upcoming book is "a collection of stories about deafness and deaf people," tentatively titled **Daddy! Get Your Elbow Off the Horn!** "I definitely want to update the current **Deaf Heritage** as soon as I can. I am even thinking ahead to a second edition. My problem is and has been having so many projects in the fire and so little time. I have two or three other books in the wings. I just hope my health and mentality hold up until I finish them!"

"I have given lectures [on Deaf history and culture] in more places than I can remember. I have spoken throughout the U.S.A. and in Greece, the Philippines, Japan, France (twice), Switzerland, Germany, and maybe some other places. I have also given somewhere around 25 commencement addresses," including Gallaudet's 127th (1996). He has received numerous honors, including MSD's first Distinguished Alumni Award (1982), NAD's Distinguished Service Award (1984), and CEASD's Edward Allen Fay Award (1986). Gallaudet awarded him an Honorary Doctor of Humane Letters degree in 1988.

"To Rosalyn I owe all the credit for whatever I have achieved. I also owe much to Gallaudet for all the opportunities I have been given, and to my co-workers, colleagues, and friends for their assistance and support. I have been a very, very lucky guy to have received so much help and support.

"I derive a lot of satisfaction from working with people and seeing the results of things we accomplish together, and out of the 'little' things in life. Humor, a smile, a hug. I get satisfaction out of a wood carving, a letter written on behalf of a friend, lending someone a hand, planting a flower or a tree . . . a walk with my dog, a moment of solitude in the country, things like that."

Top: two portraits of Ernie Hairston. Bottom: A joyous moment—receiving his doctorate in May 1994. (Courtesy of Dr. Hairston)

CHAPTER 46

Ernie Hairston

1939-

Black Deaf advocate

Ernest E. Hairston, Jr., was born on March 1, 1939, in Stotesbury, West Virginia, a company-owned coal-mining town 75 miles south of Charleston. His mother, Dorothy, was a housewife; his father, Ernest, Sr., a coal miner. There was a younger brother and sister. He says, "I had a typical childhood until I became deaf at the age of 5 as a result of spinal meningitis—that is, if living with racial segregation is typical." As he later told Mary Johnstone of **Gallaudet Today**, "Generally, white people were not much better off than black people. They lived in better parts of town and had better schools, and were *perceived* as being better. I had no feelings of inferiority in my community. We had our own stores, churches, barber shops—whatever we needed." Segregation didn't exist in the mines, where Hairston's father "worked side-by-side with white workers to send coal to the surface."

Dorothy and Ernest Hairston wanted their children to get the best possible education—the only way out of the mines and Stotesbury. Young Ernie was "quick and eager to learn," but as he prepared to start first grade, he was stricken with spinal meningitis. "Under the constant care of his mother and the town doctor," he recovered, and when school opened, enrolled. After a couple of weeks, he ran into difficulty when homework was assigned. After discovering that Ernie was deaf, the doctor recommended that Dorothy send him to the West Virginia School for the Colored Deaf and Blind (WVSCDB), in Institute, near Charleston. Initially reluctant to send "a little tyke" so far away, she finally relented.

"The move was the greatest thing that ever happened to me," Hairston later said. WVSCDB was located near West Virginia State College, "historically a college for black students," which shared campus facilities and student teachers with the children. "Fortunately, the student teachers knew little or nothing about deafness, so they came without preconceived ideas about deaf students. They taught as they normally would." He became a "bookworm."

Because so very few went to college, let alone Gallaudet, most of the "colored" or "Negro" deaf schools "provided highly skilled vocational training to their students and assured that they were hired in their given profession upon graduation, whether with a diploma or certificate of completion." Likewise, at WVSCDB, the emphasis was on trades instead of college. Students were required to master two trades before graduation. Hairston chose tailoring and barbering.

However, in 1954, the Supreme Court ruled in *Brown vs. Topeka Board of Education* that segregation was unconstitutional. West Virginia's schools were among the first to comply with the Court's integration order. In 1955, students from WVSCDB were transferred to the West Virginia School for the Deaf and Blind (WVSDB) in Romney.

Having scored highest on WVSDB's placement tests, Hairston found himself in a one-year college-preparatory program. When his English teacher, Mac Norwood, asked Ernie what he planned to do after graduation, he replied, "Be a barber." Mac "almost hit the ceiling" and retorted, "A barber, *hell*! Go to Gallaudet!" Mac became Hairston's mentor. He "advised me to take up preparatory studies at Gallaudet, which would cover two more years of high-school education because 10th grade was as high as I could get at WVSDB."

After one year at Romney, Hairston graduated at the top of his class, one of three WVSDB students selected for Gallaudet, which had only begun to accept black students in 1951 (Andrew Foster, Class of '54, being the first). "I entered the Gallaudet Preparatory Program during Fall 1956. I excelled academically as well as in athletics, and was awarded the Athlete-Scholar Award for my achievements."

After starting as a freshman in Fall 1957, he joined the varsity football and wrestling teams. He played varsity football for two-and-a-half seasons until a knee injury permanently sidelined him. But he continued—and excelled—as a wrestler. He also loved the performing arts, participated in Drama Club productions, and, showing exceptional talent as a dancer, joined the Gallaudet Dance Troupe. He served two years as President of the Gallaudet Inter-faith Council, and held various offices in the Alpha Sigma Phi fraternity. Johnstone noted: "He also earned pocket money by putting his barbering skills to work among his classmates." He was popular, and a good student. During his senior year, he won the prestigious George Moredock Teegarden Award "in recognition of excellence in creative poetry." He graduated in 1961. At the WGD in Helsinki that summer, he won a bronze medal in freestyle wrestling.

He then began his teaching career. His first job was teaching reading and literature to high-school-age deaf students, and science to ninth-graders, at the Governor Morehead School for the Deaf in Raleigh, North Carolina. He was the first black deaf teacher in the school's history. "Many of the black deaf students there saw me as a role model and aspired to go to college or further their education, seeing how college helped me 'make it.'"

In 1964, he accepted a position with the Michigan Association for Better Hearing and Speech (MABHS) in Lansing, "as a teacher of low-verbal deaf adult males enrolled in the MABHS' federal project. When the federal project was terminated in 1966, the State took over and transferred the project to the State Technical Institute and Rehabilitation Center (STIRC). I became Head Teacher and Coordinator of that project. From January to August 1967, I attended the National Leadership Training Program at San Fernando Valley State College (now CSUN) and earned my Master's degree in Administration and Supervision.

"I returned to STIRC after the training. In June 1968, I was selected to become Project Director of the newly-established, federally-funded Diagnostic, Evaluation, and Adjustment Facility

(D.E.A.F.) at the Goodwill Industries of Central Ohio Rehabilita-tion Center in Columbus. Prior to termination of the 3-year project, I helped facilitate the transfer of the project to the Columbus Hearing and Speech Center so that service to multi-disabled deaf adults could continue." During his last two years in Columbus, he also edited the Ohio Association of the Deaf's official newsletter, **Buckeye State Bulletin**.

Mac Norwood, Branch Chief of Media Services and Captioned Films for the Deaf, had followed his old student's progress, and encouraged Hairston to fill a vacancy in his department. "In May 1971, I was offered and accepted a position with the U.S. Office of Education's Bureau of Education for the Handicapped (now Office of Special Education Programs [OSEP])—as Education Program Specialist. I became Acting Branch Chief of the Captioning and Adaptation Branch in January 1988, when Dr. Norwood retired. In August 1989, I officially became the Branch Chief. As Chief of the Captioning and Adaptation Branch, I plan, direct, and implement Part F of the Individuals with Disabilities Education Act (IDEA), which includes developing policies and strategies for providing media-technology and captioning services to persons who are deaf or hard-of-hearing, as well as video-described and audio-recorded services to persons who are visually or print-disabled. These services include closed-captioned television programming and research in media technology. The National Theatre of the Deaf's Professional Theatre School and performance preparation is funded through this Branch, as are several regional and local cultural projects." 1996 marked Hairston's 25th year with the U.S. Depart-ment of Education.

He has written numerous articles and reports—for example, "Instructional Media for Mentally Retarded Deaf Children" (1972); "Digital Technologies: Impacting on Communication Needs for Persons with Developmental Disabilities" (1991); and "The Fu-ture: Hidden Captions, Videodiscs, Microcomputer, and Telecom-munications." He and Mac Norwood co-authored "Career Educa-tion for the Deaf in the '70's," in **American Annals of the Deaf**. He and Linwood Smith co-authored "Ethnic Minorities Amongst the

Deaf Population" (**Deafness Annual**, 1976); and **Black and Deaf in America: Are We That Different?** (T.J. Publishers, 1983), which won a 1985 Book Award from the President's Committee on Employment of the Handicapped.

He's a member of National Black Deaf Advocates (NBDA), NAD, TDI, GUAA, and Kappa Delta Pi Honorary Society (Pi Rho Chapter), Mabuhay, Inc. (a Filipino-American association), and D.C. Area Black Deaf Advocates. He chaired NBDA's 1985 Annual National Conference, and received its Award of Appreciation.

A karate enthusiast, he took First Place Trophy in Senior Men's Sparring Contest at the TKA 1975 Karate Tournament. He won the Director's Award of Recognition for his role as lead actor in the 1974 production of *Ceremonies in Dark Old Men* at Hughes Memorial Theatre in Washington.

Since 1989, he's worked as Sign Master for several sign-interpreted plays at Washington's Arena Stage and Kennedy Center, the Living Stage, and the University of Maryland.

He and his wife, Mencie Yaguil-Hairston, have four daughters: Darlene, Mayumi, Malaya, and Tala. They live in Bowie, Maryland.

"Without taking time off from work or family, I enrolled in Gallaudet University's doctoral program and earned a Ph.D. in Special Education Administration in May, 1994."

In 1995, Hairston returned to WVSDB to give the keynote address at its Fall Conference celebrating its 125th anniversary. He said: "Each student's educational experience is vital because education is an empowerment tool. It enables one to move ahead in his/her career or to obtain additional education. To paraphrase Jesse Jackson, education is something that cannot be taken away or robbed from you. Education is power. Unlike money, a car, a house, privileges, and other tangibles that can be earned, and can also be taken, education—once obtained—is securely yours. This concept should be instilled in students, along with the importance of making learning a life-long process. A way of keeping ahead."

Bonnie Poitras Tucker: "I want to be seen not as a deaf person but as a person, one who happens to be deaf." (Courtesy of Prof. Tucker)

CHAPTER 47

Bonnie Poitras Tucker

1939-

Attorney and Professor of Law

After they realized that their 2-year-old daughter Bonnie, their firstborn, was profoundly deaf, Thelma and Jim Poitras didn't call her "deaf;" they told everyone she was "just a little hard-of-hearing." That way, she'd be treated like everyone else.

Bonnie Poitras Tucker was born in Springfield, Massachusetts, on August 4, 1939, and had two younger brothers, Jim and Richard. (Richard began losing his hearing when he was 13; her father was late-deafened.)

After Jim Poitras was drafted during World War II, Thelma moved the children to New York, worked, and struggled, financially and emotionally. Bonnie had speech training at New York League for the Hard of Hearing, and tried to keep up with the neighborhood kids' games by "faking it." "Lipreading came easy to me, and I was a natural mimic." She received her first formal schooling at St. Matthew's Lutheran School, in classes set up in the back of an abandoned grocery store. "I hated school, both for its cruelty and its boredom." After Jim returned, the family moved to suburbia—Levittown.

"As early as the age of four I loved books and spent as much time with them as possible. I lived for the hours I could spend in my room with my books. . . . Books are my one true love. Certainly they have been the most influential force—the centrifugal force—of my life." Spending most of her childhood alone, Bonnie "read everything—biographies, autobiographies, historical novels, the classics." Although she could speechread, she missed out on much of the classroom lecture and discussion, and became a "voracious reader" to compensate for what she missed and keep pace with her classmates. She managed to get good grades.

As the only deaf student in high school, Bonnie endured the cruelty of classmates and teachers. One good teacher encouraged her to sign up for her Public Speaking class; she did well. She edited the yearbook "and even became a junior-varsity cheerleader."

She planned to major in journalism. Despite excellent grades, she was snubbed by the Cornell interviewer because she was deaf, so she chose Syracuse University instead. But Syracuse wouldn't let her major in Journalism, only Home Economics. She arranged to have a dual major, got VR assistance for tuition, adjusted to the "tyranny" of campus life, and pledged in Chi Omega sorority, faking it—until she was assigned to handle the sorority-house switchboard. She experienced raw discrimination. Frustrated with the lively class discussions that excluded her, she even took a secret bus trip to Gallaudet College, but saw that she wouldn't be happy there. "I concluded that while I may not fit perfectly in the hearing world, I didn't *want* to live in a small Deaf world. I couldn't live in an isolated enclave. I simply couldn't."

On a blind date, Bonnie met Ken Tucker—a student at Hamilton, a small, prestigious men's college. He "was considered an excellent catch." They eloped to Raleigh, North Carolina, and were married by a justice of the peace in 1960. They kept their marriage a secret—until she learned that she was pregnant. She was transferred to SU's Utica campus for her final semester while Ken finished at Hamilton.

She received a B.S. in Journalism from SU in 1961. Her original goal was "to go to New York and work on a magazine. But instead I got married, and then I had children right away, and it was just decided that I would stay home to be with the family and not go to work." They had three children: Kevin, Ronale, and Scott. Bonnie worked a bit, but was essentially a "homebody."

Just after Ken finished law school in 1966, they moved to Phoenix, Arizona. "Ken quickly became a shrewd and well-respected trial attorney," and the family prospered. But Ken grew more impatient and antagonistic towards Bonnie's deafness. Finally, after 17 years of marriage, he told her he wanted a divorce—because she was deaf. "I had to face not only a divorce, but the idea that my deafness was at the root of the divorce. I acknowledged my deafness when I got my divorce. [Before that] I wouldn't admit it." The divorce trial "was a farce." The judge's attitude was outrageous. He gave her a meager settlement to motivate her to remarry. This after Ken had divorced her *because* she was deaf! The bitter experience of injustice propelled her towards a law career.

At 37, Tucker was a "displaced housewife." She had never held a job or hired an interpreter, and couldn't use the telephone. After putting in a rewarding but ill-paid year as a respiratory therapist working with quadriplegics, she entered Arizona State University College of Law in August 1977. Warned that it would be impossible and that no one would hire a deaf lawyer, she was all the more determined to succeed.

First-year law school is a grueling experience for any student. Tucker attended classes solely for the purpose of receiving a "check" in the attendance book. Lipreading the ordinary classroom process—rapid-fire Socratic debates—was impossible. Exempted from being called on, she sat at the back of the room, often brought a book to class, and never understood a word of what was discussed. But the exam was based solely on class discussions. She obtained state VR assistance and hired three third-year law students, one per class, to take notes. It was "a workable, successful solution." To fill in the gaps, she "spent several hours a day reading legal treatises, hornbooks, law-review articles, and additional legal cases to better understand the concepts being explored," taking extensive notes. Having survived the terrifying ordeal of first-semester exams, she found, to her astonishment, that she'd gotten top grades—"first, second, or third in each course," all As. She earned a coveted spot on ASU's **Law Review**.

After a year at ASU, she transferred to University of Colorado Law School in Boulder. She attended only one class—on water law—and her classmates shared their notes with her. Some of the faculty were surprisingly helpful. She served as editor-in-chief of

CU's **Law Journal** and won the Folsom Award for the best oral performance in practice court.

Between her second and third years of law school, she clerked for a Denver law firm as a "summer associate." Her secretary functioned as an oral telephone interpreter; a friend rigged up a dual-receiver phone for them. There were many "minor hassles." But "overall, I found the summer quite productive. I learned a little bit about what the real practice of law is all about, and I learned that despite the aggravations I still wanted to be a lawyer." She graduated from CU in 1980 with a Juris Doctor degree, ranking 10th in a class of 159 (top 5%). She was awarded Order of the Coif—the law-school equivalent of a coveted Phi Beta Kappa key. She passed the Colorado, and later the Arizona and California, bar exams, and was admitted to the bar of the U.S. Supreme Court.

The first year after graduation, she "was offered the honor of clerking for the Honorable William E. Doyle, a judge on the U.S. Court of Appeals, Tenth Circuit, in Denver. During the year of my clerkship (1980-81) the Tenth Circuit decided a number of significant cases. I probably learned more about the law and our legal system during that year than I had learned in all of law school."

In Fall 1981, she returned to Phoenix and joined the law firm of Brown & Bain, P.A., as a litigation attorney, earning full-partner status in 1986. "I quickly became known around the firm as a lawyer who would get the job done well, and in a timely fashion."

Her ambition was to be an appellate-court judge. "Analyzing and writing about the law are my strengths, and that's what appellate judges do." But "the world of politics as I experienced it was so reprehensible that I reassessed my career goals."

In 1987, she took leave indefinite leave of absence from Brown & Bain to accept an associate professorship at ASU College of Law, teaching Disability Law, Criminal Law, Trusts and Estates, and Judicial Remedies. After 4 years of teaching, she became a tenured full professor. Her students consider her an effective teacher "who works hard and is always well-prepared." Said one: "If she didn't know how to answer a question, she'd be honest and get back to us the next day. She made us think and reach for answers. That's why students who like to be spoon-fed don't like her as a lecturer."

Tucker returned to teach law at CU during Summer 1990. In Spring 1993, Cornell—whose representative had rejected her in 1957 because she was deaf—invited her to teach disability law and criminal law as a visiting professor. She did likewise at San Diego College of Law, and at Monash College of Law in Melbourne, Australia—"a great adventure." She assists with disability-rights court cases on a *pro bono* basis.

From 1985 to 1989, she chaired the Arizona Council on the Hearing Impaired, and currently serves on the Advisory Council of the National Institute on Deafness and Communicative Disorders. Active on the boards of directors for AGBAD, Arizona School for the Deaf and Blind (1981-85), and Clarke School, she served 4 years on NTID's National Advisory Group (1981-85), and was the first deaf member of RIT's Board of Trustees (1988-90).

She has authored several legal books and treatises, and several dozen prominent law-review articles. These include the 2-volume **Legal Rights of Persons with Disabilities: An Analysis of Federal Law** (LRP, 1990), which she supplements twice yearly; and **Federal Disability Law in a Nutshell** (West, 1994). Her autobiography, **The Feel of Silence**, was published by Temple University Press in September 1995. She writes with wit, wry humor, perception, and unsparing honesty about being deaf, growing up "bluffing," and the anger and frustration she has experienced all her life.

In her free time, she skis, plays tennis, and goes and rafting and hiking with friends, children, grandchildren, and parents.

As she wrote in **Arizona Bar Briefs**: "As a deaf person, it is my responsibility to adapt to the hearing world; it is not the responsibility of hearing people to adapt to a deaf world. The world, or 99 percent of it, is hearing. Deaf people need to learn to talk and lipread so that they can communicate with people who do not know sign language. Although I may have to work twice as hard as a hearing person to attain the same goals, the only other option—to live totally within a deaf world—is simply not acceptable to me." She says: "I want to be seen not as a deaf person but as a person, one who happens to be deaf."

Judy Viera Tingley at Ultratec: "I have what seems to be the most interesting job in the world." (Courtesy of Teletec International Ltd.)

CHAPTER 48

Judith Viera Tingley

1939-

International businesswoman

Judith Alice Tingley was born in Oakland, California, on October 30, 1939. "My parents were also born in Oakland and I went to the same high school they went to. In fact, my father and I had the same math teacher and my mother's gym teacher was my counselor. My daughter, Jerilyn, was also born in Oakland, and she and I attended the same elementary school. I have two sisters: Jeanne, who now lives in Australia, and Kathy who still lives in . . . Oakland!

"Our father was a construction superintendent and our mother was a homemaker. My father built each house my family lived in and I think it was from him that I acquired a penchant for building things, whether they be programs or businesses.

"We were one of the first families to build a home in the hills of Oakland, which were at that time covered with Monterey pines. Their pine needles covered the hills and we had great fun sliding down the hills in cardboard boxes.

"Both of my parents have always been active in their church (Presbyterian) and community, and all three of their daughters have been outspoken on issues such as civil rights, equal opportunities, and social justice. (Jerilyn is a Presbyterian minister and shares that family trait.)

"While growing up I enjoyed playing the piano and still play it today. Our family often went camping and I still enjoy that today, too. In high school, my favorite class was Journalism and I was on the staff of the school paper. My career goal was not very clearly defined but it was in the direction of being a newspaper reporter.

"On Christmas Eve during my senior year of high school, I was hospitalized with a diagnosis of pneumococcus meningitis. I was in a coma for almost a week. When I came out of it, I was totally deaf, cross-eyed, and half of my face was paralyzed. My balance was also affected. Communication then was mostly reduced to handwritten notes. I still have the one that says 'Do you want the bedpan?' Half my hair was shaved off for surgery so by the time I was able to go home from the hospital I was quite a sight! In time, the facial paralysis went away, and a patch worn alternately on each eye gradually helped them straighten out.

"What I think is interesting is that during these first six months of being deaf, my family and I felt the need for something more than handwritten notes (lipreading still being very precarious, tear-filled, and frustrating). On our own, we 'invented' a manual alphabet, not knowing that one even existed!

"Something else that was interesting about this period was that my goal to graduate with my class was very strong and it gave me an intense focus that probably precluded my thinking very much about the permanence of my deafness.

"By a strange twist of fate, on the same night when that objective—graduation—was achieved, it was immediately replaced by another! I had been invited to a graduation party given by family friends. Their daughter attended the other high school where my tutor taught a class for deaf students and they arranged a blind date for me with a deaf fellow from that class, Richard Roman. He was fluent in sign language and he introduced me that summer to a large and active group of young deaf people that included students from Gallaudet who were home for the summer.

"My social life immediately began to revolve around this group, as my hearing friends from high school were gradually disappearing and going away to college. I wanted desperately to be accepted by these deaf people. I dove completely into the deaf community, was happily 'adopted' by a deaf family in Berkeley, Alice Amann and her three children, Frank, Astrid, and Paula, became fluent in sign language, and married a deaf man.

"I went to Gallaudet myself, graduating with a B.A. in English in

1965, and to San Francisco State for a M.A. in Education of Exceptional Children and my teaching credentials [1966]. At Gallaudet I was active on the staff of the **Buff and Blue** and **The Tower Clock** (remember my interest in journalism?)."

After Judy received her Master's, she worked as Instructor at New Mexico School for the Deaf (1966-69), then as Instructor and Personal and Social Development Specialist at NTID from 1969 to 1973, during its early years. She was a teacher at Del Campo High School in Sacramento (1973-75), Coordinator of Interpreter Training and Support Services for Deaf Students at American River College in Sacramento (1975-78), and, from 1978 to 1985, Program Manager of California's Services for Deaf Persons.

During 1985-86, she was a Fellow of the Gallaudet Institute. Established when Jerry Lee was president of Gallaudet College, "its intent was to widen the pool of potential candidates for President. It lasted only a few years but I joined Bill Marshall as the first two Fellows. The Institute allowed me to design a one-year program for myself and provided me with full interpreting support. I arranged for training from Wharton School [University of Pennsylvania], and from the American Management Association, and developed two internships with companies doing business in a regulated environment, Symbion Inc., in Salt Lake City, and Pacific Telesis in San Francisco.

"The Institute matched my salary in California for one year and provided housing on-campus. I took a one-year leave of absence from my position with the State so it was a wonderful risk-free opportunity—and I wish it were still available for others."

And so Judy made a career switch from education and community services to business. "Basically, I could see that deaf people in professional positions were very vulnerable because most were in tax-supported public-service environments such as education, rehabilitation, and community-service agencies. Also, I'd gone as far as I wanted to go in the civil service and felt that my advocacy skills were not that different from marketing in the private sector. Much of my advocacy work had been in regulated environments such as telecommunications, health care, etc., so it was logical and easy to transfer to the other side of the table.

"After completing the Gallaudet Institute experience, I returned briefly to my position with the State of California. Soon after, I joined Weitbrecht Communications as General Manager [1986-88], then moved over to Teletec International, Ltd., as President." Since 1988, she's been President of Teletec, a U.S. company with offices in the U.S. and Great Britain that handles international sales and marketing of Ultratec products (including, but not limited to, TTYs). "I focus on developing new markets and new products, both of which allow the company to grow and engage me in considerable travel abroad. Although I established the business in Great Britain and lived there full-time for 4 years, the resident staff there now is appropriately all British. This gives me more time to focus on other countries.

"Living in England was fascinating, albeit not without its challenges. I did a survey of American-owned companies in our city and found that most expatriates living there had fixed 2-year assignments, at the end of which they would be furloughed home. In addition, most companies sent two people from the U.S. to work in the United Kingdom together. Not only did I go over alone, I stayed 4 years, and also had to deal with a different set of attitudes towards women in executive positions and towards people who are deaf or disabled.

"I'd already traveled widely and knew pretty much what to expect. Like Europe in general, the U.K. is not as well-developed as the U.S. in terms of its attitudes and opportunities for people who are deaf and disabled. There is no equivalent to Gallaudet, NTID, or CSUN, for example. The most distressing aspect in Europe is the huge problem of underemployment and unemployment of deaf people. Leadership in the deaf community in Europe is achieved in spite of formidable odds that only older Americans could relate to, and I have tremendous respect for those who have managed to make a difference!

"I have what seems to be the most interesting job in the world, working with one of the finest companies, Ultratec. I would like to live and work in one more country before I retire. The insight it gives me professionally is extremely valuable."

Judy has presented and published several papers on telecommunications, particularly relay services. She edited **Deaf People in California: Demographics and Communication Needs** (California State Department of Rehabilitation, 1983), gave the keynote presentation, "Starving in the Pantry," at *Life and Work in the 21st Century*, an employment forum sponsored by the NAD in 1986, presented "TDD Relay Systems" at the National Conference on Deaf and Hard of Hearing People in El Paso in 1988, and "Relay Services: Getting Started," at The DEAF WAY, July 1989. She and psychologist Greg Kimberlin co-presented an interactive workshop, "Using VCO with Relay Service," at ALDAcon 1991.

She's also made presentations on telecommunications access and deaf/hard-of-hearing issues at numerous international conferences—Montreux, Switzerland; Madrid and Bilbao, Spain; Vienna and Graz, Austria.

She was the Founder and first Chairman of the Board, NorCal Center on Deafness, Sacramento (1976-78), a member of NTID's National Advisory Group (1981-84); and currently serves as Commissioner, Deafened Adults Concerns, International Federation of Hard of Hearing Persons (IFHOH). She also served on ALDA's Board (1993-95). She's a member of the NAD and ALDA and their English counterparts, British Deaf Association and National Association of Deafened Persons.

"My communication modes? Whatever works! I prefer sign language to lipreading. I use sign-language interpreters for all business discussions in Europe. I usually speak for myself unless the person I am meeting with has very limited English and therefore may have difficulty understanding me.

"As for a more personal side, I've appreciated the opportunity to put down roots in a new city. The quality of life in Madison, Wisconsin is excellent and I love the four seasons. I'm actively participating in a number of social events and volunteering at a hospice to work with families that include a deaf person.

"It is possible to live precariously but perfectly poised as a bicultural/bilingual happy individual!"

Henry Kisor in and out of his "Spam Can," the *Gin Fizz*.
(Top: Courtesy of Henry Kisor; bottom: courtesy of Bill Kight.)

CHAPTER 49

Henry Kisor

1940-

Journalist

Henry Kisor chose journalism by a sort of lucky accident. Or was it destiny?

He was born on August 17, 1940, to Judith (Merrell) Du Bois and Manown Kisor, in Midland Park, New Jersey. He had an older brother, Manown Jr. ("Buck"), and a younger sister, Debbie. In January 1944, while Manown was stationed at Fort Lauderdale Naval Air Station, a double whammy of meningitis and encephalitis left Hank, just short of 3-1/2, completely deaf. It also affected his sense of balance, and he stopped talking—even though he'd been "extremely precocious."

But he was blessed with stubborn, supportive parents. Judith visited AGBAD and, from an ad in the **Volta Review**, discovered a maverick private tutor of the deaf, Doris Irene Mirrielees of Montgomery, Alabama. She was eccentric, "considered a quack." Her philosophy was revolutionary. In opposition to the prevailing conventional wisdom, she trained mothers to teach their deaf children to read and write as early as possible. Although a committed oralist (true to her times, she "disapproved highly" of sign language), she didn't emphasize immediate acquisition of speech skills—literacy came first. On the Mirrielees course, Hank learned to read, rediscovered speech, and developed a knack for lipreading and an abiding love of books and language. He remembers Miss Mirrielees with fondness and gratitude: "a miracle worker."

His early start in literacy enabled him to enter public schools. Growing up in the Eisenhower era in small-town Ho-Ho-Kus,

New Jersey, Henry was "just another kid on the block." He took speech lessons to refine his "breathy monotone and foggy articulation" (he still goes in for periodic tune-ups) and acquired a hearing aid, a crude, clumsy "black brick of Bakelite" in a "brown canvas harness," which he wore for two years (to no effect).

When he was 8, the Kisors moved to Evanston, a large northern suburb of Chicago. The schools officials agreed to classify Henry as "hard-of-hearing" so he could attend the same junior-high school as his neighbors. He loved reading the **Chicago Daily News'** front-page stories and "Can This Marriage Be Saved?" in **The Ladies' Home Journal**. He made friends (including lifelong ones) and took speech lessons at the Institute for Language Disorders at nearby Northwestern University. When he was 11, he even took trumpet lessons—briefly. He joined the Evanston YMCA and became a skilled swimmer.

When he was 16, he had his first encounter with raw discrimination. He'd earned Red Cross lifesaving and water-safety certificates at the Y. Promised a lifeguard's job at Sunset Ridge Country Club's pool that summer, he was summarily rejected by the club's board of directors because he was deaf. At Camp Echo, however, he became a counselor and ran the water-skiing program.

Gradually, he became more shy, less sociable. (He still hates crowds.) He earned "respectable grades," though. English was his best subject; physics and algebra his worst. During his sophomore year, he accepted a teacher's invitation to join her journalism class. "It was the best decision I had made in my young life." He joined the school paper: "As a rewrite editor I found I had a definite knack for the shape of a story, for reducing it to its 'who-what-where-when-why-how' components and reassembling these facts in the most efficient and pleasing manner." He became managing editor, and began devouring literature—starting with Steinbeck. He graduated "a respectable 90th in a class of 591 students."

He attended Trinity College in Hartford, a "small, distinguished 'little Ivy' men's college" (where Buck had also attended, and excelled), and graduated with honors in 1962. Because of his difficulty speechreading French, the dean of the language department designed a new course for him: reading and writing about French literature. Calculus was an agony. He fared well in English-literature and European-history courses because they depended heavily on reading and writing. (English became his major; history a "strong minor.")

Most Trinity graduates went into "banking or insurance." Kisor had no idea of just what *he* wanted to do. Medill School of Journalism at Northwestern University in Evanston offered him an assistantship that he initially declined because he figured he "wasn't cut out for journalism." Urged on by a family friend, he reapplied. Medill reinstated his application. He was in.

At Medill, Kisor learned how to "assemble the facts of a story with precise and colorful thews and sinews," and to operate the cumbersome press cameras. He learned that a copyreader—journalism's "unsung hero"—was "a news story's last best hope before it is converted into type." It was an unglamorous but intellectually demanding job. Copyreaders worked mostly alone and rarely used the telephone. "I was hooked on journalism. Finally I had discovered what I was fit to do."

For several months, he worked for **One-Design Yachtsman: The Magazine of Sailboat Racing** as a temporary editorial assistant, then did layout, proofing, copyediting, writing headlines, and "most of the editorial and production work." He was even dispatched to cover regattas. But he preferred editing. Back at Medill, he earned "straight A's," and gained new confidence and poise. He received his M.S. in Journalism in 1964.

Of "half a dozen" offers, he chose the **Evening Journal** of Wilmington, Delaware. He spent 10 months there as copy editor, and wrote his first book reviews for the **Evening Journal's** sister paper, the **Morning News**. He even tried reviewing subtitled foreign films, but gave up after "bluffing" a review of a Sophia Loren film that wasn't subtitled but dubbed.

Missing Chicago and his old friends, he obtained a position at the copy desk of the Chicago **Daily News**, noted for its good writing and reportage. (Like other "big-city evening newspapers," though, it was "on its last legs.") He worked the graveyard shift, midnight to 8 a.m., later the day shift. He also worked on front-page, national, and foreign news—"fascinating, exacting work."

Previously, Kisor had had to ask his mother and Debbie to make telephone calls, even for dates. In Summer 1966, his "old chum" Sam Williamson rigged up his first (primitive) assistive gadgets. And on a blind date, he met Deborah Lee Abbott, a teacher and children's-book columnist. "On June 24, 1967, we were married, and we have been together ever since." They settled in Evanston and had two sons, Colin and Conan.

Meanwhile, Kisor gained experience in features ("soft news"), and began to contribute book reviews to **Panorama**, the **Daily News'** excellent weekend arts-and-entertainment supplement, then wrote a weekly column on paperbacks while working as **Panorama's** production editor. In March 1973, he became book editor of the **Daily News**, "writing weekly reviews and occasional long profiles of authors." Debby Abbott made the needed phone calls to solicit book reviews.

Kisor was a "slow writer," a perfectionist, laboriously retyping and correcting his way through an article. When the **Daily News** and **Sun-Times** switched to computerized phototypesetting in 1977, replacing typewriters with word processors and video-display monitors, it revolutionized his professional life. He became "a genuine literary critic as well as a book-review editor." Interviewing authors was still troublesome. He read up beforehand. Because he had to remain focused on the author's face, he couldn't take notes; he relied on a compact cassette-tape recorder. "Getting a tape transcribed was a chore." Debby willingly began producing detailed verbatim transcripts and sometimes accompanied him on interviews, where she "took copious notes."

In 1978, the ailing **Daily News** folded, and Kisor became book editor of the **Sun-Times**. He now had a "competent editorial assistant" to make phone calls and transcriptions.

For 5 years (1977 to 1982) he moonlighted as an adjunct instructor at Medill, teaching Basic Writing. By this time, he had received "a clutch of plaques and awards from newspaper and literary groups," a **Who's Who** citation, and was named a Pulitzer Prize finalist.

"The honor that meant the most to me, however, was an informal poll by the Northwestern University student newspaper that named me one of the most popular teachers on campus."

In 1982, he bought his first personal computer, an Osborne 1. "Like so many other writers who discovered the personal computer at that time, I fell head over heels in love with the technology and even became messianic about it." He began a syndicated column on the subject. After the novelty wore off, he did occasional installments of "Computing for Writers." For him, the TTY, computer, modem, and fax are "instruments of liberation."

Kisor's first book, **What's That Pig Outdoors? A Memoir of Deafness**, was published in 1990, and was, as he says, "a hit with critics." He recounts his adventures and misadventures with wit, honesty, wry humor, and style; his book is also an essay on communication, relationships, families, pride, love, work, and being human.

Zephyr: Tracking a Dream Across America, Kisor's fascinating look at the world of a cross-country Amtrak route and the people who work and travel it, was published in 1994. He and Debby collaborated on a children's book, **One TV Blasting and a Pig Outdoors** (1994). Told from Conan's viewpoint, it's an entertaining introduction to an unusual subject: what it's like to be hearing and have a deaf parent.

Realizing an old childhood dream, and eager to gather adventures for a new book (**Flight of the Gin Fizz**), he learned to fly, and joined the fledgling International Deaf Pilots Association. (He edits the quarterly **IDPA Newsletter**.) In 1993, he bought a 1959 Cessna 150 (a stout, reconditioned all-metal single-engine airplane known as a "Spam Can"), which he named the *Gin Fizz* in humorous tribute to the *Vin Fiz*. From early July through mid-October 1995, he retraced Cal Rodgers' pioneering cross-country flight, landing as close as possible to each of the 74 original landing sites of the *Vin Fiz*.

He says: "I don't think my deafness has made much difference in my work as a newspaperman, but it has of course given me a good deal to write about as an author."

Glenn B. Anderson and Shirley J. Allen.
(Michael J. Spencer/NTID; courtesy of Dr. Allen)

CHAPTER 50

Shirley J. Allen 1941-
Glenn B. Anderson 1945-

First deaf African-American Ph.D.s

Shirley Jeanne Allen was born on December 19, 1941, in Tyler Texas, and grew up in Nacogdoches, a small town in East Texas (and the oldest one in the state). "I attended all-Black schools." She was valedictorian of her class at E. J. Campbell High School (1959).

At first, she pursued a musical career—"Music was always my first love." In 1962, she was a gifted 20-year-old junior at Jarvis Christian College majoring in Music Education (emphasis on piano). After developing "some kind of fever," she was given medication, then lapsed into a coma for several weeks. After regaining consciousness, she found that she was deaf.

At first she hoped that her hearing might return, finally realizing that it wouldn't. "I did not know, until years later, that I was devastated, at some point. By that time, I suppose it was too late to be openly pitiful (sometimes I'm a bit slow!). My support system was my family, especially my grandmother [Cashie Allen], the strongest Black woman in the world. Members of my immediate and extended families have all experienced adversity in one way or another. None of them gave in to it, as far as I know. People expected me to confront this deafness thing, look into its eyes, and go on. Expectations have a profound effect on some people."

But initially "I had no idea what I wanted to do with my life." She returned to Jarvis a year later, completed her departmental re-quirements, and gave her senior music recital. "However, since I had only been in school for three years, I lacked credits to graduate. Instead of trying to become a concert pianist who happened to be deaf, I decided to try something else. This decision led me to Gallaudet College in 1963, the year in which I had previously planned to graduate with a degree in Music Education."

After attending Gallaudet for two-and-a-half years and graduating in 1966 with a B.A. in English, she had to make "another huge decision": graduate school or full-time work. "I chose working because I felt I had used up my time in school and there was a desire to test my independence; to see how I could fare away from family and structured academics. Between October 1965 and September 1967, I worked as a Classification Clerk for the Peace Corps home office, a technical editor for the Internal Revenue home office, and a distribution clerk for the post office—all in Washington, D.C." For 6 years, she worked in the Gallaudet dormitories as a supervisor ("houseparent, RA, etc."). "During this time, I also taught classes in English and Literature, attended and graduated from Howard University [in 1972] with a Master's in Guidance and Counseling." The following year, she began her teaching career at NTID/RIT as Developmental Education Specialist. Abandoning a promising career in music did bother her, but becoming a teacher was almost an automatic "substitute choice" since her father, aunts, uncles, and a grandmother were all teachers.

Now an Associate Professor in RIT's Department of Liberal Arts, Allen did her doctoral studies at UR because NTID doesn't have a doctoral program. On May 24, 1992, she became the first African-American deaf woman to earn a Ph.D. (an Ed.D., to be exact.)

"Although both [my] degrees are in Counseling, I have never worked officially as a counselor. I feel that teaching gives me freedom to associate and be in contact with my students more closely than if I were a counselor. This freedom includes the choice of using my counseling, as well as my instructional skills.

"My students are, first and foremost, the love of my life. Of course, they don't know this until years after they leave my class. I do not consider them my friends. What I enjoy most about teaching is when that rare feeling comes, telling me that I have helped someone and that they appreciate this new knowledge."

Dr. Allen has received a variety of honors and awards, and has been a guest and keynote speaker at numerous conferences and African-American/Back Deaf heritage-and-history celebrations. She's listed in **Notable Americans** (1978), **Who's Who of American Women** (1984), **Personalities of America** (1984), and **Who's Who Among Black Americans** (1994-95).

In 1992, she told the Rochester **Democrat and Chronicle**: "Deafness is now a part of me. I'm not sure I have accepted it, but I don't think it's so important that I have to worry about it." She has continued to use her voice, and also signs. "I would not call myself a 'skilled' signer. I am most comfortable speaking, so I usually use total communication [Sim-Com]. . . . This is my mode of communication in the classroom and elsewhere. . . . I'm comfortable enough with it and my students have never complained.

"My biggest challenge has been believing in myself. I'm sure many will find this hard to believe, but it's true. The self-confidence has been a long time coming. What helps me most is, I'm quite good at boosting others' confidence and trying to encourage self-esteem (especially within my students). As I watch them grow, I grow with them. I'm still learning to listen to my heart."

Glenn B. Anderson was born deaf on October 16, 1945, in inner-city Chicago. He was deafened at age 7 from medical complications of pneumonia. "My parents were hard-working people. Father was a building custodian for a junior high school, and Mother was a short-order cook in a restaurant in downtown Chicago. I was fortunate that I had some deaf friends in my neighborhood, so we formed a basketball team of five all-deaf players. We almost always beat hearing teams.

"Through sports I learned the importance of having goals and discipline. If you don't have any discipline then it's very difficult to achieve goals. I learned that fairly early. Our team used to beat all the hearing teams because we played together as a team. We had cohesion and helped each other out. The hearing teams were more individualistic in their style of play, so I learned the value of team effort. Everyone contributes to the overall goal, so all of that carried over into other aspects of my life, work, and service to the community."

Anderson was first enrolled in a day-school program with about 150 deaf students, then Parker High School—"with 2,000 students—maybe 12 to 15 of us were deaf. Most of the time I was not aware what the teacher was saying in class." No support services were provided, but he became an honor student, and before he graduated in 1964, was named Scholar-Athlete of the Year.

Planning to major in Physical Education, he enrolled at Northern Illinois University. (He received no Vocational Rehabilitation assistance.) At NIU he learned about Gallaudet College and after one semester, he transferred there. "I didn't know I had leadership potential until I went to Gallaudet. Then my whole perception of myself changed dramatically. I realized I could do more than just become a PE teacher and coach, and as a result I changed my major to Psychology." Gallaudet had "many outstanding student leaders" who influenced him—Phil Bravin, Harvey Corson, Gary Olsen, Linwood Smith.

While at Gallaudet, he was involved in many student activities: Student Body Government, the **Buff and Blue**, **Tower Clock**,, in addition to basketball and track. During his senior year in 1968, he received several honors and awards, including Who's Who in American Colleges and Universities, Olof Hanson Service Award, and Scholar-Athlete of the Year. When he graduated that spring with a B.A. in Psychology, his was the only Black family at commencement.

He earned an M.S. from University of Arizona in 1970 and a Ph.D. in Rehabilitation Counseling from New York University in 1982, becoming the first deaf African-American to earn a doctorate. In 1970, he became the first deaf person hired for a VR position in Michigan; he served two years as VR counselor for Michigan Rehabilitation Services in Detroit. From 1972 to 1975, he was Associate Research Scientist at New York University's Deafness Research and Training Center, and from 1975 to 1982, Coordinator of Continuing Education Programs for Deaf Adults at LaGuardia

Community College, City University of New York. He's now Professor of Rehabilitation Counseling at University of Arkansas. Since 1982, he has been Director of Training at UA's Rehabilitation Research and Training Center for Persons who are Deaf or Hard of Hearing. He helped establish the Little Rock chapter of NBDA, and is longtime editor of the **Deaf Arkansan** newsletter.

He's taught many university courses, made presentations at national, regional, and local conferences and workshops, and published numerous book chapters, articles, and research reports on career preparation, multicultural diversity, mental-health services, empowerment, interpreters, improving educational and employment prospects, and, in general, improving opportunities for racial/ethnic-minority deaf people. He's estimated that one-fifth of the student population at schools for the deaf are black—and they're starved for mentors. "It's very important that deaf children see deaf adults who are successful."

He and his wife, Karen Adeeb-Anderson, are active in NBDA. They have two children, Danielle and Jamaal.

In 1989, Anderson joined Gallaudet's Board of Trustees. On February 11, 1994, he made history by being chosen the first Black and second deaf Board chairman. One of his first formal duties was to read the citation on the Honorary Doctor of Laws degree awarded to President Bill Clinton at Gallaudet's 125th Commencement in May 1994.

Anderson has won numerous awards—AAAD Hall of Fame (1992), PSD's Nevil Award of Merit (1994), NAD's Frederick C. Schreiber Leadership Award (1994), ADARA's Boyce R. Williams Award (1995), and NBDA's Linwood Smith Humanitarian Award (1995). A popular keynote and commencement speaker, he gets his points across with humorous stories and parables spiced with wisdom: "You can't just give up because there's a barrier. You have to keep going around barriers until you find an open door.... Even Abraham Lincoln lost eight elections before he was finally elected President in 1860."

Dr. I King Jordan: Marathon man.
(Courtesy of Dr. Jordan)

CHAPTER 51

I. King Jordan, Jr.

1943-

First deaf president of Gallaudet University

The selection of a university president doesn't normally inspire nationwide front-page headlines or prime-time TV coverage. Yet the "Deaf President Now" uprising at Gallaudet University escalated into a national civil-rights movement for Deaf people, and sent shock waves through the world. Even though the media spotlight was brief, we are still feeling the impact of DPN.

Dr. I. King Jordan became the first deaf president in the 124-year history of Gallaudet University and a symbol of the DPN revolution—but was not a revolutionary. He describes himself as "old-fashioned," a "traditionalist." Paradoxically, he is a late-deafened adult leading a sometimes bitterly divided campus community where culturally-Deaf people scorn those who aren't. Yet he managed to win the respect of most, if not all, of the factions. A teacher and scholar who was catapulted into celebrity, he has proven a charismatic and effective leader. Gallaudet has enjoyed an excellent relationship with Congress and an unprecedented boom in endowments since he took office.

Irving King Jordan, Jr. was born in Glen Riddle, Pennsylvania, a small town west of Philadelphia, on June 16, 1943. As a student, he was bright but lazy, a likable goof-off. He loved freedom and fun. His older sisters Peggy and Betty brought home A's and B's. King didn't want to compete with them, didn't want to take academic courses, didn't want to go to college. He never wrote a research paper, never set foot in a library. He preferred taking stenography courses with the girls and trampoline-bouncing. He graduated from high school with a C average—and the honor of being named "Class Clown" in the yearbook. He *was* popular.

Hoping to find direction, he enlisted in the Navy. He didn't mind a bit of discipline, although after hours (he was stationed at the Pentagon as a clerk with the Joint Chiefs of Staff), he and his friends tore loose. He enjoyed motorcycling around Washington and socializing all night at steak-and-egg joints.

One evening in 1965, when he was 21, he was riding his motorcycle back to the barracks from a part-time job in downtown Washington, approaching the 14th Street Bridge, when a car heading in the opposite direction turned into his path at Independence Avenue. He was hurled over the hood and through the windshield. The rear-view mirror cracked open his skull and broke his jaw. Bystanders took his pulse and thought he was dead. He was rushed to George Washington University Medical Center. At first they thought he'd die—or be a vegetable.

But he survived, and his mind was clear. After 14 months, he was released. Cranial nerve VIII had been severed when his skull was fractured, leaving him profoundly deaf. He later said, "I had led a charmed life until then. I had loads of friends. I was having a good time. When I became deaf, I started to sort out the future. When you're 17 or 18 you don't think much about when you'll be 38 or 48. With a year in the hospital, I had lots of time for soul-searching. . . . You would think the accident would have narrowed my world, limited me. It did the exact opposite. I started to pay attention to the world instead of taking it for granted."

In 1967, two years after the accident, he met Linda Marie Kephart. They were married on October 12, 1968. An elementary-school teacher for over a decade, she's now a potter. They have two children: King III, alumnus of University of Colorado and graduate student at the University of Georgia, and Heidi, who attended Flagler College and now teaches at Florida School for the Deaf.

At first, Jordan saw no need to learn sign language, hoping that his deafness, as the doctors suggested, might go away. In a 1988 interview, he said, "Right after the accident, I didn't believe I'd stay deaf. So for a long time, I didn't know it was a transition. I thought it was a temporary condition." It wasn't. Was he depressed? No. "It never was depressing. By the time I realized this condition was permanent, I still had my old friends but I'd made a bunch of new friends as well. They were very supportive. My wife never knew me as a hearing person, so there was no adjustment for her." (She became a skillful signer.)

He enrolled at Gallaudet College, learned to sign, and hit the books. He graduated in 1970 with a B.A. in Psychology, and did postgraduate work at University of Tennessee, without an interpreter. Even though it wasn't required, he wrote a thesis for his Master's. This time, *he* made the grades. He received one B—and the rest were A's. He earned his Master's in 1971; his doctorate in 1973. Then he returned to Gallaudet and joined its Department of Psychology. Advancing steadily, he became an assistant professor in 1973; associate professor in 1977; a full professor in 1982, department chairman in 1983, and Dean of the College of Arts and Sciences in 1986, the same year Gallaudet became a university. He was considered an excellent psychology professor, accessible and inspiring.

In August 1987, Jerry Lee, Gallaudet's sixth president, announced his resignation. In late December, he left. A search committee was formed, and a search got underway. From a pool of some 67 applicants—an all-time high—25 were selected for serious consideration. These were narrowed down to 6 semifinalists, then to 3 finalists: Elisabeth Zinser, Vice President for Academic Affairs (Vice-Chancellor) and professor at University of North Carolina in Greensboro; Harvey Jay Corson, Superintendent of Louisiana School for the Deaf in Baton Rouge; and Dr. Jordan. Drs. Corson and Jordan were deaf, and Dr. Jordan had years of experience at Gallaudet. Dr. Zinser was hearing, with no "Deaf background." (A "broad and deep knowledge of deafness" was one major criterion.) Still, she had the most college-level administrative experience— the other major criterion.

Gallaudet alumni, GUAA, NAD, and other advocates lobbied for the selection of a deaf president. Surely the time had come, they asserted. They attempted to communicate these feelings to the

Board. Students, faculty, and staff took up the cause. The first "Deaf President Now" rally was held on March 1, 1988.

On Sunday, March 6, the Gallaudet University Board of Trustees voted 10-4 in favor of Zinser. (She received the votes of all but one of the hearing majority. The deaf members voted for Jordan. Although a Board member, Corson, a candidate, couldn't vote.) Jordan was running around the track when he received the news.

That night, a crowd of students and alumni marched to the Mayflower Hotel to confront the Board and communicate their disappointment and anger to Board Chairman Jane Bassett Spilman. Early next morning, they barricaded the campus gates and rallied. The "DPN" strike had begun.

Jordan had initially taken a "hands-off" position. He hoped to find some satisfactory compromise—somehow. But when Spilman asked him to make a public declaration of his support for the Board's decision, he found himself caught between conflicting responsibilities. Zinser *had* been elected fairly. As a loyal member of the university administration, he was duty-bound to support the Board's decision. Yet, as a deaf person, he empathized with the protesters; he couldn't support the Board's attitude. The protest did not have universal support in the Gallaudet community. He was worried about potential damage to university property, or worse, that people might get hurt.

On Wednesday, March 9, Jordan met with Zinser, then with the four student leaders. When he asked them to support Zinser, they refused. Zinser met briefly with them, then went with Jordan to a press conference, where he affirmed his support for her, saying that it was in the University's best interests. He also thanked students, staff, and friends for their encouragement and support. "Gallaudet will never be the same," he said.

Afterwards, he conferred with Linda and had a long TTY conversation with Dr. Edward C. Merrill, Jr., Gallaudet's fourth president and an old friend, who counseled him to follow his conscience: "Listen to your heart," say what you honestly believe. That night, tormented by his conscience, he couldn't sleep. Finally, he reached a decision. The next morning, he addressed a crowd in front of

Chapel Hall, admitted he had made a mistake, and that he supported the protesters. He was prepared to resign as Dean.

But Zinser, recognizing the enormity of this "social phenomenon," resigned that afternoon. On Friday, while DPN participants marched to the Capitol and rallied, the Board reconvened at Embassy Row Hotel. Jordan was picking up a friend at the airport when he was phone-paged and informed that he had been chosen president—by unanimous vote. Spilman resigned.

Celebration replaced protest. On Monday, March 14, his first day as president, Jordan thanked the DPN activists, then, at a press conference, said that he was "thrilled," discussed the events, fielded questions, and urged everyone to get back to work. His statement, "Deaf people can do anything hearing people can, except hear," was quoted and requoted everywhere. It became the Deaf community's favorite slogan.

He went to work immediately, put in exhaustingly long days at Gallaudet, gave interviews and speeches, signed autographs, testified before Congress, was lionized as a hero, a champion for Deaf rights. Throughout it all, he maintained his old warmth, patience, and humor. But his private life was utterly disrupted; his family and friends rarely saw him. They, too, coped with the sudden intrusion of fame.

On October 21, 1988, a joyous crowd of 3,500 gathered in the Field House and four other overflow locations on campus to celebrate Jordan's inauguration as Gallaudet's eighth president. He told the crowds, "Last March, we put our hands to the ground and we felt the vibrations of generations of aspirations and expectations. We felt the pulse of excellence. We came out of the huddle, and we made a beginning. And now, let us begin together."

The real challenges, he knew, were to come—budgeting, administration, the ongoing headaches of Deaf illiteracy and communication controversies, and the overall task of bringing Gallaudet into the 21st century. His commitment was to excellence. As he has said: "Every person has the right to unlimited goals and expectations."

(Top) Phyllis Frelich in *Children of a Lesser God* (1980). (Courtesy of Mark Taper Forum.)
Bottom left: With Marlee Matlin in *Bridge to Silence* (1989). (Courtesy of CBS-TV.)
Bottom right: In *The Gin Game* (1991). (Courtesy of Ms. Frelich.)

CHAPTER 52

Phyllis Frelich

1944-

Tony Award-winning actress

Eldest of nine Deaf sisters and brothers, Phyllis Frelich was born to Deaf parents on February 29, 1944, and grew up in a small farm 13 miles northeast of Devils Lake, North Dakota. She attended North Dakota School for the Deaf in Devils Lake, the same school her parents had attended. Times were hard, and when she was 13, her father gave up farming and became a printer, moving the family to town, near NDSD. Phyllis enjoyed performing in classroom skits and plays, but recalls being admonished by her deaf teachers for signing openly in public. "They told us that we would be thought of as animalistic. And indeed, I have observed that most 'polite' deaf adults will sign small in public so as to 'hide' their signs. Thus, I was taught directly and indirectly that sign language was neither respected nor encouraged."

At Gallaudet College, she majored in Library Science because she didn't know what else to study. There was no Drama degree offered back then. She took part in almost all the Drama Club productions. Her outstanding performances in the title role of Euripides' *Medea* won her the Best Actress of the Year Award. She was first seen by David Hays, founder and artistic director of the National Theatre of the Deaf, when she performed as the Leader of the Chorus in *Iphigenia at Aulis* during her junior year. The entire production was invited to perform that summer at the O'Neill Center in Waterford, Connecticut (NTD's first home). During her senior year, she appeared in NTD's first TV special (*NBC Experiment in Television*, 1967), which launched the first professional deaf theater company.

Upon her graduation from Gallaudet in 1967, she joined NTD as one of the founding members. That same year, she met Robert Steinberg, the company's technical director. He learned sign language from her, and they were married within a year. They had two sons, Reuben and Joshua, both hearing.

After touring with NTD for a year, Frelich left to accompany Steinberg, now the resident lighting and scenic designer at the Mummers Theatre in Oklahoma City. After a year of working backstage at Mummers, she rejoined NTD for another two years, playing such roles as Polly Garter in *Songs from Milk Wood* and Marie in *Woyzeck*.

When Steinberg became a professor at the University of Rhode Island's theater department, Frelich left NTD to raise the boys on a nearby farm. But she was always around the theater, as were the boys. She often took up hammer or paintbrush to help with a set, sewed costumes and even taught acting to URI theater students.

Playwright Mark Medoff was invited as guest artist to URI's theater with his new play, *The Conversion of Aaron Weiss*. Frelich was the first deaf person he'd ever met. After learning that there were no roles written especially for Deaf actors, Medoff was inspired to write a play for her. Several months later they met again in a Manhattan deli to go over the script he'd begun writing. He invited Frelich and Steinberg to be guest artists at New Mexico State University's theater during Spring 1979.

The play took shape as Medoff gained new insight into a Deaf character, and the relationship between Frelich and Steinberg. Still, the dramatization of the stormy romance between James Leeds, a speech therapist, and Sarah Norman, the young Deaf charwoman who works at her old school, is fictional. The play uses deafness as a universal metaphor for communication and relationships; the ending—reconciliation or separation?—is ambiguous.

When the script was finally completed, Medoff titled it *Children of A Lesser God* after a phrase from Tennyson's Arthurian epic, **Idylls of the King** (*"For why is all around us here/As if some lesser god had made the world/But had not force to shape it as he would?"*). It was first presented at an NMSU workshop with Frelich as Sarah and Steinberg as James. Shortly afterwards, the play was brought to Los Angeles by Gordon Davidson, Artistic Director of the Mark Taper Forum. Under his direction, it underwent changes in the script and casting. John Rubinstein took over the demanding role of James Leeds; he had to communicate in fluent signs with Frelich while voicing her half of the dialogue. The setting of the play challenged the audience's imagination. To emphasize the "silent world" of deaf people, there was very little scenery, and even the props were mimed.

It was a smash. After a successful run in Los Angeles, *Children* opened on Broadway on March 30, 1980, at the Longacre Theatre, where it won the acclaim of audiences and critics.

On a memorable June evening in 1980, at Broadway's Mark Hellenger Theatre, *Children* made a remarkable "sweep" at the annual Antoinette Perry ("Tony") Awards—it won Best Play, Best Actress (Frelich), and Best Actor (Rubinstein). The Outer Critics Circle named it "the most distinguished new play," and they hailed Frelich's intense performance as "an outstanding debut."

In the months that followed, *Children* played to packed houses and the demand for tickets continued to increase. The National Tour Company took the play to major cities throughout the United States and Canada. The Bus and Truck Company played in smaller cities in the States. The London Company took it to England, where it enjoyed a long run. Similar groups went to South Africa and Australia. In each of these, Sarah was played by a Deaf actress. By 1984, scores of Deaf performers were employed in leading or supporting roles and as understudies. That year, a Hollywood movie company starting preparing for film production. (This version, which catapulted Marlee Matlin to fame, glossed over the Deaf issues and had a happy ending.) *Children* has been performed in numerous foreign-language translations.

For over two years, Frelich performed in the original production. In Fall 1993, she said: "I didn't work for two years after *Children of a Lesser God* closed. The odds are against me for opportunities, more so now. Women over 40 are not accepted in our industry."

In 1981, North Dakota Governor Allen Olson presented her with the Theodore Roosevelt Rough Rider Award. (Her portrait hangs in the State Capital in Bismarck.) That same year, she guest-starred on NBC's much-loved sitcom, *Barney Miller*, playing a Deaf prostitute with memorable realism and humor. In March 1982, she participated in the ABC spectacle *Night of 100 Stars* for the benefit of the Actors Fund of America.

In 1984, she had the leading role in another new play written especially for her by Medoff—*Hands of its Enemy*. It was first performed (again, in workshop) by the American Southwest Theatre Company, which Medoff founded and directed. Like *Children*, it was later refined by Davidson, who formally staged it at the Mark Taper Forum that October; it later played at the Manhattan Theatre Club. It's about the relationship of an inexperienced but ambitious Deaf playwright (Frelich) and her hearing director (played by Hollywood star Richard Dreyfuss), who learns to communicate in sign language as the play unfolds. Steinberg played her best friend and interpreter. Through a clever use of interpreting and signing, the play was accessible to all theatergoers. Frelich gave another virtuoso performance.

For her stunning portrayal of the bitter, frustrated textile worker Janice Ryder in the TV-movie *Love is Never Silent* (1985), she received an Emmy nomination. (Her old NTD colleague Ed Waterstreet played her milder-spirited husband, Abel.)

She appeared with Marlee Matlin (who had won an Oscar for *her* portrayal of Sarah Norman in the movie version of *Children of a Lesser God*) in the CBS-TV movie *Bridge to Silence* (1989). In a play-within-a-movie device, the two appeared in rehearsal scenes of an ASL version of *The Glass Menagerie*. Other TV credits include *LA Law, Hunter, Spenser: For Hire, Gimme a Break*, and *Santa Barbara*.

In 1991, she was elected to the Screen Actors Guild Board in Hollywood, the highest policy-making body in the entertainment industry. She was the first deaf SAG member on the Board. That same year, Waterstreet co-founded the Deaf West Theatre Company. Frelich starred as Fonsia Dorsey in its premiere production,

D. L. Coburn's Pulitzer Prize-winning two-character play, *The Gin Game*. Once again, her performance got rave reviews. She assisted Director Stephen Sachs for Deaf West's Fall 1992 production of *One Flew Over the Cuckoo's Nest*.

Her exciting one-character play, *Lolly Foster's Daredevil Airshow*, premiered at The Kennedy Center for the Performing Arts in 1993. This was about a "pioneer spirit," a Depression-era Deaf pilot whose license has been revoked because she's "deaf and dumb" and cannot communicate by radio.

Frelich created the roles of Frances in Beth Henley's *The Debutante Ball* at the South Coast Repertory Theatre, and Esther in Medoff's *Gila* at American Southwest Theatre Company. She played Scrooge in Deaf West's adaptation of *A Christmas Carol* (1995), with Bernard Bragg as Marley.

Through her bilingual Tree House Theatre project, Frelich performed with, and for, children at the Smithsonian Institution's Discovery Theatre. She has conducted a multitude of workshops and acting classes at NTD's Summer Program, URI, NMSU, and Deaf West. And she's made extensive appearances as a guest lecturer and keynote speaker at numerous educational institutions, civic and service organizations, and corporate conferences. Among her many honors are The Outer Circle Award, two L.A. Dramalogue Awards, and the Humanitarian Award and an Honorary Doctor of Fine Arts degree from Gallaudet.

She says: "Today, I am amazed at how times and things are changing for Deaf people. I believe that at least some of the impetus for change can be attributed to such things as the NTD and *Children* for their ability to demonstrate to the world the beauty of sign language and the dignity of Deaf people—that there is no better way to change people's attitudes than through the arts. I am continually amazed at the number of people from all walks of life who are now studying sign language—often for no other reason than for the beauty of the language. This was not the case when I was growing up. The only problem is that I *still* have to hide my signs—but for different reasons: there are 'eaves-watchers' everywhere."

Top left: Jack Levesque on his Harley hawg. Top right: A youthful portrait.
Bottom: With his three children. (Courtesy of Jack Levesque)

CHAPTER 53

Jack Levesque

1945-

Leader and advocate

John F Levesque (that's how he prefers to spell it) was born on January 1, 1945, in rural Indian Orchard, Massachusetts, to Ruth M. and Edgar T. ("Ziggy") Levesque. Ziggy worked in a factory as a rigger, installing and repairing heavy machinery.

When he was about 6 months old, Jack was severely deafened in both ears, possibly by German measles, possibly by recurrent ear infections. "I had sufficient residual hearing to pick up and discriminate sounds. As a result, I learned auditorially, not through speechreading." He got some speech training at the Springfield League of the Hard of Hearing, and was enrolled in the Monson public schools. Even though he was "passed" into second grade, Jack's parents saw that he wasn't getting an appropriate education. Following a doctor's advice, they enrolled him in Clarke School for the Deaf. He remembers:

> The odd thing about my experience at Clarke was that I enjoyed my nine years there. It was much harder to communicate at home and I felt lonely there. I was a model student, a good example of a successful role model. It appears I relished that role as the center of attention. . . . I was defined as being very patient and willing to provide extra help to my classmates. I do not ever recall seeing sign language used during my term there. I was not exposed to it. We did have an Honor Roll for those who used speech all the time and did not wave hands or point. Those who could hear well and speak well had a rather easy transition at the school, whereas those who had problems speaking had a much harder time, and that spilled over to the dorm life too. The expectations of our performances were always high in every aspect of school and dorm life. The oral training was boring and quite grueling.

He graduated in 1960, and felt confident enough to take on public high school, without any support services. He sat in the front row and worked hard. "I got by. Sports carried me through school, as I was not crazy about the classrooms. The best class, and for which I am grateful today, was typing. Many of my teachers were helpful and understanding and a couple were not. I survived." He earned letters in several sports, and participated in lots of extracurricular activities, but recalls a feeling of hollowness—which he later realized was the lack of communication.

He got his first job at age 14, working at a restaurant, earning 25¢ to 50¢ an hour (I felt rich"), then worked in an auto-body shop.

After graduating from high school, he went to work in construction and carpentry, laid pipe for a gas company, made women's hats in a "sweat mill," and drove a truck. "Since most of the jobs were of the sweat-mill type, I couldn't use my hearing aid; I had to get by with gestures and what lipreading skills I possessed. The benefits from working these jobs were discipline and the merits of hard work." This schooling, too, would prove useful.

Around this time—he was 19 and still in the sweat mills—Jack "made an incredible discovery": sign language. As a member of the Mohawk Oral Club (a social club composed mostly of Clarke alumni), he helped form a softball and basketball team. They competed in regional Deaf tournaments, where he saw Deaf athletes signing to each other. He shrugged it off at first, figuring that he was "doing just fine with oral communication."

In 1965, acting on his Vocational Rehabilitation counselor's advice, Jack went to ASD and took the Gallaudet entrance exams. He got top scores. Driving down to Gallaudet with two Clarke friends in his "beat-up old 1955 Chevy jalopy," Jack experienced "a cultural shock" on his arrival. "The first person I encountered was Dr. Frank R. Turk, who was responsible for the Orientation Program then. Meeting Turk was an experience I have never forgotten. I made up my mind then that once I could understand Turk, then I would be scot-free to be able to communicate with anyone. He was my role model to understand. Since sign language was the mode of communication there, I was determined to learn how to sign and be fluent in it."

As an oralist learning ASL, he was teased and hazed. Most teachers signed and mouthed words, so he got by. "It took three years before I could comfortably understand Dr. Turk, and once I accomplished that goal, I felt I belonged. Dating girls was also a big incentive to learning signs quicker. I participated in soccer and played all intramural sports. I just got involved as a college student. It was heaven compared to working in the sweat mills."

But he left after his freshman year to go back to work, starting a trucking company with his brother. "In 1969 I returned to college, a bit wiser and more anxious to get a degree."

Back at Gallaudet, Jack majored in Sociology, joined the wrestling team, served as Vice-President of Student Publications, and was named Best Actor of the Year in 1969 for his role in *Universal Robots*. "That was the only Gallaudet production I acted in. I did join in with several Hughes Memorial Theatre productions and had fun with them." He was elected President of the Student Body Government (1970-71) and Head Senior (1971-72). **The Tower Clock** listed him as a "BMOC." He helped establish the Rathskeller (now the Abbey) and the annual rating of teachers by students.

The B. A. in Sociology he received in 1972 helped get him a job at the NAD as assistant to Fred Schreiber. He remembers his two years there as one of the best times of his life. Fred was his mentor. "There was never a dull moment working with Fred Schreiber. People loved working for and with him. He had a way with people. He was unconventional in his thinking and took chances and dared where others never thought to try. He hired me, despite opposition by several people, to work in the NAD, and the same was true for Terrence J. O'Rourke and Edward C. Carney. I am proud to be a part of that group." Jack's stint at the NAD taught him about leadership, interaction, politics, cooperation, and the bonds shared by Deaf people.

Although Jack's goal was to be Assistant Executive Director, the NAD Board had other ideas, so Fred advised him to seek another job. He contacted Dr. Richard E. Thompson ("DT") a Deaf Massachusetts psychologist, "a mover and shaker in his own right, probably the most unrecognized hero in our country today. I was able to obtain a job as a VR counselor working with the Massachusetts Rehabilitation Commission. My role was to work with six mainstreamed high-school students in Eastern Massachusetts in the newly-developed Deaf Services Office of the MRC. I am grateful to Dr. Thompson for opening the door to that job."

With DT and other Deaf leaders, Jack helped found the Massachusetts State Association of the Deaf, and served as president. When the Massachusetts Office of the Deaf (now Massachusetts Commission for the Deaf and Hard of Hearing) was established in 1977, Jack was chosen Program Development Specialist. (DT had also originated the idea of the MOD.) Along with DT, Schreiber, Jerome Schein, Doug Watson, Massachusetts Rehabilitation Commissioner Elmer Bartels, Jack helped establish the Developmental Evaluation and Adjustment Facilities (D.E.A.F., Inc.). "Because of DT, we were able to establish D.E.A.F., Inc., with Ann MacIntyre as its first Director. I served as President of the Board for several years. This whole idea came about as a result of DT's experiences with a previous program that he ran. Based on a handshake with Fred Schreiber to obtain NAD support, a meeting with Fred Schreiber, DT, Jerome Schein and myself, the idea bore fruit and the center was established. We called [it] the Frederick C. Schreiber Center. This was a most exciting venture and really put our state association on the map." D.E.A.F. is still thriving as a community-service center in Allston, a Boston suburb.

Jack entered the National Leadership Training Program at CSUN in January 1981 and graduated in August with a Master's in Administration and Education and Rehabilitation. During his training at CSUN, he interned, then joined the staff of Deaf Counseling, Advocacy, and Referral Agency (DCARA), founded as East Bay Counseling and Referral Agency in 1963. "I wondered what it would be like to work in a HAVE agency whereas my experience was in a HAVE NOT environment. DCARA was the dream place to work." Through DCARA, he was able to fulfill his old dream of having a Deaf community center that was completely Deaf-owned and operated. (DCARA's motto is "Of, By, and For the Deaf.") He has been Executive Director since 1981.

"DCARA [now located in Hayward] is the largest comprehensive Deaf Service agency in the Bay Area and is comprised of a 100% Deaf board. We have a staff of 40 people [over 60% Deaf], providing social services and advocacy to our members of the Deaf and hard-of-hearing community—to the Deaf/Blind, Latinos, the Gay/Lesbian population, Deaf senior citizens, the foreign-born group—you name it, we serve them." Under Jack's leadership, DCARA became a model agency, and he was well-known (and sometimes feared!) in the Sacramento legislature. He retired from DCARA in 1997.

Jack has been active in NAD, AAAD, WGD/U.S. Team Committee, Jr. NAD, the National Council of Agencies on Deafness, California Coalition of Agencies Serving the Deaf, the Deaf and Disabled Telecommunications Trust, CAD, Lions Club, and many others. He has given numerous presentations at conferences.

He considers fragmentation the Deaf community's biggest problem. Of deaf schools, he says: "There is nothing wrong with a residential program that a little effort, commitment, and time won't fix. Instead of tearing down such programs, we need to work together and build them much stronger, offering many different components including mainstreaming and day class programs."

Separated from Ann MacIntyre, he's the father of three hearing daughters—Aimee, Jackie, and Marie. In his spare time, he enjoys riding one his four ATVs, either of his Harley Davidson motorcycles—a 1995 13400 cc and a 1995 883 cc—or camping out in his 1961 Airstream Bambi. In October 1995, using a one-year administrative leave a bit at a time, he began a new venture: "to take two trips a year (5-6 weeks each time), visit all residential schools for the Deaf that use sign language, shoot videos and record them for posterity, interview various individuals, and see if we can record ASL stories and legends for our history and archives. All of the visits will be done on my Harley. It combines my three loves of life: Harleys, movie-making, and Deaf schools."

He considers being Deaf "the greatest gift he could ever have received."

Linda Bove and Elmo of *Sesame Street*. She's signing "friend."
(© 1995 Don Perdue/Children's Television Workshop)

CHAPTER 54

Linda Bove

1945-

Sesame Street star

Linda Bove was born to Deaf parents on November 30, 1945, in Garfield, New Jersey. She attended St. Joseph's School for the Deaf in the Bronx, then transferred to New Jersey (now Marie Katzenbach) School for the Deaf in Trenton, graduating in 1963. She then attended Gallaudet College, where, like Phyllis Frelich, she majored in Library Science. But her real interest—her heart— was in Drama. She participated in Gallaudet's Drama Club productions. During her junior and senior years, she was highly praised for her performances as Polly Peachum in *The Threepenny Opera* and as the female lead in Edgar Lee Masters' poetic-recitative *Spoon River Anthology*. She was also stage manager for Gallaudet's first all-student-cast-and-crew production of *The Man Who Came to Dinner*. Before her senior year, she participated in NTD's newly-established Summer Program. This led to an invitation to join the NTD. After graduating in 1968, she did.

At NTD, she performed with Ed Waterstreet, a Gallaudet classmate who had also joined the company after graduation. They were married two years later, becoming the first professional Deaf husband-and-wife performing team.

NTD's repertoire afforded Bove the opportunity to demonstrate her versatility as an actress. Under David Hays' direction, she worked with Bernard Bragg, Freda Norman, Dorothy Miles— among others—performing classic lead and supporting roles in multiple touring productions across the United States and abroad (e.g., Yugoslavia, Israel, Holland, France, Argentina)—Canina in

Volpone, Belissa in *The Love of Don Perlimplin and Belissa in the Garden*, and the Harlot in *Gilgamesh*. She made her Broadway debut at the Longacre Theatre as Lauretta in *Gianni Schicchi*, an adaptation of Puccini's opera. (She left NTD in 1977, after 9 years, because "there were other opportunities I wanted to explore.")

A major hit was her inspired "camp" performance in NTD's second original work, *Priscilla, Princess of Power* (1974), a pop-art/comic-strip-inspired farce directed by Waterstreet. As Priscilla, the "ordinary shmo" who turns into a Wonder Woman-type superheroine, Bove delighted audiences and critics, who praised her timing, physical comedy, and sense of melodrama.

In 1968-69, she joined Bragg, Mary Beth Miller, and Richard Kendall in establishing the Little Theatre of the Deaf, NTD's branch company for younger audiences. She directed and starred in many LTD productions, which received favorable publicity in the national and international press. **The New York Times** called LTD's 1972 Christmas Week tour "the most rewarding kid's show in town."

In 1973, Bove successfully auditioned for the role of Melissa Hayley, a Deaf character, for CBS's longest-running soap opera, *Search For Tomorrow*, becoming the first Deaf performer to appear on the "soaps." There was a romantic subplot with a young hearing doctor who could communicate in sign language because his mother was Deaf. And a happy ending: marriage without communication barriers.

Although it was typical soap opera, the storyline portrayed some of the problems Deaf people cope with in everyday life—misunderstandings, communication issues, and teaching hearing friends how to sign. Public response was positive. For 26 weeks, Bove presented an anti-stereotypical image of an attractive, independent Deaf character to millions of TV viewers.

It was but a short jump to prime-time television—appearing with Meryl Streep on PBS' *Omnibus* series. She starred in *A Child's Christmas in Wales*, a seasonal special first broadcast in 1973 and subsequently rerun. In 1974, she and Marlo Thomas received the AMITA (American-Italian) Award for outstanding work on TV.

In 1976, she signed a long-term contract with Children's Television Workshop and joined the cast of PBS' *Sesame Street* as a regular. As "Linda the Librarian"—undoubtedly the most familiar of all her roles—she worked with other adults on the cast, teaching children basic ASL and Deaf culture. This role represented a breakthrough—Bove's deafness was strictly secondary to her character. Having a B.A. in Library Science added authenticity to her portrayal. In her interviews, she told many funny stories about her experiences with Jim Henson's Muppets. When she was hired, for instance, the producers and writers automatically assumed she'd be able to read lips—or a caricature of lips—on such characters as Oscar the Grouch, Bert, Ernie, and Cookie Monster. In 1978, she starred in *Christmas Eve on Sesame Street*, which won an Emmy. During her 20-year involvement on the show, *Sesame Street* has won multiple Emmys.

Soon she had become the best-known "librarian" in the nation. Her popularity with children helped make sign language a more visible medium of communication while encouraging audiences to accept and welcome cultural diversity. (Characteristically, she also taught the basics of sign language to other cast members and technical crews she worked with.)

In 1977, Bove and Waterstreet were invited to join a primarily hearing production, *He Who Gets Slapped*, at Hartman Theatre in Stanford, Connecticut; they were written in as Deaf Clowns.

In Fall 1979, Bove participated in NTD's 30,000-mile world tour, the brainchild of David Hays, who also wrote the major production, *The Wooden Boy* (adapted from Carlo Collodi's **Pinocchio**). She played Mrs. Webb in Thornton Wilder's tragicomedy, *Our Town*. She also directed a companion piece, *The Four Fables* by James Thurber, and performed in *The Tale of the Magic Painter*, which Waterstreet directed.

The high point of the tour—a major triumph—was a visit to Japan arranged by Tetsuko Kuroyanagi, national television/film/ stage celebrity. She had previously invited Hays and Bove to come to Japan and appear on her TV show, *Tetsuko's Room*, the most popular one in Japan. Later, the NTD Company made its debut in the famed Shinjuku Bunka Center of Tokyo before an SRO audience that included the Crown Prince (later Emperor) Akihito, his wife Michiko, and Prince Hitachi. During the intermission, Tetsuko, Hays, and Bove were presented to the royal family. Akihito, who spoke fluent English, later told the press that NTD's appearance was "one of his outstanding memories of the year and that it could be of great meaning to the deaf in the future in Japan."

It was a prophetic statement. Two years later, the Japanese Deaf community, inspired by NTD, established its own professional theater company. For Bove and Hays, the world tour helped fulfill another of NTD's objectives—the successful exchange of cultural experiences in the theater arts between Deaf people of the States and those of foreign countries. Starting 1979, Japan began sending 10 representative deaf persons to NTD's annual Summer Program; one of them joined the NTD company. A strong intercultural link had been established.

In February 1980, Bove guest-starred with prime-time idol Henry Winkler on *Happy Days*, ABC-TV's ultra-popular sitcom. As Allison, Fonzie's Deaf girlfriend, she made him declare his love for her in sign language!

Sesame Street tie-ins like the colorful English/Spanish **Sesame Street Magazine** have helped Bove reach an even wider audience. She appeared in the movie *Follow That Bird!* And she wrote two popular *Sesame Street* books, **Sign Language Fun** and **Sign Language ABC**.

Bove made several appearances on Broadway. From 1980 to 1982, she was the understudy for Phyllis Frelich ("Sarah") in *Children of a Lesser God*. When the National Tour Company was formed, Bove was given top billing in major theaters throughout the States and Canada. She also appeared in the film version with Marlee Matlin. "It was the first play where a large role was written for a deaf person—a leading role, a meaty role. The play was written for a person who was deaf. I worked hard and was on the road with it for a year-and-a-half. It was the most joyful, rewarding experience I've had in my theatrical life."

Together with Waterstreet, who became Artistic Director, Bove was a founding member of Deaf West Theatre Company in Los Angeles. In 1991, she directed its first production, *The Gin Game*, starring Phyllis Frelich. Bove's version got international coverage on CNN and was critically acclaimed for its intense and psychologically compelling translation into ASL.

In 1992, Bove received the Bernard Bragg Artistic Achievement Award for her many contributions to the world of theatrical arts and the advancement of deaf people in that world. Her 18 years as "Linda the Librarian" on *Sesame Street* were cited as a landmark in "creating access for deaf children to children's educational television, promoting greater awareness in all children, and building the case for consistent use of Deaf talent in the mass media." That year, too, she received an honorary degree in Fine Arts from Gallaudet University for her excellence in the field of television.

Her *Sign-Me-a-Story* video (1988) won both the Action for Children's Television Award and the Parents' Choice Video Award. A live production directed by Waterstreet premiered at the Kennedy Center in 1993, where it enthralled both Deaf and hearing audiences, then moved to Deaf West. This interactive children's show (parents were welcome to participate) featured a cast of three actors (two Deaf, one hearing voicer) and included sign-language games, improvisations, and anecdotes about Deaf culture and people who "talk with their hands."

She produced *One Flew Over the Cuckoo's Nest* (which won a Critic's Choice Award) and *His Wife* for Deaf West's 1992 and 1994 seasons. In 1995, she had the title role in a compelling ASL production (directed by Kenneth Albers) of Euripides' *Medea*, playing the powerful sorceress who, betrayed by her lover and tormented by jealousy, wreaks bloody revenge. The children's heroine played literature's most infamous murderous mother.

From August through December, Bove works on *Sesame Street*, commuting between New York and Los Angeles. When she's not working on the show or at Deaf West, she makes personal appearances at events across the country, entertaining children and adults with highly interactive performances.

As she has said, "I like taking roads that are less traveled."

Kitty O'Neil: "I guess I like danger, and thrills. But mostly I want always to
have a goal, some dream that I can try for." (Gallaudet University Archives)

CHAPTER 55

Kitty O'Neil

1946-

"Fastest Woman on Earth"

During her career as stuntwoman and racer, Kitty O'Neil performed countless breathtaking feats. For her, doing the impossible was nothing unusual.

The daughter of a Cherokee Indian mother and Irish-American father, Kitty O'Neil was born on March 24, 1946 in Corpus Christi, Texas. (There was a younger brother, John III. Her parents later divorced; John O'Neil II was killed in a plane crash.) When she was 4 months old, she contracted measles, mumps and smallpox concurrently. A nurse packed her in ice to bring down her soaring temperature, but the fever left her totally deaf and impaired her sense of balance.

Stoic and determined, Patsy O'Neil took Kitty to Wichita Falls, Texas, and attended the University of Texas to earn teaching credentials and study methods of teaching deaf children; she established the School of Listening Eyes in Wichita Falls, and taught other deaf children. Patsy adamantly refused to learn sign language or to let Kitty learn it either. She taught Kitty to "read" throat vibrations and lips, and speak. Already a daredevil, Kitty spent a year at the Jane Brooks School for the Deaf, learned to read and write, then, aged 8, entered third grade in public school.

Ignoring the taunts of other children, she made good progress. She even studied cello and piano, and became a champion swimmer, then diver. At 14, she won the AAU Southwest District Junior Olympics Diving Championship in Texas.

When she was 16, Kitty moved to Anaheim, California, to train with Dr. Sammy Lee, a two-time Olympic diving champion who ran a free school for "Olympic hopefuls." She attended Savannah High School, put in "four rigorous hours of diving training each afternoon, and studied homework late into the evenings." Because her teacher sometimes forgot to face her and talked to the blackboard, Kitty missed portions of their lectures. "She used the weekends to catch up." According to Phil Bowie of the **Saturday Evening Post**:

> Dr. Lee couldn't use his customary method of shouting to cue her exactly when to tuck or twist in her dives, so he began using a pistol loaded with blanks. Kitty would feel the concussions and respond in mid-air. "After a couple of trials with a new, complex dive," Dr. Lee said, "she would be oriented and from then on she would actually 'feel' her way through the sequence. After that, it was just a matter of polishing and perfecting." (...)
>
> She was eighteen when she told a newspaper reporter, a bit defiantly, "I can do anything. I like to do things people say I can't do because I'm deaf. I have to work harder than some, but look at the fun I have proving they're wrong."

Dr. Lee was confident that Kitty could capture a gold medal in the 1964 Olympics, but she contracted spinal meningitis during a visit home and was left half-paralyzed. The doctors feared that she might not only never dive but never walk again. "Two weeks later I surprised everyone by walking out of the hospital," she said. She went on to win the 10-meter (33-foot) Junior Olympics Diving Championship at the 1964 AAU Nationals. She broke a wrist, recovered, and placed 12th in the Olympic tryouts.

In 1963, she graduated from Savannah High with honors. By then, she had collected 38 blue ribbons, 17 first-place trophies, and 31 gold medals in swimming and diving competitions.

Always eager for new challenges, she began exploring more dangerous sports—racing drag boats, top-fuel dragsters, production sports cars, and (for fun) snowmobiles; sky-diving, scuba-diving, and high-speed water-skiing. O'Neil told Bowie in 1977, "I guess I like danger, and thrills. But mostly I want always to have a goal, some dream that I can try for." She set two world speed records for women—racing in a high-powered boat at 285.23 miles per hour and then hitting a "phenomenal" high of 104.85 mph on waterskis (1970). Bowie noted: "She entered grueling off-road automobile and dune buggy events such as the Mint 400, the Baja 500, and the Mexican 1000, racing, and often winning, against such expert drivers as Mickey Thompson, Malcolm Smith, and Parnelli Jones." Then she mastered cross-country motorcycle racing, achieving an expert rating. She qualified for international competition—the only woman in the world to do so.

In 1970, she was diagnosed with cancer. Two operations and three years later, she was pronounced clear.

Around 1971, O'Neil met Duffy Hambleton, ex-banker and Hollywood stuntman, at a motorcycle meet in Saddleback, California. They were competitors, and Hambleton was astounded by O'Neil's fearlessness. She settled down somewhat—for a time. "After several years living on an orange ranch [in Fillmore] serving as a housewife and mother to Duffy's two [teenage] children by a previous marriage, Kitty decided she wanted to get back into some kind of action herself," Coles Phinizy wrote in **Sports Illustrated**. Hambleton taught her the tricks of his profession, including survival techniques. After two years of training, she joined him at Stunts Unlimited, a fraternity of top daredevils—"macho egomaniacs" as Hambleton humorously put it. O'Neil and Janet Brady were the first women to join. In 1976, sponsored by Universal Studios, O'Neil received her Screen Actors Guild card and "began stunting regularly" on *Bionic Woman*.

She was notably petite—5' 3", weighing 95 to 105 pounds—small but powerful. **The Saturday Evening Post** called her "the most sought-after stunt woman in Hollywood." She stunt-doubled for Lee Grant, drowning in a sinking jet plane in *Airport '77* (she hated that ordeal); for Lisa Blount, ablaze during a graveyard seance in *9/30/55*; for Lana Wood, hanging from a 6th-story ledge in an episode of *Baretta*; for Lindsay Wagner when *Bionic Woman* jumped off a speedboat; and for Lynda Carter whenever *Wonder Woman* hurdled or leaped from rooftops. Her *Wonder Woman* jump from the Sheraton Universal Hotel roof (127 feet) set a new record for women's high falls—which she soon broke.

In 1994, when Cynthia Merrifield of **Hearing Health** asked O'Neil what types of stunts she had done, she replied: "Everything! Engulfment in fire, swimming, diving, water skiing, scuba diving, horse falls and drags, transfers between horses, car rolls, cannon-fired, car driving, motorcycle racing, ice skating, skydiving fighting routines, gymnastics, snow skiing, jet skiing, golf, tennis, track and field, 10-speed bicycle racing, hang-gliding, boat handling, deep-sea fishing, airplane flying, and high falls into an air bag or water, to name a few." Her highest free-fall was 180 feet from a helicopter. That set a new record. So did a 90-foot fall while on fire. "Each stunt required about a month of training—I would run 7 to 8 miles a day, swim, and lift weights." Injuries? She burned her nose and eyebrows in one stunt, and permanently bent a finger in a motorcycle accident.

O'Neil then set out to tackle the women's World Land Speed Record (LSR). She learned about the *Motivator*, a lightweight, 48,000-horsepower, 3-wheeled "rocket-car" designed and built by Bill Frederick of Chatsworth, California. This one-of-a-kind item cost over $350,00, and was fueled by pressurized liquid hydrogen peroxide; it expelled a huge cloud of water vapor and oxygen—environmentally benign, but very, very expensive.

The first test run was held in September 1976 at El Mirage dry lake, where O'Neil clocked an unofficial 358 mph. (Countdowns were relayed to her by cue cards or hand signals.) O'Neil, Frederick, Hambleton, and her Stunts Unlimited colleague Hal Needham (who planned to beat the men's LSR), went to the Bonneville, Utah, salt flats in October, but the course was dangerously rough. They decided to move to the "marble-smooth" Alvord Desert in southeast Oregon, but were delayed by Federal red tape until early December—by which time winter was ready to close in. The *Motivator* performed flawlessly in early test runs.

On December 4, 1976, wedged into in the tiny cockpit, almost flat on her back, O'Neil blasted off and clocked 512.710 mph—a new LSR for women that beat the one set by Lee Breedlove in 1965 (305.56 mph) by 200 mph. (Photocell beams were used to time her;

the LSR rules required an immediate round trip "to eliminate any advantage derived from wind or slope." The average speed of the two runs through the timing traps became the official LSR.) This amazing feat was listed in the **Guinness Book of World Records**. At one point she neared 600 mph. "It took her more than five miles just to stop."

O'Neil wanted to break both the men's LSR (630.388 mph, set by Gary Gabelich in 1970), *and* the sonic barrier, but ran into another obstacle—a toy contract. A toy-development company had arranged for Needham to drive the *Motivator* to a men's LSR so Gabriel Industries could market a toy line featuring him. The day after O'Neil set the new women's land record and was preparing to go further and faster, Frederick was called and reminded "that he had a binding contract to let Needham try for the mark." (Needham had no experience driving the *Motivator*.) O'Neil's attempt was halted. Bad publicity and misinformation also spoiled plans for Gabriel's toy line. The next day, snow fell.

By 1981, O'Neil had set 26 LSRs. She'd been featured on magazine covers, written up in **The Saturday Evening Post, Reader's Digest, Sports Illustrated, Parade, The Woman's Almanac, Ms.,** a children's book (**Daredevil Woman**), and a memorable Cutty Sark Scotch ad, and interviewed on *Rainbow's End* and *Deaf Mosaic*. In all her interviews, O'Neil said that she wasn't worried about being deaf. It "was great for my concentration." She enjoyed the opportunity to share her message—"A handicap is not a defeat but a challenge to conquer"—with others, especially children. At the Bell Association's 1979 convention, she gave the keynote speech and received its Volta Award.

That same year, O'Neil's adventurous life became the subject of a CBS-TV movie—*Silent Victory: the Kitty O'Neil* **Story**, starring Stockard Channing. Naturally, O'Neil performed all the stunts. She later criticized its inaccuracy. Initially, she planned to write a book herself to set the record straight, but "it didn't work out. I just got fed up with publicity."

In 1982, at the peak of her career, she retired, and later moved to South Dakota.

Making history: Michael Chatoff walking across the Supreme Court Plaza
after arguing the Rowley case, March 23, 1982. (© Associated Press, 1982)

CHAPTER 56

Michael A. Chatoff

1946-

Legal advocate; Supreme Court groundbreaker

I have never been ashamed of my deafness—nor proud of it either; it's just a part of me that I can't change. I did not ask to be deaf, but I do my best despite the fact that I can't hear. I have always wanted to be known as a lawyer who happens to be deaf. Unfortunately, I have never been able to escape the view that I am a deaf lawyer. I think I have proved over and over and over again that I can hold my own with any other lawyer around, yet they are all lawyers and I'm a deaf lawyer. Inasmuch as I took the same exams as them, I think I am entitled to be referred to as a lawyer too, without any reference to my disability.—Michael Chatoff, 1995

Another precedent-setting lawyer and vigorous advocate of deaf people's rights, Michael Chatoff argued a case before the United States Supreme Court—and that argument has had a tremendous impact on the Deaf community.

Chatoff was born in New York City on August 18, 1946. All of the schools and colleges he attended were within New York's five boroughs. First came P.S. 173, J.H.S. #216, and Jamaica High. He graduated from Queens College in 1967 with a B.A. and a Senate Service Award. He graduated from Brooklyn Law School, receiving a J.D. (Juris Doctor) degree in 1971, and was admitted to the New York Bar later that year. Seven years later, in 1978, he graduated from the New York University School of Law with an LL.M. (Master of Laws), making him one of the best-educated people in the nation.

He was first employed in the Legal Department of the Chicago Title Insurance Company (in New York). In 1972, he accepted a position at West Publishing Company in Mineola, New York, becoming Senior Legal Editor in charge of the **United States Code Congressional and Administrative News,** which he calls "an up-to-date compendium of activities in Washington, primarily laws recently enacted, relied upon by members of the legal profession."

Following his first year at Brooklyn Law School, Chatoff, 22, experienced his first medical crisis. Two operations for bilateral acoustic neuromas (tumors on the auditory nerves on each side) left him totally deaf. Through his own tenacity and the support of his family, he was able to graduate. (Against all probability, the tumors later reoccurred, and Chatoff underwent repeat neurosurgeries. His *fifth* such operation was in 1987. "I take no pleasure in [saying] that, to my knowledge, I am the only person who survived five of those operations; I would not wish even a single one of those operations on my worst enemy.")

He has long been an active champion of deaf people's legal rights. "The Court Interpreters Act [P.L. 95-539] is the first recognition of the special communication needs of deaf individuals by the Federal judicial system. I wrote the original bill, introduced by Senator Charles Mathias, and worked with him on all rewrites until the bill became law."

In 1976, Chatoff took the New York Telephone Company and the New York State Public Service Commission to court. Representing himself and a friend of the family who is deaf, in *Chatoff v. Public Service Commission*, he argued that NYTC's rates discriminated against the plaintiffs, "who used telephone services because of their deafness heretofore used solely by businesses for profit-making purposes. The second-highest court in New York agreed with the plaintiffs; as a result, NYTC provides a rate reduction for deaf people." That ruling helped set a precedent for similar rate reductions throughout the country.

He has also been active in the deaf community, serving as president of the New York Center for the Law and the Deaf, and director of Westchester Community Services for the Hearing Impaired. He has written numerous articles on Deaf rights—e.g., "A Tax Credit for the Deaf" and "The Deaf Individual in a Legal Setting."

Chatoff's most famous case established several precedents. Amy Rowley was 10 years old, deaf, a bright, active fourth-grader at Furnace Woods Elementary School in Peekskill, New York. Her parents, Nancy and Clifford Rowley, were well known in the deaf community, and vigorously advocated for her right to an equal educational opportunity.

At issue was whether administrators at Furnace Woods had an obligation to provide an interpreter for her. Public-school officials had argued unsuccessfully in District Court and the Circuit Court of Appeals that she didn't need an interpreter because she was doing well enough. Both times, the courts ruled in favor of the Rowleys and decreed that Amy receive interpreting services. Hoping for a reversal, the Hendrick Hudson School District appealed to the U.S. Supreme Court.

Ultimately, the Supreme Court agreed to hear the case. What had started as a battle between a handful of school officials and a deaf student's concerned parents became something much bigger. The Supreme Court Justices would be defining what they believed to be the intent of the Education for All Handicapped Children Act of 1975 (P.L. 94-142). This federal law stipulated that handicapped students were entitled to a "free, appropriate education," and was considered a great step toward "equal-opportunity" mainstreaming for children with physical disabilities. Ever since the law was passed, there had been controversy over funding and the terms "appropriate education" and "least restrictive environment." The Supreme Court would now decide exactly what was meant by "appropriate," and its final decision would have widespread impact—affecting deaf and disabled students and school districts across the nation.

Chatoff had been the Rowleys' attorney from the beginning, representing the family and winning for them in the district and circuit courts. He successfully argued that Amy's Individualized Education Program—which included an FM amplifier, a tutor, and a speech therapist—was inadequate. Even with her excellent lipreading ability, Chatoff contended, Amy could only understand half of the classroom conversation. Accordingly, an interpreter as an additional support service was both "appropriate" and indispensable, since Amy was fluent in sign language.

During both lower-court hearings, Chatoff himself had employed support services—a notetaker. Although the notetaker was helpful, relying on quickly-scribbled notes was an imperfect solution. It was almost impossible for the notetaker to keep pace with the rapid give-and-take in the courtroom. But the method worked well enough to allow Chatoff to argue convincingly and win the cases.

Rather than depend on notetaking for the Supreme Court hearing, he wanted to use a more efficient system—Real Time Graphic Display, a computerized high-speed-translation unit. With this setup, which uses a court stenotypist and video-screen monitor, Chatoff could read the justices' questions almost instantaneously. (Chatoff spoke for himself.) Real Time Graphic Display represented another technological boon for deaf people. In Chatoff's case, however, the only problem was that nothing like it had ever been brought into the Supreme Court, and he would need approval. In fact, no video equipment of any kind—cameras or monitors—had ever been allowed within the Court's lofty walls.

Chatoff put in his request and then waited anxiously for the Justices to make their decision. In the meantime, numerous attempts were made to try and dissuade him from participating. Alexander Stevas, the Court Clerk, sent a note to Chief Justice Warren Burger, dryly noting that "efforts to persuade [Chatoff] to have other counsel argue the case have not been fruitful." To the dismay of some court-watchers, Chatoff was determined to represent the Rowleys.

Just when he thought he would have to engage a notetaker again, the Justices agreed to allow the real-time setup, thus enabling him to set two important precedents. Besides being the first deaf lawyer to argue before the Supreme Court, he was the first attorney to break the Court's entrenched ban on electronics. Setting the latter precedent helped other deaf lawyers, plaintiffs, defendants, members of the jury, spectators, and at least one district-court judge, make use of real-time setups in other cases and courts.

On March 23, 1982, Chatoff presented his case before the Justices of the Supreme Court. He lost the final decision by a very narrow margin (5-4), in which the Court ruled that Amy was doing well enough without the interpreter and that each school has the right to determine what is "appropriate" for a deaf or disabled student. To the Court, "appropriate" really meant "adequate." As Chatoff put it: "Education need only provide some educational benefits, not necessarily an equal educational opportunity."

Shortly after the decision, the Rowleys moved to New Jersey. Amy enrolled in a local public school that willingly provided her with an interpreter. Her grades soared, and she became a top student; later, a Gallaudet alumna.

After *Rowley*, Chatoff helped draft legislative guidelines for the appointment of an interpreter for a deaf defendant whose primary language is other than English.

In 1992, he sued New York City because its 911 Emergency Response System was not accessible to TTY users. "Originally, I had another attorney, but I was not satisfied with her so I took over myself. N.Y.C. agreed to enter into a Consent Judgment and provide the services I demanded. For the first time in 10 years, I was convinced that I had recovered from a decade that had begun so promisingly and ended so poorly."

Chatoff's valor and commitment to justice were not forgotten. Largely on the basis of his appearance before the Supreme Court, he has been "elected into **Who's Who in America**, together with the President of the United States, the President of Gallaudet University, and, ironically, the Chief Justice of the Supreme Court.

"Since I graduated from law school in 1971, I have wanted to see the legal profession opened up to more deaf people. I was the second deaf person to graduate from law school; at the time of the *Rowley* argument, the number of deaf people who were lawyers could be counted on the fingers of two hands. Now there are dozens of lawyers who are deaf and hundreds more in the pipeline. Many of those lawyers and law students called me and wrote to me to tell me that my argument in the *Rowley* case inspired them to persevere. Of course, that made me feel proud."

John Yeh with his fingerspelled nameplate.
(Michael Sparks; courtesy of Mr. Yeh)

CHAPTER 57

John T.C. Yeh

1947-

Entrepreneur

Although in Chinese culture, the lot of a deaf or disabled child could be tragic, John Yeh had the good fortune to be born into a "strong, supportive" family. The Yehs were devout Christians who considered all their children a gift from God, and sought to be good "stewards of this gift." "My parents encouraged us to be successful and to seek professional jobs," he later said. "They expected all of their children to get Master's or Ph.D. degrees."

Yu Yeh, a civil engineer, and his wife, Lin, had fled mainland China with their children in 1945, before Mao Zedong's 1949 revolution. John was born deaf in Taiwan on January 27, 1947, at a time when families were ashamed of "defective" children and even encouraged to kill them. The status of deaf and disabled people is still very low. John's younger sister Fanny was also born deaf. There were three older hearing brothers—James, Joseph, and Jeffrey. All the children were treated the same, except that Lin communicated by writing notes to John and Fanny. (She later learned sign language.)

In a 1988 **Parade** profile, Jack Anderson recounted how after the Yehs moved to a large city, the other children wanted to "test and tease the newcomer," so they set off a firecracker behind John's back. Of course, John, who was profoundly deaf, didn't flinch. He cried at the humiliation. But, Joseph said, instead of fighting back, "John made friends with them." He was outgoing and friendly.

Lin and Yu Yeh wanted John and Fanny to get a good education, but there weren't any good schools for the deaf in Taiwan. In 1960, when John was 13, the entire family, seeking better opportunities for them, sailed from Hong Kong to Brazil aboard a cargo ship. Their ultimate destination: the States. As Anderson recounts: "By the end of the month-long trip, John had not simply made friends with most of the crew—they treated him as an honorary deckhand.

"After two years of financial sacrifice and bureaucratic paperwork, the Yehs finally settled in the United States in 1962." John, now 15, was enrolled in KDES. He found himself placed with 10-year-olds, another humiliating situation. "I felt out of place. I knew I had the responsibility to learn, and that I had to be patient. Every year I found that I had problems to overcome." When he arrived in Washington, he knew no English. (He could already lipread and sign Chinese—but Chinese Sign Language is quite different from ASL.) So he equipped himself with a Chinese-English dictionary, memorized, studied, and mastered written English, and ASL. He graduated 3 years later, in 1966, with the other 18-year-olds.

At Gallaudet College, he founded the Rathskeller (later renamed the Abbey), still a favorite student hangout, and served as Grand Rajah of the Kappa Gamma fraternity. He also met Mary Gibbs. They had two daughters, Mei Ling-Hui (deaf) and Ming Hui-Chung (who has Down's syndrome), and a son, Jason Tai-Wei (deaf).

When John received his B.A. in Mathematics from Gallaudet in 1971, he originally planned to teach high-school math. "I was turned down. Some said because my English was weak, others said it was both my deafness and my English. If two people's skills are the same, they will choose the hearing person."

Undaunted, he enrolled in the Master's program in Computer Science at University of Maryland, where James, Joseph, and Jeffrey were already students. He was the first, and only, deaf student in the program. "The university was very hard. I worked 7 days a week on my studies. In those days, I had to find my own notetakers and interpreters." His interpreter was unfamiliar with computer terminology, which frequently created confusion for him. He received his Master's degree in Computer Science in 1973, and soon afterwards, became a U.S. citizen.

Eagerly, he made plans to enter the job market. He figured that since his brothers were thriving and his grades had been good, he'd have an easy time. He ended up searching—without luck—for a year. "I thought a person with a Master's degree in Computer Science would find many jobs open. That was back in the early 1970s, and at that time computer science was very new. But I really couldn't find a job. I sent out 100 résumés, and I didn't get a response . . . [because] I was honest. I said I was deaf, that I used sign."

As Sandra Sugawara noted in a 1989 **Washington Post** profile: "Discouraged, he reluctantly returned to the sheltered environment of Gallaudet, where worked as a computer programmer for 5 years." He helped develop Gallaudet's computer-research-information (TICCET) program. But for him, that was easy. He was ambitious; he wanted something more challenging. James, Joseph, and Jeffrey were now established in the computer field and doing well. As he watched their success, John grew increasingly restless. He finally decided to start his own company—the only way he, as a deaf person, could succeed.

He asked his brothers to help him set up a new company to develop software—an idea they "had kicked around for several years." Joseph told him, "If you really want to do it, we'll support you." Even though Jeffrey had found a good job with Ford Aerospace in California and was reluctant to leave, he saw that the company needed everyone's help to survive.

That was just the beginning of another struggle. Even though Yu and Lin offered to put up their home as collateral, every bank rejected John's loan application. In 1979, with great persistence, he managed to obtain a small loan from Small Business Administration's Handicapped Assistance Loan and the 8(a) Minority Business program that set aside federal-contract work for small minority-owned businesses. He qualified for a Handicapped Assistance loan of $100,000 with 3% interest. "But before we could get the loan, we had to be turned down by three banks. That was easy—I did it in one day." While waiting for the SBA loan to be approved, he learned accounting and business management from

SBA workshops and library books.

He named the new venture Integrated Microcomputer Systems, formed a partnership with his brothers, and incorporated. When IMS opened in January 1979, it consisted of John, James (as business manager), and an interpreter. They set up shop in the back room of a warehouse in Rockville, Maryland. Joseph and Jeffrey became vice presidents (business development and technical planning). For 7 years or so, Fanny was IMS' liaison with the Deaf community and taught sign language to workers. John was president. He was nervous at first, since he had quit a good job at Gallaudet and earned nothing the first year. Mary Yeh, a schoolteacher, brought home the sole paycheck and paid the bills.

Eight months after opening, IMS landed its first contract—"a subcontract to modify software for Computer Sciences Corp. on an Army contract," $1.5 million over 3 years.

In June 1981, IMS had 56 employees. By 1985, the offices were so crowded that the company had to find larger quarters. That year, IMS had 300 workers. By 1989, more than 400. By 1991, almost 600. Within a decade, IMS had become one of the Beltway's fastest-growing businesses, "a multimillion-dollar enterprise" specializing in software development, telecommunications, office automation, and systems engineering. In Summer 1988, reported Todd Byrd of **Gallaudet Today**, IMS served "a broad base of government and commercial organizations from four field offices and its spacious corporate headquarters near Interstate 270." 1991 revenues exceeded $38 million.

The Yehs were known as "the brothers" or affectionately by their sign-names: *J1*, *J2*, *J3*, and *J4*. Teamwork was the key to their success. John acknowledged that without their help, "the task of building IMS would have been far more difficult."

He's proud that IMS provided a comfortable, accessible, "Deaf-friendly" environment. A good percentage of IMS employees were Deaf or disabled. About half of the hearing employees knew sign language; many took classes after starting work there. Around one-third were ethnic/racial minorities. Blackboards were used to facilitate communication; TTYs and modems everywhere.

Even though he was wealthy, John continued living in the same housing development as his parents and brothers. He still put in a 70-hour week; his office door was open to all employees. Most of the profits were re-invested in IMS.

He has seen attitudes changing for the better. In 1989, he noted that IBM, which "summarily rejected" his job application in 1973, was now "proud of their disabled. . . . Society has become more aware and more educated about the disabled community." With a wry smile, he described an encounter with an officer of a bank that had rejected his loan application. "I told him about my business. His expression showed shock. He was surprised we had grown."

IMS won numerous national, state, and local awards for its contributions to the economy, and Yeh has been honored as an outstanding entrepreneur and citizen. In June 1988, he received the Gallaudet Community Relations Council's Business and Economic Development Award. He was national runner-up that year for SBA's Small Business Person of the Year award (behind the legendary ice-cream magnates Ben & Jerry). IMS was also chosen by the Defense Department and **Government Computer News** as one of nation's best small minority defense contractors.

In 1990, Yeh joined the Gallaudet University and NCI Boards. On September 30, 1991, in a gala Kennedy Center event, he was one of six recipients of the second annual America's Award, sponsored by the Positive Thinking Foundation and hosted by Childhelp USA. He was honored as a "unsung hero" who personified the American character and spirit.

IMS continued to grow. In 1993, Yeh became Chairman of IMS Technologies, the new parent company of three subsidiaries: IMS (government), IMS Service (commercial), and IMS International.

Although business is his major focus, Yeh maintains membership in numerous civic and Deaf-community organizations. He's a popular keynote speaker at entrepreneurial conferences. He considers computer technology is a booming field for deaf people, and encourages deaf children to work hard and aim high. In 1989, he said, "It's a great joy for me to be able to turn the negative energy of my early frustrations into this positive contribution."

Chuck Baird: "A painter who can act and an actor who can paint."
(Courtesy of Mr. Baird)

CHAPTER 58

Chuck Baird

1947-

Artist and actor

Chuck Baird was born on February 22, 1947, in Kansas City, Missouri, the youngest of five children. His mother collected and sold antiques; his father, a jack-of-all-trades, loved camping out. Both were hearing, but he had three deaf sisters and one hearing brother.

He attended Kansas School for the Deaf in Olathe (1951-1967). "At KSD, I had a good art teacher, Grace Bilger, the hearing wife of a great deaf football coach, an outstanding watercolorist who had won many awards." She provided encouragement and inspiration; he was one of her best pupils. She took the class to art museums, University of Kansas' Art Department, and the Kansas City Art Institute. "These last two places, especially, inspired me to eventually study art in college. The moment I saw the large canvas paintings in the university classrooms, the smell of oil [paint went through me].

"Mrs. Bilger submitted my very first oil painting to the **Scholastic Magazine** Art Contest in Kansas City when I was 13. Later, it was sent to New York, where it won the National Award in the category of oil painting at the high-school level. For each of the next five years, until my graduation, I won gold keys in the regional contest and became a finalist for the National Award in the categories of oil, watercolor, and drawing."

During Baird's senior year in high school, the National Theatre of the Deaf was formed. Through his sister, Ruth Ann, who was attending its first summer session, he learned that David Hays "was seeking two young deaf painters to serve as apprentice scenic designers at Lincoln Center in New York City. I decided to apply, and sent my portfolio to NTD. I learned that I had been accepted for the job only a short time before I received a thick envelope from Gallaudet College notifying me that I had passed their entrance exam. As a Kansas boy, I didn't feel ready to work in New York City. I decided to go to Gallaudet first, to continue my education. Hays understood and offered to wait."

Just after enrolling at Gallaudet as a prep, Baird learned that he couldn't take any art courses until his junior year. Next year, when he was a freshman, he met an NTID recruiter. "Meanwhile, I didn't keep my grades up to satisfactorily complete my freshman year, and I was dismissed from Gallaudet." He applied to NTID anyway, and was fortunately accepted. At RIT's College of Fine Arts, he majored in studio painting, actively participated in several NTID Drama Club productions, and designed and painted sets.

Bob Panara sent Baird to NTD's Summer Program in 1971. Baird later returned to the O'Neill Center for the National Theatre Institute's one-semester program. But instead of joining NTD, he completed his BFA program at RIT.

After graduating in 1974, he taught art for a year at New York State School for the Deaf in Rome. "I was the only art teacher for 200 children in the school, and I taught 20 classes a week, from first through twelfth grade." It was "an overwhelmingly difficult experience." He returned to Rochester, but due to lack of experience, couldn't find a job as a graphic artist.

Meanwhile, the 1975 World Federation of the Deaf Congress was holding an international art exhibition in Washington, D.C. Baird brought some works ("mostly acrylics of 'close-ups' of vegetables"). Ten participants met that week and discussed establishing an organization of deaf artists and a deaf art center in Austin.

Later that summer, NTD hired Baird to paint the sets for its new production, *Parade*. He then found a temporary position as a dormitory counselor at the Margaret S. Sterck School in Newark, Delaware. When he learned that the school was looking for a deaf artist-in-residence, he applied and got the job (1975-76).

After participating in the 1976 NAD Convention in Houston (he helped execute the set of a production staged there), he was invited to Austin. About 15 deaf artists and a few hearing supporters formed a new organization: "Spectrum: Focus on Deaf Artists." Then Baird executed 10 large flats for NTD's *Four Saints in Three Acts* (1976-77 tour).

He returned to Austin for Spectrum's second conference (July 11-17, 1976). "Twenty-four deaf artists from different parts of the United States attended, representing a wide variety of art fields." There were lively workshops and enthusiastic networking. That fall, Spectrum was awarded a CETA grant and hired 13 staff members. Baird was given a full-time position as photographer, and later became coordinator of the Visual Arts Program. During weekly meetings, participants shared discoveries and "had eternal discussions on the criteria and definitions of deaf art. These meetings were where I began to ask myself, honestly, whether I was a deaf artist or not."

Invited to attend NTD's Summer Program—he was "being considered to fill a vacancy in the acting company"—he declined, thinking that he'd be staying in Austin. Later that summer, though, he returned to NTD to paint a set for *The Wooden Boy*. "This time, Hays coaxed me to come back soon, as an actor." On his way back to Texas, Baird recruited more than 30 deaf visual artists and collected the names of 90 more to contact later.

He sponsored "a very successful Capitol Deaf Art Show in the rotunda of the Texas State Capitol" for the 1980 Deaf Awareness Week. But after Spectrum's third successful summer conference, President Jimmy Carter cut the CETA program, and Baird was out of a job. He finally had free time to paint. He designed and painted a backdrop for the Austin Ballet Company's production of *Nutcracker Suite*, depicting the Land of the Sugar Plum Fairy. Soon afterwards, he received a contract from NTD. "Much as I hated to let my painting go for a while, to act, I felt a need to develop my acting, to see the world more, to gain experience in order to paint even better." He hoped to return to Spectrum later, but lack of funding and facilities forced it to disband in 1981.

For 9 years, Baird acted, designed, and painted in and for "practically every [NTD] production." He continued drawing and painting on the side, and found time to mount several one-man shows. "I have found that my work as a professional actor has lent a professionalism to my painting. I've noticed my signing as a storyteller has become more confident and graceful; I feel as though I paint the words in the air as though they were images on canvas. Each craft gives the other more strength. Being an actor helps me to be a better painter, and vice versa."

Baird enjoys being "an actor who can paint or a painter who can act." In NTD's adaptation of Philippe de Broca's 1967 cult-film classic, *King of Hearts* (1988-89 tour), Baird gave a memorable performance as "The Painter." He actually painted a fresh set on huge panels covered with white wrapping paper—from scratch—during each performance. His rapid-fire paintings were part of the action: "Every time when I'd just completed the silhouettes of German and Allied soldiers, I grabbed a bucket of red paint and splashed it on them wildly as I threw out all the emotions and terrors of war—as a difficult part would be for an actor." The concept was new—acting *and* painting in front of the audience. It was a dual challenge. Every brushstroke had to be right. "An actor could ad-lib a mistake, but a painter couldn't." He was nervous during the first two or three performances, but finally relaxed and let loose. "I cherish those memories. It was the best year we ever had together!"

He'd worked closely with Dr. Betty G. Miller, the driving force behind Spectrum, in Austin. "I know her as a fabulous individual, very influential, a genius, a person with a great heart. I would call her 'Mother of DeVia.'" She emphasized the role of art in bringing Deaf people back to their roots and instilling pride. In 1989, Miller, Baird, and several other Deaf artists got together, drafted a manifesto, and developed a label: DeVia [**De**af **Vi**sual **A**rts]. DeVia expresses the Deaf experience through formal artistic elements.

For the historic DEAF WAY Conference and Festival (July 1989), he created a stunning 15' x 40' mural about the Deaf community that was installed in MSSD's cafeteria.

In 1992, Joe Dannis, President of DawnSignPress, commissioned Baird to do a series of Deaf-related paintings. The result was **Chuck Baird: 35 Plates**, a glorious full-color monograph. Signs are cleverly incorporated into still-lifes, nature, or genre scenes, many as playful images. ASL-based paintings present a challenge: how to capture motion in a motionless image. One of Baird's DawnSignPress paintings was kinetic—it had a small motor, and "signed." It was a big hit with viewers.

Baird has always experimented. And he incorporates images and techniques borrowed from all over. The elements of another DawnSignPress painting, *According to Coyote*, came from five different sources: the sky from a scientific text on weather, the canyon from a book on national parks, the rocks in the foreground from a geography book, the coyote from a zoo book, and the head of the Navajo from a picture file. These elements were modified so the lighting was consistent. The painting doesn't look like a pastiche; it's a unified whole.

Other paintings, like *Detour*, are based on his own photographs. "I always attempt to capture the spirit of the interaction between light and shadow. It's just like poetry."

In 1994, he served as artist-in-residence at The Learning Center for Deaf Children in Framingham, Massachusetts. For TLC's 25th-anniversary celebration on October 27, 1994, Baird designed an "ILY" sculpture of 3,600 balloons (the ILY sign resembles "25"), which the students set up. He also coordinated the creation of a photo-collage mural 30 inches high and 150 feet long, depicting the history and evolution of ASL, and celebrating TLC's first 25 years. It was unveiled in the TLC cafeteria on June 10, 1995.

Some DeVia artists choose a militant approach; others, lyrical. Baird's approach has been warm, tranquil, and benign. "I don't have much of anything to be angry about or deny. I simply accepted the way the world is around me. I'd rather find something beautiful in life even if we have a villain somewhere in there. I want to paint about it. I let the viewer see and celebrate with me."

Frank G. Bowe in 1990, a few months after the ADA became law: living
"a life driven by dreams." (Courtesy of Peter C. Howard/**The Hill**)

CHAPTER 59

Frank G. Bowe

1947-

Disability-rights advocate

"My family raised me to live a life driven by dreams." Frank George Bowe was born March 29, 1947, in Milton, Pennsylvania, during the optimistic "baby-boom" era, and grew up in nearby Lewisburg, near Bucknell University campus. His father, Francis, was a plant manager for a steel mill. His mother, Kitty (Windsor), a Bucknell alumna, worked as a newspaper reporter during World War II. He had a younger sister, Robin. Three successive bouts of measles left Frank completely deaf in his left ear and severely deaf in the right when he was 3.

Kitty taught him to read early; Francis drilled him in arithmetic. Ignoring a doctor's advice to send Frank to Scranton State School for the Deaf or Willowbrook, she and Francis insisted that he be enrolled at South Ward, the local public school. He was the only deaf child there. "I believe the hard way is the best way," was Francis' credo. "If you're not going to do your best, don't do anything at all." Determined to give Frank a "normal childhood," his parents enrolled him in Little League and made sure that he got a fair chance to play. He became a "champion" pitcher and an expert tennis player (like his father). Kitty even made him take piano lessons. There were lipreading lessons, too.

What was effortlessly absorbed by his hearing classmates was, for him, attained only through grueling labor. Lagging behind them in vocabulary development, he struggled to master English by reading unfamiliar books and combing through dictionaries. He often skipped recess to read. He endured taunts ("Hey, freak!"), teasing, and beatings by bullies. After one vicious gang attack, his father arranged for him for him to take private boxing lessons from a pro. He did have a few friends.

By sixth grade, "reading was becoming a pleasure." Frank "devoured every word of the **Daily Item**," the local paper. "I continued to favor novels because there, and only there, I learned what people said to each other, how they talked, and what expressions they used."

In eighth grade, he decided to take the demanding college-preparatory academic program at Lewisburg Joint High School, even though his grades were borderline (C+). He derived an unexpected benefit from learning Latin—it helped him understand English better. He graduated in 1965, a respectable 17th in a class of 188. Although he was interested in attending Gallaudet, Kitty vetoed that. He chose Western Maryland College, majored in English/Philosophy, and became its first deaf graduate.

He'd become a skilled writer. "What I wanted to do more than anything else in life was to be a reporter. Drew Pearson and Jack Anderson were my idols." After he did a report for journalism class—interviews and all—his teacher told him that he'd "made a number of factual errors." Reporting, she told him, involved a lot of interviewing and phone calls; editing even more phone-work. "In those days before professional interpreters were the norm, I could see the door closing. Teaching was out. Business was out. And now it seemed writing, the one thing I did well, was also out. I could not, for the life of me, think of what was in."

An emerging political consciousness led to his getting involved in civil rights and Appalachian volunteer work. During winter-semester break of his senior year at WMC, he impulsively drove down to Frederick and visited Maryland School for the Deaf. The children were intrigued. *Same?* signed one boy. *Same,* Bowe signed back. "I was overcome with emotion, just overwhelmed at a sudden and very powerful sense of kinship, belonging, and, yes, of being needed."

He graduated from WMC in 1969, *summa cum laude.* "The fact that I've won under these rules doesn't mean I like them," he told his parents. "Someday, I want to change the rules of the game."

He secured a fellowship to Gallaudet Graduate School's M.A. program in Education of the Deaf. McCay Vernon, "the eminent authority on the psychology of deafness," introduced Bowe to some administrators in the Department of Health, Education, and Welfare; he worked as a research assistant for them while at Gallaudet. He became fluent in sign language.

After receiving his M.A. in Special Education in 1971, Bowe created a special-education program in Bloomsburg, Pennsylvania, for deaf and multiply-handicapped children. He taught sign language, and trained student teachers and therapists, and interpreters.

With the aid of a DHEW grant, Bowe worked at New York University's Deafness Research & Training Center, pursuing a doctorate in Educational Psychology. He had interpreters in all of his classes. No more "lost syllables," no more faking it. He acquired his first TTY and used Contact, a volunteer-network relay service. He received his Ph.D. in 1976.

He met Phyllis Barbara Schwartz, a teacher, in 1973, at an NYU total-immersion sign-language retreat. They were married in 1974 and had two daughters, Doran and Whitney, who chose legal and medical careers.

At the Mayor's Office for the Handicapped, Bowe met its bold, brash director, Eunice Fiorito, blind since childhood, founder and president of the American Coalition of Citizens with Disabilities. ACCD "had no office and a budget of little more than a hundred dollars—but it had, she said, 'a heartful of hope.'" In 1976, Bowe moved to Washington and became ACCD's Executive Director and first paid employee. ACCD became a powerful political force.

Section 504 of the Rehabilitation Act of 1973 (PL 93-112) prohibited discrimination on the basis of handicap, and mandated equal access for all disabled citizens to all federally-funded facilities and programs (including public schools, colleges, housing, transportation). It wasn't enforced during the Nixon and Ford administrations. Unless regulations were issued soon, the law was, for all practical purposes, dead.

Jimmy Carter's inauguration in January 1977 "gave us the opening we sought." On April 5, 1977, 300 disabled persons—including
Deaf advocates—staged a sit-in in the Washington headquarters
of HEW Secretary Joseph Califano. Hundreds more occupied
HEW's 10 regional offices. Bowe masterminded the nationwide
protest, which Sherri Kimmel calls "the largest sit-in by disabled
people in the nation's history." When Califano politely addressed
the Washington demonstrators, promising to issue "fair" regulations "soon," Bowe replied, "Mr. Secretary, with all due respect,
that statement is not what we came here for. We've heard 'soon' too
many times for the word to have any more meaning. And if you are
serious about ending the injustices we are protesting, we ask you
to issue rules—and do it now." Feeling the heat, Califano finally
signed the 504 regulations on April 28.

On May 7, 1977, the regulations were published in the **Federal
Register**, and immediately "had the force of law." The cumulative
impact on U.S. society was tremendous.

Secretary of State Cyrus Vance appointed Bowe as U.S. Representative to the U.N. Planning Committee for the Year of Disabled
Persons (1981). Israeli Prime Minister Menachim Begin invited
him to Israel to make recommendations for accommodating disabled war veterans and civilians. He did similar work in Japan and
other countries. ("Of the 500 million disabled people, about 80%
live in the Third World," Bowe noted in a 1990 article.)

He left ACCD 1981 to form his own company. (ACCD folded in
1984 because of financial problems.) From 1981 to 1984, as president of FBA Inc., he worked as an independent consultant to Bell
Atlantic, IBM, Xerox, NYNEX, Unisys, and other major corpora-
tions. As Director of Research at the U.S. Architectural and Transportation Barriers Compliance Board (1984-87), he administered
research contracts on accessible building telecommunications-
system design. He chaired the U.S. Congress Commission on
Education of the Deaf (1968-88). **Approaching Equality** (T.J. Publishers, 1991) was his report on COED's findings. From 1987 to
1989, he was Regional Commissioner, Rehabilitation Services
Administration, U.S. Department of Education, where he admin-

istered $150 million in grants, supervised 6 VR state agencies, monitored several hundred private university/nonprofit rehabilitation facilities and training programs and independent-living centers.

He's written numerous book chapters and articles and over 25 books on disability rights, special education, employment trends, demographics, and technology, including **Handicapping America** (Harper & Row, 1978), **Rehabilitating America** (Harper & Row, 1980), **Personal Computers and Special Needs** (Sybex, 1984), **Changing the Rules** (Bowe's poignant autobiography, T.J., 1986), **Equal Rights for Americans with Disabilities** (Watts, 1992), and **Birth to Five: Early Childhood and Special Education** (DelMar, 1995). His many honors and awards include being named one of the Ten Outstanding Young Americans by the U.S. Jaycees (1982), CSUN's John Bulwer Award (1988), and **Who's Who in American Education** (1994-95). Gallaudet University awarded him an honorary Doctor of Laws (L.L.D.) in 1981.

He told Kimmel, "I was one of a number of people who said we need to expand 504 to the private sector." He and his colleagues helped create the Americans with Disabilities Act (ADA), which President Bush signed into law as PL 101-336 on July 26, 1990. Then began the implementation process.

Since 1989, Dr. Bowe has been Professor in Hofstra University's School of Education, Department of Counseling, Research, Special Education and Rehabilitation. In January 1996, he directed a national conference at Hofstra, *Access to the Information Superhighway*. He's now monitoring the implementation of the Telecommunications Act of 1996 (PL 104-104), signed into law by President Clinton on February 8, 1996. It has exciting implications for new technology and media accessibility.

He treasures university life—teaching, writing, and research. More than 40 years after launching "a life driven by dreams," he has realized yet another goal. In May 1996, Hofstra University recognized him as its "Distinguished Teacher of the Year."

"I woke up and saw the faces and went blank again." Julianna Fjeld with
her Emmy Award, September 21, 1986. (Courtesy of Julianna Fjeld)

CHAPTER 60

Julianna Fjeld

1947-

Emmy Award-winning producer; actress

Julianna Fjeld was an "army brat." Her father was an Army colonel, so the family lived on bases across the country. Always moving. She was born deaf on June 1, 1947, in Minneapolis, Minnesota, "the only deaf person in the whole family tree." Nobody ever found out why. The doctor who delivered her had immediate suspicions, so her parents were alert.

She first attended the John Tracy Clinic in Los Angeles, from 1948-53. (Founded in 1942 by Louise Tracy, wife of the legendary Hollywood actor Spencer Tracy, in honor of their son John, who was born deaf, it operates a famous oral home-study program. Julianna actually met Spencer Tracy at the Clinic when she was 4. (It was then that she decided she was going to be an actress.) Then came Kansas School for the Deaf in Olathe (1953-58). Then Percy M. Hughes School in Syracuse, New York (1958-59), a day school for the handicapped. ("That was my worst nightmare. I spent my fourth grade there, mingling with handicapped kids. From that experience I became a great political fighter—that Deaf people are not disabled. We are Deaf people with *communication* needs and disabled people are people with *physical* needs.") Then Kendall Demonstration Elementary School (1959-61) on the Gallaudet campus, back to KSD (1961-64), then California School for the Deaf (1964-65). After taking the Gallaudet Board tests and passing, Fjeld left CSD in her junior year for Gallaudet. "I got my official high-school diploma in 1966 after spending one year in prep at Gallaudet, so I officially graduated from CSD-Berkeley in 1966 and finally graduated from Gallaudet in 1970 with a B.A. degree in English Literature.

"At my schools they usually had literary-society events and holiday plays, and I was performing at KSD from time to time. My first role was Rudolph the Red-Nosed Reindeer. Fun, fun role! And I did things here and there in school plays. At Gallaudet I was involved with Gallaudet Theatre, knowing that after graduation there would be no opportunities. I was being very realistic, so I applied for teaching jobs. That was my goal. But when the National Theatre of the Deaf was born, *eureka!!!!*" She was 18 years old, home with her parents in Los Altos for the summer, when she heard "through the grapevine" that NTD was being launched. Bernard Bragg had received David Hays' invitation one month earlier. There was an NAD convention in San Francisco, "around a 45-minute drive away." She went to the convention hotel and "bumped into" Bragg.

"He was in his tux with a glass in his left hand and a script in his right hand. . . . I was very, very, *very* nerdy in looks with a broken nose, wearing a pair of glasses, very skinny, with mousy-colored short hair. I [told] Bernard, 'I would like to be an actress.' He looked at me—with his hands all occupied—and smiled and nodded."

Her boldness paid off. "My first play with NTD was *Gilgamesh.* There were other plays—**The Dybbuk, Candide, Parade**—but *Gilgamesh* was my favorite because it was my first play with NTD, and the rest were beautiful experiences, especially traveling with the company." She also performed in LTD.

"While we were touring with NTD, we stopped in Denver, Colorado, and we met Joanne Greenberg, the author of **I Never Promised You a Rose Garden** and **In This Sign**. I was so amazed at her when I first met her, because while I was a senior at Gallaudet, the book **In This Sign** came out and I read it. That book hit home and I didn't like it, because at that time I was a little embarrassed to be deaf—growing pains." (**In This Sign** [1970] is about a Deaf couple and their often stormy relationship with their hearing daughter, and her own family; it spans three generations.) After rereading it, Fjeld "wanted to do something about" the book.

"To let hearing people see and understand."

Her friend Gregg Brooks "was a student at American Film Institute in Hollywood. He was the very first Deaf person ever enrolled there, and I heard a lot about AFI—a great place for future filmmakers, producers, and writers, and I also realized that Audree Norton [an NTD founding member who was the first Deaf performer to do a TV commercial] was there already as a great actress, doing guest spots in various series." So on July 23, 1977, Fjeld flew to Los Angeles. "And Gregg took care of me. He taught me all the ropes around Hollywood."

She had a small role as a nurse in the 1982 TV-movie version of *Johnny Belinda* (the classic tearjerker about a young deaf, languageless woman, which has never been played by a Deaf actress), starring Rosanna Arquette as Belinda and Richard Thomas as her teacher-benefactor.

Children of a Lesser God first opened at the Mark Taper Forum— "my home in Hollywood"—in 1980, starring Phyllis Frelich. "I was consultant for the production at Taper and on Broadway, and eventually I became Phyllis' understudy during the last 6 months, and I had a great chance going up and performing. I saw that more people were being open to Deaf-culture issues. Right after Broadway, I came back to L.A. and dove into this **In This Sign** project completely. I didn't perform at all for 4 years so I could focus my whole energy to get **In This Sign** off the ground while the air was hot. Then . . . *boom*, it happened."

When she visited the *And Your Name Is Jonah* location during filming, Bernard Bragg "introduced her around." He worked with Darlene Craviotto on a sequel to *Jonah*; Fjeld (an old friend) tutored her in sign language. After CBS turned down the sequel— Bragg says they "felt it was sort of anti-mainstream"—Fjeld gave Craviotto **In This Sign**. Craviotto wrote a teleplay, *Love is Never Silent*, an adaptation of the first half of the book.

Then the legwork began. "My heart was full of joy and faith and patience and love. Lots of frustrations, yes. I was so poor—no money—so I was just barely surviving. Then the word about the project spread, more ripples hitting more people in this town." In the days before California Relay Service, "I had interpreters with me all the time, making phone calls and setting up appointments to meet producers. . . . I have my formula for success—the right project at the right time with the right people. For 10 years, I usually had the right project with the right people but at the wrong time, or the right project at the right time but with the wrong people. So I stuck to it with stubbornness to get the right project at the right time with the right people."

Craviotto arranged a meeting with Marian Rees. "My heart 'clicked' immediately with her, knowing that she meant well, loved the book, and was willing to do it, as long as we could have Deaf actors play the leads." Hallmark was willing to sponsor it. Rees was Executive Producer, Fjeld was Co-Executive Producer, and Dorothea Petrie was Producer. "We were a great team, knocking on the networks' doors."

Then came the pre-production tug-of-war. At first, CBS was involved. CBS wanted "big superstars"—Paul Newman and Joanne Woodward—as Abel and Janice. I said *NO!!!* And Marian fought for me and Deaf actors in general. We disagreed with CBS, so CBS backed out. NBC jumped and got us and told us that [they were] letting us do what was right. So we had Phyllis Frelich and Ed Waterstreet (as Janice and Abel) and Mare Winningham (as Margaret). [We had] wonderful feelings with NBC, and such a good time on location in Vancouver, British Columbia, Canada, where we filmed *Love is Never Silent.* Most of the crew had never worked with Deaf actors before, but the experience—and outcome—was positive." (Fjeld had a tiny but memorable part as Barbara, Janice's Deaf co-worker in the textile mill who gets injured on the job.) Joseph Sargent, who had previously worked with Fjeld (in *Golden Girl*), directed. *Love is Never Silent* premiered on the *Hallmark Hall of Fame* in Fall 1985.

The 1986 Emmy Awards night on September 21 "was the most mind-blowing experience for [us]." There were four other "tough" contenders for Best Picture: *Amos* with Kirk Douglas; *Mrs. Delafield Wants to Marry* with Katharine Hepburn; *Early Frost*, directed by John Erman; and *Death of a Salesman* with Dustin Hoffman.

When Joseph Sargent won Best Director, "I was the happiest gal in the universe and was so satisfied; I didn't think we would win. But—when Linda Evans announced the [Best Picture] winner, it was like a bomb blasting, and no vision in front of my eyes, just a blank. And I couldn't remember my going up with Marian and Dorothea and Michael Ennis, my date who could Sign, until I saw the handwritten card announcing the winner, on the [lectern]. I woke up and saw the faces and went blank again until we entered the wing, where Linda Evans fingerspelled 'I love you' to Dorothea, Marian and me."

Afterwards, "I got a lot of lecturing offers all over the country, and I thought I should do that, so I did, for 4 years, including 3 years of directing school plays at CSD-Fremont, to try something new—*Sign Me Alice* by Gil Eastman; Gibson's *The Miracle Worker*; and *Into Hiding*, based on two different points of view between Anne Frank and Miep Gies (who helped hide the Jewish family in that attic). And I decided I was ready for Hollywood again; came back with new projects and my new production company, White Rose Productions."

After a stint as Co-Artistic Director of the NTD (1991), Fjeld worked as a Vocational Rehabilitation counselor in Boston, then as Managing Director of SignRise Cultural Arts, Inc., then located in Silver Spring, Maryland. She played Blanche DuBois in SignRise's Fall 1994 production of Tennessee Williams' *A Streetcar Named Desire*. After that, she became a producer for *Deaf Mosaic* at Gallaudet University, and worked as Sign Master (developing theatrical sign language with, and directing, a team of two interpreters) for two major productions of *The Follies of Will Rogers* and *Miss Saigon* at the Kennedy Center for the Performing Arts.

When *Deaf Mosaic* ended its 10-year run, Fjeld decided it was time to move back West—this time to Seattle, Washington. In Fall 1995, she began working on "two theatrical projects [for] Abused Deaf Women's Advocacy Services." In early 1996 she became ADWAS' Education/Outreach Coordinator. She's still advocating for Deaf rights, representation, and roles. "And I am still waiting for the infamous word 'novelty' to be erased completely."

Lou Ferrigno: "Never say never!"
(© Globe Photos)

CHAPTER 61

Lou Ferrigno

1951-

Bodybuilder and actor

Lou Ferrigno is still best-known as the star of CBS-TV's popular "comic-book" series (1976-1981), *The Incredible Hulk*. As the "green Goliath" who crushed steel, broke through walls, and terrorized the nastiest villains, he appeared larger-than-life—a 6' 5", 275-pound titan with a 59" chest and 23" biceps. What makes his story all the more poignant is that he was once a shy, skinny, abused kid.

He was born on November 9, 1951, and grew up in Brooklyn, New York. When he was 3, he contracted an ear infection that, undetected, resulted in a 75% hearing loss. Because the available hearing aids (the body-pack variety) were relatively bulky, clumsy, and primitive, he developed "very defective speech. That was harder to deal with than the hearing loss, because people assumed I was dumb when they heard me talk," he told **People Weekly** in 1981. "I was very introverted and always isolated from my class-mates."

For a while, he attended P.S. 47. He later transferred to Brooklyn Technical High School and took lessons in speech and lipreading on Saturdays. Still, he was misunderstood and called "dumb Louie" by the tough kids in his neighborhood. And picked on. "So I fought back, but at the same time I was heartbroken."

He came from a "macho Italian family." His father, Matt, a cop, was a "very strict, domineering" character who pumped iron and psychologically abused and bullied his son. The world of Marvel Comics provided a temporary escape from the nasty realities of everyday life. "I avidly read all the comics and had a huge

collection of them," he told Bill Reynolds of **Muscle** in 1980.
"Superman, Batman, Captain America, The Incredible Hulk—I
loved reading about these super-heroic figures who were all built
like Mr. Universe. I used to have all these fantasies, like growing
up to be a giant of a man, fighting off all sorts of scurvy characters,
and winning the heart of every pretty lady for miles around. But in
reality, I was skinny, too shy even to talk to girls, and pathetically
weak. My fantasies allowed me to escape from all this."

Tired of being taunted, he decided to take up bodybuilding when
he was 12-1/2. "I had a major inferiority complex. . . . I thought that
if I became strong, I could gain respect from people."

When Lou began lifting weights in the basement of his house, his
mother, Victoria, thought he was crazy. His father jeered. He later
attributed his success to sheer determination and "genetic potential," because at first he did many things wrong. When he was 19,
he entered his first contest—Open New Jersey Mr. Hercules—and
finished in 22nd place. Some people advised him to forget about
bodybuilding. Instead, he trained relentlessly. The results were
spectacular. Lou entered the AAU Teenage Mr. America competition and finished fourth. The same year—1971—he won the Teenage Mr. America contest and a free trip to Switzerland.

He was now ready to try big-time competition. In 1972, age 20 (6'
5", 225 pounds), he swept the Mr. Eastern America and Mr.
America titles, then competed in the Mr. Universe contest as the
underdog against 90 experienced opponents. He won by unanimous decision—the youngest competitor ever to win the title. As
TV historian Tim Brooks noted, "By 1974 he had won all of
bodybuilding's major titles including Mr. America (1972), Mr.
Universe (1973 and 1974), and Mr. International (1974)." But he lost
the Mr. Olympia world-class competition to the mighty Arnold
Schwarzenegger. Both rival champs were featured in the
now-classic documentary, *Pumping Iron* (1975).

Although Ferrigno was winning trophies, the prize money wasn't
enough to live on. His first paying job was as a $10-an-hour
sheet-metal worker in a Brooklyn factory. He had learned the trade
at Brooklyn Technical High. Although he stayed on the job for 3

years, he didn't enjoy the work, which was hard and dangerous. After a friend and co-worker accidentally sliced off a hand, Ferrigno decided to look elsewhere for employment.

His first stop was Canada, where he signed on as a defensive tackle for the Toronto Argonauts of the Canadian Football League. After playing in a couple of games, however, he pulled a leg muscle, and after it healed, he quit professional football. He declared that it wasn't for him.

In 1976, he went to Los Angeles, having heard that Universal Studios was looking for a bodybuilder for the nonspeaking *Incredible Hulk* role. He auditioned and got the job. A TV-movie debuted in November 1977, leading to a TV series. Co-starring with Bill Bixby, Ferrigno played the alter ego of irradiated scientist David Banner, who periodically—and unwillingly—metamorphoses into a raging green monster. The chemistry between Ferrigno and Bixby was good. "There's a little bit of The Hulk in everyone," Ferrigno told Bill Reynolds. "The way I play the character, he's a hero who doesn't bother keeping his emotions bottled up inside himself. Everybody feels the urge to hulk out occasionally, but he actually does it!" Later he said, "I have a lot of anger and I grew up with a lot of anger, and in some ways I consider acting like therapy—I'm able to get a lot of these inner emotions out."

Preparing for the role was almost as difficult as the role itself. "It was a nightmare," Ferrigno recalled in 1991. "Making the change from professional bodybuilding to show business was like shock treatment." The makeup procedure took around 2-1/2 hours every day. He was fitted with green contact lenses, false scalp, putty eyebrows, and wig. Then his body was sprayed with green paint. The waiting was nerve-wracking. The work was punishing, and he even had to do his own stunts, which were sometimes dangerous. Once he jumped off a 30-foot-high wall. Another time, he was expected to run through a prop wall supposedly constructed of flimsy breakaway material. But somewhere along the way, the prop crew had made a mistake, and the wall was almost rock-hard. When Ferrigno hit it while running at full speed, he bounced away like a rubber ball. Even the green paint couldn't conceal all of his black-and-blue marks.

After 5 very successful seasons, *The Incredible Hulk* ended its run in 1981. Initially "devastated," Ferrigno, now a seasoned actor, pursued other roles, preferably speaking ones. (He's a accomplished lipreader and wears two hearing aids.) Determined to succeed, he continued to take lessons in speech therapy to improve his speech (which he considered a bigger challenge than bodybuilding). His most enthusiastic booster was his wife, Carla. (A previous marriage—a brief one—had ended in divorce.) They met in 1979 when she was working as a manager at TGIFriday's, and Lou found her to be sensitive and understanding about his deafness and imperfect speech. They also found they shared a common interest, as Carla had previously worked with deaf children as a psychotherapist at UCLA's Neuropsychiatric Institute. She became his business partner. They bought a cheerful house in Santa Monica, and had three children—Shawna, Carla, and Lou Jr.

In May 1981, Ferrigno served as national chairman for Better Hearing and Speech Month. He was also named honorary director of the National Hearing Association "for his singular accomplishment in athletics and acting, and for his courageous example to all the hearing-impaired youth of America that they, too, can be champions." As he himself said: "We are all handicapped, some more noticeably than others."

In 1982, he was chosen for the title role in a remake of the 1959 Steve Reeves movie he'd seen long before—*Hercules*. He began a demanding weight-training regimen at Gold's Gym to develop an ultra-superhero physique. "I'm training for the *Hercules* movie as if it were the Mr. Olympia contest," he told Bill Dobbins of **Muscle & Fitness**. The movie was released in 1983 to indifferent reviews, but critic Leonard Maltin, who called it "silly," acknowledged that Ferrigno was "undeniably well cast." Also in 1983, Ferrigno played a paramedic in ABC-TV's short-lived *Trauma Center*—his first speaking role. In between roles, he did posing seminars and worked as weight-trainer to stars such as Chuck Norris and Mickey Rourke. He and Carla made a weight-training video, *Body Perfection*. Together, they marketed a line of sportswear

("Perfetto").

He starred in other bicep-flexing epics and action flicks: *The Seven Magnificent Gladiators* (1983); *The Adventures of Hercules* (*Hercules II*), 1985); *Desert Warriors* (1988); *Sinbad of the Seven Seas* (1989); *The Cage* (1989), "a pointless and violent film;" *All's Fair* (1989), an unfunny war-of-the-sexes romantic comedy; *Liberty & Bash* (1990); *Superforce* (1990); *Hangfire* (1991); and *Extralarge* (1991), a TV-movie. Some of these bombed. But one of his best vehicles was *The Making of . . . And God Spoke* (1993), an amusing satire of god-awful Biblical epics, in which he played Cain. He also ventured into stage acting, playing Jonathan Baxter in a Chicago production of *Arsenic and Old Lace* , and starring in *Requiem for a Heavyweight* (both 1985).

There were occasional TV appearances (e.g., *Battle of the Network Stars; Celebrity Challenge of the Sexes*), and a few *Incredible Hulk* TV-movies. Seven years after the original series ended, Ferrigno teamed up with Bill Bixby again and returned to green paint and shredded shirts in *The Incredible Hulk Returns*, a 2-hour TV-movie that aired on NBC on May 22, 1988. A "final installment," *The Death of the Incredible Hulk*, aired in 1990.

When asked if he'd be returning to competition, Ferrigno replied, "Never say never!"

After repeated setbacks, he took second place at the 1994 Masters Mr. Olympia competition.

Bill Graham and Kathie Skyer Hering in Chicago, 1996.
(Pat Condon, courtesy of Bill Graham)

CHAPTER 62

Bill Graham 1952-
Kathie Skyer Hering 1950-

Champions of late-deafened adults

It started with a small list of names and a get-together. Around 1985, Kathie Skyer Hering of Glenwood, Illinois, a social-services worker, formed an informal support group for late-deafened adults. Science editor Bill Graham and two others from the Chicago area showed up in 1986. They came to discuss the major problem they faced—isolation—and to give each other the support they weren't getting elsewhere.

In March 1987, 11 late-deafened people came to Graham's house for a party. He'd gotten their names from Hering, who had compiled a contact list of 25 persons. Something "clicked." Says Graham: "The party was a smash success. Although most of us were total strangers who had never so much as spoken to another late-deafened person, we found it easy to be in one another's company. There was a special feeling in the room—a feeling of belonging, of unspoken understanding, of patience with our similar communication difficulties. A week after the party, I wrote a letter to all the people on the mailing list, expressing my view that something extraordinary had occurred. The enthusiastic response to that letter led me to begin a regular newsletter, through which we consolidated a group that eventually became known as the Association of Late-Deafened Adults (ALDA)." ALDA swiftly became the fastest-growing deaf organization in the United States. Within three years, it had gone international.

With 23 chapters in cities throughout the States and Canada, ALDA offers support groups, social activities, advocacy, and a yearly conference. Says Graham: "Born-deafness is a state of being. Late-deafness is being in a state of disrepair. In ALDA, people can be the way they are without apologizing for their inability to hear. It's okay to be deaf. It's not the end of the world—for many of us who have found ALDA, it can be the start of a wonderful new world. One that is different from the world that we used to know, but no less satisfying."

In 1993, ALDA received a state grant to create a program for people with adult-onset hearing loss. This became the pioneering Hearing Loss Link Program in Chicago. Offering counseling, advocacy, referral, education and outreach, it serves as a national model. For Graham, it was a dream come true. "ALDA fills a tremendous need to meet and share with others who have traveled the same road," he says. "But late-deafened adults usually have problems that can benefit from professional help and guidance. Link fills this need."

Bill Graham was born on September 15, 1952, and grew up in a tough blue-collar neighborhood on Chicago's South Side. "I grew up with a slight impairment, but went through high school without thinking about it much. I considered myself perfectly normal and I don't think many, if any, people outside my family knew I didn't have normal hearing.

"I had hearing aids since I was about 14, but the first kind I had was built into my glasses and I hated wearing glasses, so there was no way you'd find me in them. Sometimes, when the lights were low at home and I was watching television in the front room by myself, I put them on. But no way would I wear them with people nearby. Later, as my hearing deteriorated, I started to wear aids— the smaller behind-the-ear models. After I started to accept my hearing loss better, I wore aids all the time; I figured people would see them and treat me better, as a hearing-impaired person.

"I attended an all-boys Catholic high school with a predominantly black student body. I played varsity baseball and intramural everything else. I loved sports. I didn't try too hard in the classroom—except maybe in math-related classes—but ranked in the upper eighth of students. I wrote for the student newspaper and won a national award my senior year."

At Illinois Institute of Technology, he originally majored in Architecture. "My hearing started to go downhill fast. By the end of my freshman year, I often couldn't understand what teachers were saying. I had trouble coping. (By the time I was 25 I couldn't hear on the phone anymore. So I consider myself to be deaf since age 25.) I quit the architecture program, then planned my future courses and major so I would have to spend as little time as possible in the classroom. I graduated from IIT with a Bachelor of Science degree in English.

"After college I knocked around a bit, worked in an electro-coating factory, with a hard hat, operating a crane. Then I went to Colorado State's graduate-school program in creative writing. I finished all of the coursework but didn't get through my oral examinations because of communication misunderstandings. As a result, I never graduated. After leaving Colorado State, I worked for about a year writing scripts for educational videotapes, then **World Book Encyclopedia** in Chicago found me. I worked at **World Book** from 1977 through 1995." He was Life Sciences Editor for 13 years. In January 1996 he began work as an editor for Microsoft's **Encarta** encyclopedia in Redmond, Washington, north-east of Seattle. His wife, Karina (hearing), whom he married in 1991, is a noted advocate and clinical social worker.

He began learning sign language around 1982. "I'm not very good at it, but it's not stressful and the only way I can be sure what a person says. With lipreading, I am *not* sure. I taught sign language to about 150 people at **World Book**. Some of them got good enough to serve as emergency interpreters for me [there]. Since coming to Microsoft, I've started biweekly sign-lunches."

In February 1991, Graham became the youngest member of Gallaudet University's Board of Trustees. His appointment gave the Board a 51% deaf majority. That November, he became ALDA's first Executive Director at the princely wage of $1 per year. In

February 1993, he resigned from that position and as editor of **ALDA News,** to take the helm as Executive Director of Hearing Loss Link. In September 1993, he received the I. King Jordan Outstanding Achievement Award for serving as the primary force in ALDA. He's a board member of Lighthouse for the Blind's Center for Aging and Vision Loss (New York), VITAC (the Pittsburgh-based captioning/media-access company), and is on **DEAF LIFE's** Advisory Board.

In Summer 1995, Graham underwent cochlear-implant surgery, and was hooked up just before ALDAcon 95, where he delivered a speech in his characteristic style—honest, upbeat, and funny.

Kathie Skyer Hering knew that deafness was inevitable. Neurofibromatosis Type 2 ran in her family. She recalls: "At my brother's high-school graduation in 1973, my two sisters, my brother, and I placed ourselves strategically around the table to accommodate our 'bad ears.' Bilateral acoustic neuromas would deafen all four of us between 1975 and 1978. These tumors don't develop until the second decade of life or later, just when young adults are busy making career and lifestyle choices."

Even though she went through a period of denial, there was support and acceptance in her family—of deafness and sign language. "A lot of late-deafened people didn't have that kind of support. No one understood them when they talked about isolation or some of the empty feelings you have.

"I was born February 24, 1950, in Chicago. My family moved to the suburbs in 1960. I graduated from high school in 1968. I attended University of Illinois at Chicago and obtained my B.A. in History Education." In Fall 1975, she entered UIC's M.A. Program. Her tumors were diagnosed and she underwent her first surgery that year. "Not believing that I would lose my hearing, I completed my coursework for the M.A. program. I suddenly lost the hearing in my 'good' ear in August 1978." At age 28, she was deaf. Because she could no longer teach in a regular classroom, she returned to graduate school to earn a degree as a rehabilitation counselor.

The worst barrier was other people's attitudes. "I wanted stability in my life. To achieve this, I completed my degree, married my significant other [John Hering], and moved to a house. I took my comprehensive exams the following spring. Meantime, John and I attended a sign class and I took speechreading classes and sign-language tutoring. I enrolled in NIU's Counseling Program in Fall 1979 and obtained my M.A. in Counseling with Deaf People in 1981.

"Immediately after high school, I was hired by the U.S. Post Office as the first full-time female Career Carrier in Park Forest, Illinois (whoopee). I was told when I took my work physical, that women were too "frail" to be mail carriers. I just went to another doctor and 'passed' my exam, my point being: if I am told I can't do something, then I try much harder. I was told, 'No one can learn to sign well enough in one year to use an interpreter.' Well, I did. It was not easy to do, but I needed to do it, so I did."

Hering initially worked as counselor and program manager at Kennedy Job Training Center in Palos Park with minimum-language-skill deaf adolescents and adults. In 1988, she joined the Board of Directors of the Will-Grundy Center for Independent Living and served as Board President several years. She's been ALDA Chicago Chapter President since 1991, and is editor of its newsletter, **ALDA Chicago Style**. She's served on the National Board of Neurofibromatosis, Inc., promoting public awareness of NF-1 and NF-2, and is a member of the Link Board of Directors.

"[Since I began networking with other late-deafened people], I have regained my confidence. For my Chapter work, I received the 1991 ALDA Fearless Leader Award. I would rather nominate others for awards than receive them myself. Some people deserve the recognition for their achievements—Steven Wilhelm for developing ALDA Crude [a real-time setup], and Holly Elliott for her many years of research and training about the needs of people with adult-onset deafness. Both of them have demonstrated dedication to improving the quality of the lives of deaf and deafened people. Others, like Roy Miller, work to quietly improve opportunities for our future. ALDA's growth has enabled links between these people. It feels good knowing that I was a part of that."

Mary Lou Novitsky co-hosting *Deaf Mosaic*.
(Courtesy of Gallaudet University TV Department)

CHAPTER 63

Mary Lou Novitsky

1954-

Deaf Mosaic co-producer and co-host

Mary Lou Novitsky is best known as producer (1987-1991), co-producer (1995-95), and co-anchor of *Deaf Mosaic*, which enjoyed a 10-year run as the only nationally-broadcast program for and about deaf people. For her work on it, she won five Emmy Awards, television's highest honor.

"I was born deaf on July 18, 1954, in Johnstown, Pennsylvania. Both of my parents were deaf, but my older sister, Theresa, is hearing. My parents were on the staff of the local hospital. I fondly remember visiting them at work, sometimes joining them for meals in the hospital cafeteria. It was in this setting that I became interested in helping people, which later led to my decision to major in Psychology at Gallaudet.

"I attended the Western Pennsylvania School for the Deaf in Pittsburgh and was very active in soccer, volleyball, basketball, and softball. I was also a member of the student council. My current position as a television producer probably stems from my early interest in media. At WPSD we were required to take vocational courses, and I took them all—cooking, sewing—you know the kind. During my senior year, I didn't want to cook any more, so I enrolled in a media course instead. I was hooked—I found television and photography fascinating." She graduated in 1974.

At Gallaudet, Novitsky minored in Communications, graduating in 1979 with a B.A. in Psychology. (At that time, Gallaudet had no TV major.) For the next two years, she worked as a researcher and captioner at the National Captioning Institute. Using specialized equipment, she converted scripts from television programs and movies into captioned text, which she then recorded onto floppy disks for reference and storage. In 1981, she joined the staff of Gallaudet's Department of Television, Film and Photography as a production specialist—its first full-time deaf employee, and, for 3 years, its only one. "Even my parents said I couldn't do TV," she told Elizabeth Levy-Malis of **Producers Quarterly** in 1990. "I thank God I had the guts and the stubbornness to ignore all the people who said I couldn't." She provided pre-to-post-production support for studio and remote assignments, including camera operation, lighting, floor management, technical direction, character generation, editing, and captioning. From 1984 to 1986, she was an associate producer there. Her responsibilities included developing and producing story concepts, developing scripts and production plans, and working with senior members of the production team.

Deaf Mosaic's predecessor was *Images*, an on-campus program produced, taped, and edited by Novitsky. "When a new administration took over, I was given more responsibility, since I knew the Deaf community better than anyone in TV. Dr. Marin Allen, Chair of Gallaudet TV, came up with the catchy title *Deaf Mosaic*." Hosted by Gil Eastman during its first two years, it began airing in April 1985, a lively half-hour magazine-format show and the only Deaf programming on "mainstream" television.

In 1988, Novitsky was promoted to Senior Producer/Director and became the producer and co-host of *Deaf Mosaic*. She also represented the TV Production Department at public functions in the States and abroad. She produced and directed other on-campus projects, including a video version of Gil Eastman's book, **From Mime to Sign**.

For 6 years, *Deaf Mosaic* aired weekly on more than 100 PBS affiliates, then, in August 1990, debuted on The Discovery Channel, reaching more than 65 million homes nationwide. Viewers who tuned in were greeted by the sight—which must have been exotic to some—of two attractive professionals using sign language, with synchronized open captions and voice-overs to ensure full accessibility. There were also music and sound effects. Particular care was taken to ensure the highest-quality audio track for the benefit of hard-of-hearing and moderately-deaf viewers. So *Deaf Mosaic* had a fully-equipped post-production audio room.

For thousands of hearing viewers, no doubt, *Deaf Mosaic* was their first exposure to sign language and Deaf issues. Deaf viewers, needless to say, were hungry for Deaf-oriented programming. *Deaf Mosaic* filled that need.

Deaf Mosaic featured stories about deaf people from around the world, and covered events and issues of importance to the national Deaf community—cochlear implants, mental health, prisons, AIDS. There was footage of the Deaf NAMES Project Memorial Quilt—panels commemorating the ever-increasing number of deaf victims of the AIDS epidemic. Deaf personalities, many pursuing professional careers—architects, lawyers, authors, entrepreneurs, community activists—were spotlighted. Interviews were conducted in sign language. There were profiles of historical figures, and contemporary folks with unusual hobbies—a skydiver, for example. It often focused on the arts, including the National Theatre of the Deaf and other performing groups, and chronicled important social, political, and cultural events in the Deaf community—sports tournaments, World Games for the Deaf, NAD conventions. World Congress of the Deaf, and The DEAF WAY.

Novitsky—and *Deaf Mosaic*—took an international view and ventured into new territory. A major production priority was to enrich viewers' awareness and respect for deaf people and Deaf culture throughout the world. *Deaf Mosaic* production teams traveled all over the States and Canada, the Caribbean, Europe, Australia, and New Zealand. As Levy-Malis noted, "*Deaf Mosaic* was the only program to visit the Canadian location of the film version of *Children of a Lesser God* and aired the first television interview with Marlee Matlin, who went on the win the Academy Award for her role as the deaf lead in the film." *Deaf Mosaic's* DPN special was internationally honored, and its exclusive video footage of that historic week was extensively rebroadcast in the States and abroad.

In its decade-long run, *Deaf Mosaic* and its staff received a total of 18 Emmys, the National Academy of Television Arts and Sciences (NATAS) Board of Governors' Award, 4 Council on International Nontheatrical Events (CINE) Golden Eagles, 6 Cindy (Association of Visual Communicators), and 4 Telly awards, and many other honors from the Deaf and hearing communities.

In 1987, Novitsky's outstanding work was recognized by NATAS when they honored her with her first Emmy Award. She subsequently received several other television awards from Council of Advancement and Support of Education (CASE), CINE, National Educational Film and Video Festival, and other professional organizations for her talent-exposure and special-interest programs. Plus NAD's Achievement in Television Production Award in 1988, GUAA's Outstanding Young Alumnus Award in 1989, **The Tower Clock** Dedication and School of Communication Dean's Award in 1991, and WPSD's Distinguished Alumni award in 1994.

Since 1986, she's given numerous presentations and workshops on television production to various groups and organizations. In September 1989, she presented a seminar, "Working in Tandem: The Production of Deaf Mosaic/Magazine Programs for the Deaf," at an international conference, *European Broadcasting Union on Educational Television*, in Stockholm, Sweden. She was a panelist at the National Federation of Local Cable Programmers conference in Washington, D.C., in July 1990. And she was a commencement speaker at North Carolina School for the Deaf in 1991 and Alabama School for the Deaf in 1994.

She married Jerry Mabashov, After-School Program Coordinator at KDES (which was just a few feet away from the *Deaf Mosaic* studio), on June 10, 1989. ("He's deaf, too. He graduated from Fanwood in 1978.") They live in the Beltway suburb of Crofton, Maryland. In Fall 1990, she took a 3-month leave to take care of her first child, Michael Alexander, who was born on October 23, 1990. Their second, Dan Arthur, was born on June 30, 1993.

By the time Gallaudet's TV Department announced that *Deaf Mosaic* would cease production, it had been seen by countless millions of viewers across the States and in England, Europe, Asia,

Australia, and South Africa. On June 25, 1995, *Deaf Mosaic* aired its final show on The Discovery Channel. Novitsky said, "We're feeling some sadness about bringing *Deaf Mosaic* to a close, but we're also looking forward to creating new programs to educate and entertain the Deaf and Hearing communities."

Novitsky is now Production Supervisor at Gallaudet TV. She says: "I have traveled extensively, both as a producer for *Deaf Mosaic*, and as an invited lecturer on deaf life and my experiences. I think I've been to most of the continental United States, as well as Germany, Sweden, Finland, England and Italy.

"I believe it's important that deaf people become involved in any and all activities. If you do not, then you'll be a victim and cripple future generations. It means that we must put into action all that is best for the deaf community and deaf people.

"I truly enjoyed my tenure as producer and host of *Deaf Mosaic.* It was really a pleasure meeting people from all walks of life and from all over the world. Each individual I met was special and unique. I learned so much from them and I will treasure all the experiences I encountered.

"I hope my contributions to television have had a small impact on the deaf and hearing communities. *Deaf Mosaic* was a terrific avenue for me to share our varied interests and abilities. It was also an instantaneous and proficient procedure for disseminating important news, such as AIDS awareness, or changing federal regulations and laws to the deaf community.

"Now that *Deaf Mosaic* ended its run, I am working on other projects such as developing teleconferences, distance learning, and mentoring Gallaudet students in the field of television. I will be producing and directing programs for Gallaudet, and continue to lecture about television for and by deaf people.

"Not everyone stops with the accomplishment of one goal; she must pursue new goals—and I am. My future interests are varied and I look forward to what lies ahead."

Top: Bruce Hlibok in the "Hubbell's Nightmare" scene, *Runaways*, 1978. (Martha Swope.) Bottom right: In *The Deaf-Mute Howls*, 1988. (Ellen Roth.) Bottom left: Around the time *Lovelost* was produced, 1990. (All photos courtesy of Albert and Peggy Hlibok)

CHAPTER 64

Bruce Hlibok

1960-1995

Actor, playwright, ASL teacher

Bruce Michael Mackintosh Hlibok was born on July 31, 1960, Peggy (O'Gorman) and Albert Hlibok's firstborn. The Hliboks—with their three other children—Stephen, Gregory, and Nancy—became one of the best-known families in the Deaf community.

Bruce was precocious. At 2 years, he could read books independently, although his parents read to him every night. At 2 years, 6 months, he started his schooling at Lexington School for the Deaf. He loved to draw, built airplanes and paper houses, and was always "very active except during reading time." After 8 years at Lexington, he attended P.S. 107 for a year, then spent 7 years at Horace Mann School, where he excelled in English. (He ultimately wrote over 100 poems and prose pieces.)

When he was 13, he was local and national Jr. NAD President. In 1975, he wrote and directed two versions of the annual fundraising play for the Metro NYC chapter of Jr. NAD, a revue, *That's Entertainment!*, and edited the Youth Leadership Camp newsletter, **Daily Drum**.

In 1977, when he was 17, he made theater history. In May, he auditioned and was cast for Elizabeth Swados' off-Broadway musical, *Runaways*. **The New York Times** called it "an inspired musical collage about the hopes, dreams, fears, frustration, loneliness, humor, and perhaps most of all, the anger, of young people who are estranged from their families and are searching for themselves." Swados said she cast him "because I think signing is beautiful." Hlibok later told a **Daily News** reporter that she "asked three deaf teenagers up for the role to draw a picture of what life would be like for runaways. The other two drew model houses with trees and picket fences. 'I drew guns and figures of death and violence.' He got the part."

Runaways played for 2-1/2 months Joseph Papp's Public Theater Cabaret in Greenwich Village, and in May 1978, moved uptown to the huge Plymouth Theater on Broadway until it closed on December 31. It got several Tony nominations, good reviews, and extensive publicity. In short, it was a hit. As Robert Swain noted in **The Deaf American**:

> Bruce supplied a lot of the spirited energy. He was the first to spring to action after the lights went up. (His name headed the cast listing in the playbill.) Not a moment did he relax during the musical's two hours; he danced, jumped and bounced around with the members of the cast. And his nimble hands and fingers were never idle as he lustily "sang" and spoke in sign language.

His dynamic performance as Hubbell was noticed by the critics, who admired his expressive signing (quite a novelty on Broadway). Lorie Robinson, who voice-interpreted for him, also got an enthusiastic response. Favorable reviews appeared in **The New York Times**, **New Yorker**, **Newsweek**, and **Rolling Stone**, all mentioning Bruce. He was a beautiful young man, with an angelically handsome face and tousled dirty-blond hair.

He had spirit, too. He told a reporter in 1978, "The theater group in high school wouldn't let me act. They said I was useless, that I wasn't needed. But when I got the part in *Runaways*, they came to see me and told me they were sorry. I made it in spite of them." He managed to juggle schoolwork and Broadway. Swain noted that he had to leave immediately after his own commencement ceremony at Horace Mann to prepare for that evening's performance.

Runaways gave Hlibok his "first break in mainstream theater." "I was the first deaf person to play a deaf character on Broadway, and the first deaf person to be in a Broadway musical," he later told another reporter. "It was thrilling." Nonetheless, he still felt like an outsider. "I wanted to be part of the team, but somehow I was always different."

He appeared on ABC-TV's *1978 Tony Awards* telecast as a guest performer, and, around the same time, in *The Baxters' Night Out* and *The Baxters' Christmas Special* (WCVB-TV, Boston); HBO's *Christmas in New York*; and PBS' *Search for Solutions* and *Rainbow's End*. Later he appeared in an episode of CBS' *The Equalizer*, and ABC's *20/20*.

He spent a year (1ᶜ '9-80) in Gallaudet College's Honors Program, performed the title role in *Androcles and the Lion*, and was voted "Best Actor." He attended the 1980 National Theatre of the Deaf summer program, and presented a staged reading of his play, *Going Home*. That fall, he transferred to New York University. He studied playwriting at NYU's Gallatin Division/University Without Walls, and received his B.A. in English/Playwriting in 1985.

His first full-time job was as a sign-language instructor at New York Society of the Deaf. Beginning 1981, he taught ASL, Deaf Culture, new teaching methods, and interpreting techniques, and ultimately became director of its Sign Language/Interpreter Training Program. In a 1990 interview, he said, "Last night . . . one [student] explained he was studying sign language so that he could get to understand deaf culture and to find a cure for the disease of deafness. I was so angry I was ready to castrate him, but, being a teacher, I kept my temper under control and pointed out that Hitler thought Jews were also diseased people."

He was a GED Instructor for Deaf adults in New York City Technical College in Brooklyn. He counseled and tutored NYU doctoral/graduate students on their theses and dissertations. He was a sign-language consultant and researcher at City University of New York and NTID, working with graduate students, and a sign-language/theatrical-interpretation consultant to various theaters and agencies.

He wrote **Silent Dancer**, a children's book about his sister Nancy, then a 10-year-old Lexington student enrolled in the Joffrey Ballet's after-school class for deaf dancers. Beautifully photographed by Liz Glasgow, it was published in 1981. It was, and remains, one of the most positive and anti-stereotypical books about deaf children.

During the '80s, he and Ellen Roth—a Deaf friend from NYU days—presented and hosted several parties: "How Shocking!", "Mindtrip," "New York," "After Dark," "Let's Party!", and "Halloween Madness!"

He emceed a few state-level Miss Deaf America pageants, conducted workshops, participated in panel discussions, and presented lectures (e.g., NYU, NTID) on Deaf Culture/ASL issues. In October 1991, he participated in the second ASL Literature Conference at NTID. He directed all evening-entertainment shows during the DEAFantasy SIGNsail cruise in August 1992.

Best known for his theater work, Hlibok enjoyed a successful—if controversial—career as a playwright and actor. He wrote more than 12 plays, of which several were produced, mostly in small Manhattan theaters or public facilities. (Others were put aside for future development.) Many producers rejected his work after learning that he was deaf, and wrote plays that were performed in sign language. *Short Lessons in Socially Restricted Sign Language* (1982-3) was performed in a school auditorium. In 1983, he founded his own theater company, Handstone Productions, trying to make sure "deaf theater becomes professionally recognized—and not as a novelty." Using "a core group of Deaf and hearing actors," Handstone produced a variety of theater pieces for Deaf/Hearing audiences. Most were original Off-Off-Broadway productions: *WomanTalk* (1984); *The Passion of Rita H.*, a "SignOpera" (1985; also played in Boston and Washington, D.C.); *Rainfall* and *Anna and Danilo* (1988); *Lovelost*, his last produced play, a "musical a cappella" and a staged reading of *Deafwatch: Silence!* (1990). He performed in several of his plays.

The Deaf-Mute Howls was a one-man show based on the 1930 autobiography of Albert Ballin, a Deaf actor, writer, traveler, and advocate. After its 1988 off-Broadway premiere, Hlibok performed abridged versions at the 1988 NAD Biennial Convention and The DEAF WAY Festival in July 1989. He toured Europe twice (1990-91), playing International Visual Theatre in Paris and HandTheatr in Amsterdam.

His work received mixed reviews. Hlibok insisted that it wasn't "sign-language theater . . . just theater." Ellen Roth says that Hlibok's plays were years ahead of their times—too bold, too outspoken. *WomanTalk* was about an abused wife who kills her husband; *Rainfall*, the anguish of a Deaf man with AIDS. Raymond Luczak describes *Lovelost* (which Hlibok himself said was "about how people react to being lost, being abandoned by the people they love") as "uneven" but "nakedly honest." Plays like these depressed and irritated Deaf audiences, who wanted cheerful works.

Bruce also took roles in "mainstream" productions. In September 1991, he played off-Broadway in *Another Person is a Foreign Country*. In June 1994, he returned to Broadway and once again got rave reviews, playing John Singer in Avalon Repertory's production of *The Heart is a Lonely Hunter*—the first *theatrical* adaptation of Carson McCullers' novel. In the movie version, Alan Arkin had played Singer, the "tragic deaf-mute" who "listens" to everyone else's sorrows and never expresses his own, but Hlibok invested the role with a passion and authenticity no hearing actor could have done. **The New York Times** praised his "mysterious melancholic dignity" and vivid signing. It was his last role.

Bruce's health had begun to fail in Fall 1993. Diagnosed with AIDS, he remained busy as long as he could. There was so much left undone—plays, books, projects, return visits to Amsterdam, a city he loved. He bequeathed his collection of over 400 theater books and videos to Gallaudet's Theatrical Arts Department. And he designed his own panel for the NAMES Project AIDS Memorial Quilt, which his friends sewed together. It showed the masks of tragedy and comedy, peeking from a rich maroon-velvet, gold-fringed curtain and making the ILY sign, with his name in a spotlight. (Bookplates with a similar design were inserted in the books and videos of his Gallaudet bequest.) Later, Peggy and Al began working to establish a memorial endowment at Gallaudet. There would be other memorials, other remembrances.

He died on June 23, 1995—just over a month before what would have been his 35th birthday. His life and career were cut short; his death became yet another tragic statistic of the AIDS epidemic.

Marlee Matlin helped make sign language chic—and being Deaf glamorous.
(Courtesy of Bragman Nyman Cafarelli)

CHAPTER 65

Marlee Matlin

1965-

Oscar-winning actress

For better or worse, Marlee Matlin has become the best-known Deaf face in Hollywood. A celebrity. A *superstar*. As everyone knows, she was "discovered" by Hollywood while performing in the stage version of ***Children of a Lesser God*** and given the chance to star in Paramount's film version with veteran film actor William Hurt. And the rest, as the saying goes, is history.

She was born in Morton Grove, Illinois, on August 24, 1965. Her mother, Libby, worked in a jewelry store; her father, Don, was a used-car dealer. There were two older brothers, Eric, a stockbroker, and Marc, an auto-loan officer.

When she was 18 months old, she developed a case of roseola (a strain of measles), accompanied by a series of high fevers. Her deafness was diagnosed 6 months later, when she was 2 years old. She first attended an oral school, and began learning sign when she was 5. Growing up deaf could be frustrating and lonely. She later described herself as "an angry child," stubborn, "paranoid" about being deaf and getting stared at. Acting was an outlet for the pent-up feelings. She started in summer camp. At the Children's Theater of the Deaf sponsored by the Center on Deafness in Des Plaines, Illinois, Marlee, 7, made her stage debut as Dorothy in ***The Wizard of Oz***. She had lead roles in ***Peter Pan***, ***Mary Poppins***, and ***A Chorus Line***. She later told Lou Ann Walker: "We did plays all over Illinois, Nebraska, and Indiana." When she was 12, Henry Winkler went backstage after one of her performances and signed "I love you." (They became friends.)

When she entered John Hersey High School in Chicago (which had a deaf program), she put acting on hold—"it started to become competitive, and I hate competition."

At William Rainey Harper College in Palatine, Matlin considered a career in law enforcement—as a probation officer for deaf criminals—and took two semesters of criminal justice. (She had always loved TV cop shows.) She was in her third semester when a friend urged her to audition for a touring-company production of *Children of a Lesser God*. She took the secondary role of Lydia. (She knew that a movie was being planned, but didn't attempt to audition, as she figured there'd be plenty of deaf actresses competing for the lead role. She was right. Dozens auditioned in New York, Los Angeles, Chicago, and Canada. But the one chosen wasn't considered suitable.) A Paramount talent scout saw Matlin's first performance. Afterwards, each cast member was videotaped. Soon afterwards, an astonished Matlin got a phone call from Paramount, asking for a videotape of her as Sarah Norman. Director Randa Haines flew her to New York for another audition, then to Los Angeles for two more. The "obvious chemistry" between Matlin and Hurt helped her clinch the role. She was 19, Hurt 35. Filming was done August to November 1985.

The movie version blunted much of the play's political bite, reducing it to a conventional love story and sweetening it with a happy ending. But Matlin's fiery ASL performance got raves. **TIME's** Richard Schickel called her "a beautiful young woman and an actress of awesome gifts. . . . she has an unusual talent for concentrating her emotions—and her audience's—in her signing. . . . *Children of a Lesser God* cannot transcend the banalities of the play. But Matlin does. She is, one might say, a miracle worker." **Newsweek's** Jack Kroll correctly predicted that her performance was "so good that she is likely to be the first deaf actress to get an Oscar nomination." She was.

Also nominated for Best Actress of 1987 were veterans Jane Fonda (*The Morning After*), Sissy Spacek (*Crimes of the Heart*), Kathleen Turner (*Peggy Sue Got Married*), and Sigourney Weaver (*Aliens*). Beating the odds, Matlin won. She accepted the Oscar statuette from Hurt. As Joanna Powell noted in **Glamour**: "It was a moment straight from the Hollywood fantasy mill." She was only the fourth actress to win an Oscar for a debut performance, and, at 21, the youngest ever to win Best Actress. She also won the Golden Globe that year in the same category. She was now a superstar. Gallaudet University bestowed an honorary doctorate on her—not without criticism. She said: "I feel honored to represent deaf people . . . and I also feel scared."

Her next movie role, a small one, was with Ed Harris in Alex Cox's *Walker* (1987), based on the real-life adventures of William Walker, an American filibuster (soldier of fortune) who briefly took control of Nicaragua and declared himself president in 1856. Matlin played Ellen Martin, a wealthy socialite, Walker's fiancée and political opponent—and actually deaf. She spent two weeks in that war-torn country and, as **Glamour** reported, gave her free time to charity, making day trips to deaf schools where they signed in Spanish." The film "died at the box office."

The next year, at the 1988 Academy Awards telecast, she sparked a firestorm of controversy in the Deaf community. Before presenting Michael Douglas with his Oscar for Best Actor, she signed, then lowered her hands and used her voice to announce the nominees. She was proudly showing off the results of voice coaching. As she told Lou Ann Walker: "I'm not trying to be hearing. I take advantage of the hearing I have. But I don't like being labeled 'the deaf actress.' I'm an actress who happens to be deaf." Later, she told another reporter, "The first thing that comes to mind when people hear my name is, 'Oh, she's the deaf one!' I've learned to accept that kind of attitude."

Ever since *Children*, she had struggled with the problem facing all deaf performers in Hollywood: a scarcity of suitable scripts. She used her clout to collaborate with producers to get scripts written for her. To this end, she formed her own company, Solo One Productions, to acquire and develop projects she could produce or act in.

CBS-TV's *Bridge to Silence*, shot on location at Lake Simcoe near Toronto, and first aired in April 1989, was Matlin's first speaking role. (Actually, she spoke and signed, Sim-Com style.) Although she'd been speaking all her life, she took speech-therapy sessions with Dr. Lillian Glass, a well-known Beverly Hills speech-and-voice pathologist. Her pronunciation was improved considerably.

Matlin made the covers of **People**, **Us**, **IN Fashion**, and **Cable Guide**. In 1987, **Harper's Bazaar** chose her as one "America's 10 Most Beautiful Women." One critic noted that it was hard to take your eyes from her. She was petite, with chestnut hair and translucent skin, and a wonderfully expressive face, hands, and body. She was uninhibited, earthy, her signing peppered with profanity.

In Spring 1990, Matlin and her ginger-vanilla cat Billy Joel ("B.J.") got prime-time exposure on a delightful 30-second Whiskas cat-food commercial. It was in ASL with open-captions. She also appeared in national ads for Target, Cheerios, and Apple computers, and PSAs for AmFAR and Amnesty International.

In Summer 1991, ripples of excitement went through the media and Deaf community: Matlin was going to co-star in NBC's new prime-time TV series, *Reasonable Doubts*. She played Assistant District Attorney Tess Kaufman, opposite Emmy nominee Mark Harmon, as police detective Dicky Cobb. She was quoted in **Entertainment Weekly**: "Speaking on the show was a decision I was terrified of. I am insecure about my speech; I know deaf people do not speak as well as hearing people."

Reasonable Doubts premiered on September 27, 1991. Matlin had become the first deaf performer to star (not guest) in a prime-time TV series. The series got mixed reviews—critics felt that Harmon was miscast and Matlin wasted, but everyone liked her feisty character. It lasted two seasons. Matlin was nominated for a People's Choice Award and two Golden Globe Awards.

Reasonable Doubts was followed by a few small parts and cameos. Matlin played Jeannette, "a beehive-hairdoed cashier," in *The Linguini Incident* (1992), about a Manhattan restaurant. **Film Journal** called it a "zany but uneven romantic spoof." She won a coveted cameo in Robert Altman's *The Player*.

In Robert Greenwald's romantic thriller *Hear No Evil* (1992), she starred as a fitness trainer stalked by a cold-blooded killer seeking a stolen rare coin hidden in her beeper. Critics liked Matlin's spirited performance but hated the movie. "Terminally dull," yawned **Variety**. It was another box-office dud.

In February 1993, Matlin became engaged to policeman Kevin Grandalski, whom she met on the set of *Reasonable Doubts*. They were married that August at Henry Winkler's Los Angeles home. The engagement and wedding were publicized in **People**. Their first child, Sarah Rose, was born in January 1996.

In 1994, she played the title role in Lifetime's *Against Her Will: The Carrie Buck Story*, about a woman whose 1927 Supreme Court case made it legal to sterilize "mental defectives" against their will. This was her first "non-deaf" role. It was nominated for a Cable ACE Award. She also appeared in comic roles on *Picket Fences* and *Seinfeld* and got Emmy nominations for both performances. In March 1995, she returned to *Picket Fences* to reprise her role as Laurie Bey, the "Dancing Bandit," and became a series regular in September 1995. She appeared in *It's My Party* (1996)—about a gay man with AIDS who decides to throw one last party before committing suicide. She starred in another computer commercial—for Macintosh. And on numerous TV specials.

Matlin has had profound impact on the hearing community. A deaf actress's winning an Oscar in an ASL role made deaf performers that much more visible. Her high visibility in the hearing community, coupled with her refusal to limit herself to "deaf" or non-speaking roles, has caused some controversy within the Deaf community.

Yet, among her political and volunteerist involvement (e.g., AIDS), she has maintained her commitment to "Deaf" causes. As celebrity spokeswoman for the National Captioning Institute, she has successfully advocated increased closed-captioning on TV and home videos. She participated in the Deaf Performers' panel at The DEAF WAY (July 1989), and lent support to the Center on Deafness, GLAD, TRIPOD, and other "good causes." She loves to visit deaf schoolchildren wherever she works or travels. And, indisputably, she helped make sign language chic—one could even say that she made being Deaf glamorous.

Top: March 13, 1988: The student leaders give a victory cheer. (Courtesy of Tim Rarus.)
Bottom: A 5th-anniversary portrait (1993). Left to right: Rarus, Covell, Bourne-Firl,
Hlibok. (Jim Dellon, GU TV/Photography Department, courtesy of Ms. Bourne-Firl)

CHAPTER 66

Jerry Covell 1965-
Tim Rarus 1966-
Greg Hlibok 1967-
Bridgetta Bourne-Firl 1967-

DPN student leaders

The "Deaf President Now!" uprising at Gallaudet University (March 6-13, 1988) captured the world's attention, however briefly. For the first time in history, deaf people and their concerns got front-page, prime-time exposure.

When two qualified deaf candidates for president were by-passed in favor of a hearing administrator who didn't yet know sign language, students (and many faculty and staff) went on strike to protest the Board of Trustees' decision and closed down the campus. As we know, the nonviolent strike was successful, and had some immediate positive effects: the appointment of Gallaudet's first deaf president and, soon afterwards, a deaf Board majority. Across the nation, schools for the deaf began actively seeking and hiring qualified deaf candidates as superintendents, administrators, faculty, and staff. The ADA was signed into law on July 27, 1990. DPN helped provide impetus.

The DPN leaders were chosen by the Gallaudet student body. All were student-government leaders. All are from Deaf families. DPN has had a profound impact on their careers and lives.

Gerald Lee Covell was born on February 4, 1965 in Spokane, Washington. He attended Washington State School for the Deaf in Vancouver, various public schools with deaf programs, Texas School for the Deaf in Austin, and then graduated from Maryland School for the Deaf in Frederick in 1984. He entered Gallaudet College in 1984, and received his B.A. in American Government in 1988. He received his M.A. in American Government and Voting Behavior from University of Maryland in December 1995.

Covell was the most actively involved of the DPN student leaders. He was instrumental in the organization of the protest.

He worked at KDES as instructor's aide and instructor and Head Residence Education Assistant for Student Life at MSSD; Paralegal Assistant for Student Life at Gallaudet; Assistant Manager's intern at Federal Bureau of Prisons and Litigation Assistant Intern for the Civil Rights Division, both at the Department of Justice. He's given numerous presentations nationwide on Deaf awareness, rights, and empowerment.

As Executive Director of the Missouri Commission for the Deaf, he continues his "commitment to equality of access and treatment for all deaf persons," working with state legislature, agencies, organizations, and the grassroots community.

He's on several committees that have direct impact on the people he serves: State Rehabilitation Advisory Council (governor-appointed); State Task Force on Education of the Deaf (Chair); Interpreter Training Program Advisory Board, William Woods University; Gallaudet University Regional Center/JCCC Advisory Board; Department of Mental Health/Bureau of Deaf Services Steering Committee; Missouri Deaf and Hard of Hearing Coalition (Founder); Missouri School for the Deaf Advisory Board (Liaison); and Relay Missouri Advisory Board. Also, he has drafted, found sponsors, testified, and successfully lobbied for various legislation "that assures equality, respect, independence, and accessibility for all individuals with hearing loss."

He is married to Laura (Fitzwater), who works at Missouri School for the Deaf. (She's hearing.) They live in Fulton with two Dalmatians and a cat.

Tim Rarus represents the fourth generation of a Deaf family. He was born on May 28, 1966, in Hartford, Connecticut, and attended American School for the Deaf until 1974, then California School for the Deaf, Riverside, for nearly a year, returned to ASD for the next two years; then Arizona School for the Deaf and Blind until he graduated in 1983. He entered Gallaudet that fall and received his B.A. in Government in 1989. He did graduate work at the University of Missouri Kansas City, majoring in Public Administration, and planned to enter law school in 1997.

"My grandfather, Edgar Bloom, has been one of my greatest role models. As a young deaf man in the early 1900's he overcame many of the obstacles that prevented deaf Americans from succeeding as they do today. A graduate of Columbia University with two Master's, one in Chemical Engineering and the other in Chemistry, he taught me that the world could open for me if I fought hard enough. He lived in an era where there were no interpreters and where services for the deaf were scarce. He opened many doors during his time, and it is my hope that I can follow in his footsteps.

"My mother, Nancy Rarus, is no stranger to advocacy. She has always told me, 'Being deaf is a full-time job.' As a child, I would watch her argue for the rights of deaf people with NAD and other state organizations. Having two strong role models as my grandfather and mother, I have always known I would enter the field of advocacy."

After graduation, Rarus worked with Senator John McCain (R-Arizona) at as Staff Assistant at the U.S. Capitol for two years, then moved to Overland Park, Kansas, where, for the next three years, he served as Assistant Director/Workshop Manager at the Gallaudet University Regional Center at JCCC. In 1991, he married Brandi Sculthorpe (Miss Deaf America 1988-90). They relocated to Austin, Texas, where Brandi works for Sprint as the Account Manager of Relay Texas. "I am currently employed as the Executive Director of Vaughn House, Inc., which provides vocational and residential-program options for deaf people with additional disabilities. Our kids at the moment are our cocker spaniels."

Gregory Hlibok was born on June 24, 1967, and grew up in Flushing, New York. "I attended Lexington School from K-12 with one slight interruption," during first grade, when he was sent to a nearby public school where he was ignored and unfairly punished. "It was a dreadful experience. So I had a 'silent protest' by not communicating with my family much and insisting that I return to Lexington School. I was sent back to Lexington afterwards. So that was where I gained my experience in protesting!"

At Gallaudet, he was elected student-government president shortly before DPN, and was the most prominent of the student leaders. On March 9, 1988, he made a memorable appearance on Ted Koppel's *Nightline.*

"Since DPN, I have been in schooling with a one-year break, working at the prestigious law firm Milbank, Tweed, Hadley & McCloy in Manhattan as a legal assistant. It helped me decide on becoming a lawyer. Studied law for 3 years at Hofstra Law School on Long Island." He graduated in 1994. "Was actively involved with its activities, like being participant of its Pre-Trial Litigation program, President of ACCESS (Disability Law student organization), participant in Trial Technique, and recipient of the Robin Cohen Award (for the student who has an excellent record of student-activities participation with high academic standing). From time to time, I have given speeches at some conferences and graduation ceremonies across the country."

Hlibok participated in the August 1994 protest at Lexington Center for the Deaf, in which the selection of a hearing Executive Director sparked community-wide protests. This, too, succeeded.

"Currently, I am an associate at the Law Office of Ralph G. Reiser, who is also a deaf attorney. Our firm does general practice but concentrates mostly on negligence, discrimination, matrimonial, and contract-dispute cases.

"One of my best memories since DPN is the evening when I proposed to my fiancée [Charmaine Jacobs]. I practically drove all the way from New York to Washington D.C., under [a] heavy storm, from midnight to 4 a.m.!" They were married in September 1995, and live in Flushing, New York.

Bridgetta Bourne was born in 1967. She attended preschool at Gallaudet's Speech Center, the oral Camelot School ("I became an early oral failure"), then Maryland School for the Deaf (1973). "I remember my first day at MSD—I couldn't believe it when I saw EVERYONE signing in the cafeteria. I grew up at MSD." She graduated in 1985.

"I graduated from Gallaudet University in May 1989 with a Bachelor's degree in Government." After an adventurous summer backpacking through Europe with friends, Bourne interned at the National Academy. She planned two regional seminars: women's employment and leadership for young adults. "Then I became a program-development specialist. While working full-time, I was in Gallaudet's graduate program in Administration and Supervision studying Public Administration, took evening and weekend classes, and graduated in May 1992. By then, the coordinator's position, which required a Master's degree, was open and I was promoted to it." She became "an expert on the implications of the ADA for the deaf community and became involved in disability advocacy. I contributed to Joseph P. Shapiro's book, **No Pity**, and began reviewing other people's articles and books to make sure they were sensitive to the deaf community—including the Department of Education's training materials on the ADA and a genetic counselors' manual for working with deaf clients."

She married Leslie Firl (Gallaudet '87), in September 1990. Their son, Jared, was born in July 1994.

In May 1992, as a result of Gallaudet's Vision Implementation Plan, the National Academy was disbanded; Bourne-Firl was "displaced." "Being laid off was a difficult and devastating time." She found a new job as conference coordinator in the Conference Management Unit within the College of Continuing Education, managing a group staff focusing on developing, planning, implementing, and evaluating conferences held in the new Gallaudet University Kellogg Conference Center. Concerned about the low percentage of deaf employees at Gallaudet, she helped found the Deaf Employees' Caucus, a revival of the old workers' organization, and was elected its first Chair.

Kenny Walker signing "tackle." From a triple sequence, "Tackle your dreams,"
taken during his Denver Broncos days, 1992. (Philip Saltonstall)

CHAPTER 67

Kenny Walker

1967-

Pro football player

There have been two deaf players in the history of the National Football League. Bonnie Sloan played for the St. Louis Cardinals from 1973 until 1974, when a preseason knee injury ended his career. And then there's Kenny Walker.

He was born in tiny Crane, Texas, on April 6, 1967, the youngest of Julia and Fred Walker's six children, and the only deaf kid in town. (Julia was a cafeteria worker; Fred an oil-field worker.) At age 2, Kenny contracted spinal meningitis. For 5 days he ran a high fever and was in a coma. When he woke up, he was deaf. He considers himself "blessed" to have survived. (He was left with about 11% hearing in his left ear; an aid helps him modulate his speech and registers extremely loud sounds.)

Times were hard in Crane, and Julia and Fred separated when Kenny was 4. Julia and the children moved to Denver so Kenny could attend a deaf program at University of Denver, where he learned sign language and speechreading. He mixed with hearing kids, who didn't think he was much of an athlete; when they chose teams they picked him last. After seeing how good he was, they began picking him first. One season, he led Baker Junior High's basketball team from last place to the league championship.

He never thought of himself as "handicapped." He told **Sports Illustrated for Kids**: "If I felt sorry for myself, my brother Gus would beat me up!" Gus, one year older than Kenny, interpreted for him, encouraged him, and goaded him on: "You're not going to be a quitter. Your deafness can't prevent you from doing anything you want to do." Of Kenny, he said: "I'm his ears and he's my inspiration."

Denver was an expensive place to raise a family, so Julia and the children moved back to Crane when Kenny was 15. For him, the uprooting was traumatic. He'd made many deaf friends in Denver, his "hometown," but Crane had no Deaf community. He'd had support services in class. In Crane, there were none. Still, he enrolled as a sophomore at Crane High School, instead of commuting 60 miles to the Regional Day School for the Deaf because he wanted to spend time with friends, not on the road. He struggled to speechread his teachers. (He had some helpful ones.) He overcame his shyness, made friends, and became popular. He played basketball and ran track. Even though he had never played organized football before—just the rough-and-tough street version— he joined the school team in 10th grade, where he made the starting team as a defensive end and, on offense, as a split end. By the time he was a senior, he was a *bona fide* star. The **Dallas Morning News** rated him one of the top 20 high-school players.

The "Southwestern powerhouse football colleges"—Texas A&M, Baylor, University of Oklahoma—wanted to recruit such a hot prospect. But Walker wanted to go to University of Nebraska ("Big Red"), and wanted an interpreter provided as part of the deal. "There is too much happening to read everyone's lips," he said. NU agreed to provide one, so that's where he went, its first deaf scholarship player.

Mimi Mann, who worked as a freelance interpreter at NU's Handicapped Services Office, was recruited to interpret for Walker. An admitted non-fan ("Sports leave me cold"), she "knew absolutely nothing about football." She first met Walker in 1985, when he visited NU on his recruiting trip. At first, she felt very much out of place. But she made a 5-year commitment, took a crash course in football terminology, studied the playbook, worked diligently with the Cornhuskers' coaching staff, absorbed endless hours of instruction, covered meetings, watched videos, asked questions, and, along with Walker, earned herself a place in Husker history. She and Walker developed a "field vocabulary" of 500 signs so he'd know immediately what the coaches wanted him to do. She accompanied him to his classes and every team meeting, even halftime chalkboard sessions. She made a much-quoted remark: "The least important thing about Kenny Walker is his deafness. The most important thing about him is his heart." (To her, the Huskers were "beloved players" and "dear, sweet coaches." Walker's roommate Morgan Gregory, NU starting split end, helped "keep him abreast" of things he missed when Mann wasn't around.)

Mann's interpreting allowed Walker to focus on his academics. He majored in Fine Art at NU and maintained a B average.

And with Mann on duty, the once-reticent Walker was able to tackle interviews. When asked if opposing players got angry when he tackled them, he replied, "Yes. I saw a player, here, say to me, 'Read my lips,' then he cussed me out. I just ignored that." He explained that he didn't use his hearing aid during games. As for "late alignment changes," he said: "We have signals before the snap, where a tap on the hip or my back gives me the last-second switch in plays. I can read the linebacker's lips to get the play calls." A teammate or linebacker would tap him on a particular spot on his back, leg, or rump when the ball was snapped; a defensive tackle might crouch and give him a quick hand-signal.

With the Huskers, Walker kept getting shifted to different positions—outside linebacker, middle linebacker, defensive tackle— and finally, after two years, defensive end. That's where his strength was and where he wanted to stay. As John G. Hubbell noted in **Reader's Digest**, "By his senior season, he had become a dominating defensive end." According to a 1990 writeup, "With a time of 44.58 seconds in the 40-yard dash, Walker is Nebraska's fastest lineman, and the sixth-fastest player on the squad."

He finished the 1990 season with 73 tackles, and led the Huskers in tackles for a loss (21), 11 quarterback sacks, and 21 quarterback hurries. He made all three Big Eight Conference teams, and was the first deaf player named to AP's All-America first team, the first Husker to make it since 1988. UPI chose him as its Big Eight Defensive Player of the Year. He was AAAD's Athlete of the Year.

One unforgettable moment occurred in early November 1990,

before his final home game with the Huskers. There's a tradition for senior NU players to be introduced alphabetically. As each jogs onto the field, fans stomp and cheer. Local media and NU's sports-information office "engaged in a conspiracy." The Omaha **World-Herald** illustrated the ASL version of an ovation ("flying hands")— hands held high, palms out, fingers spread, wrists rotated quickly. Mimi Mann and Julia Walker, who had come to see Kenny play, made sure that he didn't see any newspapers that morning. Little danger of that—he was preoccupied with the upcoming game. Waiting his turn in the Memorial Stadium tunnel, he could feel the vibrations in his shoulder pads as the capacity crowd of 76,464 fans cheered each senior Husker. But when he jogged out, he felt only silence. Puzzled, he stopped and looked up. The fans—all of them—were giving him a standing ovation with "flying hands." Kenny turned to all corners and signed back, "I love you!"

The Denver Broncos picked him in the eighth round of the 1991 NFL draft, one of four defensive players. He could have been drafted higher, but teams were doubtful about a deaf player's ability to succeed in the league. He was determined to play as well as anyone else. At 6' 3", 265 pounds, Walker was smaller than many NFL linemen, but strong (a 375-pound bench press), quick, smart on the field, and *very* determined to succeed. During his first NFL season, he played in all 16 Broncos games, had 16 tackles, and 3 sacks. (He appeared in 6 different football-card series—the first deaf player ever to hit the cards!)

As Adam Schefter wrote in **Game Day Spotlight**: "Walker's upper-body strength is a tremendous asset in the heat of battle; his gentle demeanor makes him one of the most popular Broncos." The kids—hearing and deaf—loved him. Off-season, he made PSAs and public appearances on behalf of NCI and charitable causes. Among his honors was CSUN's 1992 John Bulwer Award for "daring to be different." He was already thinking ahead to his post-football career—possibly advocating for Deaf rights, pursuing a career in commercial art, or both.

At a college party in 1988, he'd met Martina Offenburger, a student at Creighton University in Omaha, who was seeking a mentor for her 10-month-old son Tommy, newly diagnosed as deaf. They were "just friends" for two years, started dating in April 1990, and were married at Boys Town on Valentine's Day, 1992. As **World-Herald** columnist Michael Kelly wrote:

> [T]heir marriage, you could say, was improbable.
>
> She is Catholic, he is Baptist. She hears, he does not. She is white, he is black. Parents on both sides must have worried about the differences.
>
> "I sat down with Kenny and Marti once," said Dan Offenburger, her father, "and asked, 'Are you aware of the challenges you face in crossing the racial gap?'
>
> "Kenny looked at me and said, 'We're not worried about that. The bigger challenge we face is the gap between the hearing world and the deaf world.'"

When Marti gave birth to Kenny Bo (hearing) in October 1992, Walker was there in the delivery room—with his interpreter, Guy Smith. As Schefter wryly noted: "After the baby was born and everyone in the room had a chance to see him, Marti concluded Bo had her nose. Kenny concluded Bo had his brown eyes. And Guy, not to be left out, concluded Bo had his fuzzy black hair."

Smith, who wore a coaching-staff uniform on duty, was knowledgeable about football jargon. But none of the Broncos knew sign language. On the field at Mile High Stadium, as he had done at Memorial, Walker made do with speech-and-face-reading, and simple gestures. Although Smith was interpreting for Walker fulltime at practice games and team meetings, he was on standby on the sidelines during games, and couldn't trespass onto the field. The biggest problem was when linebackers shouted out changes. Even the defensive-line coach admitted it was a problem.

After two seasons as defensive end with the Broncos, Walker was informed that he'd been put on waivers (i.e., cut). According to the Broncos, he was pushed out by two draft picks—younger, fresher talent. Others suspected that the Broncos had gotten tired of dealing with a deaf player. He was released in August 1993.

After the Broncos dropped him, Walker played with three teams in the Canadian Football League before retiring from pro football. He's now a teacher, counselor, and coach at Iowa School for the Deaf. His autobiography, **Roar of Silence: The Kenny Walker Story**, was published in September 1998.

Shelley Beattie as Siren in *American Gladiators*.
(Courtesy of Ms. Beattie)

CHAPTER 68

Shelley Beattie

1967-

Champion bodybuilder, American Gladiator

Shelley Beattie was born in Santa Ana, Orange County, California, on August 24, 1967, and spent her first 11 years in Corona, a Los Angeles suburb. She had two younger brothers and a sister. When gangs began moving into the neighborhood, the family relocated to tranquil, small-town Monmouth, Oregon.

She was "very hyperactive" and "got into everything." When she was 3, she overdosed on aspirin—she got into the cupboard one day and ate 20 adult-strength tablets. "Why I loved eating aspirin and kept on eating so much I'll never know." Later she learned that it *could* cause severe hearing loss. Being "hyper" kept her alive. "A normal 3-year-old kid would have died—that's what the doctor told us. I went into a coma after they pumped my stomach, and afterward I had a lot of hearing problems"—recurrent ear infections. Tubes were surgically inserted to drain them. Her hearing fluctuated wildly. She ended up with a severe nerve-damage loss in her left ear, profound in her right.

She had what she calls a "messed-up" childhood and adolescence. She was mainstreamed, wore hearing aids, and had speech therapy. No accommodations were made for her at school. "I always felt left out. I *was* very good at reading lips and deciphering words, and I still do that today.

"There was a lot of denial in my family. My parents, instead of accepting my hearing loss, called me things like 'stubborn,' 'rebellious.' My teachers had notes on my report cards like 'Doesn't pay attention, easily distracted.' My peers called me 'airhead,' 'stuck up,' and 'weird.' I was *not* a rebellious or bad kid—just confused."

Because her parents could no longer care for her, between ages 14 and 17 she was placed in three different foster homes and attended three different high schools. "It was horrible. All my problems got worse. I felt abandoned and unlovable." She refused to switch on her hearing aids. "I was hyper; I was losing my hearing slowly. I couldn't deal with it, and neither could they. I had problems communicating with anyone. As I lost more and more hearing, I preferred to be alone."

Her progressive hearing loss, not so paradoxically, motivated her as an athlete. At the urging of her coach, she began weight-training when she was 14 to improve her track-and-field performance, in which she excelled. "The weights were also a method of escape for me. I was introverted and tired of being introverted. Developing strength and muscles disguised my insecurities. I had a natural amount of physical strength. When I started lifting I added to that. Lifting made me more aggressive. I loved the attention it got me. The guys thought I was unreal. I was stronger than the [other] girls. In fact, I could compete with the boys when it came to pure strength. I felt secure, I felt safe. People were more afraid to call me names due to my hearing problem because I was becoming a pretty tough girl—with muscles!"

She attended Western Oregon State College, majoring in Child Psychology. (She didn't graduate because although she'd managed to keep up with a full-time-job her first two years, she took on another full-time job during her third and fourth, and had to cut her class load in half. "I was pretty stressed out.") She worked as assistant manager of a co-dependent group-home for children with a variety of handicaps—mental, emotional, physical.

During her first year at WOSC, she learned ASL, began using interpreters in her classes, and met and made friends with other deaf and hard-of-hearing people. "In many ways it was easier to be deaf rather than in the middle. Now I've found a balance of both worlds. I need to have both hearing and deaf cultures in my life." She also studied jazz dance and choreography, and for two years was a member of the Disco Dance Theatre. She put her expertise to good use in her posedown routines, which incorporated "trendy video-dance moves," as one reporter put it.

"I entered my first contest when I was 19—the 1985 Portland Rose Cup. I placed fourth, weighing then about 126 pounds. I was a skinny kid with lots of energy. I loved competition. I knew I was hooked. Bodybuilding is an individual sport. I'm better at singular sports. I like having control of how I do, based on my own actions." She worked her way up in the competition circuit, and also made her mark in handcar racing, which involves old-fashioned hand-pumped railroad cars, each with a team of two athletes operating the crossbar. She took 1988 and 1989 national and world records for fastest time with co-ed handcar teams. Those records still stand. She still holds high-school track and heptathlon and college weightlifting records. Her best bench press is 315 pounds.

She entered 6 bodybuilding contests in 1989, winning Heavy-weight class and Overall titles at the Vancouver National Champi-onships, Western Oregon, and Portland Rose Cup and Emerald Empire competitions. In late 1989, she placed second to Nikki Fuller at the Emerald Cup and Pacific Coast Championships, and in 1990, again won class and Overall titles there. "Then"—as **FLEX** put it—"came a sensational—albeit unexpected—overall victory" at the 1990 National Physique Committee (NPC) USA. In her first national competition, she bested Fuller (who came in second), and won both Heavyweight and Overall titles. The muscle magazines raved. Typical comment: "Shelley Beattie's proportions were dy-namite" (Ruth Silverman, **Ironman**). At the 3rd Ms. International (1991), her first pro show, she placed third.

During 1990 and 1991 she did "guest-posing appearances" across the States and in Russia and Finland. "*WOW!* What an experience meeting all the Russians and Europeans! We were treated like queens and kings. I learned so much about other cultures—it really made me appreciate being free and American!"

She placed 7th at the 1992 Ms. International. "My proudest achievement so far was placing third at the 1992 Ms. Olympia. I never worked so hard in all my life." She credits her "huge improvements" to John Romano, whom she first met at the 1991

Ms. International. An accomplished bodybuilder and nutritionist, author of **Muscle Meals**, he was training Tonya Knight, who took first place, and was later "Gold" on *American Gladiators*.

She participated in an anti-steroids/drug MTV spot, and had an endorsement contract (1990-92) with Joe Weider Health and Fitness—doing TV, magazine advertisements, photo shoots, Q/A columns and articles (especially for Weider's **FLEX**), videos, and personal appearances. She also lobbied in support of closed-captioning on ESPN, and insisted on having her videos and TV spots captioned. In 1992 she signed a 5-year endorsement contract with Twinlab, a leading sports-supplement company, and represents **Muscular Development Fitness and Health**.

Summer 1992 marked Beattie's debut on *American Gladiators*, as "Siren." Romano, acting as Beattie's agent, "made the endless calls to the producers to have me try out, and convincing them that my hearing loss would *not* affect my athletic performance *or* communication with them. When I got called to try out I was *sooo* thrilled! I ended up breaking the old records: 57 pushups in a minute, 4.5-second 40-meter sprint, and knocking down Gladiators in a match of Powerball and Joust. The first reaction from the producers was: 'She's a *machine!*' But it wasn't over yet. The fact that I was hearing-impaired was the only obstacle for them—not *me*—THEM. I was told later I'd be an alternate Gladiator—and promised 2 shows (of the 26), but if another Gladiator got hurt I'd be the first in. The girl they picked at first was "Lace." But after the first day she was *fired* and I was in. They told me later that they were really sorry and they made a big mistake—but that I had been a *godsend* to their show.

"My most memorable experience on the show was my first day's first event—when unexpectedly, as I came out to do Slingshot (bungee-game), the entire audience stomped their feet and waved their hands for me! I couldn't hold back the tears. It felt so good to be a Gladiator. I wanted to win for the *kids*—the *fans*. I just love them. I felt for the first time, I was accepted for my deafness."

In November 1992, she had a bit part in *Hot Shots 2*, with Charlie Sheen and Leslie Nielsen, playing herself as Siren. *American*

Gladiators, of course, had lucrative tie-ins. There was a Siren Action Figure, a team poster, and other goodies.

In 1994, Beattie took on a new challenge: getting one of the 26 coveted spots on *America³*, the first all-women crew to compete in the 1995 America's Cup, the world's top sailboat race. She was one of 650 women to try out. Although she had no sailing experience, she applied anyway, and was chosen as a finalist. "A grueling 10-day tryout on the boat impressed them that I was coachable." She was a grinder—cranking the winch that kept the sails tight—which requires tremendous strength.

By that time, Beattie had accumulated an impressive list of TV appearances—*Entertainment Tonight, Good Morning America, NBC Evening News, ABC World News Tonight, CBS Interview with Connie Chung and Ted Koppel, CNN Headline News, MTV Sports*, a Lifetime documentary, and numerous profiles, interviews, and cover stories in muscle and sailing magazines, **Sports Illustrated, Mademoiselle, Mirabella, Glamour, DEAF LIFE, Los Angeles Times, Boston Globe Sunday Magazine**, and **People Weekly**. She's enjoyed the publicity and gotten positive response.

"I used to coach for Special Olympics—track and field, mostly, but also basketball and weightlifting. It gave *me*, as well as my 'kids,' a lot of pride and joy." She's continued her involvement in the Special Olympics and participated in other good causes—the Make-a-Wish Foundation, a PSA for BHI, and a visit, as Siren, to hospitalized survivors of the April 1995 Oklahoma City bombing.

In August 1995, Beattie and Romano moved from San Diego to Orlando, Florida, where she began preparing for a live version of *American Gladiators* that opened in December. She was thinking about getting a spot on the Women's Kayak Team in the 1996 Olympics.

In her interviews, she's talked about growing up, fitness, and the frustrations and complexities of deaf/hearing communication. And attitude. "I'm a survivor," she says. "If you are patient and disciplined, there is nothing you can't do if you believe in it. Don't let others define who you are or limit you. Don't doubt your abilities. And never fear change."

Curtis Pride, at a field near his home in Silver Spring.
(Courtesy of Joe Rizzo/Better Hearing Institute)

CHAPTER 69

Curtis Pride

1968-

Pro baseball player

Curtis John Pride was born in Washington, D.C., on December 17, 1968, the second child of Sallie Curtis Pride, a former registered nurse, and John Pride, a former track star and specialist in disabilities at the Human Resources Department. Sallie had contracted rubella (German measles) during the 1968 nationwide outbreak. (Her two daughters, Jackie and Christine, were hearing.) At 17 months, Curt was diagnosed as congenitally deaf with a profound (95%) sensorineural loss. A hearing aid amplifies the 5% he hears, but it's just undecipherable noise.

When he was 2, the Prides moved to Silver Spring, Maryland, and enrolled him in the Montgomery County Public School System's Auditory Services infant program. He spent his grade-school years in special-education oral classes. As Pat Jordan noted in a **Sporting News** cover story, "But even as a child, Pride refused to learn sign language. He saw that as a sign of defeat. He insisted he not be categorized by his deafness." He has always relied on lipreading.

He was always "crazy about sports." Sallie and John encouraged him to participate in sports, and when he was 6, enrolled him in a local T-ball league. He loved it. After his very first game, he declared, "I'm going to be a baseball player!"

As a fourth-grader, Curt took his first mainstreamed classes. It was a traumatic introduction to the cruelty of other children. He came home after the first day, vowing never to go back. Sallie comforted him: "There will always be cruel people. But you can never, ever let them stop you from doing what you want to do." Pat Jordan says, "He was teased and shoved around by other kids," but finally knocked down a tormentor and earned their respect.

When Curt was ready to enter junior high, John and Sallie wanted to send him to "a special school for the deaf," but Curt insisted on enrolling in a nearby public junior-high school. He was fully mainstreamed in neighborhood schools until he graduated from John F. Kennedy High in 1986. As the only deaf kid in school, he took his lumps. Predictably, his classmates taunted him.

Through junior and senior high, he struggled to lipread the teachers (who sometimes absent-mindedly turned their backs on him while lecturing) and tried in vain to follow classmates' conversations. He enlisted the help of a shy classmate, Steve Grupe. When the teacher spoke facing the board, Steve mouthed the words to Curt, and helped him with his notes. Curt helped Steve with his baseball. The two became fast friends. Curt's reputation as a top athlete gained him popularity. He was a straight-A student.

At Kennedy, he broke several county records and virtually all of the single-season and career records for soccer, basketball, and baseball. When he was 16, he toured China with the U.S. National all-star soccer team, competing for the 1985 Junior World Cup at Beijing Stadium. He scored two of the U.S. team's 3 goals and assisted on the third. Afterwards, **Kick Magazine** named him one of the top 15 youth soccer players in the world, and the only American. (Kennedy's soccer coach Jeff Schultz later told the **Washington Post**, "I still think soccer is his best sport. I almost cried for soccer's sake [when Pride concentrated on basketball and baseball].") He excelled in wrestling, swimming, track, and gymnastics as well. He was a **Parade** All-American in basketball—his basketball prowess gained him a full scholarship. (He was recruited by more than 200 colleges.) But baseball was his first love.

He signed a baseball contract after being drafted by the New York Mets just before he graduated from Kennedy High (he was a 10th-round free-agent amateur-draft pick), but also worked out an unusual deal whereby he could attend the College of William and Mary (Williamsburg, Virginia) on the basketball scholarship, play-

ing baseball part-time (during the summer). The Mets uncondi-
tionally released him each fall and re-signed him in June. (He
signed a standard rookie contract: $7,500 plus $700 for every
month he played.) The NCAA ruled that he could play pro baseball
while maintaining amateur status in other sports. At W&M, Pride
was a 4-year starter as point guard on the basketball team, averag-
ing 9 points per game.

He graduated in 1990 with a degree in Finance. "Education is
very important to me. There are no guarantees in baseball. I need
something to fall back on." (Possibly a future career as a financial
consultant.)

After he finished each year of college, the Mets assigned him in
midseason to a minor-league club. Since he could only practice
during summer, missing spring and postseason trainings and half
a season each year, his development was slowed down and his pro
career got off to a frustrating start. He spent his first three summers
(1986-88) in the Appalachian Rookie League (Kingsport, Tennessee, Class A), batting .109 his first season, .240 his second, and .284
his third. As Jordan put it: "The following three years, still in A ball,
he managed a total of only 21 home runs and in his last year with
the Mets ('92), he hit only .227 in the Eastern League." After 7
erratic years with the Mets, he would advance only to Class AA.

In 1989, he batted .259 in 55 games, with 6 home runs and 231 RBI
for the Pittsfield (Massachusetts) Mets of the New York-Penn
League. In 1990, he held the starting left-field position for the
Columbia (South Carolina) Mets of the South Atlantic League
(.267, 6 home runs in 51 games). In 1991, having graduated from
W&M, he attended his first spring training and put in his first full
season—a disappointing one—with Port St. Lucie of the Florida
State League, where he batted .260 (team lead) and hit 9 home runs
in 102 games. He was good enough to get promoted to an AA club,
but, with a .247 career batting average, wasn't considered a major-
league prospect.

He spent 1992 with the Binghamton (New York) Mets of the
Eastern League, enduring a batting slump.

After hitting .227 with 10 home runs and 42 RBI in 1992 at

Binghamton, Pride chose not to re-sign with the Mets. As a minor-league free agent, he could sign with any club. He chose the Montreal Expos. "I just wanted to find a better situation. The Expos liked me, and I thought it was a better fit." He was promised an opportunity to play every day—he'd ended up benched in Binghamton.

During his first season in the Expos' organization, Pride developed—or exploded—into a major-league prospect. He began the 1993 season with the AA Harrisburg (Pennsylvania) Senators, a farm club for the Expos. After 50 games, during which he led the Eastern League by hitting .356 with 15 home runs, 39 RBI, and 21 stolen bases, he was promoted on June 21, 1993, to the Expos' "sizzling" AAA Ottawa Lynx. In his first 24 games there, he hit .344 with 7 doubles, 2 triples, 9 RBI, and 9 stolen bases. (The season's totals were .302, with 6 home runs, 22 RBIs, and 29 steals.) He made "incredible" improvements in his hitting. After batting a combined .324 with 21 home runs and 50 stolen bases in AA and AAA, he looked like a sure prospect for the majors. On September 11—in midseason—he was "called up" to the Montreal Expos. After a lapse of 48 years, a deaf player had broken into the major leagues.

A muscular 5' 11", 195 pounds, he's a lefthanded batter and righthanded outfielder, a powerful, aggressive player. Jordan described his batting style as "a short, quick, powerful stroke." Expos Manager Felipe Alou called him a "terrific fastball hitter."

Pride finished his initial major-league season with a solid .444 batting average, including a 9th-inning pinch-hit home run to defeat the Florida Marlins during the last week of the season.

On August 11, 1994, the major leagues went on strike. Pride didn't have a chance to return to Montreal until June 1995. Returning briefly to Ottawa that August, he helped them win their first International League championship; he won a coveted championship ring. In January 1996, he signed with the Detroit Tigers.

Jordan noted, "He talks with great difficulty, his words garbled, his features contorted, as if for him speech were a painfully difficult physical act. . . . Pride is forced by his hearing loss to communicate beneath his level of intelligence, humor and personality, which is his real loss."

Being deaf, Pride told reporters, motivated him: "My handicap forces me to focus better. It frees me from unpleasantness around me. I can't let my mind wander. All my life, I worked hard to be normal. To prove I wasn't stupid. I never thought there was anything I couldn't do. I'm not afraid of anything. My handicap taught me not to quit. Not to need sympathy from people or have them treat me differently. I think I've been fortunate. I had talent, a good family, people to support me. . . . I'm lucky."

Still, Pride takes the responsibilities of his celebrity status seriously, and capitalizes on the opportunities it gives him to encourage young people, especially those with disabilities. As spokesman for Better Hearing Institute, he's made numerous appearances at benefit events. He receives a lot of fan mail—hundreds of letters each year, many of them from kids with disabilities, or their parents—and, with the help of his family, tries to personally answer each one. For several years, during the off-season, he's been a special-education instructional assistant in Montgomery County, including Kennedy High, working with physically- and learning-disabled students, and as volunteer assistant soccer coach.

He's received many awards for his achievements and his community service, including W&M's James Kratzer Award, given to an exceptional senior, the National Council on Communicative Disorders' Youth Achievement Award, and **The Washington Post's** All-Met Distinguished Alumni Award. In January 1995, he was selected by the U.S. Junior Chamber of Commerce as one of the 10 "Outstanding Young Americans" of the year.

As he told John Smallwood: "I'm happy because I'm starting to get some recognition for my performance on the field. I think I've surprised a lot of people. But I've always had a lot of confidence in myself and a determination to be successful in whatever I do. . . . I never considered my deafness a handicap. I get great satisfaction out of proving people wrong. I want to be a role model to show other people with handicaps that they can do anything you set your mind to. I'm just like anyone else, except that I can't hear. But we're all a little different. And none of us are perfect."

Atlantic City, September 17, 1994: Kimberly Aiken, Miss America 1994, crowns Heather Whitestone, Miss America 1995. (© Globe Photos)

CHAPTER 70

Heather Whitestone

1973-

Miss America 1995

When her name was announced, she didn't hear it. Cullen Johnson, Miss Virginia, the first runner-up, turned and emphatically pointed both forefingers towards her, and said, "You won. You won." The cameras caught the look of momentary astonishment on Heather Whitestone's face as she tried to comprehend. A few moments later, Kimberly Aiken, the outgoing Miss America, placed a rhinestone crown on Whitestone's head as she clutched her hands to her heart, overwhelmed with emotion, blinking back the tears. The expression on her face was delightful: awed, stunned, terrified, joyful. Aiken then handed her a Waterford Crystal scepter. She took the winner's walk down the famed runway, and flashed an "ILY" sign. She beamed, but her eyes were brimming. On either side of the runway, the cameras crackled like fireworks. Heather Whitestone, Miss Alabama, had won the crown. She had become the first deaf Miss America—possibly the most controversial one ever.

She came from a "struggling middle-class" background. Her mother, Daphne Gray, had always been strong-minded and independent. Her father, Bill Whitestone, was a furniture salesman and metallurgist. They lived in Dothan, Alabama, and had two older daughters, Stacey and Melissa. When their third daughter was born on February 24, 1973, they named her Heather because Bill had just returned from a trip to Scotland, and Daphne loved his photographs of the happy, rosy-cheeked children.

When Heather was 18 months old, she contracted a bacterial infection, *Haemophilus Influenzae*. She was given two antibiotics in the aminoglycoside family—gentamycin and ampicillin—which are ototoxic (known to cause damage to the auditory nerves). These—or the *H-influenzae* itself—left her totally deaf in her right ear and profoundly deaf in the other.

An essential ingredient of Whitestone's success story is the choice her mother made—a choice that many Deaf people—as survivors—disapprove of. First came the diagnosis and the stereotypical low expectations. According to one account, "Doctors told her parents to teach her sign language and not to expect much for the little girl's future." Gray told a reporter: "They said it's typical for a lot of hearing-impaired kids to end up with a third- to sixth-grade education, because academically, they tend to have some problems." Naturally, she refused to accept this.

Gray learned of, and visited, the Doreen Pollack Acoupedics Center at Denver's Porter Memorial Hospital. She was impressed with it. (In acoupedics, students neither learn nor use sign language.) She persuaded Heather's speech therapist to enroll at the Center, and they learned how to teach Heather at home. It took several grueling years, but Heather became increasingly proficient at lipreading and speaking. "It took me 6 years to say my last name correctly," she said later in a widely-reported remark. She also said that she supported her mother's choice, and appreciated her fight to get the best possible education for her. They were always been close.

As part of her therapy, she began ballet lessons when she was 5. Said Gray: "I wanted Heather to understand there is a natural rhythm in the voice. The fluctuations of ballet music and movement helped her grasp that." With her talent and extensive training, Heather was a good enough dancer to consider a professional career, but balked at idea of having to live with her mother—dancers get meager paychecks. She wanted to be independent.

After the communication struggle came the academic struggle—"having to work twice as hard as the others." Heather attended public schools, with one exception. At age 11, because her reading scores were low, she began 3 years of study at Central Institute for the Deaf in St. Louis. CID calls her "an extraordinary student. In just 3 years at CID, she made 6 grade levels of improvement in reading and was ready for high school." She graduated in 1987. She didn't learn sign language until high school, and no one else in the family signed.

When Heather was 15, her parents divorced. To pay for Heather's college education, Gray enrolled her in the Shelby Junior Miss Pageant. She didn't win, but received enough scholarship money to finance her first year of college.

She lost her next scholarship pageant (Miss St. Clair) because she bungled the interview. The officials asked her questions that she couldn't understand, and she was too embarrassed to ask them to repeat. "Instead, she guessed at what they were saying, answered questions incorrectly, and blew her shot at the crown," noted a reporter.

"Know your problems, but don't let them master you," she later told her audiences. "I thought I didn't win Miss St. Clair because of my deafness. But my family watched the videotape of that interview and said I didn't win because I didn't master the situation." At the next pageant—Miss Jacksonville State University— she was upfront about being deaf. She asked the judges to speak slowly. They accommodated her, and she won the 1992 title.

The Miss JSU Pageant is a steppingstone to the Miss Alabama Pageant. But the real "turning point" came in September 1993, when Daphne and Heather went to Atlantic City see the Miss America Pageant. As **Redbook's** Candace Bushnell noted, "That was the night Heather decided she would give it her all, that she would dedicate the upcoming year to nothing but training for the crown, that she would indeed endure the rigors of reentering the local, then the state pageants, in hopes of making it all the way to Atlantic City."

After returning home, she began "refining her platform"—the year-long community-service project undertaken by Miss America. A strong platform is essential. Hers was titled "Anything is Possible." She developed her appealing 5-point STARS Program ("Success Through Action and Realization of Your DreamS"): have a positive attitude; believe in a dream, especially education;

face your obstacles; work hard; and build a support team.

Whitestone was 21 by that time, a junior at JSU. She attracted some pre-Pageant publicity because she was deaf. She was, of course, a skilled lipreader, and her speech was described as clear, nearly normal, with a slight "foreign" intonation. She wasn't the first deaf competitor in the Miss America Pageant. (In 1989, Jennifer Wall, Miss Washington State, was a Top 10 semifinalist.) Says Whitestone, "The Miss America Pageant allowed me to have an interpreter, but I chose to read their lips."

Whitestone won both the talent and swimsuit competitions, the only 1995 contestant to do so. Pageant-watchers generally agreed that her talent routine clinched the crown. Most other competitors sang. Her flawless ballet performance, to Sandy Patti's pop-religious anthem "Via Dolorosa," got a 3-minute standing ovation from the judges and audience (and moved some to tears). The last hurdle was the final question of the final onstage interview before the final judging on September 17. Co-host Regis Philbin asked her how she would motivate youth. She nodded and replied, "My good attitude helped me get through hard times and believe in myself." Said the **Washington Post**: "The crowd exploded." Minutes later, she was taking the victory walk down the runway.

The next day, she made headlines fielding a question at her first press conference. "You keep flashing," she gently chided the photographers. "You make it hard for me to see his lips. Can you hold for a minute?"

Said Gigi Anders in a **USA Weekend** cover story:

> She flawlessly signed *The Star-Spangled Banner* at the Super Bowl. Whereas 40 million Americans watched her speak and not sign at September's pageant, 120 million saw her sign and not speak at January's game. (...)
>
> Three weeks after capturing the crown in Atlantic City . . . she was a guest at the White House, where the Clintons privately advised her on handling critics. From there it was on to meetings with members of Congress and the Cabinet, all of whom fell under her spell.

In addition to a $35,000 scholarship and a new red convertible Camaro, she was expected to earn at least $200,000 in appearance fees. The booking-scramble began immediately. Everyone wanted her. Having her as a guest speaker guaranteed a sellout crowd.

Although ambitious, Whitestone was evidently stunned by her victory—and unprepared for the controversy she aroused. In a **TIME** article, David Van Biema wrote: "While participating in a Miss Deaf Alabama contest, she has said, she realized that 'sign language puts more limits to their dreams." She adds: "As long as they don't use English, it's not going to help them be successful.' She prefers SEE. . ." Deaf people expressed dismay at this statement. Whitestone later told Anders, "I've *never* said that," insisting that she respected everyone's choices.

Over and over again, she had to face the same questions. And the same issues—speaking and signing. Unwittingly, she was caught up in the politics of the Deaf community, which are often hot, sticky, and unresolvable. She quickly learned that to take a stance that pleased one faction was automatically to alienate the other factions. All this could be, and was, very tiring. Her answers were terse and careful. She insisted on remaining true to herself, and abiding by the choice she felt most comfortable with—speaking. She told Anders, "I never imagined becoming Miss America would throw me into a communications war. I feel caught between the hearing and deaf worlds. It's been very frightening."

Her victory meant a bonanza of free publicity for oralists, which worried some Deaf advocates. (E.g., a CID press release: "Heather Whitestone is a special inspiration for deaf children and their parents, who can see by her example just how much a deaf child who can talk can achieve.") Others were concerned about the hostile feelings Whitestone unwittingly aroused in the Deaf community, and what this could mean to other deaf women who might also like to compete for the crown.

After her "term of service" was over, she was considering switching her major to business administration. And she hoped to buy a condo at the beach and "have a normal life back." She continued to give inspirational talks around the nation. Her engagement to John McCallum, former Congressional aide and Atlanta-based financial advisor, was announced in late 1995.

Honorable Mention

Authors' note: This listing represents a mere fraction of current and historical notables. It does not attempt to present a comprehensive roster.

Contemporaries

Alan R. Barwiolek ("Al B.") (d. 1996)
Co-founder, New York Deaf Theatre; advocate

M.J. Bienvenu
ASL advocate, Bicultural Center co-founder

Ramy Bustamante and **Glenn Eichensehr**
Entrepreneurs (PYRAMerica Enterprise)

Phil Bravin
First deaf Chairman of the Gallaudet Board of Trustees

H. Latham Breunig, Nancy Breunig, Jess M. Smith
TTY-network pioneers; TDI co-founders

Lee Brody
TTY entrepreneur

Judge Richard Brown
Wisconsin judge

Kathy Buckley
Comedienne

Gerald "Bummy" Burstein
Parliamentarian and storyteller

Clifton F. Carbin
Author, **Deaf Heritage in Canada**

Edward Carson Carney
Teacher, advocate, and leader

Dorothy Casterline and Carl Croneberg
William Stokoe's assistants and collaborators

Peter Cook
ASL poet and performer

Harvey Jay Corson
Gallaudet University's first deaf provost

Father Thomas Coughlin
First deaf man ordained as a Catholic priest

Joe Dannis
Founder and publisher, DawnSignPress

Gil Eastman
Performer, playwright (*Sign Me Alice*), *Deaf Mosaic* co-producer and co-host

Russell Errigo
Auto racer

Jane Kelleher Fernandes
Administrator

Alexander Fleischman
Community leader

Victor Galloway
Chemist, teacher, RSA executive

Mervin D. Garretson
COSD Director, author, educator, leader

Loy E. Golladay
Teacher and writer

Jerry Hassell
Texas Deaf Caucus and Native American activist;
teacher and advocate

Burma Young Holder
First deaf exhibition skater

Leo Jacobs
Author, **A Deaf Adult Speaks Out**

Katherine Jankoswki
Administrator, superintendent

Jerald M. Jordan
Professor; World Games for the Deaf Director

Tom Kane (d. 1995)
Deaf Gay activist, originator of Deaf NAMES
Project Memorial Quilt

Barbara Kannapell
Founder of Deafpride

Nancy Kensicki
First deaf person to earn a Ph.D. in English

Harry G. Lang
Science teacher, researcher, biographer

Herb Larson
Director, National Center on Deafness at CSUN

Ella Mae Lentz
ASL teacher, poet

Raymond F. Luczak
Poet, writer, anthologist
(Eyes of Desire: A Deaf Gay and Lesbian Reader)

Eric Malzkuhn ("Malz")
Actor, teacher, storyteller

Betty G. Miller
"Mother of DeVia," artist and advocate

Audree Norton
First deaf actress to be featured in a TV commercial

Judith Pachciarz
Biochemist and physician;
First deaf woman in the U.S. to hold M.D. and Ph.D. degrees

Shirley Platt
AAAD President

James C. Marsters and Andrew Saks
Co-developers of TTY coupler

Tony Landon McGregor
Artist, gourd-crafter, advocate

Shanny Mow
Actor, playwright, artistic director

Freda Norman
Actress (NTD, *Rainbow's End*)

Gary Olsen
NAD leader, advocate

Carol Padden and Tom Humphries
Co-authors, **Deaf in America: Voices from a Culture**

Kim Powers
Deaf-blind actress, Kaleidoscope Network personality

Terrylene Sacchetti
Performer, playwright, advocate

Howie Seago
TV and theater performer, producer, director

Ann Silver
Artist and designer

Michael Schwartz
Former Manhattan assistant district attorney

Howard E. "Rocky" Stone
Founder and first Executive Director of SHHH

Andy Vasnick
Actor, teacher

Ed Waterstreet
Founding Artistic Director, Deaf West Theatre

Barbara Jean ("B. J.") Wood
Commissioner and leader

Historical personalities

Lucy Truman Aldrich
Rhode Island aristocrat; collector of Japanese Noh robes

Albert Ballin
Author (**The Deaf-Mute Howls**); actor; storyteller

Frederic A. P. Barnard
President of Columbia College (now Columbia University),
1863-1888

Mabel Hubbard Bell
Hostess, wife of Alexander Graham Bell

John Brewster
Early-American folk portraitist

Eliza Boardman Clerc
Wife of Laurent Clerc;
partner in the first deaf marriage in U.S.A.

Alice Cogswell
First student at American School for the Deaf

Sam Edwards
Co-founder of New York Deaf Theatre, performer,
Deaf Gay advocate

Kathleen Fettin
Actress; first deaf woman to direct a film

John Jacobus Flournoy
Co-founder of Georgia School for the Deaf;
advocate of Deaf separatism

Sophia Fowler Gallaudet
"Mother Gallaudet," "Queen of the Deaf Community;"
T. H. Gallaudet's wife and E.M. Gallaudet's mother

John R. Gregg
Creator of the Gregg shorthand system

Agatha Tiegel Hansen
One of the first women to graduate from Gallaudet College;
Olof Hansen's wife

Olof Hansen
Architect

Paul Hubbard
Probable inventor of the football huddle
at Gallaudet in 1894

Frederick H. Hughes
Gallaudet College professor and drama coach

Wesley Lauritsen
Teacher at Minnesota School for the Deaf

J. Schuyler Long
Publisher of **The Sign Language: A Manual of Signs**,
the first illustrated sign-language dictionary

Alto M. Lowman
First woman to receive a degree from Gallaudet College

William Mercer
First known deaf American artist

Dorothy Miles
Actress and playwright

Edward B. Nitchie
Founder of New York League for the Hard of Hearing;
creator of Nitchie lipreading system

Peter N. Peterson
Originator of the idea of NTID

Granville Redmond
Artist; actor; teacher and friend of Charlie Chaplin

Emerson Romero
Inventor, actor, pioneer film captioner

Ben M. Schowe
Recruiter of deaf workers for Firestone;
employment authority

George W. Veditz
NAD leader; early Deaf-rights and ASL advocate

David Otis Watson ("El Sordo")
Texas pioneer, father of David O. Watson
(**Talk With Your Hands**)

Eliza Willard
Co-founder of Indiana School for the Deaf;
William Willard's wife

Harry R. Williams
Artist

Background:
The Co-Authors
by
Linda Levitan

Matthew Scott Moore in three favorite roles: (top) as Mercutio in NTID's *Romeo and Juliet* (1979); (bottom left) as Felix Unger in *The Odd Couple* (1982); and (bottom right) as publisher during MSM Productions' early days, 1987.

Matthew Scott Moore

1958-

Publisher, advocate, entrepreneur, actor, poet

Poet, performer, playwright, businessman, publisher, editor, community leader—Matthew S. Moore personifies the "Deaf Renaissance" spirit.

He is an example of a culturally-Deaf person whose first language is ASL and second language English—but who is comfortably bilingual. He is able to communicate with any person—Deaf, hard-of-hearing, hearing, oral-deaf, Deaf-blind. He does *not* use his voice, a political decision; he refuses to allow himself to be judged or measured by the quality of his speech. He has provided encouragement for young deaf people, and reassurance to anxious hearing parents, that deaf people can succeed in untraditional endeavors.

Moore was born on December 31, 1958, the first child of JoNelle (Painter) and Scott Moore of Indianapolis. He has a younger brother and sister—Mark and Terri, both hearing.

JoNelle Moore had been exposed to rubella (German measles) during her pregnancy. Matthew seemed perfectly healthy. His deafness wasn't diagnosed until he was 18 months old. Since he was bright, alert, and had already started babbling, they thought he was "normal." But one day, JoNelle entered Matthew's room while he was playing in his crib, and called loudly to him: "Matthew!...MATTHEW!" No response. She then placed her hands on the crib rails. Matthew turned, looked up, and smiled. Immediately, she suspected he was deaf.

JoNelle was a very young mother (only 18), and didn't know what to do. After Matthew was diagnosed as deaf, a doctor told her to send him to a special clinic at Indiana University twice a week.

As with many other parents of deaf children, there were ongoing debates about schooling. JoNelle, wanting "the best" for her son, thought he should board at Indiana School for the Deaf.

Matthew was enrolled in ISD at age 4. "It was a great thing," he recalls. "I saw these diagrams of signs and the objects they represented. I recognized that signs could represent things. I learned ASL from another boy who came from a Deaf family." He boarded at ISD several years. Then beginning its pioneering Total Communication program, ISD was acquiring a reputation as one of the top schools for the deaf. In his senior year, Matthew took an advanced-reading class and was forced to devour, then write term papers on, an abnormal quantity of college-level texts. "It sort of turned me off reading for pleasure." He edited the high-school newspaper, **The Reflector** (which won a state award for excellence), participated in school plays ("my first taste of theater") and Youth Leadership Camp (1976—he edited **The Daily Drum**), collected honors and awards, and was valedictorian of his class (1977).

He chose the National Technical Institute for the Deaf at Rochester Institute of Technology. "I'd grown up in a Deaf institution. I wanted a different experience, even though most of my classmates encouraged me to go to Gallaudet." He first majored in chemistry "because I had a bent for science. Then I realized that I enjoyed working with people." He switched to social work and minored in photo/media. Both disciplines proved useful.

In 1979, a good friend saw how expressively he signed, and she urged him to audition for NTID's production of *Romeo and Juliet*. At first, he put her off, but she persisted, and he finally assented. They auditioned together. Matthew recited the "Queen Mab" speech. It was a hit. He discovered that he had a talent for performing. He played Mercutio, whose sign-name (M-to-the chest) became his own. That's when Bob Panara first saw him. "He came to me . . . 'Marvelous! . . . You played Mercutio *perfectly!*'"

From that point on—"my theater career just took off." He appeared in a variety of roles: Henry (*The Fantasticks*, also 1979); Chrysalde (*The School for Wives*, 1980); Billy (*One Flew Over the Cuckoo's Nest*, 1981) and *C'est Autre Chose* (a musical revue that he co-wrote, co-produced, and directed, also in 1981); Felix (*The Odd Couple*, 1982); Marley (*A Christmas Carol*, 1983); *Cue Up* (an experimental play); and Renfield (*The Passion of Dracula*, 1985). He was noted for his incandescent technique and the beauty and power of his signing, and he was a "show-stealer" as well. One night when he was playing Marley in *A Christmas Carol*, a spark from a special-effects smoke-squib fell into his trouser-pocket and ignited. Without missing a beat, "Marley" calmly improvised a line, excused himself, turned around, slapped out the flame, and resumed his part of the dialogue.

He won the Irene Ryan Award as a Regional Finalist in the American College Theatre Festival (1980) and NTID's coveted Golden Hand Award for excellence in theater (1982). He also served as House Manager of the Performing Arts Department for 2 years, and participated in NTD's Professional Theatre School (1980). He directed the television production of an experimental silent video, *Table*, first shown in 1983 at Rochester's Little Theatre. It won second place in the American Film Institute's Eastern Regional Competition.

In 1982, he received the Davis Scholarship Award for "Outstanding Leadership at RIT;" in 1983, the Dr. Robert Frisina Scholar Award, RIT's highest award in Community Services, "for bridging the communication gap between hearing and deaf students."

He was a resident advisor for 2-1/2 years, and a VR counselor for 7 months. His VR work afforded him valuable insight into the Deaf community. By this time, he had become a firm believer in the power of the mass media to influence and change people's attitudes. Instead of working one-to-one with clients, he reasoned, why not utilize the media to make maximum impact on the maximum numbers?

In 1981, he founded the Student Communication Center as a way to give NTID students hands-on experience in producing a newspaper and a television series. **NTID Perspectives** debuted in 1981;

the TV show premiered after he graduated in 1983.

After incorporating an independent small business, he co-pro-duced, wrote, and directed a pilot magazine-format program, *Deaf Magazine*, which aired on WOKR, Rochester's ABC affiliate, on June 1, 1984. His friend Tom Connor wrote the jazzy theme song and helped with production. It drew unanimously favorable re-sponse. Moore sought funding for more installments, but couldn't secure any commitments. He decided to start an independent monthly magazine as a way of getting the revenue he needed for the show. He first shared his idea with Charles F. Bancroft, who had worked with him at SCC. The Trial Issue of **DEAF LIFE** was published in July 1987. **DEAF LIFE** began monthly publication in July 1988, and the MSM team "never looked back."

In September 1992, MSM Productions published its first book, **For Hearing People Only**, under the Deaf Life Press imprint. Matthew and I collaborated on it. It was an immediate success. The first edition sold out by May 1993, by which time the second edition (expanded and revised) was ready. Its first printing sold out in February 1994; the second printing in early September 1994; the third printing in July 1995; the fourth in June 1996; whereupon the fifth was made ready . . .

Deaf Life Press's second book was Bernard Bragg and Jack R. Olson's **Meeting Halfway in American Sign Language**. This took a good 3 years of painstaking computer-graphics work—it fea-tured over 2,000 sequential-action sign-language photos by Denise Stenzel—and was the most lavishly-photo-illustrated sign-lan-guage text ever published.

The third book was **St. Michael's Fall**, a collection of autobio-graphical poems by Raymond Luczak.

And Deaf Life Press's fourth book is the one you are reading now: the revamped, expanded, and updated second edition of **Great Deaf Americans**. Still other books are in various stages of plan-ning.

MSM Productions' motto is "Deaf awareness is our business." Upcoming projects include books, videos, and multimedia—all with a Deaf Awareness theme. "My ultimate dream is to produce a high-quality, first-class movie," Moore says.

If the community can be said to be experiencing a "Deaf Renaissance," Moore is a key figure. As a public character, he's charismatic, a powerful, even formidable presence onstage. In private life, he's a thoroughly engaging personality—energetic, sensitive, kind, generous, funny, and charming. He's noted for his stories, songs, witty and imaginative signplay, and bawdy jokes.

At NTID's 25th Anniversary Alumni Reunion in July 1993, he received the NTID Alumni Association's first Outstanding Alumni Award "for valuable service on behalf of deaf citizens and for contributing to the betterment of the Deaf community and to NTID/RIT." Not wanting to be outdone, the Gallaudet University Alumni Association gave him its prestigious Alice Cogswell Award "for valuable service on behalf of the Deaf Community" at its April 1994 Charter Day Banquet.

Moore can be found attending to several projects at once, or off on a lecture tour. He's been invited to talk about his experiences by schools, universities, and agencies, to audiences across the nation—e.g., his native Indianapolis, Kansas City, California, Texas, Missouri.

Nothing has given him more pleasure than seeing his work having an impact on public perceptions of deaf people. "Money and fame mean nothing to me," he says. "Seeing people's attitudes improve—accepting us for what we are, respecting our language, ASL, granting us equal rights as U.S. citizens while allowing us to keep our own Deaf identity—*that's* something."

—Linda Levitan

Top: Shirley and Bob Panara (holding a Panara Theatre plaque), at NTID. Bottom left: Onstage, RIT's Ingle Auditorium. Bottom Right: Bob holds a paperback copy of the first edition of **Great Deaf Americans** (1983); with Shirley and John. (Courtesy of Bob Panara)

Robert F. Panara

1920-

Author, poet, teacher

Speak the speech, I pray you, as I pronounced it to you, trippingly on the tongue. But if you mouth it, as many of our players do, I had as lief the town crier spoke my lines. Nor do not saw the air too much with your hand, thus, but use all gently, for in the very torrent, tempest, and (as I may say) whirlwind of your passion, you must acquire and beget a temperance that may give it smoothness. . . .

Be not too tame neither, but let your own discretion be your tutor. Suit the action to the word, the word to the action, with this special observance, that you o'erstep not the modesty of nature.

—William Shakespeare, *Hamlet*, III.i, "Hamlet's advice to the players"

This is one of Bob Panara's favorite quotes. Baseball buff, historian, biographer, researcher, chronicler of Deaf literature and literary images, poet, Shakespearean teacher—he is a veritable "walking encyclopedia" of lore and letters. His sign-name, incorporating the initial "P," is a play on the ASL sign for "exaggeration" or "discoursing at length"—with the "P" bounced four times.

Robert Frederic Panara was born on July 8, 1920, and raised in the Upper Bronx area of New York City. When he was 10, he contracted spinal meningitis and afterwards discovered that he was "stone-deaf." He didn't know of any schools for the deaf in those days, so he returned to Public School 103, and "just read my way through school. By then I had become a good reader. My cousins had brought me loads of books while I was recuperating, and began reading: **Treasure Island**, **The Three Musketeers**, many Westerns by Zane Grey, and **Tarzan** books by Edgar Rice Burroughs."

He "followed the gang" to all-boys' DeWitt Clinton High School, "a powerhouse in sports. I used to read books—poetry, novels— during classes. Couldn't or didn't try lip-reading the teachers; they moved all around. No interpreters or notetakers, just read my way through. But I was very outgoing, hung around with my gang, played sports—nuts about sports (swimming and baseball) in fact, which helped me integrate with my hearing peers. I think becoming deaf at age 10 was somewhat fortunate since I could bounce back, but I was withdrawn a lot, couldn't participate in the small-talk or jokes. Even dating was out, but sports was the catalyst for integrating and getting accepted by the boys and that helped my morale a lot, although I didn't realize what I was truly missing all during those elementary and high school years, nor did I truly identify myself as a Deaf person."

After he graduated, his family moved to Fall River, Massachusetts, where his father had found a good job. It was still the Depression. Not knowing what to do or where to go next, young Bob Panara worked part-time in a clothing factory, then decided to try University of Massachusetts. He met with the Dean, who knew something about Gallaudet College and gave him the address of its president, who in turn advised him to try the American School for the Deaf in West Hartford, Connecticut. "First day of school I felt like a 'stranger in a strange land.' Decided to pack up and take the first bus home, but a young hearing teacher, Dr. Lloyd Harrison, who had trained at Gallaudet, talked me out of it. Said to be patient, that I would learn sign soon enough, and just love Gallaudet College. He was right. I stuck it out, learned sign and became a human semaphore in 2 months. Also played sports and became one of the gang."

Finally, he went on to Gallaudet, where he "got involved in many things... never a scholar during the first 3 years." But he met Dr.

Powrie Vaux Doctor, a hearing professor of English and editor of **American Annals of the Deaf**. "A great teacher," Panara recalls. "He influenced me to pursue my innate interests in English and literature, and said I would make a good teacher of English to Deaf students. I also was in awe of a Deaf professor, Frederick Hughes, who taught dramatics and economics. He had a dynamic style of teaching, very visual and dramatic. I sort of tried to imitate his style but added voice: i.e., total [simultaneous] communication, which was used by hearing teachers at Gallaudet but was not the vogue of most Deaf teachers, but that was how Dr. Powrie Doctor taught. So that became my trademark from the very beginning of my teaching career."

After graduating from Gallaudet, he was employed at New York School for the Deaf in White Plains—"Fanwood"—where he taught English literature *and* algebra, "believe it or not." He notes proudly that four of those students became professors at Gallaudet: Bernard Bragg, Alan Sussman, Suleiman Bushnaq, and Eugene Bergman. "A funny thing—after teaching at Fanwood for 4 years and going to New York University at night, on Saturdays, and during summers for my Master's in English (without interpreter or support services), I was asked to teach at Gallaudet, and I again taught those four boys, or rather, men. They are all great leaders and educators now." Bragg and Panara founded the Drama Club at Fanwood and "had a ball" producing plays. During one summer vacation, Panara met Shirley Fischer of St. Louis, Missouri, a star athlete; they eventually got married.

Panara returned to Gallaudet as instructor of English, and rose to the rank of associate professor. His own early experiences at Gallaudet helped him "develop the confidence to give numerous teaching demonstrations to educators, Congressmen, visiting dignitaries from Europe, newspaper reporters, you name it—they always brought them to watch me in action." He also studied at Catholic University in Washington, D.C. He had wanted to write his doctoral dissertation about Deaf characters in literature but lost his advisor; the work remained unfinished.

By that time, however, the "NTID Act" had passed through

Congress. Panara was asked to serve on the National Advisory Board on the Establishment of NTID (National Technical Institute for the Deaf). The only Deaf member, his responsibilities included writing guidelines for the future NTID and reviewing all the proposals received from about 30 colleges and universities. The board finally chose Rochester Institute of Technology (RIT). When Dr. Robert Frisina, a Gallaudet dean, was chosen as president of NTID, he asked Panara to "come on board" as the first Deaf staff/ faculty member. "I never got that Ph.D. degree, but 4 years later I was rewarded with the rank of full professor at NTID/RIT, so I didn't need that Ph.D. title after all!"

His years at NTID were very busy ones. "Whew, I wore many hats during the first 5 years!" He set up the English Department, founded the Drama Club, served as Education Specialist—coordinating interpreters, notetakers, and tutors in the College of General Studies (now Liberal Arts)—taught "Literary Studies" to deaf and hearing students, and later initiated two courses in "Deaf Studies." With the first, "Deaf in Literature," he was able to make his "dream dissertation" come to life; with the second, "Creative Interpretation of Literature in Sign," he brought the theater into the classroom for full college credit. He notes with amusement, "I can boast of being the only teacher, deaf or hearing, who has taught at Gallaudet University, NTID, RIT, CSUN, University of Massachusetts, and University of Rochester."

In 1945, he became the first recipient of the Teegarden Medal for Creative Poetry, and published many poems written in classically perfect meter and rhyme (his forte). "On His Deafness" won the Grand Prize of $1,000 from **World of Poetry**.

He wrote many articles on Deaf Studies and methods of teaching English and literature to deaf students. While at Gallaudet he had co-edited **The Silent Muse: An Anthology of Poetry by the Deaf**. At NTID, he co-authored, with his son John, the first edition of **Great Deaf Americans** (T.J. Publishers, 1983). He dedicated it to Shirley, "a great gal Friday;" she had helped prepare the manuscript. He also served as an associate editor and contributed several articles on Deaf Studies, culture, and performing arts to the

Gallaudet Encyclopedia of Deaf People and Deafness, a hefty 3-volume reference work (1987). He gave numerous workshops at schools, colleges, and teachers' conventions around the country.

In 1985, MacMurray College in Jacksonville, Illinois, conferred upon him the honorary degree of "Doctor of Public Service," and a year later, Gallaudet University conferred the honorary degree of "Doctor of Humane Letters." He adds: "But what topped it off were the honors that NTID bestowed on me: establishment of the Robert F. Panara Scholarship Fund, and the naming of the theater after me. That truly is the highlight of my professional career."

On May 19, 1988, Bob and Shirley Panara were attending an awards presentation in the NTID Theatre when they were summoned to the stage and presented with a plaque commemorating the renaming of that theater in his honor—it's now the Robert F. Panara Theatre. The Panaras were caught totally by surprise. Two identical plaques at the entrances to the Panara Theatre highlight his contributions:

> Teacher, author, actor, poet . . . Robert F. Panara was RIT's first deaf faculty member; founder and first chairman of NTID's Department of English; and founder and first director of NTID's Experimental Educational Theatre Program. Professor Panara's two decades of service to NTID at RIT, and his firm belief in the talent and potential of young deaf people, will always be remembered by those with whom he has shared his wisdom and vision.

Now retired from NTID, he is able to enjoy the things he couldn't do regularly while working, such as writing letters to students and friends, reading books at a leisurely pace, going to baseball games, rooting for his two grandchildren, Bill and Erin, in their Little League ballgames, "and getting the chance to date Shirley any time I feel like it!"

—Linda Levitan

Select Bibliography

Profiles are listed alphabetically. Listings are organized alphabetically by (1) books; (2) periodicals and unpublished material, including works-in-progress; (3) videotapes. Correspondence material—letters, *curricula vitae*, and other documentation obtained directly from the "profiles" themselves—is indicated by an envelope dingbat (✉) after that person's name. Other unlisted material (copies of old newspaper clippings, records, biographical data, etc.) obtained from library archives, family, colleagues, etc., is indicated by a pencil dingbat (✏). Sources are listed in "Acknowledgements."

COLLECTIVE & GENERAL WORKS; OVERVIEWS

Profiles in the Arts: a joint project of the National Endowment for the Arts and the President's Committee on Employment of the Handicapped, 1986.

Bowe, Frank G., and Martin Sternberg. **I'm Deaf Too: 12 Deaf Americans**. Silver Spring: NAD, 1973.

Braddock, Guilbert C. **Notable Deaf Persons**. Florence B. Crammatte, editor. Washington, D.C.: Gallaudet College Alumni Association, 1975.

Fischer, Renate, and Harlan Lane, editors. **Looking Back: A Reader on the History of Deaf Communities and their Sign Languages**. Hamburg, Germany: Signum, 1993.

Gannon, Jack R. **Deaf Heritage: A Narrative History of Deaf America**. Silver Spring, Maryland: National Association of the Deaf, 1981.

Holcomb, Mabs, and Sharon Wood. **Deaf Women: A Parade Through the Decades**. Berkeley: DawnSignPress, 1989.

Lang, Harry G. **Silence of the Spheres: The Deaf Experience in the History of Science**. Westport, Connecticut: Bergin & Garvey, 1994.

Lang, Harry G., and Bonnie Meath-Lang. **Deaf Persons in the Arts and Sciences: A Biographical Dictionary**. Westport, Connecticut: Greenwood Press, 1995.

Neisser, Arden. **The Other Side of Silence: Sign Language and the**

Deaf Community in America. New York: Knopf, 1983. Washington, D.C.: Gallaudet University Press, 1990.

Van Cleve, John V., Editor-in-Chief. **The Gallaudet Encyclopedia of Deaf People and Deafness**. 3 vols. New York: McGraw-Hill, 1987. (**GEDPD**.)

Van Cleve, John V., and Barry Crouch. **A Place of Their Own: Creating the Deaf Community in America**. Washington, D.C.: Gallaudet University Press, 1989.

SHIRLEY J. ALLEN ✉

"Dr. Shirley Allen: 'My students are, first and foremost, the love of my life.'" **DEAF LIFE**, October 1995.

"'Positive influences.'" **DEAF LIFE Plus**, July 1992.

GLENN B. ANDERSON ✉

Anderson, Glenn B., and Cynthia A. Grace. "Black Deaf Adolescents: A Diverse and Underserved Population." In **Adolescence and Deafness**. Edited by Oscar Cohen and G. Long. Washington, D.C.: **The Volta Review**, 1991.

Anderson, Glenn B., and D. Watson, eds. **Black Deaf Experience: Excellence and Equity**. Little Rock: University of Arkansas Rehabilitation Research and Training Center for Persons Who are Deaf or Hard of Hearing, 1993.

Redding, Reginald, and Glenn B. Anderson. "Does Full Inclusion Offer an Rx for Enhancing the Education of Minority Deaf Students?" **American Annals of The Deaf**, 139 (2), April 1994.

Overstreet, James. "Speaker urges deaf students to overcome barriers." **Clarion-Ledger** (Jackson, Mississippi), February 1994 [no date].

Uyttebrouck, Oliver. "LR professor committed to helping black deaf children beat harsh odds." **Arkansas Democrat Gazette**, February 10, 1992.

"A Conversation with Dr. Glenn Anderson." **DORS Opener**, October 1994.

HILLIS ARNOLD ✐

Sonnenstrahl, Deborah, "Hillis Arnold." **GEDPD**, Vol. 1, 34-36.

"Expressing the Sounds of a Silent World." **Monticello Alumnae Bulletin**, July 1960.

Althoff, Shirley. "Art and Altar." St. Louis **Globe-Democrat Sunday Magazine**, November 6, 1966.

Arnold, Meda. "The story of a little boy who couldn't hear." Unpublished paper, n.d., Lewis & Clark Community College files.

N. Hillis. "A Deaf Sculptor." **Volta Review**, June 1967.

Degener, Patricia. "A Retrospective of Arnold Sculpture." **St. Louis Post-Dispatch**, May 1, 1983.

Helmkamp, John. "Genius in a Silent World." Unpublished paper, May 12, 1972, Lewis & Clark Community College files.

Johnson, Dennis. "'Olin Statue'—A sign of new growth." Lewis & Clark Community College files.

Kowalewski, Felix. "Hillis Arnold: American Deaf Sculptor." **The Deaf American**, November 1972.

—"Profiles of Selected Deaf Artists." **Gallaudet Today**, Summer 1981.

Klope, L. Allen. "Sculptor Hillis Arnold designs 'Destiny' Eagle." **Alton Telegraph**, March 27, 1964.

Lane Helen. **The History of Central Institute**. St. Louis: CID, 1981.

Wahonick, Nancy. "'Discovering' Hillis Arnold." **December Rose**, July/August 1988.

CHUCK BAIRD ✉

Baird, Chuck. **Chuck Baird: 35 Plates**. San Diego: DawnSignPress, 1993.

—"My life as an artist." Manuscript. 1989.

"Mini-Galley: Chuck Baird." **DEAF LIFE**, December 1988.

Bodnarchuk, Kari J. "Learning Center mural speaks volumes for the deaf." **Middlesex News**, June 11, 1995.

Gurdak, Dorree. "Learning Center for Deaf Children turns 25." **Middlesex News**, October 28, 1994.

Loynd, Ray. "Theatre of the Deaf's Merry 'King of Hearts.'" Review. **Los Angeles Times**, n.d.

DONALD L. BALLANTYNE ✉

"Shattered Lives: forgotten victims of infamous crimes." **People Weekly**, April 3, 1995.

Carr, Steven. "Bloomfielder, Dr. Ballantyne, probes the small world of microsurgery." **Essex Journal**, Bloomfield, N.J., August 23, 1979.

Milner, Louise B. "Dr. Donald Ballantyne—Deaf Researcher in Transplants." **The Deaf American**, November 1965.

Williams, Gurney III. "Lifesaving Surgery—Under a Lens." **Popular Mechanics**, March 1979.

WILLIAM BEADELL ✏

Olson, Michael J. "Editors and journalists in literature: William W. Beadell." **GEDPD**, Vol. II, 171.

"William Wolcott Beadell." **The Iowa Hawkeye**, October 1, 1931.

"William Wolcott Beadell: Editor and Publisher." **Special Commemorative Number, printed by the Employees of the** *Arlington Observer*, New Jersey, July 1931.

Van Winkle, Daniel. "William Woodruff Beadell, Journalist." **History of the Municipalities of Hudson County, New Jersey**. 3 vols. New York and Chicago: Lewis Historical Publishing Co., 1924.

SHELLEY BEATTIE ✉

"Woman of Steel: Heavyweight bodybuilding champion Shelley Beattie balances career and competition." **DEAF LIFE**, July 1991.

"The 'Woman of Steel' is aiming for the gold." **DEAF LIFE**, December 1992.

Bradford, Reg. "Shelley 'Wonder Woman' Beattie: NPC USA Champion." **Muscular Development** [no date].

Dobbins, Bill. "Shelley Beattie Goes to Hollywood...and then goes home...to train for her pro debut." **Muscle & Fitness**, February 1991.

Grannis, Lori. "Shelley Beattie: Muscling in on a Better Life." **Women's Physique World** [no date].

Luoma, T.C. "1990 NPC USA Bodybuilding Championships." **Muscular Development**.

Reynolds Bill. "Oregon Gold." **FLEX**, December 1990.

Silverman, Ruth. "Rally in Raleigh." **Ironman**, November 1990.

Skita, Max. "1990 American Airlines USA Championships." **NPC News**, January 1991.

Teper, Lonnie. "Loud and Clear: Despite a hearing impairment, Shelley Beattie rings sharp on bodybuilding and Gladiator stages." **Ironman**, December 1993.

EDMUND BOOTH ✎

Booth, Edmund. **Edmund Booth: Forty-Niner.** Stockton, California: San Joaquin Pioneer and Historical Society, 1953.

Crouch, Barry A. "History: A Deaf Commonwealth." **GEDPD**, Vol. 2, 61-63.

Representative Deaf Persons of the United States of America. Edited and published by James E. Gallaher, Chicago, 1896.

Van Cleve, John V. "Edmund Booth." **GEDPD**, Vol. 1, 143-144.

Booth, Frank Walworth. "Edmund Booth: A Life Sketch." **Association Review**, 7: 225-237, 1905.

"Edmund Booth." **The Silent Worker**, ca. Spring 1905.

"Edmund Booth, M.A." **Silent World** (Toronto, Canada), April 15, 1881.

LINDA BOVE ✉

"Deaf West Theatre Company Goes Corinthian!" **Community Ear**, April 1995.

"Linda Bove: At Work in the Medium." **Gallaudet Today**, Winter 1973.

Sesame Street Magazine, to date.

Cergol, Susan. "Beyond Sesame Street." **NTID Focus**, Summer 1989.

FRANK G. BOWE ✉ ✎

Bowe, Frank G. **Approaching Equality: Education of the Deaf.** Silver Spring: T.J. Publishers, 1991.

—Changing the Rules. Silver Spring: T.J. Publishers, 1986.

Kimmel, Sherri. "Freedom Fighter." **The Hill** (Western Maryland College), November 1990.

—"Interview with Frank Bowe, April 15, 1996." Work in progress.

MacGugan, Kirk. "Frank Bowe: Spokesperson for the American Disability Rights Movement 1976-1990." Dissertation, Hofstra University, 1990.

BERNARD BRAGG ✉

Bragg, Bernard. **Lessons in Laughter: the Autobiography of a Deaf Actor. As signed to Eugene Bergman**. Washington, D.C.: Gallaudet University Press, 1989.

Bragg, Bernard, and Jack R. Olson. **Meeting Halfway in American Sign Language: A Common Ground for Effective Communication Among Deaf and Hearing People**. Rochester: Deaf Life Press, 1994

Levitan, Linda. "All the World's a Stage: A Tribute to Dr. Bernard Bragg." **DEAF LIFE**, February 1989.

Powers, Helen. **Signs of Silence: Bernard Bragg and the National Theatre of the Deaf**. New York: Dodd, Mead, 1972.

An Interview with Bernard Bragg: The Man Behind the Mask. Videocassette. San Diego: DawnSignPress, 1995.

MORRIS BRODERSON ⊠ ⏎

Mannes, Judy P. "Morris Broderson. **GEDPD**, Vol. I, 159-161

"Morris Broderson." Tucson: University of Arizona Museum of Art, 1975.

"Artist Morris Broderson attends reception at College." **On the Green**, December 7, 1981.

Ankrum, Joan. "Biography of Morris Broderson," 1975.

—"Broderson Exhibit Ankrum Gallery Finale." Press release. October 1, 1989.

Barrett, Robert. [Commentary.] Fresno Art Museum, September 1993. Reprinted in "Morris Broderson: Recent Paintings," NTID, November 10-December 31, 1993.

Canaday, John. "Morris Broderson." [**The New York Times**? October 1978].

Cleave, Jane. [Commentary.] Fresno Arts Center and Museum, 1988.

Cleek, Patricia Gardner. **Gallery Notes**, Santa Barbara Museum of Art, July 1981.

Hines, Diane Casella. "Morris Broderson/Speaking Through His Art." **American Artist**, October 1980.

McCloud, Mac. "Visual Epiphanies: Morris Broderson at Ankrum Gallery." **Art Week**, December 7, 1989.

Reynolds, Judith. "Fast Forward: A return to the tragic in art." **City Newspaper** (Rochester, New York), December 2, 1993.

DOUGLAS J. N. BURKE ✏

Burke, Douglas J.N. **Love's Source of Grace: The Sonnets of Douglas J.N. Burke**. Mansfield, Texas: Latitudes Press, 1989.

Panara, Robert F. "Cultural Programs." **GEDPD**, Vol. 1, 216-222.

Prospectus, SouthWest Collegiate Institute for the Deaf, 1981.

"Doug Burke Passes Away." **NAD Broadcaster**, November 1988.

"SWCID Celebrates!" **DEAF LIFE Plus**, April 1990.

Burke, Douglas J.N. "On Founding SWCID: Why and How." Presentation, SWCID, Fall 1987.

Campbell, Daniel G. "Dr. Douglas J.N. Burke." Eulogy. SWCID, 1988.

Johnstone, Mary. "A Lifetime of Service, a Legacy of Love." **Gallaudet Today**, Winter 1988-89.

McQuerry, Delaina. "Educational leader brings expertise to HC." **The Hawk Reporter**, February 15, 1980.

Partlow, David. "Unique college draws unique leader." **The Hawk Reporter**, March 5, 1980.

JOHN CARLIN

Domich, Harold J. "John Carlin: A Biographical Sketch." **American Annals of the Deaf**, Vol. 90, No. 4, September 1945.

Higgins, Francis C. "John Carlin." **GEDPD**, Vol. I, 178-179.

MICHAEL CHATOFF ✉

"Deaf Lawyer Seeks Special 'Hearing.'" **Newsday**, February 3, 1982.

Chatoff, Michael A., and Barry G. Felder. "Education of the Handicapped Act: Rowley v. Board of Education." **GEDPD**, Vol. 1, 383-386.

Mann, Jim. "Deaf lawyer wants to make case his way." **Los Angeles Times**, March 23, 1982.

Walker, Lou Ann. **Amy: The Story of a Deaf Child**. Photographs by Michael Abramson. New York: Dutton, 1985.

LAURENT CLERC ✏

Clerc, Laurent. **Diary of Laurent Clerc's Voyage from France to America in 1816**. West Hartford: American School for the Deaf, 1952.

DeGering, Etta. **Gallaudet, Friend of the Deaf**. 1964. Washington, D.C.: Gallaudet University Press, 1987.

Gannon, Jack R. "Laurent Clerc and His Legacy." **Kaleidoscope of Deaf America**. Silver Spring, NAD, 1989.

Golladay, Loy. "Laurent Clerc." **GEDPD**, Vol. 1, 190-193.

Lane, Harlan. **When the Mind Hears: A History of the Deaf**. New York: Random House, 1984.

Neimark, Anne E. **A Deaf Child Listened: Thomas Gallaudet, Pioneer in American Education**. New York: Morrow, 1983.

Clerc, Laurent. "Laurent Clerc—In His Own Words." **The American Era**, Winter 1991-Spring 1992. Reprinted from Henry Barnard's **Tribute to Gallaudet** (Hartford, 1852).

Coats, G. Dewey. "The Two Glorious Lives of Laurent Clerc." **The Kentucky Standard**, December 14, 1967. Reprinted from **The Missouri Record**.

Golladay, Loy E. "Laurent Clerc: America's Pioneer Deaf Teacher." **The Deaf American**, March 1980.

Parsons, Frances M. "In Search of Laurent Clerc, or: Never Underestimate the French Femmes!" **DEAF LIFE**, December 1995.

Thorkelson, Chris, compiler. "Years Ago at the American School." Series. **The American Era**.

Truffaut, Bernard. **Cahiers de l'Histoire des Sourds**, 0-5.12. St. Jean de la Ruelle, France, 1989-1990.

Wiltse, Lyle. "Laurent Clerc." **The Pelican** (Louisiana School for the Deaf), April 1969. Reprinted from Gallaudet Day program, Gallaudet College, December 10, 1946.

Laurent Clerc (1785-1869). Videodocumentary. Carlsbad, California: DeBee Communications, 1995.

LEROY COLOMBO ✏

"Death Takes Famed Lifeguard." **The Deaf American**, October 1974.

"LeRoy Colombo Wins Long Swim/Cinto Colombo Second in Marathon." Unidentified newspaper clipping, *circa* 1926-1929.

Scarlett, Harold. "Russ Colombo Trains on Beer, Defies Undertow . . . He's Galveston's Life Saver." **Houston Post**, May 8, 1966.

GREAT DEAF AMERICANS

ROBERT DAVILA ✉ 🖨

"Assistant Secretary Addresses U.N." Press release, USDE, October 13, 1992.

"Davila to head OSERS." **The Progress Report** (Pre-College Programs, Gallaudet University), Spring 1989.

"Vice President Quayle swears in Davila as new OSERS Secretary." **NAD Broadcaster**, August 1989.

Cooper, Kenneth J. "Deaf official moves from advocate to insider." **Washington Post**, February 20, 1990.

"Room at the Top: Dr. Robert Davila." **DEAF LIFE**, November 1990.

DPN LEADERS ✉

Christiansen, John B., and Sharon N. Barnartt. **Deaf President Now! The 1988 Revolution at Gallaudet University**. Washington, D.C.: Gallaudet University Press, 1995.

Gannon, Jack R. **The Week the World Heard Gallaudet**. Photographs by Jeff Beatty and Chun Louie. Washington, D.C.: Gallaudet University Press, 1989.

Manning, Anita. "From roots of protest, deaf power thrives." **USA Today**, March 5, 1996.

Shook, Nancy B. "Gallaudet's Deaf President Now Movement: Views of our student protest leaders a year hence." **Kaleidoscope of Deaf America**. Silver Spring: NAD, 1989.

"DPN's 5th Anniversary: Special Issue." **DEAF LIFE**, March 1993.

Zinser, Dr. Elisabeth. "Breaking the Silence." **DEAF LIFE**, November and December 1991.

LOU FERRIGNO

Brooks, Tim. **The Complete Directory to Prime Time TV Stars**. New York: Ballantine, 1987.

Ferrigno, Lou, and Douglas Kent Hall. **The Incredible Lou Ferrigno**. New York: Simon & Schuster, 1982.

O'Donnell, Owen. **Contemporary Theatre, Film and Television**. Vol. 8. New York: Gale Research, 1990.

Adelson, Suzanne. "No longer silenced by hearing loss, the Hulk debuts in a speaking role." **People Weekly**, February 9, 1981.

Dobbins, Bill. "Lou Ferrigno Arm Training." **Muscle & Fitness**, September 1982.

Dougherty, Margot, and Suzanne Adelson. "Green with indignation, Lou Ferrigno is back in bulk as The Incredible Hulk." **People Weekly**, May 16, 1988.

Elkins, Jon. "Mr. Incredible." **Rochester Athletic Monthly**, January-February 1991.

Ferrigno, Lou, as told to Bob Wolff. "When Fate Has DIFFERENT Plans." **Muscle & Fitness**, March 1995.

Reynolds, Bill. "The Two Faces of Lou Ferrigno." **Muscle**, April 1980.

JULIANNA FJELD ✉

"Julianna Fjeld: From the NTD to Hollywood and back again." **DEAF LIFE**, June 1991.

ANDREW JACKSON FOSTER

"Dr. Andrew Foster." **Gallaudet Today**, Summer 1975.

Dively, Valerie L. "Andrew Jackson Foster." **GEDPD**, Vol. I, 430-431.

PHYLLIS FRELICH ✉ ✏

Gilbert, Laura-Jean. "Backstage with Phyllis Frelich." **Gallaudet Today**, Fall 1980.

Kakutani, Michiko. "Deaf since birth, Phyllis Frelich became an actress—and now a star." **NAD Broadcaster**, May 1980.

Morris, Rebecca, "Interview: Phyllis Frelich." **Stagebill**, The Kennedy Center for the Performing Arts, October 1993.

GERTRUDE S. GALLOWAY ✉

Newman, Larry, editor. **NAD President's Book**. Silver Spring: NAD, 1996.

"Galloway would have made Bailer proud." **The Hill** (Western Maryland College), Fall 1995.

Boller, Donna E. "School for Deaf leader moving to help students in N.J." **Howard County Times**, December 12, 1990.

Galloway, Gertrude Scott. "We, the Outsiders." **Gallaudet Today**, Summer 1984.

Leusner, Donna. "First Deaf Superintendent/Pupils feel special bond at school for hearing impaired." Newark **Star-Ledger**, March 4, 1991.

Van Tassel, Priscilla. "Finding new paths in education for deaf." **The New York Times,** December 23, 1990.

BILL GRAHAM & KATHIE SKYER HERING ⊠

"A safe haven, an ever-increasing load." **DEAF LIFE Plus**, October 1993.

Hering, Kathie Skyer. "Presidential Perspectives." **ALDA Chicago Style**, 1990 to date.

Holmes, Vincent. "Bill Graham: Building a New Field of Dreams." **DEAF LIFE**, May 1991.

Levitan, Linda, and Vincent Holmes. "Out From In Between: The ALDA Experience." **DEAF LIFE**, May 1991.

McCullough, Gayle. "Interview with Bill 'Another year, another dream' Graham." **Life After Deafness**, January 1994.

ALICE HAGEMEYER ⊠

"The Never-Ending Story: Finishing off a distinguished 34-year library career, Alice Hagemeyer starts a new adventure." **DEAF LIFE**, January 1992.

ERNIE HAIRSTON ⊠

Hairston, Ernie. "Education: An Empowerment Tool." Presentation, WVSDB, Fall 1995.

Johnstone, Mary. "Making an Impact." **Gallaudet Today**, Winter 1990-91.

EUGENE "SILENT" HAIRSTON ⊠ ⊜

La Motta, Jake. **Raging Bull: My Story**. New York: Prentice-Hall, 1970.

"Where Are They Now? Eugene (Silent) Hairston." **The Ring**, July 1982.

"Silent Hairston." **Ebony** [no date, *circa* 1951].

BRUCE HLIBOK ✐

"Leading Light: a Tribute to Bruce Hlibok." **DEAF LIFE**, September 1995.

Gussow, Mel. "Stage: Inspired 'Runaways.'" **New York Times**, March 10, 1978.

Dowling, Colette. "The Making of a Runaway Hit." **Playbill**, May 1978.

Hlibok, Albert J. "We still feel his presence." Letter. **DEAF LIFE**, February 1996.

Holden, Stephen. "The Desperation of Life in McCullers Country." **New York Times**, June 1, 1994.

Kroll, Jack. "Babes Up in Arms." **Newsweek**, March 27, 1978.

Luczak, Raymond, and Ellen Roth. "Two Tributes: Bruce Hlibok." **DEAF LIFE**, October 1995.

Mandell, Jonathan. "Responding to the Hearing World." **Newsday**, June 28, 1990.

Perlow, Mavis. "Deaf playwright strives to be heard." New York **Daily News**, May 29, 1990.

Swain, Robert. "Deaf Teenager A Runaway Success on Broadway." **The Deaf American**, January 1979.

FRANK P. HOCHMAN ✉

"Breaking the Sound Barrier: Lack of hearing hasn't meant lack of success." **San Jose Mercury News**, March 15, 1988.

"One of the first deaf doctors practicing in Newark." **The Sunday Review, The Argus** (Fremont), April 1, 1990.

Eickmann, Lori. "Deaf man followed his calling, became a successful physician." **San Jose Mercury News**, May 12, 1986.

Tye, Larry. "Deaf doctor offers dose of empathy." **Boston Globe**, May 14, 1995.

ROY HOLCOMB ✉

Holcomb, Marjoriebell Stakley. **The Holcomb Heritage**. Fremont: self-published, 1990.

—**The Sounds of Silence**. Fremont: self-published, 1992.

Holcomb, Roy. **Hazards of Deafness**. Northridge: Joyce Media, 1977.

—"The Present State of Total Communication" and "Mainstream—the Delaware Approach." **Proceedings of the International Congress on Education of the Deaf, Tokyo, 1975**.

Moores, Donald F. **Educating the Deaf: Psychology, Principles, & Practices**. Third Edition. Boston: Houghton Mifflin, 1987.

Scouten, Edward L. **Turning Points in the Education of the Deaf**. Danville: Interstate, 1984.

Toole, Darlene. **Courageous Deaf Adults**. Beaverton, Oregon: Dormac, 1980.

WILLIAM E. "DUMMY" HOY 🖎

The Baseball Encyclopedia. New York: Macmillan, 1990.

"The Oldest Red." **Cincinnati Reds Official Souvenir Book**, April 1944.

Davis, Mac. **100 Greatest Baseball Heroes**. New York: Grosset & Dunlap, 1974.

Neft, David S., Richard M. Cohen, and Jordan Deutsch. **The Complete All-Time Pro Baseball Register**. New York: Grosset & Dunlap, 1979.

Ritter, Lawrence S. **The Glory of Their Times**. New York: Morrow, 1984.

Smith, Ira L. **Baseball's Famous Outfielders**. New York: Barnes, 1954.

"The Colorful Legacy of 'Dummy' Hoy." **DEAF LIFE**, November and December 1992.

"Houcktown's Deaf Baseball Hero." **Toledo Magazine**, October 11, 1981.

Dawidoff, Nicholas. "His Actions Spoke: Dummy Hoy should be a Hall of Famer." **Sports Illustrated**, October 31, 1988.

De Vries, Jack. "Crowd's roar escaped deaf center fielder: Dummy Hoy used speed to succeed." **USA TODAY Baseball Weekly**, September 2-8, 1992.

Fisher, Randy. "William 'Dummy' Hoy and the Invention of Umpire Hand Signals." **The Vintage & Classic Baseball Collector #6**, May/June 1996.

Hunter, Bob. "Man says he won't stop until deaf hero's in Hall." **Columbus Dispatch**, February 3, 1996. Reprinted as "The best friend a slugger could have," **DEAF LIFE Plus**, April 1996.

Overfield, Joseph M. "Three to the Plate!" **Baseball Digest**, 1960.

—"William Ellsworth Hoy, 1862-1961: The remarkable life of a man called 'Dummy.'" **The National Pastime**, 2 (Fall 1982).

Panara, Robert F. "'Dummy' Hoy inducted into Ohio Baseball Hall of Fame," and "William 'Dummy' Hoy" (poem). **DEAF LIFE Plus**, July 1992.

Swope, Tom. "Game's first 'Dummy' marks 86th birthday: topped .280 for 18-year O.B. career." **The Sporting News**, June 2, 1948.

Woodward, Stanley. "Enshrine the Dummy." **New York Herald Tribune**. Reprinted in **The Sporting News**, January 25, 1961.

REGINA OLSON HUGHES ✏

Agricultural Research Service of the United States Department of Agriculture. **Selected Weeds of the United States**. 1970. Reprinted as **Common Weeds of the United States**. New York: Dover Publications, 1971.

Crammatte, Florence. "Regina Olson Hughes." **GEDPD**, Vol. 2, 77-79.

"Mileposts." **GCAA Bulletin**, May 1, 1981; March 15, 1982.

"Regina Hughes...something of a holotype herself." **Gallaudet Today**, Summer 1979.

"Regina Olson Hughes, '18." **Gallaudet Today**, Spring 1991.

King, Merrill Robert, and Harold Robinson. "The Genera of the Eupatorieae (Asterceae)." **Missouri Botanical Garden**, 1987.

Langrall, Peggy. "Regina Hughes lends her skills to SI botanists." Smithsonian Institution **Torch**, January 1987.

Peterson, Cate. "A brush in her hand." **Magazine of the Midlands**, Omaha **World-Herald**, October 11, 1987.

Read, Robert W. "Artists and Botanists." **Journal of the Bromeliad Society**, January-February 1983.

Tangerini, Alice R. "Biography of Regina Olson Hughes." **Guild of Natural Science Illustrators Newsletter**, September 1994.

GEORGE E. HYDE ✏

Hyde, George E. **Life of George Bent Written from His Letters**. Edited by Savoie Lottinville. Norman: University of Oklahoma Press, 1968.

—**The Pawnee Indians**. Norman: University of Oklahoma Press,

1951.

—**Red Cloud's Folk: A History of the Oglala Sioux Indians**. 1957. University of Oklahoma Press, 1968.

—**Spotted Tail's Folk: A History of the Brulé Sioux**. Norman: University of Oklahoma Press, 1961.

Panara, John. "George E. Hyde." **GEDPD**, Vol. 2, 79-80.

Stensland, Anna Lee. **Literature By and About the American Indian: an Annotated Bibliography for Junior and Senior High School Students**. Urbana, Illinois: National Council of Teachers of English, 1973.

"Indian-study expert dies/'Dean of Historians' was 86 years old." Omaha **World-Herald**, February 3, 1968.

"Omahan won essay contest, but—elbow-bending Buffalo Bill left him waiting for prize." Omaha **World-Herald**, March 20, 1961.

Logan, Wilfred D. "Omahan published new book on early Indians." **Sunday World-Herald Magazine**, August 4, 1963.

Mattes, Merrill J. "Omahan George Hyde's 'Spotted Tail' splendid." **Sunday World-Herald Magazine**, March 19, 1961.

McDermott, John Dishon. "A Dedication to the Memory of George E. Hyde." **Arizona and the West: A Quarterly Journal of History**, University of Arizona Press, 17(2), 1975.

McGrath, Mary. "Historian Hyde left puzzling lines." Omaha **World-Herald**, April 23, 1969.

Smith, Ralph. "'No sob stuff'; Hyde's book on Pawnees solid history." Omaha **World-Herald**, July 22, 1951.

I. KING JORDAN, JR. ✉ 🖎

"Pride and Joy: Gallaudet Celebrates Dr. Jordan's Inauguration as President." **DEAF LIFE**, November 1988.

"'There is no way I'm going to fail!' Dr. Jordan visits NTID." **Deaf Rochesterians' Newsmagazine**, December 1988.

Adelman, Ken. "Loud and Clear: 'Of a thousand things about deafness, nine hundred ninety-eight are good.'" **The Washingtonian**, March 1991.

Fussman, Cal. "The Nonstop Hero." **Washington Post Magazine**, December 18, 1988.

Ivey, Lisa. "Gallaudet President I. King Jordan Continues to 'Keep the Streak Alive." **Deaf Sports Review**, Winter 1995.

Johnstone, Mary. "First-rate First Lady." **Gallaudet Today**, Fall 1988.

Levitan, Linda, and Wilma Santiago. "'Deaf people can do anything...except hear': an exclusive interview with Gallaudet's first deaf president." **DEAF LIFE**, July 1988.

Naughton, Karen, and Bonnie Rudy. "Interview with Dr. I. King Jordan, Edinboro University, May 12, 1991." Manuscript.

Walter, Vickie. "Off & Running: Gallaudet's new president takes the helm." **Gallaudet Today**, Summer 1988.

HENRY KISOR ⊠

Abbott, Deborah, and Henry Kisor. **One TV Blasting *and a* Pig Outdoors**. Illus. Leslie Morrill. Morton Grove: Albert Whitman, 1994.

Kisor, Henry. **What's That Pig Outdoors? A Memoir of Deafness**. New York: Hill and Wang, 1990.

—**Flight of the Gin Fizz**. [In progress. See Cal Rodgers' listing.]

—**Zephyr: Tracking a Dream Across America**. New York: Times Books/Random House, 1994.

Hack, Carol. "Deaf pilot flies the route Cal Rodgers did in 1911." **State Journal-Register** (Springfield, Illinois), August 30, 1995.

Kisor, Henry. "What's That Pig Outdoors? A Journalist Explores the Humor and Hazards of Growing Up Deaf." **People Weekly**, June 18, 1990.

ART KRUGER ✒

"Kruger, Smith Honored." **NAD Broadcaster**, June 1982.

Atkinson, Charlie. "Art Kruger: The Man Behind the U.S. Deaf Olympic Team." Morganton **News Herald**, July 2, 1981.

Carney, Edward C. "In Memoriam Art Kruger." Eulogy. March 1992.

Elliott, George B. "The Art Kruger Story." Program Book, 15th Annual AAAD National Basketball Tournament, Atlanta, Georgia, April 1-4, 1959.

Schreiber, Herb. "Art Kruger—a study." Program Book, 22nd Annual AAAD National Basketball Tournament, Boston, Massachusetts, March 30-April 2, 1966.

Sutcliffe, Ronald E. "Art Kruger, Tradition Builder." **Dee Cee Eyes**, April 1992.

JACK LEVESQUE ✉

Allphin, Lisa. **The Best of "Jack's Corner."** DCARA, 1992.

—"John F Levesque: Portrait of a Deaf Leader." Manuscript, 1995.

Levesque, Jack. "Jack's Corner." Editorial. **DCARA News**, 1985 to date.

JULIETTE GORDON LOW ✏

Brown, Fern G. **Daisy and the Girl Scouts**. Illustrated by Marie DeJohn. Morton Grove: Albert Whitman, 1996.

Choate, Anne, and Helen Ferris (editors). **Juliette Low and the Girl Scouts**. New York: Doubleday Doran, 1928.

List, Ely. **Juliette Low and the Girl Scouts**. New York: Girl Scouts of the U.S.A., 1960.

Pace, Mildred M. **Juliette Low: Founder of the Girl Scouts**. New York: Scribner's, 1947.

Shultz, Gladys Denny, and Daisy Gordon Lawrence. **Lady from Savannah: The Life of Juliette Low**. Philadelphia: Lippincott, 1958.

Woods, W[illard]. H. "Juliette Gordon Low: Girl Scout Founder." **The Deaf American**, February 1974.

THOMAS SCOTT MARR ✏

"Thomas Scott Marr." **Tennessee, the Volunteer State 1769-1923**. Vol. IV. Chicago and Nashville, S. J. Clarke, 1923.

Mannes, Judy P. "Thomas Scott Marr." **GEDPD**, Vol. 2, 204-205.

Woods, W[illard] H. **The Forgotten People**. St. Petersburg: Dixie Press, 1973.

"New building one of finest in Nashville." Nashville **Banner**, November 18, 1934.

"Thomas Scott Marr: our alumnus and architect." **100th Anniversary Book**, Tennessee School for the Deaf, 1845-1945.

Boatner, Edmund Burke. "Thomas Scott Marr: A Biography." **Nebraska Journal**, June 1936. Reprinted from **The American Era** (ASD).

Chandler, Mrs. J. B. "Thomas Scott Marr, Architect." **The Silent Worker**, June 1929.

[Woods, Willard H.] "Thomas Scott Marr, Deaf Architect." **Digest of the Deaf**. Reprinted from **Silent Observer** (TSD), October 1939.

ERNEST MARSHALL ⌧ ⎙

Schuchman, John S. **Hollywood Speaks: Deafness and the Film Entertainment Industry**. Chicago: University of Illinois Press, 1988.

—"Television and Motion Pictures: George W. Veditz Film Collection: Ernest Marshall and Movies for Deaf Audiences." **GEDPD**, Vol. 3, 280-281.

"Ernest Marshall: "Reel-to-Reel Life." **DEAF LIFE**, February 1995.

Weinrib, Melinda. "A Study of the Minority Status of Independent Films in the Deaf Community: Implications for Deaf Studies Curriculum Development." Master's thesis, University of Arizona, 1994.

Moving Pictures, Moving Hands: The Ernest Marshall Story. Videocassette. San Diego: DawnSignPress, 1995.

The Projectionist. Videocassette. Ernest Marshall.

MARLEE MATLIN ⌧ ⎙

"Captionwatch: Rated ZZZ..." **DEAF LIFE Plus**, April 1994.

"The grit and the glamour." **DEAF LIFE Plus**, December 1994.

"Marlee Matlin: Prime-Time Breakthrough." **DEAF LIFE**, October 1991.

"News & Notes: Flashes." **Entertainment Weekly**, August 30, 1991.

"'Oh, No! Not Again!' Criticizing the critic." **DEAF LIFE Plus**, May 1995.

"Who's Purring Now? Marlee Matlin's new ASL commercial is the cat's meow." **DEAF LIFE Plus**, July 1990.

Chanko, Kenneth M. "Feisty Marlee." **Celebrity**, July 1988.

Chapman, Art. "Without a doubt, Marlee Matlin and Mark Harmon will have a hit." Rochester **Democrat and Chronicle**, August 20, 1991.

Colapinto, John. Review of *Reasonable Doubts*. **US**, September 1991.

Davis, Anna Byrd. "Marlee Matlin/Deaf actress hopes America is getting the message from her new TV series." **Lawrence Eagle-Tribune**, January 30, 1992.

Freeman, Patricia, and Lois Armstrong. "Actress Marlee Matlin builds a Bridge to Silence in her first speaking role." **People Weekly**, April 10, 1989.

Kroll, Jack. "Children of a Lesser God." Review. **Newsweek**, October 20, 1986.

Lipton, Michael A., and Julie Klein. "Law and Ardor." **People Weekly**, March 15. 1993.

Matrango, Stuart. "Hark the Sound: Marlee Matlin portrays a woman caught in our nation's past hysteria." **Cable Guide**, October 1994.

Mills, Nancy. "Marlee Matlin's determination speaks for itself." **Los Angeles Times**, April 7, 1989.

Powell, Joanna. "Is there life after the Oscar? Yes!" **Glamour**, January 1988.

Rosenberg, Howard. "Matlin crosses a new 'Bridge.'" **Los Angeles Times**, April 7, 1989.

Schickel, Richard. "Children of a Lesser God." Review. **TIME**, October 20, 1986.

Steele, Nick. "The Mystique of Marlee Matlin." **Art & Understanding: The International Magazine of Literature and Art About AIDS**, December/January 1996.

Walker Lou Ann. "'I want people to see me for who I am.'" **Parade**, May 22, 1988.

MARCELLA M. MEYER ✉ ✇

"'Excessive Force': an update on the McComb case—and some notes on slanted coverage." **DEAF LIFE Plus**, May 1995.

"Found in DEAF VALLEY." **The GLAD News**, Summer 1995.

Klugman, Marge. "'I refuse to be victimized': Deaf, hard-of-hearing, and hearing Californians rally to protest police brutality against a respected Deaf advocate." **DEAF LIFE Plus**, April 1995.

—"6.8 Earthquake Changed a Lot of Lives." **The GLAD News**, Spring 1994.

Levitan, Linda, and Matthew S. Moore. "Of, By, and For the Deaf: Greater Los Angeles Council on Deafness." **DEAF LIFE**, July 1989.

Meyer, Marcella M. "Marcella's Musings." **The GLAD News**, Spring 1994.

MATTHEW S. MOORE ✉

"Dedication." **NTIDLife Yearbook**, 1983.

Moore, Matthew S., and Linda Levitan. **For Hearing People Only: Answers to Some of the Most Commonly Asked Questions About** the Deaf Community, its Culture, and the "Deaf Reality." Second Edition. Rochester: Deaf Life Press, 1993.

"'A Labor of Love': the not-so-secret history of **DEAF LIFE**." **DEAF LIFE**, July 1993.

Hoy, Mary, and Robert Hoy. "Interview with Matthew S. Moore." **Community Ear**, December 1994.

Levitan, Linda. "N.T.I.D. celebrates its 25th anniversary." **DEAF LIFE**, September 1993.

Livadas, Greg. "The deaf get 'a magazine of their own.'" Rochester **Times-Union**, June 17, 1987.

Pessin, Beth M. "Editor, publisher, entrepreneur: what Moore?" **NTID Focus**, Fall 1990.

LOWELL MYERS ✉

Myers, Lowell J. "Court Decisions: People v. Lang." **GEDPD**, Vol. 1, 210-212.

Tidyman, Ernest. **Dummy**. Boston: Little, Brown and Co., 1974.

"Book reviews: **Dummy**, by Ernest Tidyman." **Gallaudet Today**, Fall 1974.

"Lowell Myers: the times and trials of a veteran lawyer." **DEAF LIFE**, April 1993.

"Unlocking A Prisoner of Silence." **TIME**, January 17, 1977.

Fegelman, Andrew. "Blind woman still reaches out to accused killer." **Chicago Tribune**, June 28, 1993.

Witt, Linda. "After years in legal limbo, a murder trial approaches for the deaf-mute known as 'Dummy' Lang." **People Weekly**, June 27, 1977.

—"'Dummy' lawyer Lowell Myers takes aim at rights for the deaf." **People Weekly**, June 4, 1979.

MAC NORWOOD ✏

"Breaking the Sound Barrier: The Caption Center turns 20," and "A Caption Center Timeline & Highlights of Captioning History," **DEAF LIFE**, March 1992.

"In Memoriam: Dr. Malcolm J. Norwood, 1927-1989, the 'Father of Captioning.'" **DEAF LIFE**, July 1989.

"In Memory of Malcolm J. Norwood." **NAD Broadcaster**, May 1989.

Sullivan, Frank. "Eulogy for Mac Norwood." **NAD Broadcaster**, May 1989.

MARY LOU NOVITSKY ✉

"Deaf Mosaic nabs 6 more Emmys." **DEAF LIFE Plus**, August 1993.

"'Time to move in new directions': *Deaf Mosaic* ends decade-long run." **DEAF LIFE Plus**, April 1995.

Barwick, Scott. "Being Heard." **TV Time**, August 24-30, 199-

Levy-Malis, Elizabeth. "Reaching Around the Deaf World." **Producers Quarterly**, Spring 1990.

—"Audio for Deaf Mosaic." **Post: The Magazine for Animation, Audio, Film & Video Professionals**, June 1990.

Reed, Ron. "Expanding the Message of Gallaudet University." **Prime Times** (NATAS), November-December 1990.

Prakash, Snigdha. "Award-winning show gets a third Golden Eagle." **Washington Post TV Week**, December 2-8, 1990.

"Also on Discovery: *Deaf Mosaic*." **Assignment Discovery: Spectrum**, August 1990.

KITTY O'NEIL

Harries, Joan. **They Triumphed Over Their Handicaps**. New York: Franklin Watts, 1981.

Ireland, Karin. **Kitty O'Neil: Daredevil Woman**. New York: Harvey House, 1980.

Bowie, Phil. "The Fastest Woman on Earth." **Saturday Evening Post**, March 1977.

Merrifield, Cynthia. "Interview." **Hearing Health**, August/September 1994.

Phinizy, Coles. "A Rocket Ride to Glory and Gloom." **Sports Illustrated**, January 17, 1977.

Satchell, Michael. "The Fastest Women on Wheels." **Parade**, May 6, 1979.

T.J. O'ROURKE ✐

A Basic Course in Manual Communication. Silver Spring: NAD, 1973.

Bowe, Frank G. **Changing the Rules**. Silver Spring: T.J. Publishers, 1986.

Humphries, Tom, Carol Padden, and Terrence J. O'Rourke. **A Basic Course in American Sign Language**. Silver Spring: T.J. Publishers, 1980.

"In Memoriam: Terrence J. O'Rourke." **DEAF LIFE Plus**, February 1992.

"T.J. O'Rourke." **DEAF LIFE**, March 1992.

Kotite, Erika. "Personal Best: When Abilities Outshine Disabilities." **Entrepreneur Magazine**, April 1991.

ROBERT F. PANARA ✉

Levitan, Linda. "A Tribute to Dr. Robert Panara." **DEAF LIFE**, September 1988.

Panara, Robert F. "The Deaf in America: Two Hundred Years of Progress." **NTID Focus**, October/November 1976.

—"The Deaf Writer in America from Colonial Times to 1970." Parts I and II. **American Annals of the Deaf**, September and November 1970.

Van Cleve, John V. "Great Deaf Americans." Review. **Gallaudet Today**, Winter 1985.

PEGGIE PARSONS ✉

Parsons, Frances M., with Donna L. Chitwood. **I Didn't Hear the Dragon Roar**. Washington, D.C.: Gallaudet University Press, 1988.

Parsons, Frances M. **Sound of the Stars**. New York: Vantage Press, 1971.

"A crusade to help the deaf." Unidentified Bombay newspaper, September 1976.

"Parsons sees fruits of her labor in developing countries." **On the Green**, February 28, 1994.

"Parsons' working vacation in France proves productive." **On the Green**, August 17, 1992.

"Peggy Is Back!" **Gallaudet Today**, Spring 1977.

"The deaf of the world find a vigorous champion in Frances Parsons." **People Weekly**, May 1976.

Monaghan, Charles. "Signs of Amity: An American in China." **Washington Post**, August 14, 1988.

Parsons, Frances M. "Around The World in 86 Days." **The Deaf American**, November 1969.

—"Diary Of Frances 'Peggie' Parsons . . . as condensed by Hortense Auerbach." **The Deaf American**, July-August, September, and October 1978.

—"Gallaudet's 'World Ambassador': Helping the Deaf to Communicate." **Rehabilitation/WORLD**, Summer 1977.

—"How 'Sound of the Stars' Started." **The Deaf American**, November 1972.

Scott, Nadine W. "Don't give up ship, parents of deaf/Expert with affliction to speak Thursday." **Honolulu Star-Bulletin**, January 1, 1980.

Welzenbach, Michael. "Listening with the eyes." **Washington Post**, October 12, 1983.

DAVID PEIKOFF ✆

Carbin, Clifton F. **Deaf Heritage in Canada**. Toronto: McGraw-Hill Ryerson Ltd., 1996.

"A champion of champions." **DEAF LIFE Plus**, February 1995.

"PAH! is the word!" **DEAF LIFE Plus**, March 1995.

Carbin, Clifton F. "'Service Above Self': A Canadian tribute to the late David Peikoff." **DEAF LIFE**, May 1995.

Gannon, Jack R. "He Makes Money Immortal." **Performance** (President's Committee on Employment of the Handicapped), January 1972.

—"Two Roads...and David Peikoff: an Appreciation." Excerpts from a eulogy. February 2, 1995.

Trabish, Marilyn. "Forty years of service features life career of Dr. David Peikoff." **The Buff and Blue**, December 1964.

Williams, Mel. "David Peikoff...Man of Action." **The Silent Worker**, July 1951.

CURTIS PRIDE ✆

Bowker, Michael. "The Loudest Cheer." **Reader's Digest**, May 1994.

Giannone, John. "Pride of the Mets Conquers Deafness." **New York Post**, June 26, 1990.

Gildea, William. "Seeing Pride in His Accomplishments." **Washington Post** [no date, *circa* August 1994].

Koenig, Bill. "Minor League Beat: Pride communicates in power and grace." **USA Today Baseball Weekly**, April 22-28, 1992.

Smallwood, John. "Special, but...deafness isn't what is getting player noticed." Rochester **Democrat and Chronicle**, July 16, 1993.

Jordan, Pat. "Baseball's Pride and Joy." **The Sporting News**, May 2, 1994.

CAL RODGERS ✏

Boyne, Walter. **The Smithsonian Book of Flight**. Washington, D.C.: Smithsonian Books/Orion Books, 1987.

Ethell, Jeffrey L. **Frontiers of Flight**. Washington, D.C.: Smithsonian Books/Orion Books, 1992.

Kisor, Henry. **The Flight of the *Gin Fizz***. (Work-in-progress; projected publication 1997.)

Lebow, Eileen F. **Cal Rodgers and the *Vin Fiz*: The First Transcontinental Flight**. Washington, D.C.: Smithsonian Institution Press, 1989.

Kisor, Henry. "Hearing Impaired Pilot a Pioneer in 1911." **IDPA Newsletter**, Spring 1995.

FRED SCHREIBER

Schein, Jerome D. **A Rose for Tomorrow: Biography of Frederick C. Schreiber**. Silver Spring, Maryland: NAD, 1981.

"Deaf People Throughout the World Mourn Loss of Fred Schreiber." **NAD Broadcaster**, September 1979.

Carney, Edward C. "A Great Leader Passes On." **NAD Interstate**, No. 3, 1979.

BILL SCHYMAN ✉

"Schyman: Standout DePaul Cager." **Chicago Sun-Times**, January 27, 1952.

Gamble, Bob. "Bill Schyman—One of Us—One of You." **IAABO Sportorials**, (International Association of Approved Basketball Officials), March 1979.

Parezo, Stephen A. "Schyman Named Head Olympic Basketball

Coach for the Deaf." **The News Leader** (Laurel, Maryland), November 20, 1980.

Yengich, Karen. "To Be Inducted in the AAAD Hall of Fame." **The News Leader** (Laurel, Maryland), March 29, 1979.

LAURA REDDEN SEARING ⊜

Gannon, Jack R. "Laura Searing." **GEDPD**, Vol. 3, 11-13.

Glyndon, Howard [Laura Redden Searing]. **Echoes of Other Days**. San Francisco: Harr Wagner Publishing, 1921.

—**Notable Men of the House of Representatives**, 1862.

—**Of El Dorado**. San Francisco: C. A. Murdock, 1897.

Olson, Michael J. "Writers in literature: Laura Redden Searing." **GEDPD**, Vol. 2, 178.

Reed, Richard D. "A Forgotten Alumna of the Missouri School for the Deaf." **Missouri Record**, March-April 1995.

—"Rediscovering Laura Redden Searing, 19th-century journalist." **DEAF LIFE Plus**, October 1995.

ERASTUS "DEAF" SMITH ⊜

Ford, Marjorie Winn, Susan Hillyard, and Mary Faulk Koock. **The Deaf Smith Country Cookbook**. New York: Macmillan, 1973.

Huston, Cleburne. **Deaf Smith: Incredible Texas Spy**. Waco, Texas: Texian Press, 1974.

Williams, John Hoyt. **Sam Houston: A Biography of the Father of Texas**. New York: Simon & Schuster, 1993.

Nevin, David. "'Fight and be damned!' said Sam Houston." **Smithsonian**, July 1992.

Sandy, Steven R. "Battle of San Jacinto." Letter. **Smithsonian**, September 1992.

Swain, Robert L., Jr. "The hero who gave his name to Texas' Deaf Smith County." **The Deaf American**, December 1969.

MARTIN STERNBERG ⊠

"'A Perfect Marriage': **ASL Dictionary** on disk." "**DEAF LIFE Plus**, June 1994.

Sternberg, Martin. "The Adventures of Martin L.A. Sternberg: Communications pioneer, scholar, actor, and Jaguar man." **DEAF LIFE**, February 1996.

LUTHER H. "DUMMY" TAYLOR ✏

McGraw, John J. **My Thirty Years in Baseball**. 1923. Introduction by Charles C. Alexander. Lincoln: University of Nebraska Press, 1995.

Nash, Bruce, and Allen Zullo. **Baseball Hall of Shame 3**. New York: Pocket Books, 1987.

Dawson, Kimberly. "Major League Baseball Loved Luther Taylor." **Deaf Sports Review**, Winter 1993.

Lanigan, Harold W. "Dummy Taylor, who let fast ball and curve speak for him when with Giants, puts his story on paper." **The Sporting News**, December 24, 1942.

Mann, Arthur. "Mute Testimony." **Baseball Magazine**, September 1945.

Warshawsky, Leonard. "The Taylor-Made Story." **The Silent Worker**, September 1952.

RHULIN THOMAS

"Deaf Pilot to leave in Cub coupe today on flight to coast." **Washington Evening Star**, October 26, 1947.

"Deaf Star Employe[e] who piloted plane across nation gets medal." **Washington Evening Star**, September 30, 1948.

"Rhulin A. Thomas." **The Missouri Record**, October 1981.

"White House honors deaf mute for flying plane across U.S." **Washington Evening Star**, September 16, 1948.

"White House is the scene of presentation ceremonies for Thomas flight award." **The Cavalier**, September 30, 1948.

Golladay, Loy E., editor. "Deaf pilot spans continent in own Piper Cub." **The American Era**, May-June 1948.

Mossel, Max. "Rhulin Thomas stops at School on California hop." **The Missouri Record** (MSD), November 22, 1947.

DOUGLAS TILDEN ✏

Albronda, Mildred. **Douglas Tilden: The Man and His Legacy**. San Francisco: Self-published, 1994.

Runde, Winfield Scott. "Douglas Tilden, Sculptor." **The Silent Worker**, December 1952.

JUDITH VIERA TINGLEY ✉

Tingley, Judith Viera, editor. **Deaf People in California: Demographics and Communication Needs**. Sacramento: California State Department of Rehabilitation, 1983.

—"Deafened Adults: Who We Are and What We Need," and "A Model National Organization for Late Deafened Adults." Proceedings, *5th International Congress, International Federation of Hard of Hearing People*, Graz, Austria, August 1996.

—"Ergonomia y Nuevas Tecnologias." *Conferencia Internacional Sobre Empleo de Personas con Discapacidad*, European Community CERMI and HELIOS, Bilbao, Spain, February 1994.

—"'Help! Emergency!' Text Telephone Access." Proceedings, *XIIth World Federation of the Deaf Congress*, Vienna, Austria, July 1995.

—"Issues in Relay Services: Administration, Planning, Procedures, and Evaluation." Proceedings, *European Community COST 219 Seminar on Relay Services*, Montreaux, Switzerland, March 1992.

—"Relay Services: Getting Started." Presentation, *The DEAF WAY*, Washington, D.C., July 1989.

"Starving in the Pantry." Keynote presentation on employment/ Proceedings, *Forum: Life and Work in the 21st Century*, NAD, Las Vegas, Nevada, 1986.

—"TDD Relay Systems." Presentation, *National Conference on Deaf and Hard of Hearing People*, El Paso, Texas, September 1988.

—"Teléfono para sordos: Independencia social y económica." Proceedings, *Simposio Internacional sobre Supresión de Barreras de Comunicación*, FIAPAS and INSERSO, Madrid, Spain, July 1993 and March 1994.

Tingley, Judith Viera, and Greg Kimberlin. "Using VCO with Relay Service: An Interactive Workshop." Proceedings, *ALDA Annual Conference*, Chicago, November 1991.

BONNIE TUCKER ✉

Tucker, Bonnie Poitras. **The Feel of Silence**. Philadelphia: Temple University Press, 1995.

"Achieving Personal Best: 200 Words on Lear's Women: sign of justice/Bonnie Tucker/Phoenix litigator." **Lear's**, May 1990.

"Welcome On Board: Bonnie Tucker brings a fresh perspective to RIT's Board of Trustees." **NTID Focus**, Summer 1989.

Caldwell, Jean. "Succeeding in a world she can't hear." **Boston Globe**, June 18, 1987.

Coates, Bill. "How does she do it?/Deaf lawyer teaches at ASU, chooses speech over sign language." **Phoenix Gazette**, September 5, 1988.

Cole, Rochelle Mackey. "Seasoned Survivor of a Silent World." **Arizona State**, Winter 1990.

Hansen, Midge. "Deaf lawyer speaks up." **Sunday Camera**, July 29, 1990.

Johnson, Richard. "Classroom communications no bar for totally deaf lawyer." **Denver Post**, July 9, 1990.

Keller, Roseanne. "Deaf attorney makes most of handicap." **Arizona Business Gazette**, August 17, 1987.

Morrison, Melissa. "Fair Hearing: Lawyer-prof refuses to let deafness bar her." **The Arizona Republic**, June 16, 1987.

Tucker, Ronale. "Litigating in Silence." **Arizona Bar Briefs**, July 1986.

FRANK R. TURK ✉

"Frank Turk: Energy, leadership, and inspiration—but no shortcuts." **DEAF LIFE**, August 1989.

"Greensboro closing: update." **DEAF LIFE Plus**, March 1995.

"The axe falls—on the Central School." **DEAF LIFE Plus**, February 1995.

Solomon, Barry J. "Deaf Youth's Champion—Dr. Frank R. Turk." **DeafNation**, November 1995.

Turk, Frank R. "From the Director's Desk." **The DSD/HH Insider**, Fall 1991 to date.

KENNY WALKER ✏

Walker, Kenny, and Bob Schaller. **Roar of Silence: The Kenny Walker Story**. Grand Island, Nebraska: Cross Training Publishing, 1998.

Barfknecht, Lee. "Walker giving scouts a 'rush.'" Omaha **World-Herald**, October 19, 1990.

Blayvelt, Barry. "For deaf player, the cheering is eloquent." **USA Today**, December 31, 1990.

Doleman, Bill. "Kenny Walker: a special player." **Sidelines** (College Football Association), November 1988.

—"A Mann and her tackle." Unidentified clipping.

Hambleton, Ken. "Brotherly love carries Walker." Omaha **World-Herald**, November 2, 1990.

Hilgers, Laura. "Tackle Your Dreams." **Sports Illustrated for Kids**, August 1992.

Hubbell, John G. "Kenny Walker listens with his heart." **Reader's Digest**, October 1993.

Kelly, Kevin. "Walker returns fans' love." Omaha **World-Herald**, November 4, 1990.

Kelly, Michael. "A silent roar for Kenny Walker." Omaha **World-Herald**, November 3, 1990.

Maly, Ron. "His happiness is in her hands." Des Moines **Register**, August 31, 1990.

Schefter, Adam. "The Silent Game." **NFL Game Day**, October 11, 1993.

Tayman, John, and Vickie Bane, "Quiet thunder for a rookie." **People Weekly**, October 7, 1991.

Warshawsky, Lenny. "The Spotlight." **The FRAT**, July-August 1994.

Wolf, Mark. "Broncos get a rusher, and a role model." **Rocky Mountain News**, April 23, 1991.

CADWALLADER WASHBURN ✑

Sonnenstrahl, Deborah. "Cadwallader Washburn." **GEDPD**, Vol. 3, 338-340.

Bowe, Frank G. "Missions Impossible...The Incredible Story of Cadwallader Washburn." **The Deaf American**, November 1970.

Chitwood, Donna L. "Washburn: Gallaudet's Noted Artist-Correspondent." **Gallaudet Today**, Winter 1977.

Kowalewski, Felix. "Profiles of selected deaf artists." **Gallaudet Today**, Summer 1981.

ROBERT WEITBRECHT ✑

"Robert Weitbrecht." **Gallaudet Today**, Summer 1974.

"TTY history described in plenary address." **GA-SK Newsletter**, Summer 1995.

Sternberg, Martin. "The Adventures of Martin L.A. Sternberg:

Communications pioneer, scholar, actor, and Jaguar man." **DEAF LIFE**, February 1996.

HEATHER WHITESTONE ✉ 🖢

Gray, Daphne, and Gregg Lewis. **Yes, You Can, Heather: The Story of Heather Whitestone, Miss America 1995**. Grand Rapids: Zondervan, 1996.

—**Heather Whitestone**. Grand Rapids: Zondervan, 1996.

"Gally Goings-On." **DEAF LIFE Plus**, January 1995.

"Mixed Victory?" **DEAF LIFE Plus**, October 1995.

"Star Pupil"; "Example or exception?" **DEAF LIFE Plus**, November 1994.

"Whitestone wows NTID." **DEAF LIFE Plus**, March 1995.

Anders, Gigi. "Beauty and the Battle." **USA Weekend**, March 3-5, 1995.

Bonillas, Paula. "There She Is...*Really*!" **Hearing Health**, October/November 1994.

Bushnell, Candace. "Miss America's Mom." **Redbook**, February 1995.

Jobe, Kim. "Miss America encourages others to strive for success." **Daily Corinthian** (Corinth, Mississippi), November 25, 1994.

Kemp, Kathy. "Miss America taught optimism by mother." **The Journal**, Washington, D.C., October 4, 1994.

Min, Janice, and Jeff Schnaufer. "Cut to the Chaste." **People Weekly**, April 1, 1996.

Roberts, Roxanne. "Beautiful Dreamer/Miss America's reign gets off to a sunny start." **Washington Post**, September 18, 1994.

Shapiro, Joseph P. "Miss America meets the disability lobby." **U.S. News and World Report**, October 17, 1994.

Swingle, Chris. "Silent cheers for Miss America." Rochester **Times-Union**, September 23, 1994.

Van Biema, David. "Beyond the Sound Barrier." **TIME**, October 3, 1994.

WILLIAM WILLARD 🖢

Coffey, Bill, editor. **The Hoosier**, Sesquicentennial Issue, Fall 1993.

NELLIE ZABEL WILLHITE ✏

"Services Friday for aviation pioneer Nellie Willhite, 98." **Argus-Leader** (Sioux Falls), September 4, 1991.

Messmore, Ann. "Nellie Willhite, Ex-Barnstormer." **Northliner**, Spring 1974. Reprinted in **The Deaf American**, February 1975.

Nelson, Todd. "Aviation pioneer dies at 98: Willhite was South Dakota's first female pilot." **Argus-Leader** (Sioux Falls), September 3, 1991.

Smith, Clayton F. "Dakota Images." **South Dakota History**, Summer 1993.

—"Nellie Zabel Willhite: South Dakota's First Aviatrix." Presentation, 20th Annual Dakota History Conference, Madison, South Dakota, April 8, 1988.

Weinstein, Dorene. "Our First Lady of the Air." **South Dakota Magazine**, 1989.

BOYCE R. WILLIAMS ✏

Adler, Edna [Paananen]. "Boyce Robert Williams." **GEDPD**, Vol. 3, 340-342.

"Thirty-Three Years." **The Deaf American**, September 1978.

"Tribute to A Friend in Sound & Sign: Dr. Boyce R. Williams." **Gallaudet Today**: Fall 1970.

Bowe, Frank G. "Dr. Boyce R. Williams—Foremost in Rehabilitation of the Deaf." **The Deaf American**, June 1973.

Hoag, Dr. Ralph L. "Federal Program Activities Providing Additional Educational and Employment Opportunities for the Deaf." **The Silent Worker**, July-August 1964.

Kaika, Mike. "Boyce R. Williams—The Class of '32 is still going strong!" **Gallaudet Today**, Winter 1984.

Shaposka, Bert. "Boyce Williams: The VRA Investment in the Future of the American Deaf." **The Silent Worker**, May 1964.

Williams, Boyce R. "Journey into Mental Health for the Deaf." **Rehabilitation Record**, September-October 1970.

FRANCES WOODS ✉

Bray, Billy. **The Wonder Dancers Woods and Bray**. Youngstown, Ohio: Billy Bray, 1975.

"Duo dances six decades." **The Daily Courier** (Connellsville, Pennsylvania), October 11, 1991.

Brownfield, Cathy. "Woods, Bray are veterans of ballroom dancing steps." **Canfield News**, June 5, 1993.

Cochran, Joan. [Commentary.] Unidentified article [*circa* 1980].

JOHN YEH ✉

Anderson, Jack. "Success in a World of Silence." **Parade**, January 31, 1988.

Byrd, Todd. "Realizing the Dream: John Yeh's entrepreneurial spirit opens doors to success." **Gallaudet Today**, Fall 1988.

Sugawara, Sandra. "Signs of Success for Deaf Entrepreneur." **Washington Post**, March 20, 1989.

Acronyms & Terms

AAAD . . . American Athletic Association of the Deaf; renamed
USA Deaf Sports Federation (USADSF) in 1998

ADA . . . . . Americans with Disabilities Act, 1990

AGBAD . . Alexander Graham Bell Association for the Deaf

ALDA . . . Association of Late-Deafened Adults

ASD . . . . . American School for the Deaf in West Hartford,
Connecticut

ASDC . . . . American Society for Deaf Children

ASL . . . . . American Sign Language

BHI . . . . . . Better Hearing Institute

CAD . . . . . California Association of the Deaf;
Canadian Association of the Deaf

CAID . . . . Convention of American Instructors of the Deaf

CEASD. . . Conference of Executives of
American Schools for the Deaf

COED. . . . Commission on Education of the Deaf (1986-1988)

COSD . . . . Council of Organizations Serving the Deaf (1967-1973)

CSD-B . . . California School for the Deaf, Berkeley
(relocated to Fremont)

CSD-F. . . . California School for the Deaf, Fremont

CSD-R . . . California School for the Deaf, Riverside

CSUN . . . . California State University, Northridge
(formerly San Fernando Valley State College)

DHEW . . . Department of Health, Education and Welfare
(now Department of Education and
Department of Health and Human Services)

DPN . . . . . Deaf President Now! movement, March 6-13, 1988

FCC . . . . . Federal Communications Commission

GCAA . . . Gallaudet College Alumni Association, now
Gallaudet University Alumni Association (GUAA)

IAPD . . . . International Association of Parents of the Deaf, now
American Society for Deaf Children (ASDC)

ICED . . . . International Congress on Education of the Deaf

IDEA . . . . Individuals with Disabilities Education Act

JCCC .... Johnson County Community College in
Overland Park, Kansas
KDES .... Kendall Demonstration Elementary School, on
Gallaudet's Kendall Green campus
KSD ..... Kansas School for the Deaf;
Kentucky School for the Deaf
MCDHH . Massachusetts Commission for the Deaf and
Hard of Hearing
MSD ..... Maryland School for the Deaf;
Missouri School for the Deaf
MSSD .... Model Secondary School for the Deaf, on
Gallaudet's Kendall Green campus
NAD..... National Association of the Deaf
NBDA ... National Black Deaf Advocates, Inc.
NFSD .... National Fraternal Society of the Deaf ("FRAT")
NLTP .... National Leadership Training Program, San Fernando
Valley State
NTD ..... National Theatre of the Deaf
NTID .... National Technical Institute for the Deaf, one of 8
colleges of Rochester Institute of Technology (RIT)
NYSD .... New York School for the Deaf, White Plains
("Fanwood")
NYSSD... New York State School for the Deaf, Rome
OSD ..... Ohio School for the Deaf
OSERS ... Office of Special Education and Rehabilitation Services
OVR ..... Office of Vocational Rehabilitation
PCEPD... President's Council on Employment of People with
Disabilities (formerly President's Council on
Employment of the Handicapped)
P.S. 47.... New York's public school for the deaf
RID ...... Registry of Interpreters for the Deaf
RSA ..... Rehabilitation Services Administration
TSD ..... Tennessee School for the Deaf
VR....... Vocational Rehabilitation
WFD..... World Federation of the Deaf

Note: *Cerebrospinal meningitis* is also called *spinal meningitis*. Old terms are "spotted fever" and "brain fever."

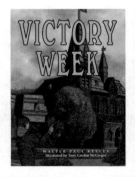

ORDER FORM

Please print clearly!

Name: _____

Address: _____

City: _____

State: _____   Zip: _____   Phone:(_____) _____

ITEM	COST EA.	QTY	TOTAL
1. DEAF LIFE (12 issues—see p. 512)	$27.00 X	__ =	_____
2. For Hearing People Only/PB	$19.95 X	__ =	_____
3. For Hearing People Only/HC	$35.00 X	__ =	_____
4. Great Deaf Americans: 2nd Edition	$24.95 X	__ =	_____
5. Victory Week	$18.95 X	__ =	_____
6. St. Michael's Fall	$12.95 X	__ =	_____
7. Meeting Halfway in ASL	$39.95 X	__ =	_____

see p. 512

SUBTOTAL _____

NY State: add 8% Sales Tax (Except DEAF LIFE) _____

Add $3.00 ea. for S/H (Except DEAF LIFE) _____

GRAND TOTAL $_____

☐ MasterCard ☐ VISA ☐ DINERS CLUB INTERNATIONAL

Credit Card #

__/__/__/__/__/__/__/__/__/__/__/__/__/__/__/__/__/ Expiration date__/__

Signature_____

Canadian/Foreign orders: Please add $10.00 each—must be **U.S. funds**.
Handling time, prices, postage, etc., subject to change without notice.
Orders take 2 to 6 weeks for delivery.

A $20.00 fine is charged on all bounced checks.

Send this order form with check or money order payable to:
DEAF LIFE PRESS, c/o MSM Productions, Ltd.
1095 Meigs Street, Rochester, NY 14620-2405
FAX (716) 442-6371
http://www.deaflife.com

Photocopies of this form accepted.